Visual, Material and Print Culture in Nineteenth-Century Ireland

Visual, Material and Print Culture in Nineteenth-Century Ireland

Ciara Breathnach & Catherine Lawless

EDITORS

FOUR COURTS PRESS

Set in 10 on 12.5 point Bembo for
FOUR COURTS PRESS LTD
7 Malpas Street, Dublin 8, Ireland
e-mail: info@fourcourtspress.ie
and in North America for
FOUR COURTS PRESS
c/o ISBS, 920 N.E. 58th Avenue, Suite 300, Portland, OR 97213.

A catalogue record for this title
is available from the British Library.

ISBN 978-1-84682-231-5

Printed in England
by MPG Books, Bodmin, Cornwall.

Contents

Illustrations

TABLES

Abbreviations

BG	Board of Guardians
BL	British Library
BL AP	British Library: Althorp Papers, Additional Manuscript 77110
BM	British Museum
BM FC	British Museum: Department of Prehistory and Europe, Fountaine Collection, Original Documents File
CPM	*Catholic Penny Magazine*
ESRC	Economic and Social Research Council
GPO	General Post Office
IRCHSS	Irish Research Council for the Humanities and Social Sciences
IMMA	Irish Museum of Modern Art
NCAD	National College of Art and Design, Dublin
NIVAL	National Irish Visual Arts Library
NLI	National Library of Ireland
NUIM	National University of Ireland, Maynooth
PMLA	*Publications of the Modern Language Association of America*
PPM	*Protestant Penny Magazine*
PRIA	*Proceedings of the Royal Irish Academy*
PRONI	Public Records Office Northern Ireland
QUB	Queen's University Belfast
RHA	Royal Hibernian Academy
RIA	Royal Irish Academy
SSNCI	Society for the Study of Nineteenth-Century Ireland
SSPL	Science and Society Picture Library
TCD	Trinity College Dublin
UCC	University College Cork
UCD	University College Dublin
VAA	Victoria and Albert Museum Archive
VAA RP	Victoria and Albert Museum Archive: Department of Science and Art, Fountaine Collection File, MA/2/F, containing numerous documents, each item being identified by a Received Paper (RP) number.

Contributors

ELIZABETH BOYLE is a Leverhulme Early Career Fellow in the Department of Anglo-Saxon, Norse & Celtic at the University of Cambridge. She works on eleventh- and twelfth-century religious history and intellectual culture, and is also preparing for publication the selected correspondence of the Celtic scholar Whitley Stokes (1830–1909).

CIARA BREATHNACH lectures in History at the University of Limerick. Her publications include *The Congested Districts Board of Ireland, 1891–1923: poverty and development in the west of Ireland* (2005); (ed.), *Framing the West: images of rural Ireland, 1890–1920* (2007); with Aoife Bhreatnach (eds), *Portraying Irish travellers: histories and representations* (2007).

JUSTIN CARVILLE lectures in Historical & Theoretical Studies in Photography and Visual Culture at the Institute of Art, Design & Technology, Dun Laoghaire. He recently guest-edited a special Ireland-themed issue of the journal *Early Popular Visual Culture* and is currently researching the connections between photography, ethnography and the visualization of Irish identity, for which he received an IRCHSS Research Fellowship for 2008–2009.

OLIVIER COQUELIN holds a doctorate in English and Irish studies from the University of Rennes 2 (France), and is a tutor at the University of Western Brittany (Brest/Quimper). He is also an associate researcher at the Centre for Breton and Celtic Research (Brest). His research focuses on the history and ideological analysis of Irish political and social movements in modern times, and more specifically in the Union era (1801–1922).

VIRGINIA CROSSMAN is Reader in History at Oxford Brookes University. She has published widely on governance and administration in nineteenth-century Ireland. She is currently directing a major, ESRC-funded project on welfare regimes under the Irish poor law, 1850–1921.

EMILY CULLEN completed her doctorate in English at NUI Galway, where she was an IRCHSS Government of Ireland scholar between 2004 and 2007. Her thesis explores the cultural functions of the Irish harp as visual icon, literary trope and musical instrument in the construction of an Irish self-image. She has published articles on political representations of the harp in bardic discourses, as well as twentieth-century, and contemporary Irish poetry.

ROBIN J. KAVANAGH is currently a Post-doctoral Research Fellow at An Foras Feasa (AFF), NUIM, in the ICT Innovation and Digital Humanities stream. As Principal Investigator on a new project entitled 'Irish inc: images from the nineteenth-century periodicals', she is working with the AFF technical team to create a digital library of visual images from selected nineteenth-century Irish illustrated periodicals housed in the Russell Library, Maynooth. This research tool is due for completion in October 2010. She has worked on the IRCHSS project entitled 'Religion and social identity in Ireland: the role of parish confraternities and associations, 1775–1965'. Dr Kavanagh worked with AFF technicians and computer scientists to create an online research tool providing free access to the research data through a variety of search avenues. The Irish Confraternities website is available at www.irishconfraternities.ie.

CARLA KING is a Lecturer in Modern History at St Patrick's College, Drumcondra. She has published various works relating to Davitt, including *Michael Davitt* (1999; 2009); *Michael Davitt: collected writings, 1868–1906* (8 vols, 2001), *Michael Davitt: jottings in solitary* (2003); *Lives of Victorian political figures, part II, vol. 4: Michael Davitt* (2007); and co-edited with W.J. McCormack, *John Devoy's Michael Davitt: from the Gaelic American* (2008). She has also published articles on Davitt in scholarly and popular journals. She is writing a biography of Davitt's later life to be published by UCD Press.

GEORGINA LARAGY is a post-doctoral scholar at the University of Limerick. She has published on suicide and murder in nineteenth-century Ireland, with articles such as 'Suicide among the Irish and English emigrants in 1870s New York', *Proceedings of the Associação Portuguesa de Estudos Anglo-Americanos, XXVII Encontro, 'Crossroads of History and Culture' I* (2007); 'Eluding the care of their guardians: suicide, their families and the state in post-Famine Ireland', forthcoming in C. Cox and M. Luddy (eds), *Practices and cultures of care in Irish medical history* (2010), and 'Murder in nineteenth-century Cavan, 1809–91', *Breifne: Journal of Cumann Seanchais Breifne* (2009). Her monograph, *Suicide in Ireland, 1831–1921: a social and cultural study*, is forthcoming.

FELIX M. LARKIN has recently retired from the Irish public service. He studied history at UCD in the years 1968–72, and has written about that experience in an essay in *Dublin in the medieval world: essays in honour of Howard B. Clarke*, edited by John Bradley, Alan J. Fletcher and Anngret Simms (2009). Vice-chairman of the National Library of Ireland Society, he edited *Librarians, poets and scholars: a Festschrift for Dónall Ó Luanaigh* (2007) on behalf of the Society. In 2008, he was a founder-member of the Newspaper and Periodicals History Forum of Ireland (www.newspapersperiodicals.org).

CATHERINE LAWLESS is a lecturer in the History of Art, specializing in fourteenth- and fifteenth-century Florentine art, with a particular emphasis on religious and devotional imagery, the relationship between religious belief and representation, text and image, hagiography and iconography, and representation and gender. She has published widely in these fields, and some of her recent publications include Christine Meek and Catherine Lawless (eds), *Victims or viragos? Women in late medieval and early modern Europe* (2005), and Christine Meek and Catherine Lawless (eds), *Pawns or players? Women in late medieval and early modern Europe* (2003).

MAXIME LEROY has been a lecturer at the Université de Mulhouse (France) since 2007. He graduated in 2003 with a PhD from the Université d'Angers on authorial prefaces from Walter Scott to Joseph Conrad. He has published several articles on the use of paratext in Scott, Thackeray and James. He is currently preparing a book on authorial illustrations in nineteenth-century British and Irish novels.

KIERA LINDSEY teaches at the University of Melbourne and is currently completing a PhD concerned with the 200 Irish bride thieves who were transported to the Australian colonies in the first half of the nineteenth century. In 2008, she was awarded a U21 Visiting Scholarship and was based at UCD.

LEON LITVACK is Reader in Victorian Studies at QUB. He has a special interest in Ireland and the visual arts in the nineteenth century, and is the editor (with Glen Hooper) of *Ireland in the nineteenth century: regional identity* (2000) and (Colin Graham) *Ireland and Europe in the nineteenth century* (2006). He has also authored a host of works on Charles Dickens. He is a Past President of the Society for the Study of Nineteenth-Century Ireland.

SEÁN LUCEY is an IRCHSS post-doctoral scholar at TCD. His previous publications include *The Irish National League in Dingle, County Kerry* in the Maynooth Local History Series (2003). His forthcoming monograph (*Land and popular politics in County Kerry, 1872–86*) will be published by UCD Press.

CATHERINE MARSHALL is currently on secondment from the Irish Museum of Modern Art. She is co-editor of Volume V of the Art and Architecture of Ireland Project (Royal Irish Academy and Yale University Press). She has published widely on modern and contemporary Irish art.

PATRICK MAUME is a graduate of UCC and QUB in History, English and Politics. He has taught in History and Politics departments and is currently a researcher with the Royal Irish Academy's Dictionary of Irish Biography. He has contributed to several SSNCI publications and has edited several texts for the UCD Press Classics of Irish History series, as well as publishing biographies of Daniel Corkery and D.P. Moran and *The long gestation: Irish nationalist political life, 1891–1918* (1999). He has a particular interest in newspaper and periodical history.

PHILIP MCEVANSONEYA is a lecturer in the History of Art at Trinity College Dublin. He has published widely on painting in Europe, 1600–1900, with particular reference to Britain, Ireland and France. Some of his recent publications include '"A thing to be seen": creating the Crampton collection of English watercolours in the 1850s', *Journal of the History of Collections*, 21:1 (2009), 95–110, and 'Making choices: Hugh Lane's selection of works by Degas, Monet, Pissarro and Puvis de Chavannes for the gallery of modern art' in B. Dawson et al. (eds), *Hugh Lane: founder of a gallery of modern art for Ireland* (2008), 36–43. His current research is on aspects of Irish art, 1800–50.

PATRICK NAUGHTIN is currently at the University of Melbourne completing a PhD on Irish nationalism in colonial Victoria during the Parnell era. He has a masters degree in Australian Studies from Monash University, where he studied the Irish in nineteenth-century Australian society. In a long teaching career, he has taught history extensively in secondary schools in Australia and overseas.

SEÁN Ó DUINNSHLÉIBHE is a College Lecturer in the Department of Modern Irish, UCC. His research interests include post-classical Irish prose writings, Gaelic scribal activity of the later period (seventeenth to nineteenth centuries), the field accounts of collectors working for the Irish Folklore Commission, in particular those kept by full-time folklore collector Seán Ó Cróinín, and the portrayal of eighteenth- and nineteenth-century Gaelic literary figures in later oral narrative. He is one of the founders and editors of *Béascna* (UCC Journal of Folklore and Ethnology).

NIAMH O'SULLIVAN is Professor of Visual Culture at the National College of Art and Design, Dublin. She writes on Irish and Irish-American art and popular culture. Her book, *Aloysius O'Kelly: art, nation, empire* (2010) was published by Field Day.

OLWEN PURDUE is a post-doctoral scholar currently working at the Institute of Irish Studies, QUB, on poverty, welfare and public health in nineteenth- and twentieth-century Belfast. Her recent publications include *The Big House in the north of Ireland: land, power and elites, 1878–1960* (2009) and *The MacGeough Bonds of The Argory: an Ulster gentry family, 1880–1950* (2005).

SARAH RODDY holds an MA in Irish History from QUB, and is currently completing a PhD thesis on clerical attitudes towards emigration from nineteenth-century Ireland.

Introduction

CIARA BREATHNACH &
CATHERINE LAWLESS

In a 2001 book, Roy Porter confessed that as a historian he was as 'a child of Guttenberg', having spent most of his professional life 'trapped in a web of words'.[1] While art historians and historians of visual culture do not hesitate to cross disciplinary boundaries, the same cannot be said about mainstream historians, who continue to have difficulties reconciling documentary, two-dimensional and three-dimensional sources. Given the inconsistent nature of documentary sources, non-textual sources are essential to the study of nineteenth-century Ireland.[2] This volume, like Úna Ní Bhroiméil and Glenn Hooper's *Land and Landscape*, feeds into a shift in wider historiographical trends, where historians and literary scholars of both Irish and English are increasingly using images as integral primary sources and not just as frontispieces or last-minute centrefolds.[3] It also reflects advances in publishing practices that allow for cheaper image reproduction.

Emanating from the 2008 Society for the Study of Nineteenth-Century Ireland Conference of the same name, this volume brings together scholars engaging with multi-media primary sources, and reflects the vibrancy of such research. The strong emphasis on illustrated texts highlights a growing interdisciplinary approach to scholarship of Ireland. There are discussions of various symbols, and the plurality of Irish identities is expressed in many of the chapters. This volume highlights the development and application of digital humanities in nineteenth-century Irish research agendas, which has gone some way towards reconciling issues surrounding access but, more importantly, is allowing for greater disciplinary fluidity. Thematically, this volume can be roughly divided by the type of source material used, beginning with art history and what can be broadly termed 'aesthetic nationalism', forming the basis of the first six chapters. The use of illustrated texts incorporating the gradual use of photography as well as news print culture provides the basis for the central chapters, while a miscellany of writings – ego-documents, translations and official records – are used in the closing chapters.

The volume begins with Catherine Marshall's piece on the difficulty of memorializing the Great Famine from historical and contemporary perspectives. Few

1 Roy Porter, *Bodies politic: disease, death and doctors in Britain, 1650–1900* (London, 2001), p. 9. 2 Jordanova uses a wide explanation of non-textual sources to include art, photography, music, material culture, seals and maps, to mention but a few: see Ludmilla Jordanova, *History in practice* (2nd ed., London, 2006), pp 163–7. 3 Arising from the 2005 SSNCI conference held at Mary Immaculate College, Limerick, Úna Ní Bhroiméil and Glenn Hooper (eds), *Land and landscape in nineteenth-century Ireland* (Dublin, 2007).

scholars have attempted such a challenge and Marshall explains why by discussing issues of famine and identity through a juxtaposition of nineteenth-century and modern artistic interpretations.[4] Problematizing the impact that famine had on collective Irish memory, and locating her discussion within a wider discourse of historical trauma and commemoration, Marshall concludes that, with the exception of isolated efforts, the event was too painful to visually document until relatively recently. In stark contrast with Marshall's chapter, which points to a visual hiatus, Niamh O'Sullivan focuses on cultures of display in early nineteenth-century Dublin. Her account of the exposition of Gericault's *Raft of the Medusa* (1821), is located in a broader discussion of trends of display at that time. She notes the popularity of panoramas among Dublin's elite, while the critics and the public at large paid little attention to Gericault's masterpiece. In this chapter, O'Sullivan explains why the painting met with little appreciation in the early decades of the Union. Philip McEvansoneya's chapter details how the Royal Irish Academy raised funds to buy a reliquary of national significance. In the process, the Academy managed to fend off stiff competition from the British Museum and wealthy antiquarians. The eventual location of the reliquary, as McEvansoneya carefully shows, involved varying degrees of diplomacy and set precedents for acquisition policies. This chapter also recognizes the crucial role of the Academy in the absence of a National Museum. Although the function of the former did little to promote an appreciation of antiquities among the public at large, it did encourage the historical awareness of the potential for antiquities to possess a value and significance in terms of national identity. Staying with the concept of objects concerning national identity, Cullen's analysis of the role of the harp in authenticating other Irish symbols, like the Milesian Crown, gives us an interesting insight into how such contested elements of identity became institutionalized in nationalist iconography. She carefully traces the use of the Harp from the revival of ancient symbols in Bunting's eighteenth-century publications to O'Connell's repeal movement. She also notes the derogatory usage of Irish symbolism by *Punch*. Cullen's analysis of harp aetiology raises a number of questions about the authenticity and use of other nationalist and national symbols.

The exploration of a renewed interest in the medieval is continued in the contribution by Elizabeth Boyle, which takes issue with Young's appraisal of the work of Margaret Stokes on medieval Irish saints and evidence of Irish *Peregrini* in Europe. Boyle argues that those who brush Stokes aside as superficial fail to take account of gender constraints in nineteenth-century Ireland and therefore underestimate the importance of the style of her delivery. Boyle also notes the maturity between volumes, with a certain toning down of 'picturesque language' employed in early writings to more of an emphasis on historical evidence in later work.

4 Margaret Kelleher, *The feminization of famine: expressions of the inexpressible* (Durham, NC, 1997). This seminal work tackles the issue of representing famine in literature. Hedda Friberg, Irene Glisenan Nordin and Lene Ydind Pedersen, *Recovering memory: Irish representations of past and present* (Newcastle, 2007). Various essays in this volume deal with various concepts of 're-covering' collective memory in Irish literature.

Catherine Lawless' chapter examines the role of religious iconography as public art. In the aftermath of the Synod of Thurles, Ultramontanism grew exponentially and church-building flourished. Lawless traces how certain cults were chosen and represented status in post-Famine Ireland. She recognizes the function of the hierarchy in the promotion and proliferation of religious iconography, which in turn fuelled an international trade in stained glass, statues, altars and other ecclesiastical objects. Providing further social and religious context for Lawless, Patrick Maume focuses on the writings of Margaret Anna Cusack (1829–99), more popularly known as the 'Nun of Kenmare', and in particular her Ultramontane phase, although she was later to renounce this stance and, indeed, her Catholicism. He shows how, through her works, she reflected, and at times participated in, many of the religious controversies of her day.

Robin Kavanagh's chapter eases the transition from thematic discussions of fine art, antiquities and high church politics to illustrated texts. Kavanagh presents a fascinating case-study and sketches exactly how powerful the Catholic illustrated press became during the course of the 1830s. Kavanagh makes great use of carefully chosen images to emphasize the importance of the visual in conveying a Catholic message to the masses (of varying levels of literacy) when the church was faced with opposition from proselytizing Evangelical magazines. Maxime Leroy examines the role of illustration in the literary work of Samuel Lover's *Handy Andy*, and their centrality to textual enhancement. Noting an even dispersion of images throughout the novel, Leroy draws our attention to how Lover wished the images to work with the action scenes.

Leon Litvack traces advances in photographic techniques and highlights the competitiveness of the Dublin industry in order to contextualize James Robinson's photographic reproductions of Wallis' (1830–1916) painting of the purported suicide of the tragic Thomas Chatterton (1752–70). A complicated copyright case ensued, as the owner of the painting had sold the copyright to a third party who held reproduction rights with tenacity and held Robinson to account. Litvack's chapter highlights the voracious Victorian appetite for visual representations, how it drove rapid changes in the field of professional photography and that this in turn forced copyright law to maintain a similar pace. Justin Carville's piece focuses on how quickly the use of photography was absorbed by nineteenth-century ethnographers as a scientific method in their fieldwork. He examines the role of the RIA, anthropologists and scientists of physiognomy in the attempt to locate 'the Irish face' in the racial hierarchy. Carville, using images reproduced from the *Proceedings of the Royal Irish Academy*, highlights how important it is to examine the function of photometric anthropometry in the context of the dialogue between photographer and subject. He notes how this conversation has been overlooked by scholars and advises that the term 'visual economy' rather than 'visual culture' be employed in such studies.

Carla King's chapter accounts for Davitt's career as a journalist at a time when that profession had begun to rise in social stature. King weaves the history of nationalism with an account of the crucial role played by the national and regional press in achieving a sense of a collective identity. This essay gives us an impression of Davitt's working life and the difficulties he faced at a time when critical decisions in news-paper official appointments hinged largely on social and political networks. Indeed, his own journalistic writings were polemic offerings to what King terms a 'counter-culture' to Parnellism. Following on from King's essay, Olivier Coquelin juxtaposes the function of two sets of ego-documents in an attempt to ascertain the experience of incarceration for political reasons. Using the prison writings of John Mitchel and Michael Davitt, Coquelin traces how these late nineteenth-century writings informed and shaped later republican works. Crossman, Lucey, Purdue and Laragy's piece on Welfare Regimes in mid- to late nineteenth-century Ireland argues that the general understanding of the Irish Poor Law is limited because of the 'relatively under-developed state of social history in Ireland, but not, it should be emphasized, a lack of source material'. This chapter gives a distillation of the findings of the Welfare Regimes project, which identifies a number of sources and suggests creative ways in examining and augmenting such material.

Echoing King's appraisal of Davitt's career in the Irish media, Felix Larkin gives us a succinct analysis of the influence of two key figures in the development of the *Freeman's Journal* from 1892 to 1916. Detailing their political and religious origins, Larkin highlights how small were the political and journalistic circles during that period and how such identifiable links led to the dwindling circulation of the *Freeman's*. Faced with stiff competition from the cheaper and better financed *Irish Independent*, both men withdrew or were replaced post-1916 by a newer wave in editorial and journalistic practices. Pat Naughtin's treatment of the *Melbourne Advocate* provides us with an understanding of how Ireland was portrayed in diasporic terms. Both King and Larkin highlight how the Irish press fed a voracious appetite for news from home and helped to maintain a two-way contact between Ireland and those emigrants who might be more appropriately called 'the exiled'. Naughtin links the success of the survival of the *Advocate* with strong backing from the Catholic hier-archy and its growing congregation. Identifying Irish birth, nationalist tendencies and Catholicism as key characteristics of its founders, the aims and achievements of the newspaper were fairly predictable. Naughtin, however, challenges historiographical perceptions that the *Sydney Freeman's Journal* was more significant than the *Advocate* in raising awareness about Irish political agendas.

In the interests of regional continuity, and offering a different perspective of Irish identity in Australia, this volume continues with Kiera Lindsey's study of stage Irishism, albeit in an earlier period. Lindsey tells us that Edward Geoghegan's *Currency Lass* was the first representation of an Irish character, and Lindsey uses the play as a prism on Sydney society. It offers a different perspective of the social posi-tion of the Irish in early colonial life. Lindsey, through her analysis of this play notes how some of the newly arrived Irish managed to share the same social platform as native-born, first-generation Europeans, as distinct from the native aboriginal peoples. Locating Geoghegan's play within the stage Irishman genre, Lindsey informs us that in the Australian context, the nuances of language require further contextualization in an increasingly layered social fabric that clearly assigned class and related privileges. Lindsey's chapter unveils Geoghegan's real underlying agenda as identifying the possibility of the reinvention of Irish identity in the remote outposts of empire, even if the play was short-lived.

Sarah Roddy's essay adds to the discussion about the role of personal letters in fuelling the diaspora and draws attention to the role played by clergy to counteract some of the falsehoods and exaggerated accounts of wealth and conditions. Roddy provides a fair representation of denominational counter-literature to such emigrant claims. These resulting guidebooks, as Roddy notes, were useful to a point and offered little solace to emigrants going to remote areas that did not offer the infrastructures associated with organized religion. The last contribution is Sean Ó Dúinnsléibhe's assessment of de Barra's surviving translations. Noting a considerable dearth in research in this area among scholars of Gaeilge, this contribution adds to a general understanding of the how literate the Gaelic Irish were.

We hope that the volume will be a significant contribution to the growing interdisciplinarity among scholars of nineteenth-century Ireland, with essays from the fields of art history, print culture, literary history and social history.

History and memorials: fine art and the Great Famine in Ireland

CATHERINE MARSHALL

In a self-portrait called *The Bogman* from 1995, Robert Ballagh (1943–) represents himself as an archaeologist, digging into the landscape for clues to his own identity (fig. 1.1). His pose, notwithstanding the spade he digs with, in typical self-deprecation, mimics that of *Cúchulainn* in the iconic statue by Oliver Sheppard (1865–1941) in the GPO in Dublin, a reference made all the more explicit through the presence of a bird on his shoulder, like Cúchulainn's raven of death (fig. 1.2). Ballagh the modern man, references both the heroic myth and the site of the struggle for Irish Independence in 1916, yet he does not stop there. The digging figure and the framing, fictive Romanesque arch, with its Irish language inscription, suggest that there are other histories beyond those immediately visible; other realities not alluded to by the mythical pose.

We are all rightfully concerned with history and what it tells us about ourselves and our collective heritage. The desire to commemorate defining moments from the past appears to be universal, but we must understand what precisely we are about when we do it. Jean-François Lyotard claims that memorializing great events is problematic because the words or images used to perpetuate the memory of the event paradoxically lead us, instead, to forget it.[1] Lyotard has a number of issues with memorializing historical moments; the memorial comes to stand in place of the thing it represents and, in so doing, displaces the original. In Lyotard's view, the memorial is usually too specific, too representative of a particular perspective of the original experience and hence blocks access to wider readings of the event. It gives ownership of the event to some rather than to all. Most importantly, it is generally associated with traditions of the grand-narratives of history and therefore denies the experience of the individual.

To take Lyotard seriously, we have to reconsider the value of grand memorializing projects such as the twentieth-century attempts to commemorate the Great Famine in Ireland and in those areas of the world where the Irish settled in their struggle to escape it. Since most of those commemorative projects have a strongly visual aspect, it is informative to briefly outline the visualities surrounding that particular event in Ireland's past.[2] Difficulties with the term 'the Famine' prove Lyotard's

---

1 Jean François Lyotard, *The post modern condition: a report on knowledge* (Paris, 1979; repr. Manchester, 1984), ch. 5. Sarah Kofman, *Smothered words*, trans. Madeleine Dobie (Chicago, IL, 1995). Kofman here discusses Lyotard's theory in relation to attempts to commemorate the suffering of the Jews during the Holocaust. **2** The term 'visualities' refers to the ways

1.1 Robert Ballagh, *The Bogman* (1997). Oil on canvas, 200 × 122cm.
Reproduced with kind permission of Robert Ballagh

1.2 Oliver Sheppard, *Cúchulainn* (1911). Bronze, 150 × 62cm. GPO, Dublin. Reproduced with kind permission of An Post.

point, since the country continued to produce great quantities of food while those dependent on the potato were allowed to die when that crop failed between 1845 and 1850 and on other occasions throughout the remainder of the century. The presence of the word displaces the reality. Far from the grand memorializing project, however, it is the absence of visual representation of the Hunger that is the most obvious thing to an art historian.

The history of the representation of the Famine in fine art has been rehearsed elsewhere, so a brief outline will suffice here.[3] Only a small handful of artworks directly referencing the 'Hunger' are known to have been produced in the nineteenth century, of which Daniel McDonald's *The Irish Peasant Family Discovering the Blight of their Store* (1847; Folklore Department, UCD) is the only known painting of the subject by a contemporary Irish artist. McDonald's untimely death at the age of thirty-two means that very little of his work survives. Most of the other contemporary paintings of the Famine and its impact on the lives of the peasants in Ireland that have come to light are by English artists. G.F. Watts (1817–1904) and F. Goodall

'in which vision is constructed in various ways; how we see, how we are able, allowed, or made to see, and how we see this seeing and the unseeing therein': Hal Foster (ed.), *Vision and visuality* (Seattle, WA, 1988), p. ix.   **3** Catherine Marshall, 'Painting Irish history: the Famine', *History Ireland*, 4: 3 (1996), 46–50.

(1822–1904), in keeping with contemporary taste for social realism, produced sympathetic depictions of it. Others, such as the Scottish artist, Erskine Nicol (1825–1904), who worked in Ireland between 1845 and 1850 and produced picture after picture of Irish peasants for the London art market, were much less sympathetic. Nicol's paintings, on the whole, suggested that the Irish peasants were not as badly off as the newspapers and nationalist politicians claimed, and served to reassure both the government and art collectors in England that the Irish neither required nor were worthy of government assistance.

The story of the food shortages and attendant social upheaval is represented in a series of illustrations for a number of new journals, most particularly for the *Illustrated London News*. Particularly interesting in relation to the first set of illustrations – those by James O'Mahoney, Wakeman, Topham and others – is the relatively sanitized picture they present compared to the graphic verbal descriptions that accompany them.[4] Another point to note is that although James O'Mahoney went on to paint the visit of Queen Victoria to the Great Exhibition in Dublin in 1853, there is no evidence that he ever attempted to paint the history of the Famine, although Cork, his native county, was particularly affected by it.[5] The omission is notable since for most artists it was their role as painters not illustrators that guaranteed their place in the hall of fame.

While a number of pictures of evictions and emigration scenes exist, in a discipline where the depiction of history was considered to be the single most important goal of the artist, the general scarcity of paintings of the Famine and its impact on Ireland is quite shocking. The clichéd and superficial explanation offered for this is that the Irish were visually illiterate and unaccomplished. It would certainly be fair to say that access to and education in the visual arts was confined to a very small sector of the population, not only in the nineteenth century but also for most of the next one. A study of the relevant visualities, however, points to more complex reasons. Standard art histories, informed by connoisseurship, investigate those artworks that exist in a stylistic way. They give less if any attention to the factors that pre-empt the artistic exploration of a subject or the factors governing the means of production. Since the emergence of what used to be described as 'the new art history' in the 1960s and 1970s, inspired by the works of Marxist and feminist writers, such a narrow focus is no longer tenable. New art history demands, instead, that a study of the visualities governing the creation of an artwork should provide an in-depth analysis of the context of its making, Attitudes to race, nationalism, fashion, patronage, market forces and psychological factors can impact on art production and are particularly relevant to representations of trauma on the scale encountered in mid-nineteenth-century Ireland.

4 For fuller discussion of this see Niamh O'Sullivan, *Aloysius O'Kelly: re-orientations* (Dublin, 1999). **5** For further information see Michelle O'Mahony, *Famine in Cork city: famine life at Cork Union Workhouse* (Dublin, 2005); Colman O'Mahony, *Cork's Poor Law palace: workhouse life, 1838–1890* (Cork, 2005).

Undoubtedly, when faced with disease and death from hunger, one's first incli-
nation is surely to alleviate distress, if possible, rather than to paint it. The fact that
many artists had to emigrate means that they were not in the country to record the
disaster, which they may also have found too disturbing. Thomas Hovenden (1840–
1895) may be a case in point. Orphaned at the age of five in 1845, he went on to
enjoy a successful career as a history painter in the USA, but never attempted to paint
anything of the scenes he must have witnessed as a young man growing up in Co.
Cork. Since he and his wife were actively opposed to slavery and he painted sympathetic pictures of African Americans, the absence of Irish subject matter suggests that
he found it too painful.[6]

Whatever their personal inhibitions, the need for patronage must have made it
impossible for Irish artists to paint the subject of the Famine. Apart from a brief
period in 1847, the government in England provided little in the way of Famine
relief, preferring to view the failure of the potato crop as a natural solution to Anglo-
Irish difficulties.[7] There is significant anecdotal evidence to suggest that government
circles and their wider social networks in Ireland were likely to find Nicol's caricatures of drunken, lazy peasants more to their taste than accurate portrayals of
deprivation. Letters to the newspapers at the closure of the Ordnance Survey
Memoir two years before the first outbreak of the potato blight indicate that there
was a strong belief that the government had closed it because they considered that
educating the Irish in their own history would nationalize them.[8] To draw attention
to one's Irishness was to reduce opportunities for patronage. One of the most
successful artists in Victorian London, William Mulready (1786–1863) found it necessary to deny his Irish birth,[9] while James George O'Brien (1779–1819) a generation
earlier changed his name to Oben, as it seemed less Irish.[10] Frederick William
Burton's (1816–1900) reluctance to represent Irish history as his friend Thomas Davis
had exhorted him to do, was rewarded when he was appointed Director of the
National Gallery in London in 1874.[11] As late as 1890, the critical reception afforded

6 Julian Campbell, 'Thomas Hovenden (1840–95): a Cork artist in Brittany and America' in
Jane Fenlon, Nicola Figgis and Catherine Marshall, *New perspectives* (Dublin, 1987), pp
187–93.   **7** British governmental attitudes to the Famine and famine relief in Ireland are
well documented in Peter Gray, 'Ideology and the Famine' in Cathal Poirtéir, *The Great Irish
Famine* (Cork, 1995), pp 86–103. For a good discussion of them in relation to an artwork,
see Kevin Whelan, 'Immoral economy: interpreting Erskine Nicol's, 'The Tenant' in Adele
Dalsimer and Vera Kreilkamp (eds), *America's eye: Irish paintings from the collection of Brian P.
Burns* (Boston, 1996), pp 57–67.   **8** See letter from 'Protestant Conservative', May 1842, in
the Larcom Papers, Ms 7554, National Library of Ireland, and letters to *The Evening Mail*, 8
Mar. 1843 and *The Freeman's Journal*, 11 Mar. 1843; *The Nation*, 6 Apr. 1943.   **9** Marcia
Pointon, *William Mulready* (London, 1986).   **10** 'The artist though long much esteemed in
Dublin, was not at the opening of the exhibition [at Parliament House, Dublin, 1801]
recollected by anyone. The pieces of O'Brien had often been admired, but Oben had never
been heard of, at length it was discovered that the idea of foreign workmanship being
preferred in the London market, had induced him to Germanize his ci-devant appellation',
Anonymous diarist, Royal Irish Academy Ms 24K14, pp 258–9.   **11** For Davis' plea to

to the painting *An Irish Eviction* by Lady Elizabeth Butler (1846–1933), despite her position as Britain's most noted painter of battle pictures, would also have warned others to avoid this subject matter.[12] These are just some of the indicators that an artist had to be careful about references to Ireland if he wanted to succeed. Racist cartoons in *Punch* in London and *Harpers Weekly* in New York by Thomas Nast (1840–1902) and J.J. Rogers created such a negative picture of Irishness that it was particularly difficult for an artist to record sympathetic impressions of Ireland and hope to find a market for them in the years immediately following the Famine.[13]

Ultimately, the failure to record the Famine in painting and sculpture in the nineteenth century offers proof if proof is needed, of Lyotard's theory of the grand narrative. The one million people who died from fever and starvation and the millions who emigrated were all individuals, but their personal stories never conform to the concept of the grand-narrative. They were not victors whose lives became the source of future myth and so their history was not commemorated or monumentalized. Clearly, the task of making sense of this history for the large numbers of people who endured hunger, death and loss could not be addressed until major political and social change had taken place. Even with the development of Irish independence and a slow but steady rise in living standards, the difficulty of coming to terms with the history of the Famine was too traumatic for subsequent generations. When, in 1946, the National College of Art hosted an exhibition dedicated to Irish history, it was felt that the Famine was still too painful to form its central theme. Although the planning for the exhibition took place in the centenary year of the first appearance of the potato blight, the exhibition was dedicated instead to the memory of Thomas Davis, whose name lent itself more readily to the notion of a grand narrative.[14]

Speaking at the Civil Art's Enquiry in Dublin in 2003, Irit Rogoff pointed out that '[T]raditionally, the task of commemoration has always been perceived as the replacement of an absence with a presence'.[15] By the end of the twentieth century, following the 150th anniversary of the Great Famine and in a very different social context from the original one, several 'presences' in the form of bronze sculptures began to appear around Ireland, the United States, Canada and Australia; wherever the emigrant Irish had established themselves since that event. Nearly a century of self-government and growing prosperity gave Irish artists the confidence to face their complex emotions in relation to this heritage of loss. It is important to consider what they achieved. What do these presences amount to? Images of ragged emigrants

Burton see Thomas Davis, *Literary and historical essays* (Dublin, 1846), pp 213–15. Burton became Director of the National Gallery in London in 1874, for which he purchased over 450 important artworks.   **12** Ann Crookshank, the Knight of Glin, *Ireland's painters, 1600–1940* (New Haven and London, 2002), p. 263. Also Paul Usherwood, Jenny Spencer-Smith, *Lady Butler: battle artist, 1846–1933* (Stroud, Gloucestershire, 1987), pp 94–5.   **13** See L.P. Curtis, *Apes and angels: the Irish in Victorian caricature* (Washington DC, 1971).   **14** 'The Thomas Davis Young Ireland Movement Centenary Exhibition: pictures of Irish historical interest', National College of Art, Dublin, 1946.   **15** Irit Rogoff, 'Making art in public, reading the agreement' in *The civil arts enquiry, documents 1–6* (Dublin, 2003), p. 101.

heading for coffin ships or beggars by the roadside provide some insight into one set of experiences, but they are one-sided and exclusive. A better model of this kind of memorial is offered by the German artists Jochen Gerz (b. 1940) and Esther Shevez Gerz, in their Harburg Anti-Fascist Memorial in Hamburg, built between 1986 and 1993. For this work, the artists built a 12m-high tower, in eight stages, each one of which was visible long enough for passers-by to mark it with their own impressions, memories and feelings about the historic event and its ongoing impact on them. As each section was filled with such marks, it was lowered into the ground and the next section was made available, until the whole edifice had been discussed, graffitied and even shot at. The completed tower, with some 60,000 visual reactions to it, is now completely hidden and can only be glimpsed through a window.[16] It remains as both a presence, partially visible to those who seek it out, and an absence, because, like the history that it commemorates, it is no longer physically evident. The process of engagement with the artwork mimics the process of engagement with the history itself.

Holocaust studies indicate that the act of commemoration is central to an understanding and healing of the original trauma.[17] In the Irish poetic imagination, the country, Ireland, was for centuries personified as a beautiful woman who appealed, through the poets, for a prince to rescue her from her distress and to comfort and restore her. Generations of Irish men, during and after the Famine, were critically disempowered by their inability to fulfil this role. Their response, finally, in the late 1990s, supported by a sudden period of prosperity, was to create traditional, bronze memorials, paradoxically fixing the image of Irish poverty for all time in expensive and durable materials. The question posed by these monuments is 'to what extent do these new presences fulfil the task of commemoration?' Or do they, as Lyotard suggested, displace the original with a too-specific perspective on the real historic event?

A number of artworks by Alanna O'Kelly offer wider possibilities. In these works, photographs of the landscape overlaid with text, and tape/slide or DVD installations, the artist combines images and sounds of life, birth, nurture, nature and death. In *Sanctuary/Wasteland* (1994; Irish Museum of Modern Art), the artist's own voice is heard, keening for the dead, a traditional mourning ritual from prehistoric times in Ireland, and singing the *Caoineadh Airt Uí Laoghaire* (The Keening of Art O'Leary) (fig. 1.3).[18] In another work from the same trilogy, *No Colouring Can Deepen ...The*

---

16 Monument against fascism, Hamburg-Harburg, 1986–93. Collaborative work with Esther Shalev-Gerz. A commission by the city of Hamburg. www.c3.hu/scca/butterfly/Gerz/cv.html, accessed 11 Oct. 2009.   17 Monica Bohm-Duchen, 'After Auschwitz: art and the Holocaust' in Stephen Feinstein (ed.), *Absence/presence: critical essays on the artistic memory of the Holocaust* (Syracuse, NY, 2005), pp 55–69. See also Kofman, *Smothered words.* 18 Caoineadh Airt Uí Laoire, a lament for a young Irishman, allegedly shot for possession of a horse in Kerry during the period of the Penal Laws, is attributed to his wife, Eibhlín Ní Chonaill. Eileen O'Connell, *Caoineadh Airt Uí Laoghaire*, nuachóiriú le Seán Ó Tuama (BÁC, 1979). See works by Angela Bourke, 'The Irish traditional lament and the grieving process', *Women's Studies International Forum*, 11:4 (1988), 287–91.

1.3 Alanna O'Kelly, *Sanctuary/Wasteland* (1993), detail. Tape/slide installation, various dimensions. IMMA. Reproduced with kind permission of Alanna O'Kelly.

Darkness of Truth, a baby's first cry mingles with wind and the waves, or the whispering murmur of voices intoning the names of homelands from which they have been displaced.[19] The use of the Irish language in many of these works reminds us of the impact the Famine had on Gaelic Ireland. O'Kelly's multi-faceted process both embodies and symbolizes the expansive effects of the original event and its ongoing effect on Irish people. Just as pertinently, by introducing sounds from other places, such as pipe music from India or Australian didgeridoo sounds, O'Kelly reminds us that the Irish experience was not unique and that death by starvation, whether caused by climate change or political action, is still a presence in the world. This internationalizing of the Famine is not new, as suggested by the 1848 text superimposed by O'Kelly on one of the photographs in *The Country Blooms: a Garden and a Grave* (1990; Crawford Municipal Art Gallery, Cork) (fig. 1.4):

> *The rock of Gibraltar grows no corn*
> *The County of Cork does.*
> *Such is the admirable working of the Union of Ireland and England;*
> *The Garrisons and citizens of Gibraltar live well, feed abundantly.*
> *They care no more for the potato rot*

19 *No colouring can deepen the darkness of truth*, by Alanna O'Kelly, was installed permanently in the Workhouse in Carrick-on-Shannon, Co. Letrim, in 2008.

1.4 Alanna O'Kelly, *The Country Blooms: a Garden and a Grave* (1990), detail.
2/6 photomontage panels, 50 × 70cm and 50 × 50cm. Crawford Municipal
Art Gallery, Cork. Reproduced with kind permission of Allana O'Kelly.

Than they do a deficient date crop in Arabia,
While in Co. Cork, in Skiberreen whole families
Of men, women and children
are lying in heaps in the corners of hovels,
Some dead, some alive,
Skiberreen starves and raves and dies
That Gibraltar, St Helena and the rest of them
Be kept in good condition.[20]

In an article about O'Kelly's work for the 1996 São Paulo Bienal, the art curator and
critic Jean Fisher referred to the writing of the philosopher Giorgio Agamben, to
highlight the importance of language for human development. Agamben identifies
the moment of passage from language to discourse as the moment of history.
Agreeing with this, Fisher believes that the loss of the mother tongue is tantamount
to de-humanizing.[21] The Famine therefore, caused a double de-humanizing through
death and through loss of the mother tongue. Irish people have been struggling to
come to terms with this double loss ever since, and it is only through understanding
that process and allowing the grief that accompanies it to be expressed that this
trauma can be healed. The sincerity of that grief can be tested through our reactions
to contemporary famine. Only then can we begin to fill the absence Rogoff speaks
of.

'What is it that a work of historical commemoration wishes to achieve?', she
asks.[22] Rogoff is concerned that we must not turn history into an event. 'Those who

20 *The country blooms: a garden and a grave*, 1990 (Crawford Municipal Art Gallery, Cork).
21 Jean Fisher, *Alanna O'Kelly* (Dublin, 1996). **22** Irit Rogoff, 'The aesthetics of post-
history: a German perspective' in Claudia Mesch and Viola Michely (eds), *Joseph Beuys: the
reader* (London, 2007), pp 270–84 at p. 270.

perpetrated crimes against the innocent in the names of political ideologies or political expediencies are now confronted with the need to remember as part of some form of reconciliation with history. At the same time, the victims, or what remains of them in altered forms, are simultaneously confronted with the spectre of their reinscription into history as a potential healing of the very trauma of their initial excision', she points out.[23] To prevent the commemoration of the Famine from becoming just such an event, the thing that displaces the actual history, we must look to artwork like O'Kelly's that is suggestive and inclusive, rather than prescriptive, and which embraces the original event from various perspectives. It must resist efforts to mythologize the event and enable the viewer to enter an imaginative space where mourning and healing can begin.

23 Rogoff, 'Making art in public', p. 100.

Troubled waters: high art and popular culture, Dublin, 1821

NIAMH O'SULLIVAN

The shipwreck of the French frigate, *Méduse*, on 2 July 1816 off the west coast of Africa inspired Théodore Géricault (1791–1824) to paint one of the defining visual statements of Romanticism, *Le radeau de la Méduse* (*The Raft of the Medusa* (1818–19), Musée du Louvre, oil on canvas, 491cm by 716cm).[1] In addition to many other paintings, the *Méduse* has been the subject of a striking number of treatments in film, novel and music, and has also lent itself to extensive political, historical and cultural debate.[2] Arguably, had it not been for Géricault's memorable canvas, the subject would have faded into arcane shipwreck history. Such was the power of Géricault's image that it has spawned almost 200 years of recollection and reference, commentary and homage, and almost every generation claims its relevance to its own day.[3] While

---

1 I am very grateful to Prof. Luke Gibbons, Prof. Fintan Cullen and Dr Philip McEvansoneya for discussions related to this essay. 2 Examples include plays by W.T. Moncrieff, *The fatal raft* (1820), and Georg Kaiser, *Das Floß der Medusa* (1940–3); Iradj Azimi's film, *Le radeau de la Méduse* (1994); Hans Werner Henze's oratorio *Das Floß der Medusa* (1968); novels, such as Peter Weiss, *Die asthetik des widerstands* (1975–81), Julian Barnes, *A history of the world in 10 and a half chapters* (1989) and Arabella Edge, *The raft* (2006). It has featured on album covers, such as Great White's *Sail away* (1994) and the Pogues', *Rum, sodomy and the lash* (1985), and been imbricated into popular culture in *Astérix légionnaire* (1967) and *The Silence of the Lambs* (1991), for example. Contemporary Irish artists, among others, Andy Folan (2003) and Robert Ballagh (2009), have also revisited the painting and explored its meaning for today. 3 From contemporary accounts written by survivors, to the work of modern day art historians and cultural theorists, the literature on the shipwreck itself, as well as Géricault's painting is vast. Albert Alhadeff, *The Raft of the Medusa: Géricault, art and race* (Munich, London and New York, 1988); Clément Charles, *Géricault: étude biographique et critique avec le catalogue raisonné de l'oeuvre du maître* (Paris, 3rd ed., 1867); Jonathan Crary, 'Géricault, the panorama, and sites of reality in the early nineteenth century', *Grey Room*, 9 (autumn 2002), 5–25; Thomas Crow, *Emulation: David, Drouais and Girodet in the art of revolutionary France* (New Haven and London, rev. ed., 2006); Lorenz Eitner, *Gericault's 'Raft of the Medusa'* (New York, 1972); Lee Johnson, 'The Raft of the Medusa in Great Britain', *Burlington Magazine* (Aug. 1954), 249–53; Suzanne Lodge, 'Géricault in England', *Burlington Magazine* (Dec. 1965), 616–27; Jonathan Miles, *Medusa: the shipwreck, the scandal, the masterpiece* (London, 2007); Christine Riding, 'The Raft of the Medusa in Britain' in Patrick Noon and Stephen Bann (eds), *Crossing the Channel: British and French painting in the age of romanticism* (London, 2003), pp 15–16, 72; Christine Riding, 'The fatal raft', *History Today*, 53 (Feb. 2003), 38–44; J.-B. Henri Savigny and Alexandre Corréard, *Naufrage de la frégate Méduse, faisant partie de l'expédition du Sénégal en 1816* (Paris, 1817), transl. as *Narrative of a voyage to*

Géricault's subject matter addressed many of the individual issues of his time – the future of the monarchy, political corruption, class and slavery – in its universality, it suggested that it was concerned with nothing less than civilization itself.

Yet, when the London impresario William Bullock brought Géricault's painting to Dublin in 1821, it clashed, with disastrous commercial consequences, with Marshall's peristrephic panorama of the same event. Why did the people of Dublin shun the painting and attend the thrice-daily showings of the multi-sensory spectacle in huge numbers? The shipwreck and its visual dramatizations are not only highly informative of a contemporary scandal of considerable national import, but also richly indicative of significant changes in art practices and consumption. The painting prompted the panorama, and the panorama was proleptic of cinema; their respective receptions in Dublin were testament to dramatic developments in new visual technologies and patterns of spectatorship that gathered momentum throughout the nineteenth century.

The story has been narrated by countless historians, and the original painting analysed by numerous cultural theorists. The salient points, therefore, will be only briefly revisited here. The *Méduse* was the flagship of a convoy bringing soldiers and settlers, as well as the newly appointed French governor of Senegal, Colonel Julien-Désire Schmaltz, on the important expedition to repossess the colony of Senegal. From the outset, internal dissension was rife; before long, the incompetence of its captain became obvious, and the *Méduse* ran into the treacherous ocean shoals of the Arguin bank, and was grounded. The results were catastrophic. In France, the scandal was embroiled in internecine Bourbon-Restoration politics, tensions between the Liberals and Royalists, France's colonial ambitions, and the octane subject of the slave trade. Responsibility for the debacle lay with the inexperienced captain, Comte Hugues Duroys de Chaumareys, a minor aristocrat from the *ancien régime*, who was rewarded with the commission by the Minister for the Marine for past political services.

The voyagers set out with great optimism, but that did not last long. As they approached dangerous sandbars and reefs, de Chaumareys refused to listen to experienced advice. The ship ran aground, sixty miles from the coast. Attempts to re-float it failed. Initially, it was intended to use the longboats to ferry all the passengers and crew to shore. But Schmaltz ordered the making of a raft (20m by 7m), ostensibly to take provisions, but in reality to take what he considered the excess human cargo. On 5 July, when the frigate showed signs of breaking up, panic set in, and the captain ordered the immediate evacuation of the *Méduse*. Approximately 250 people fought their way onto six lifeboats, leaving the rest – some 150 ordinary soldiers, low-ranking officers and a motley collection of civilians – to the rickety raft.[4] It was clear from the beginning that those who designed the raft had no intention of occupying it; the captain and senior officers all privileged their own safety.

Senegal in 1816, comprising an account of the shipwreck of the Medusa (London, 1818; abridged, Dublin, 1818).   **4** A further seventeen stayed aboard the *Méduse*, three of whom were discovered alive fifty-four days later when de Chaumareys sent a salvage expedition to recover gold from the ship.

Initially, it was intended that the lifeboats would tow the raft to *terra firma* and, from there, all would proceed on foot. But, almost immediately, on the order of the governor, the captain cut the ropes; those on the raft were cut loose, with only some biscuit paste and a few barrels of wine.

After three days, most of those fortunate enough to have secured a place on the lifeboats got to land and started the long walk to St Louis, Senegal. There was much anxiety about captivity, enslavement and cannibalism from local tribes. Meanwhile, back on the raft, things were not going well. Although the occupants had been assured that they would be towed to land, according to two of its survivors, Alexandre Savigny and J.-B. Henri Corréard, the ropes were deliberately cut, casting them adrift. With few provisions, no marine officer and no navigational equipment or charts, the situation rapidly deteriorated. Of the 150, there was one woman, a butcher, a baker, a barrel-maker, many domestics and some twenty soldiers and sailors, a ragbag of mercenaries, captives and ex-convicts, including a handful of Irish. On the first night, twenty died. Due to stormy weather, only the centre of the raft was secure. Dozens died either in fighting to get to the centre, or because they were washed overboard by the waves. By the fourth day, all survivors were practising cannibalism. After five days, there were only thirty left. On the eighth day, in order to extend the remaining provisions, the fittest among the survivors were instructed to throw the injured and dying overboard, leaving just fifteen. The final fifteen survived another five days, until their rescue. Shortly afterwards, five died, leaving ten survivors in all.

Given what had happened before, during and after the shipwreck, it was not surprising that everyone concerned ran for cover. An elaborate whitewash ensued. At his court martial in 1817, de Chaumareys was found guilty of incompetent navigation and of abandoning the *Méduse* and its passengers. But even though this verdict carried the sentence of death, it was commuted to only three years in jail. The cover-up caused the surgeon, Savigny, and the engineer, Corréard, who had taken command of the raft, to retaliate. Savigny submitted *his* account to the authorities. This was leaked to the anti-Bourbon newspaper, the *Journal des Débats*, on 13 September 1816. Although by now illegal, slavery had long been integral to the French colonial project, and the new governor, Julien Schmaltz, had profited handsomely from the slave trade. As Savigny and Corréard had a major score to settle with Schmaltz, they intended to cause maximum embarrassment to the governor by insinuating this into the debate. When they were denied the compensation they sought, they began to court public attention and published their own highly self-serving account, *Naufrage de la frégate la Méduse* (1817; also published to acclaim in English, German, Dutch and Italian), which became an international bestseller. Here, Savigny and Corréard narrated the full horror of the shipwreck: negligence and nefariousness, brutality and betrayal, mutiny and murder. The story enthralled not only France but also Europe in the post-Napoleonic period.[5]

At this very time, the young 25-year-old artist, Théodore Géricault, was casting

---

5 Savigny and Corréard, *Narrative of a voyage to Senegal in 1816*, p. 108.

about for a subject. He wanted something of the moment, that would hitherto have been considered impossible: a history painting that would thrill the masses. The shipwreck and the abandonment of crew and passengers had it all: contemporary subject; political significance; news value; high drama; criminality; cowardice and cannibalism. What more could he have wanted?

Géricault was born in Rouen in 1791 into a royalist family. He moved to Paris as a teenager, where he came under the mantle of his wealthy uncle, Jean-Baptiste Caruel. In 1807, the 50-year-old Caruel married Alexandrine de Saint Martin, a young woman of 22. When Théodore's mother died the following year, Alexandrine's sympathy for her husband's 17-year-old nephew developed into a tempestuous affair. During this time, with Caruel's unsuspecting patronage, Géricault's financial independence allowed him the indulgence of only occasionally studying with master painters, Carle Vernet and Pierre-Narcisse Guérin. He was thus able to largely reject formal teaching and to pursue what Thomas Crow calls 'the cult of precocious originality', courting spontaneity and innovation, rather than control and draughtsmanship.[6] From the outset, he embodied – perhaps one might even say invented – the concept of the romantic temperament.

Géricault now set out to win the most prestigious reward for an artist, the Prix de Rome. Although unsuccessful, he left for Rome alone, where he spent over a year immersed in the work of the old masters, acquiring the skills and experience that the prize would have accorded him, had he actually won a place at the Academy in Rome. When he returned to Paris in August 1816, only weeks after the *Méduse* shipwreck, he did so with heightened and honed classical skills, unusual in a self-taught artist. He now sought a subject that would satisfy his ambitions, almost opting for the murder of a liberal official – a story of conspiracy, transvestism and ritual murder – but finally settling on the wreck of the *Méduse* on its journey to Senegal in 1816.

An axiomatic principle of Romanticism was an insistence on 'the truth', however unpalatable that might be. Notwithstanding the copious commentaries on the event, which Géricault devoured, he carried out almost forensic enquiries of his own into the scandal. He went to extraordinary lengths to ascertain the facts about the shipwreck, and even met and empathized with the victims. He arranged for the surviving carpenter of the raft to build a model that he actually tested on water. And, importantly, he interviewed Savigny and Corréard extensively. He even used them as models for the two central figures on the mast – as themselves they authenticate and concretize the event.

Géricault rented a studio opposite the Beaujon hospital in Paris, so that he could make anatomical studies of the dying, and he visited the morgue to study the dead. In his studio, he even kept amputated body parts – decaying, putrefying and stinking – to intensify the experiential act of painting. Indeed, by all accounts, he painted the *Raft* in a heightened state of tension himself. But this is no cheap novel of a painting: we do not *see* the emaciation or the cannibalism. Géricault's heroic physiognomies

6 Crow, *Emulation*, p. 281.

belie the reality of sun-scorched bodies, ravaged by fifteen days of dehydration, starvation and violence. As the *Dublin Inquisitor* observed:

> Perhaps the most prominent defect in this picture is the fullness of limbs which is given to the different figures. We must recollect that they had been thirteen days on the raft – that during that time they had eaten but two scanty meals, one of spoiled biscuits, the second of some fish which were caught between the raft-timbers – that life had been sustained only by sparingly distributed rations of wine – that while they had undergone every privation, hunger, thirst and cold, their minds had been equally agitated by all the most horrible conflicts of passion and despair – and can we reconcile to ourselves the idea of their presenting the human frame in its full strength and proportion? We are also unable to account for the nakedness of the figures, as we have been led to believe that, on leaving the ship, they were all fully clothed – with respect to the dead bodies which are introduced, we are assured that, about two days before, the sick and wounded, whose prolonged existence would have reduced the provisions too quickly, were thrown overboard, and that the fifteen who were on the raft were all living. There are few marks of their sanguinary conflicts, and none whatever of the effect of the salt water in stripping off their skin – the picture is also too dry; for although the construction of the platform on the centre of the raft raised them from their constant immersion in the water, yet the waves still washed frequently over them. The dead soldier is lying in an awkward position, and we find it difficult in imagination to suppose what part of the raft is occupied by his feet.[7]

Significantly, the *Dublin Inquisitor* went on to remark 'that most of these defects cease to be such, if we consider it merely as a specimen of the limner's art'.[8] This is perspicacious: the painting is thus conceptually realist, but aesthetically transcendent. What Géricault does is invoke Renaissance and Baroque art to rise above the parochial detail: the bodies are Michelangelesque, the dramatic thrust Rubenesque, the colour Caravaggesque. Familiarizing himself with death was part of the means by which he intensified the *sense* of death: he was not concerned with the religious or symbolic aspects of death, but the meaninglessness of it all. In its verisimilitude, it is a new kind of real. Jonathan Crary argues that the painting occupies an

> unstable position between two distinct historical worlds – between the enclosed order of reference organized around the rhetoric of the human body in the art of antiquity and the Renaissance and an unbounded heterogeneous

---

7 It was was also noted that the 'fine figure of Corréard is (we suspect) copied from a figure in Raphael's celebrated picture of "Christ appeasing the storm"': 'Remarks on M. Jerricault's [sic] "Picture of the surviving crew of the Medusa Frigate"', *Dublin Inquisitor* (Mar. 1821), 196–8. **8** Ibid.

informational field of journalistic, medical, legal, and political sources of evidence, testimony, fact, and other guarantees of the real.[9]

In French academic theory, the hierarchy of genres codified the categories of painting, with history painting at the top. Each genre had its own imperatives: history painting must exude coherence, clarity and completeness; it needed to be edifying, exhortative and enriching. The subject had to have metaphoric or allegorical significance, and be based on an acknowledged text (mythological, historical, biblical or literary). In short, history painting had to be morally, intellectually and aesthetically uplifting. And in its execution, it was necessary for the subject matter, treatment and scale to be appropriate.

When it was exhibited at the Salon of 1819, the *Raft of the Medusa* was considered a real paradox: beautiful yet repellent, a history painting of a contemporary event, conventional yet revolutionary. Its critics were divided: some thought that it did not go nearly far enough in its condemnation of the event; others felt that the painting undermined the very principles at stake. Artistically too, the painting was considered problematic. Géricault disregarded hallowed tradition and introduced idiosyncratic elements that were unacceptable in his day. Remarkably, the fact that he actually expected a government prize suggests that he himself did not anticipate much official opposition to the painting, notwithstanding the fact that it flaunted the conventions of history painting in all important respects: style, subject and treatment.

In history painting, a composition capable of carrying the scale of the narrative was essential and, of course, scale could not be sustained without exemplary drawing skills, epitomized here in the heroic pinnacle figures. At 491cm by 716cm, the picture is twice as large as life – a scale considered entirely suitable for subjects of historical significance: great battles, religious paintings and mythological scenes – but entirely inappropriate for contemporary events, reported in newspapers, such as a shipwreck of the day.

Compositionally, the structure of the painting is unusual. What was also considered abnormal was the eclectic blending of styles and compositions from myriad, even incompatible sources. Moreover, as one art historian after another has noted, the universalizing strategies of history painters, who subordinate all details in the interests of a single unifying whole, are here marked by breaks, ruptures and discontinuities. Such complexities were not untypical of Romantic painting – Delacroix, Goya and Turner all experimented with style and subject matter. And yet, notwithstanding its unorthodoxies, Géricault produced a monumental depiction of a contemporary event that transcends the local and addresses universal experience, giving the painting, as Michael Fried has identified, the authority to claim an overarching theme: suffering.[10]

Initially, Géricault intended to produce a sequence of paintings, believing that the

9 Crary, 'Géricault', 13. **10** Michael Fried, *Absorption and theatricality: painting and beholder in the age of Diderot* (Chicago, IL, 1980), p. 154.

event needed temporal narration. One of the problems in representation is how to convey a dynamic sequence in a static scene, how to condense into a single image a whole story. Pre-Renaissance artists did so by comic book techniques, illustrating different stages in the story, on the same page, as it were, leading to very idiosyncratic results. From the Renaissance onwards, history painters conceptualized narrative complexity, not by representing the climax of a story or event, but by identifying what was known as the 'pregnant moment'. The painter, according to Gotthold Ephraim Lessing in 1766, must select 'one single moment of the action, and must therefore choose the most pregnant, from which what precedes and follows will be the most easily apprehended', by which Lessing meant, the artist must represent the moment that best encapsulates what has already happened, and what is about to happen.[11] In the *Oath of the Horatii* (1784), for example, Jacques-Louis David chose the moment of the pledge rather than the victory for maximum dramatic impact.

Eventually, Géricault selected the sighting of the *Argus* by the survivors on the raft as the moment on which he should hang the narrative. Thus, he chose neither the cutting of the rope, when they were cast adrift, nor the moment of their rescue, but the tensest moment of all, when the raftists see the *Argus* in the distance and try to signal to it. Corréard and Savigny describe the moment:

> A captain of the infantry looking towards the horizon, [caught sight of] a ship, and announced it to us by an exclamation of joy; we perceived that it was a brig; but it was at a very great distance; we could distinguish only the tops of the masts. The sight of this vessel excited in us a transport of joy which it would be difficult to describe; each of us believed his deliverance certain … yet fears mingled with our hopes; we straightened some hoops of casks, to the end of which we tied handkerchiefs of different colours. A man, assisted by us all together, mounted to the top of the mast and waved these little flags.[12]

Fried argues that Géricault was the first painter to address the burden of the beholder in 'its insuperable or tragic form', evidenced by the efforts of the men on the raft to attract the attention of the *Argus* (coincidentally, Argus, in mythology, was a giant with a hundred eyes, who was also called Panoptes [all-seeing]). But that burden also extends to the need of the victims to escape our gaze, to stop being beheld by us – as Fried says, 'to be rescued from the ineluctable fact of a presence that threatens to theatricalize even their sufferings'.[13] Corréard and Savigny continue:

> For above half an hour, we were suspended between hope and fear; some thought they saw the ship become larger, and others affirmed that its course

---

11 G.E. Lessing, on the *Laocoön*, quoted in Hugh Barr Nisbet, *German aesthetic and literary criticism: Winckelmann, Lessing, Hamann, Herder, Schiller, Goethe* (Cambridge, 1985), 3, p. 99. 12 Savigny and Corréard, *Narrative of a voyage*, p. 74.   13 Fried, *Absorption and theatricality*, p. 154.

carried it from us; these latter were the only ones whose eyes were not fasci-
nated by hope, for the brig disappeared. From the delirium of joy, we fell into
profound despondency and grief.[14]

At a late stage in the painting, Géricault provocatively added three black figures to
the raft. He shared with Corréard and Savigny an enlightened attitude towards slaves
who, they believed, should be prepared for their emancipation by instruction and by
the gradual improvement of their conditions. This rhetoric conveniently drew a veil
over Savigny and Corréard's own treatment of the Africans on the raft – especially
the black soldier and two sailors who were compelled to get rid of those who were
going to die anyway, in order to provide supper for the remaining survivors, including
Savigny and Corréard themselves. As the painting was exhibited to considerable
political reaction, not only did it bring about an end to the policy of excluding experienced Bonapartist officers from service under the Restoration but, more
importantly, it also contributed significantly to abolitionist discourse in and about
France.

The story of the *Méduse* is as much about the abuse of authority as the shipwreck.
The raft threw together civilians, officers and conscripted men who were forced to
rely on their own wits to survive, rather than a standard chain of command or the
goodwill of others. But, as various commentators have observed, the notion that the
painting represented democratic values is as much related to its aesthetic as its political meanings. The sense of order imposed by Géricault is clearly an aesthetic one, in
which the bodies are assembled to rise to a classical apex, but the meaning of the
painting concerns itself with humanitarian ideals – the painting cuts across not just
class issues, but ethnic ones as well. Crow maintains that Géricault 'found new life in
the old dicta of formal and thematic unity, so that a non-hierarchical vision of
common social purpose could intrude on an event conceived to celebrate the
Bourbon repudiation of social equality'.[15]

The scale of the painting, no less than its treatment, produces paradoxical effects
of universality and intimacy, reflected in Géricault's indecision over the hanging of
the painting. Initially, it was hung low, but Géricault objected, and when it was being
hoisted up over the portal of the huge Salon Carré in the Louvre, he realized that he
had made a mistake. Its distance from the spectator had the immediate effect of
diminishing its impact. As Delacroix (one of the young artists who posed for the
painting) noted, the spectator must 'believe he has one foot in the water to perceive
all of the merit'.[16] In the *Raft*, Géricault produced a passionate painting of high moral
import, but one of *contemporary* significance and, therefore, one that was accessible to
the common man – all the more reason for it to be hung in direct line with the point
of view of the spectator. Géricault went to great lengths to connect with the spectator: note the extended hand of the dying young man lying in his father's lap. The

---

14 Savigny and Corréard, *Narrative of a voyage*, p. 74.   **15** Crow, *Emulation*, p. 292.
16 Ibid., p. 292.

open hand is, as Crow puts it, 'so involving in its emotional invitation that, once accepted, any disinterested vantage point outside the composition disappears'.[17]

When Géricault exhibited his *Raft* in the Salon of 1819, it was only a qualified success, and that was perhaps more on account of the scandal than the painting. And although he did receive a medal, it was not then purchased by the government.[18] A severe depression followed, during which he produced that truly extraordinary series of portraits of the insane (which may reflect a period of time in an asylum himself).[19] Indignant at the reception of his *Raft*, Géricault decided to bring it to England, entrusting it to the remarkable William Bullock, who exhibited it in his Egyptian Hall from 12 June to 31 December 1820, and later in Dublin from 5 February to 31 March 1821.

From a showman family, Bullock collected natural history specimens (stuffed birds and animal groups which he displayed in simulations of natural habitats), arms and armour, ethnographic material, art and antiques (Napoleon's carriage, for example, was said to have earned Bullock the modern equivalent of one million pounds). His 'living exhibition' of a family from Lapland was set in front of a panorama painting that provided the contextual information, a device taken up by other museums and waxworks, especially when it came to exhibits of an educational nature. Bullock thus had a huge influence on the collection and exhibition of material culture in nineteenth-century Britain.

As information was commodified, new forms of visual consumption emerged: natural history displays, freak shows, curiosities, magic lantern shows, vaudeville, ventriloquism and panoramas became increasingly popular. Somewhere between painting and panoramas were fascinating new phenomena, such as the Mechanical Theatre or Eidophusikon (a small stage on which were performed light and image scenes, such as storms at sea or shipwrecks); the Royal Menagerie, in which live, exotic animals were displayed in front of painted scenery simulating their natural habitat; or the display of 'noble savages' or what were considered freaks of nature, such as the *Hottentot Venus* (with her enlarged genitalia) who was put on display in Piccadilly in 1810, providing much opportunity for what Linda Nochlin described (in another context) as 'lip licking and tongue clicking'.[20] Bullock differed from other impresarios in that his displays of 'other' people were not only presented as spectacle to be consumed, but opportunities for culturally uplifting experiences.

In the early nineteenth century, physiological discussions on the subjectivity of vision questioned whether the perception of space was innate or learnt. Concern was expressed, moreover, that the dissolution of social boundaries and the mixing of social classes could lead to what might be considered fairground unruliness in public spaces. Such considerations resulted in the repositioning of the observer, socio-culturally,

---

17 Ibid., pp 291–2. **18** It was purchased by the Louvre in 1824. **19** Géricault's biographer lists five of the ten portraits of the insane painted for Dr Georget, alienist on the staff of the Salpêtrière hospital. Clément, *Géricault*. **20** Linda Nochlin, *The politics of vision: essays on nineteenth-century art and society* (London, 1989), p. 44.

leading to the formation and expectations of modern audiences. Direct stimulation, inciting visual curiosity and pleasure, and the solicitation of attention through surprise and shock, were now increasingly prized.

In Bullock's Egyptian Hall in Piccadilly, paintings such as Le Thière's *The Judgment of Brutus on his Sons* (1811), Haydon's *Christ's Triumphal Entry into Jerusalem* (1820) and Géricault's *Raft of the Medusa* were shown in his 36m-long Roman gallery. Size was a crucial factor in their success. The Géricault exhibition opened in June 1820, and Bullock emphasized the scale of the painting and its disturbing content in order to get at the popular end of the market, but it also attracted huge interest from the upper echelons of society: members of the Royal Academy, the church and the nobility. In contrast to France, it got rave reviews in London, but considerably fewer, as we shall see, in Dublin.

In 1787, the Irish landscape and portrait painter Robert Barker painted a perspectively correct 360° view of London, enclosed it in a rotunda and put it on show, thereby creating the first panorama. Here, the eye was drawn to the centre of the picture but, also, the peripheral vision could see, as in nature, the outer corners of the view. This gave the sense that there was no boundary, other than the limitations of the eye. Put into a circular room, it deceived the eye into believing that it was looking, not at a painting, but at reality itself. The panorama thus provided an almost palpable sense of reality and was, in effect, an immersion within a virtual environment. Stephen Oettermann describes it 'both as an instrument for liberating human vision and for limiting and "imprisoning" it anew', arguing that it represents the first true mass medium.[21] The new representation technologies that emerged in the 1790s mirrored, in many respects, contemporary discourses of virtual reality and pre-empted many aspects of avant-garde aesthetics. As Barker explained:

> my invention, called *La Nature à Coup d'Oeil*, is intended, by drawing and painting, and a proper disposition of the whole, to perfect an entire view of any country or situation, as it appears to an observer turning quite round; to produce which effect, the painter or drawer must fix his station, and delineate correctly and connectedly every object which presents itself to his view as he turns round, concluding his drawing by a connection with where he began. He must observe the lights and shadows, how they fall, and perfect his piece to the best of his abilities. There must be a circular building or framing erected, on which this drawing or painting may be performed; or the same may be done on canvas, or other materials, and fixed or suspended on the same building or framing, to answer the purpose complete. It must be lighted entirely from the top, either by a glazed dome or otherwise, as the artist may think proper. There must be an inclosure within the said circular building or framing, which shall prevent an observer going too near the drawing or painting, so as it may, from all parts it can be viewed, have its proper effect ...

21 Stephen Oettermann, *The panorama: history of a mass medium* (New York, 1997), p. 7.

> The entrance to the inner enclosure must be from below a proper building
> or framing being erected for that purpose, so that no door or other interrup-
> tion may disturb the circle on which the view is to be represented.[22]

In other words, everything must be done to conceal the mode of production and
increase the sense of total immersion experienced by the spectator. From a description of the peristrephic panorama of the *Battle of Navarino*, exhibited in Dublin in
1828 by the Marshalls, we get a sense of what a later version of that felt like:

> You enter a small theatre, the curtain draws up, and behind it is discovered the
> pictures which represent, in a grand whole, the series of several incidents of
> the fight. The canvas does not hang straight down, but is stretched in a convex
> semicircle, and moved off slowly upon rollers, so that the pictures are changed
> almost imperceptively, and without any break between scene and scene. A
> man describes aloud the objects represented; and the distant thunder of
> cannon, military music, and the noise of the battle increase the illusion. By
> means of panoramic painting, and slight undulation of that part which repre-
> sents the waves and the ships, the imitation almost reaches reality.[23]

Throughout the nineteenth century, panoramas depicted spectacular events and
places. Some, as we have seen, were stationary, continuous circular representations in
the round, hung on the walls of specifically constructed rotunda, the most celebrated
being in Leicester Square, London; these required the spectator to walk around the
image. Later, the moving panorama attached to spindles or cylinders allowed the
scene to slowly move past a stationary audience, creating the illusion of motion,
simulating a journey, often on water, to the accompaniment of music, and the narration of a 'barker' (the precursor of the modern lecturer) who gave a running
commentary, spiced up with salacious anecdotes. In 1822, Louis Daguerre, a painter
who had been designing stage sets for the Paris Opera, set up the Diorama, or theatre
of illusion. Large pictures (14m by 21m) were painted on both the front and the back
of semi-transparent theatrical gauze. By shifting the lighting through shuttered
skylights, from front to back and top to bottom, one image dissolved into another,
implying a lapse of time or even motion. Using a *camera obscura* to produce the paintings, Daguerre's drive for an even more realistic representation led him to
experiment with a way to permanently fix the image, culminating in photography
(and ultimately cinema).

Some of the purported facts about panoramas were greatly exaggerated (the
Freeman's Journal, for example, reported one panorama as being four miles long)
but they *were* impressive enterprises, requiring large investment, bringing together

---

22 Quoted in R.D. Altick, *The shows of London* (Cambridge, MA, and London, 1978), p. 132.
23 Quoted in John Fullerton and Jan Olsson (eds), *Allegories of communication: intermedial
concerns from cinema to the digital* (Bloomington, IN, 2005), p. 225.

financiers, architects, designers and painters.[24] Thus, they required major distribution systems, organized by impressive entrepreneurs throughout Europe and America, so that investment could be recouped. When George IV determined to have a coronation that would outshine Napoleon's – costing over £9.5 million in today's money – it was to be replicated in representational terms, leading to the production of a most elaborate panorama, consisting of, it was said, 100,000 figures in a narrative sequence of three scenes. A crude representation of movement was conveyed as the figures in the coronation procession passed before the viewers' eyes, as though the viewers were watching the procession itself pass a fixed point.

Actually, panoramas could be up to 15m high, up to 5km long, and up to 365kg each. Inevitably, they were subject to rapid deterioration, due to the constant rolling, unrolling and transportation. The panorama painters originally worked in tempera on paper, moving on to paper backed with linen, and eventually painting in oil. Teams of highly skilled artists worked together, taking up to twelve months to paint one panorama. There is no doubt but that the gradual perfecting of technique, which rendered perspective on a curved surface, reproducing an angle of vision greater than the standard forty-six degrees in a traditional painting, caused a sensation throughout the nineteenth century.

The Marshall brothers perfected the moving panorama, a considerable advance technically on the stationary one. In 1821, their *Peristrephic Panorama of the Frozen Regions* toured the British Isles, and had a very profitable run in Dublin, where many panoramas had been shown successfully over the previous twenty years. But when Géricault's *Raft* opened in the Rotunda on 5 February 1821, it clashed with one of Marshall's best: the *Marine Peristrephic Panorama of the Wreck of the Medusa French Frigate and the Fatal Raft*, shown in a pavilion, down the road from where the painting was on exhibition.[25] Paradoxically, although Dublin had a rotunda that might have lent itself to the display of the panorama, the two-dimensional painting, with finite frame, was hung in the Rotunda complex, while Marshall's panorama was exhibited in a conventional space in Lower Abbey Street.

From the outset, the Géricault painting struggled to attract audiences, while the panorama played to full houses. In contrast to London – where the painting was ecstatically praised for its subject, its execution and its sentiment – relatively few reviews appeared in Dublin. Lee Johnson confirms that important newspapers such as *Saunders's News Letter*, the *Dublin Evening Post*, the *Dublin Journal*, the *Weekly Register* and the *Freeman's Journal* all allowed the painting to come and go unremarked, nevertheless, Philip McEvansoneya shows that there was some interest in other papers: The *Correspondent*; the *Hibernian Journal*; the *Irish Farmer's Journal*; the *Patriot*; the *Dublin Journal* and *Carrick's Morning Post and Daily Advertiser* all commented on the painting.[26]

24 'Four thousand miles of American scenery – the four-mile panorama of the Mississippi', *Freeman's Journal*, 15 Sept. 1849. **25** No records of the exhibition of the painting have been traced in the archives of the Rotunda to date. **26** Johnson, 'The *Raft of the Medusa* in Great Britain', 249–53; Philip McEvansoneya, 'The exhibition in Dublin of Géricault's *Raft of the*

Notwithstanding such attention, it was far from a success. It is difficult in the first instance to understand why it was brought to Ireland at all, but it is even harder to know why it was such a failure.

Certainly, Dublin in the 1820s was far from being a cultural wilderness. In the eighteenth century, the city was famous for its court, its social life and even its learnedness. Much of its elegance was due to the work of the Wide Streets Commission, especially its reorientation on its north-south axis. Sackville Street was enhanced at its northern end with the Rotunda, the centre of much of the glittering social life of the period. The Rotunda gardens were the site of many cultural events, especially musical, and the Rotunda itself, with its plain outside and elegant interior, was considered to be one of the most magnificent circular rooms in the British Isles. But, from its status as a major European city in the late Georgian period, post-Union Dublin, in the early decades of the nineteenth century, did lack lustre. Although there were increases in population, and a growth in the new professional classes, there was less money, and this may have been a factor in the failure of the painting in Dublin, where the admission was a not inconsequential 1s. 8d. (although the *Description* which accompanied the painting was reduced from its London price, from 6d. to 5d.). Indeed, one subscriber wrote to the *Freeman's Journal* demanding to know why the public is charged 1s.8d. for viewing the 'exhibitions of Panoramas, Dwarfs, and the Raft of the Medusa Frigate, whilst in London they were exhibited for One Shilling. The loss of the Medusa Frigate, &c. was exhibited at Paris for One Franc, or Tenpence', thereby making the case that Ireland was a less wealthy nation than France or England.[27]

So what went wrong in Dublin for Géricault? It was demonstrably not the subject matter, given the success of the Marshalls' panorama of the same theme. Moreover, visually, things naval tended to thrive: Robert Barker's *Battle of Waterloo* made a huge profit, and was toured on both sides of the Atlantic. And paintings of shipwrecks were always successful; the panorama of the *Russian Grand Fleet at Spithead, 1791,* was apparently so convincing that Queen Charlotte was said to have felt seasick while looking at it (by fitting the observation platform out as a poop deck of a frigate, the entrepreneurs dramatically increased the sense of veracity).

In Dublin, shipwrecks were especially popular subjects in all media. The dangerous coastline led to many a disaster in Dublin Bay around this time – 124 in one five-year period around the turn of the century.[28] An abridged version of Savigny and Corréard's book was published in Dublin in 1818, and did well. Typically, when painting shipwrecks, artists depicted little boats buffeted by high seas, or dashed

Medusa', *Burlington Magazine,* 150 (May 2008), 325–6. According to McEvansoneya, the *Dublin Observer,* the *Dublin Mercantile Advertiser* and the *Weekly Freeman's Journal,* then in circulation, are unavailable for these dates. **27** *Freeman's Journal,* 16 Feb. 1821. **28** For further discussion, see Wes Forsythe, Colin Breen, C. Callaghan and R. McConkey, 'Historic storms and shipwrecks in Ireland: a preliminary survey of severe synoptic conditions as a causal factor in underwater archaeology', *The International Journal of Nautical Archaeology,* 29 (2009), 247–59.

onto dangerous rocks, with tiny figures clinging to the mast. The forceful focus adopted by Géricault, which zooms in on the victims of the catastrophe, was unusual for its time and intensified the sense of immediacy and veracity. This focus was typically associated with panoramas, and perceived as part of their success, which makes the failure of the painting even more puzzling.

Its failure certainly was not from want of trying to engage the interest of the public. The first advertisement for the painting appeared on 5 February 1821, and was followed repeatedly on the front pages of numerous newspapers. It tended to follow the same format:

> Mr Bullock begs to acquaint the Nobility, gentry and public, that M. Jerricault's great picture from the Louvre (24 feet long by 18 high) of the surviving crew of the Medusa, French frigate, on a raft at the moment they descry the vessel which rescues them from their dreadful situation, is now open for inspection at the Rotunda. This magnificent work of art, painted under the direction, and containing portraits of the principal survivors, excited the greatest admiration in Paris, and was visited in London by upwards of 50,000 persons. Admission, 1s. 8d. – Descriptions, 5d.[29]

But, only two weeks later, on 19 Februrary1821, the infinitely more exciting offer of a panorama on the same theme was on offer. Its advertisements also tended to follow a format:

> Messrs Marshall respectfully beg leave again to solicit the kind patronage of the nobility, gentry and public of Dublin, and its vicinity, for their lately finished, entirely novel *Marine Peristrephic Panorama of the Wreck of the Medusa, French Frigate and Fatal Raft*. Also the Ceremony of Crossing the Line. Each view accompanied by a full and appropriate band of music. The picture is painted on nearly 10,000 square feet of canvas, under the direction of one of the survivors in a superior style of brilliancy and effect – the figures on the raft and in the boats being the size of life, and the picture being of the peristrephic form, give it every appearance of reality. The following are the principal subjects displayed together with the musical accompaniments:
>
> Grand Naval Overture.
> First – The French Expedition, consisting of the *Medusa* frigate of 44 guns, the *Echo* corvette, the transport, *La Loire*, and the brig *Argus* under the command of Captain Chaumareys, setting sailing from the Island of Aix, on the coast of France, to take possession of colonies on the West coast of Africa, which were restored to them by the British at the peace of 1815.

29 *Freeman's Journal*, 6 Feb. 1821.

The Mariner's Trumpet March.

Second – The deck of the *Medusa* Frigate (from the midships looking aft) in the Tropics with a lively display of the ludricous ceremony of Crossing the Line &c.

Grand Simphonia and French Air.

Third and Fourth – The shipwreck representing the *Medusa* as she struck upon the reef of rocks on the Bank of Arguin at the moment she was abandoned by the Raft and boats.

Bay of Biscay

Fifth – The Raft towed by the boats with 150 human beings crowded upon it, partly immersed in water, 135 of whom perished.

Storm – *Vive Enrico*.

Sixth – The Raft with 15 survivors out of 150 after being 13 days and nights partly immersed in water and without provisions at the moment they descried the *Argus* brig which rescued them from their dreadful situation.

The day exhibition will commence at one, two and three o'clock, brilliantly illuminated at eight and nine o'clock in the evening. Admission front seats 1/8 – Back seats 10*d.* – Children in the front seats half price. Monthly tickets (not transferable) 5*s.* – Renewable for the same period 3*s.* Books descriptive of the picture, and giving an interesting account of the shipwreck extracted and translated from the narrative of Savigny and Corréard to be had at the door, price 5*d.* The Pavilion is always rendered perfectly comfortable by patent stoves.[30]

Given such multi-sensory excitement, it is not hard to understand the popularity of the panorama over the painting. Over the next weeks, Bullock upped his campaign in the hope of engaging interest in the painting but by early March was forced to drop his admission price: 'In order that all ranks may have an opportunity of viewing this stupendous production of the pencil, the price of admission during the short time it remains in this city, will be reduced to ten pence', he declared.[31] Nevertheless, the results continued to be disappointing, and he resorted to pleading with those who 'understand the highest department of painting, to visit the Rotunda today', where 'the admission is now reduced to a mere trifle.[32]

He even tried to create the *illusion* of interest, by begging to inform the 'ladies and gentlemen who wish to examine at their leisure this magnificent work of art that

30 *Freeman's Journal*, 19 Feb. 1821. 31 *Freeman's Journal*, 5 Mar. 1821. 32 *Freeman's Journal*, 7 Apr. 1821.

the time less crowded is from 10 to 1'.[33] But, to no avail. Desperate, he even made the excuses of the public for them, entreating those who have been inconvenienced by the badness of the weather to overcome their discomfort and make the journey to see the picture.[34]

Although initially the same admission charge was set for both the panorama and the painting, the panorama won the attendance war, hands down. And even though Bullock lowered his price, not eight weeks into its run, he had to close, ostensibly to forward the painting on to Edinburgh (although there is no evidence that it did go there). Meanwhile, the panorama continued triumphantly, showing three times a day, without reduction, until 9 June.

How do we account for this? Obviously, the panorama was more literal and therefore, arguably, more accessible than the painting. But any convincing explanation must be more complex than that. In discussing the relative merits of paintings and panoramas, the binary opposition between high art and popular culture is commonly, but not necessarily usefully, invoked. The fact is that contemporary critics regularly treated panoramas as serious works of art, and they were frequently reviewed in prestigious periodicals, such as the *Art Journal*. And the corollary also pertains: paintings, such as the *Raft of the Medusa*, were also appreciated by popular audiences, as spectacle. Nevertheless, there were meaningful differences. History painting was considerably more sophisticated in its demands of its audience – the viewer, by virtue of his education, being complicit in producing the meaning. The panorama viewer, on the other hand, was understood to be a more passive consumer; the explicit, melodramatic nature of the panorama was thought to pander more to the 'unintelligent' eye. In this instance, however, there were more similarities than usually pertain, in that both the painting and the panorama provided thrilling opportunities for vicarious sensation.

It is worth noting, on the one hand, that the numbers viewing the painting in London clearly indicated a mass audience and, on the other, that the panorama in Dublin was visited as much by the upper echelons of society as by the lower. The assumption, therefore, that the high art of painting was appreciated by the elite, and the popular art of the panorama by the common man, is far from the simple truth. From 1794, numerous newspapers noted the interest that the nobility and connoisseurs of the day took in the various panoramas that passed through Dublin. The *Freeman's Journal*, for example, reported that

> no great metropolis had presented such a deficiency of public fashionable recreation during the day, as Dublin. Until evening arrives, and the theatre arrives, our *beau monde* have no other resource against *ennui* than to go shopping … It must be pleasing to think that this frightful vacuum no longer exists. The Panorama has effected a great revolution in the distribution of the leisure hours of our *town*. It is universally become the fashionable afternoon's

33 *Freeman's Journal*, 15 Mar. 1821.   **34** *Freeman's Journal*, 3 Apr. 1821.

lounge. On Saturday, Sackville-street exhibited a crowd of superb equipages, a blaze of beauty, and all the splendour of the Irish Court. Their Excellencies the Duke and Duchess of Richmond honoured the PANORAMA with a visit, accompanied by Sir C.B. Littlehales, and a long train of persons of distinction. Their Graces were highly pleased with the admirable effect of this exquisite painting.[35]

Clearly, there was considerable overlap and mutual influence. The development of panoramas adumbrated the large narrative paintings typical of the Victorian period. And, panoramas, designed for mass audiences, taught ordinary people to see art in a certain way: those who saw the Géricault *Raft*, for example, would have transferred their visual skills from the panorama to the painting, seeing it basically as a section of a circular painting. By this means, panoramas could be said to form part of the democratization of culture in the nineteenth century.

The two major aspects of panoramas – large size, and detailed delineation – naturally evoke the sublime. In fact, during much of this period, the words 'panoramic' and 'sublime' were interchangeable (until Samuel Coleridge and Charles Lamb initiated the concept of the material sublime and demonstrated the antithetical nature of the two).[36] Consequently, the sublime was elevated to an aesthetic, and the panoramic relegated to the popular. However, simple binary oppositions – between the elite and the popular – often need to be reconsidered in more nuanced ways. This is certainly the case when it comes to attendances at cultural events at which some cross-class intermingling was a definite feature at the time.

The painting was on exhibition for six months in London and, according to Bullock, was viewed by upwards of 50,000 persons. From contemporary sources, we know that Géricault earned around 20,000 Francs which, with an average admission price of 1/-, would put the attendance at about 40,000, with around 25% purchasing the *Description* at 6d. (a more realistic figure than Bullock's 50,000). Géricault's London cut would thus have been around 18,000 Francs. In Dublin, the admission was increased to 1s. 8d. and the *Description* reduced to 5d. By the same calculations, we can speculate that the number viewing the painting in Dublin was about 4,000 visitors, netting Géricault 2,000 Francs, thus accounting for 20,000 in total. Self-evidently, this number comprised people from more than the upper echelons of Dublin society.

So, what were the implications of all this for both art and popular culture? Édouard Manet is usually credited with breaking the mould, rupturing the normativity of the Renaissance, signalling the end of art, as it was known. But Géricault got there first, and it was a relatively short journey from his hybrid aesthetics to those of mass culture; Crary argues that

---

35 *Freeman's Journal*, 17 Feb. 1812. **36** For further discussion, see J.J. Jones, 'Absorbing hesitation: Wordsworth and the theory of the panorama', *Studies in Romanticism*, 45 (fall 2006), 357–75.

the break with classical models of vision in the early nineteenth century was far more than simply a shift in the appearance of images and art works, or in systems of representational conventions. Instead, it was inseparable from a massive reorganization of knowledge and social practices that modified in myriad ways the productive, cognitive, and desiring capacities of the human subject.[37]

Photography also usurped representationalism, resulting in what Crary calls a 'confusing bifurcated model of vision' – representationalism persists, on the one hand, but is shunned on the other, leading to the view that realism dominated popular art practices (such as panoramas), while experimentation was particular to modernist art.[38] But when the two renditions of the *Raft of the Medusa* came to town, it was a tilting point: the triumph of the panorama was undoubtedly evidence of modernity in the making, and it is interesting that it was in Dublin, historically on the periphery of momentous cultural developments, that the battle between the painting and the panorama might be said to have adumbrated the society of the spectacle.[39]

37 Jonathan Crary, *Techniques of the observer: on vision and modernity in the nineteenth century* (Cambridge, MA, 1990), p. 3.   **38** Ibid., p. 4.   **39** See Guy Debord, *The society of the spectacle* (Paris, 1967).

'… merely an antiquarian curiosity':[1] the purchase of the reliquary of St Lachtin's arm in 1884

PHILIP McEVANSONEYA

The reliquary or shrine of St Lachtin's arm is a well known item of Irish metalwork (fig. 3.1). Made in the early twelfth century, possibly in or near Cashel, it serves as an excellent but rare representative example of its era. The reliquary is 39cm long and is made of cast and engraved bronze plates around a wooden core that originally housed a piece of bone from the saint's arm, now lost. It is decorated with panels of gold and silver, and gilt wire, engraved with interlace and motifs of plants, animals and snakes. An analysis of the shrine, exemplary in its detail and comprehensiveness, was given in a recent essay by Griffin Murray, and it is not proposed to comment here on the reliquary's manufacture, the symbolism of its decoration or its inscriptions.[2] This article, which is based largely on manuscript sources, concentrates on the circumstances of its purchase by and for the state, the symbolic role of the reliquary in the 1880s and its construction as an object of Irish national heritage.

The reliquary was probably obtained in Ireland by Sir Andrew Fountaine during his service in 1707–8 as Gentleman Usher of the Black Rod to the Lord Lieutenant, the Earl of Pembroke. In the nineteenth century, it became quite a well known arte-fact, being exhibited to specialists at intervals and to broader audiences in 1853 at the International Industrial Exhibition in Dublin and in 1862 at the Special Exhibition of Works of Art of the Medieval, Renaissance and More Recent Periods, held at the South Kensington Museum in London.[3] The reliquary remained part of the Fountaine collection at Narford Hall in Norfolk until 1884 when, with several hundred other items, it was brought to London for sale at Christie's. The workman-ship of the reliquary and its unusual form were admired in 1853 and 1862 as unique to Ireland,[4] but its 'Irishness' was not then an issue in the sense that there were no

1 BL AP, Powerscourt to Spencer, 13 June 1884.   2 G. Murray, 'The arm-shaped reliquary of St Lachtin: technique, style and significance' in C. Hourihane (ed.), *Irish art historical studies in honour of Peter Harbison* (Dublin, 2004), pp 141–64, which is an abbreviated version of his MA dissertation, 'St Lachtín's arm-shaped reliquary: an analysis of its metalworking techniques and art styles', UCC, 2002.   3 *Official catalogue of the Industrial Exhibition*, 4th ed. (Dublin, 1853), p. 142, no. 1839; J.C. Robinson (ed.), *Catalogue of the special exhibition of works of art of the medieval, renaissance, and more recent periods* (London, 1862), p. 47, no. 898. 4 'Museum of Irish antiquities', *Athenæum*, 1356 (22 Oct. 1853), pp 1256–7; 'Mediæval art-workmanship', *Art Journal*, n.s. 1 (1862), p. 157.

3.1 The reliquary of St Lachtin's arm (National Museum of Ireland 1884:690)
(photograph © National Museum of Ireland).

demands for its repatriation, perhaps from respect for private property. In 1884, as soon as it was put up for sale and the opportunity was created to obtain it, the reliquary was attributed with an essential Irish status. On that occasion, following a short campaign of public and private lobbying, it was bought for the Irish nation in particular, rather than the British nation in general, and deposited in Ireland.

There was a three-way tussle to obtain the reliquary. Among those who wanted it for Ireland, there was competition as to whether it should go directly into the incipient Dublin Science and Art Museum (SAM) or to the museum of the Royal Irish Academy (RIA); it was also coveted by Augustus Wollaston Franks for the collections of the British Museum (BM) in London. The final decision that it should go to Ireland was made by an Anglo-Irishman with a British peerage, Chichester Fortescue, Lord Carlingford, formerly MP for Co. Louth from 1847–74. He, as Lord President of the Council, had Cabinet responsibility for education and museums. His decision was dependent on budgetary considerations as much as on historic associations, institutional claims or moral rights.

The two principal figures in the rapidly mounted campaign to buy the reliquary for Ireland were Sir William Gregory of Coole Park, Co. Galway, who seems to have initiated it, and Mervyn Wingfield, the seventh Viscount Powerscourt, who successfully saw it through. Both had useful political connections and both had a large measure of influence over cultural policy and cultural institutions. Gregory sat as MP for Dublin and then Co. Galway at various times between 1842 and 1871 when he became governor of Ceylon, where he was instrumental in establishing what is now the National Museum in Colombo. He took a hands-on approach as a trustee of the National Gallery in London between 1867 and 1892 and was a small-scale collector with a fashionable interest in Spanish art. Gregory had been prominently involved in the state-funded purchase of the Tara Brooch in 1868. Powerscourt served in many public capacities, often in the cultural field, and sat as an Irish representative peer in the Lords at Westminster from 1865 to 1904, where he took a particular interest in education in Ireland. He was elected a member of the RIA in 1875. In 1884, Powerscourt was chair, and Gregory a member, of the committee overseeing the design and, from 1885, the construction in Kildare Street, Dublin, of the new Science and Art Museum, later renamed the National Museum of Ireland.

Gregory knew by 7 June 1884 that the reliquary was to be sold on 19 June, the final day of the sale. The campaign to purchase the reliquary for Ireland really took off when Powerscourt, who seems to have found out about the sale on the 12 June, buttonholed both the Prime Minister, William Gladstone, and the Chancellor of the Exchequer, Hugh Childers, who were present at the private view. Gregory and Powerscourt concluded that the reliquary should be bought at public expense for retention in an Irish collection, so they promptly mounted a three-pronged attack, institutional, public and private. The first element was the involvement of the RIA.

In the 1860s, the well-diffused belief in the 'national character' of the RIA collection received official endorsement, and by the 1880s the museum had long had de facto official status as the repository of items deemed to be of national interest, for example receiving material recovered by state bodies such as the Shannon Commission and the Board of Works, and items of treasure trove.[5] The Academy successfully promoted its claim to be the national repository, and its records show that national sentiment was a strong motive when it came to adding to its collection of Irish antiquities. For example, in 1870 Dr Charles Todd was praised for his 'liberality and patriotic feeling' when he lowered the price of St Patrick's bell and shrine from £700 to £500 'if bought for the Academy'.[6] In 1883–4, the Revd Charles Burton sold a torque and other gold items to the Academy at a lower price than he could have obtained in London or Copenhagen, feeling that 'such articles of Irish antiquity should come into the keeping of an Irish Institution'.[7] Although Gregory alerted the Academy on 7 June, it did not have the capacity to act swiftly and did not arrange a meeting to discuss the reliquary until the day after the sale. It preferred to develop the case for the RIA as the ultimate repository in a lengthy memorial to the Lord Lieutenant, Earl Spencer. Therein it cited its devotion since 1786 to preserving ancient relics, treasures 'representing the ingenuity and skill of the Early Irish Artist', which had often 'been snatched from destruction and placed in safe and suitable surroundings, for the delight and instruction of all the lovers of ancient art'.[8]

The second part involved trying to raise public awareness in letters to the Irish press in which Powerscourt and Gregory made the same points: that the reliquary and other rare works of early Irish art should be secured for Ireland, 'the country to which they properly belong', and be placed in the RIA, and that the purchase of the Tara Brooch was a precedent for doing this. Powerscourt underlined the national claim with his comment that he would deplore the loss of the reliquary and similar works 'to some foreign [i.e. English] museum where they would have no special national interest'.[9] It is no coincidence that the reliquary was linked by him and Gregory with the Tara Brooch; this was done not only to exploit a precedent but also to characterize the status of the reliquary. Within a few years of its discovery in 1850, the Tara Brooch had become an object of great historic, symbolic and commercial interest, being described in 1868 by Dr W.K. Sullivan of the RIA as 'a national monument of ancient Irish art'.[10]

The third prong involved canvassing politicians behind the scenes. For example, in the private correspondence between Powerscourt and Spencer, there are several letters advocating and discussing the purchase of the reliquary which Powerscourt thought

5 E. Crooke, *Politics, archaeology and the creation of a national museum of Ireland, an expression of national life* (Dublin, 2000), pp 111–12. **6** RIA, Museum Committee Fair Minute Book, entries dated 2 and 5 Nov. 1870. **7** RIA, Minutes of the Committee of Polite Literature and Antiquities, 6, pp 400–1, 24 Sept. 1883; pp 420–1, 4 Feb. 1884. **8** RIA, Council Minute Book, 20, pp 353–58, 20 June 1884, 'Memorial of the Council of the RIA to the Lord Lieutenant'. **9** 'An antique relic', *Freeman's Journal*, 14 June 1884, p. 5; 'An Irish national relic. To the Editor of the *Irish Builder*', *Irish Builder*, 15 June 1884, p. 185. **10** RIA, Council Minute Book, 14, pp 256–7, 3 Feb. 1868.

... it might be well to try to get for the Royal Irish Academy, or the new
Science and Art Museum in Dublin. Could it so be arranged to send Dr Ball
over to buy it by a government grant? I saw *Mr Gladstone* and *Mr Childers*
about it, they were both at Christie's this morning but unfortunately the
Reliquary was not there yet, having been sent for examination to the Society
of Antiquaries. Could a Govt. commission be given to buy this, it would be
a great thing I dare say it will not be a very ruinous affair? I suppose £1000
would probably be the outside? But if there was a commission it would be a
hit to lose it for a few pounds.[11]

Valentine Ball was the director of the Dublin SAM, which was then housed in the
premises of the Royal Dublin Society (RDS) and comprised the collections of the
RDS and the former Museum of Irish Industry (MII). Unbeknownst to
Powerscourt, Ball had already set in motion his own somewhat half-hearted plan to
obtain the reliquary even though, as he admitted, he had no idea of its commercial
value.[12] Powerscourt would surely have had in mind not only the scale of the new
museum he was responsible for and the need to add items of 'special national interest'
to its holdings, but also the scheme, agreed in 1877 and implemented in 1890, to
amalgamate the combined collections of the RDS and MII with the holdings of the
RIA in the new museum.

Powerscourt and Gregory also had to counter the opinions of two powerful
adversaries, J.C. Robinson and Franks, who both believed that the reliquary should
go to the BM. Robinson, a connoisseur, collector and dealer, was reported by
Powerscourt as saying that the reliquary

ought to be in the British Museum, and I told him that Ireland was the place
where it ought to be, & that if the Govt made up their minds to that, it would
be very hard to stand in the way of its going to Ireland. He said that Ireland
would gain by its being in the British Museum, but I said that, as an Irishman,
I felt most strongly that it ought to go to a public museum *in Ireland*, as a
purely Irish thing. He saw that, and I am sure that at any rate he will not
compete.[13]

Franks, the curator of the Department of British and Medieval Antiquities and
Ethnography at the BM, had long been keen to augment the Museum's holdings of
Irish material. He tried to persuade Gregory why the reliquary should come to the
Museum:

I think we ought to come to a clear understanding about the Irish reliquary
in the Fountaine Collection. From the very first, I pointed it out to the

11 BL AP, Powerscourt to Spencer, 12 June 1884, emphasis in the original.   12 VAA,
RP27441, Ball to [Col. John Donnelly] secretary of the Department of Science and Art, 11
June 1884. If a reserve price was set, it has not come to light.   13 BL AP, Powerscourt to
Spencer, 13 June 1884, emphasis in the original.

Trustees of the British Museum as the most important object to be secured for the national collection it appeared prominently in the report I made asking for a special grant for the sale ... The British Museum I look upon as the Museum of the Empire, & Irish Antiquities might be properly represented in it especially as we have already a few examples but no shrine. The shrine has been for more than a century ~~in~~ on this ~~country~~ side of the water & the only adequate ~~representation~~ engraving of it has been published by an English society ... if this object was about to be sold in Ireland I should not have thought of interfering. I should have a perfect right as a *private individual* to bid for this object & perhaps might succeed in purchasing it.[14]

Gregory replied, 'I cannot agree in your reasons why the B.M. shd have the reliquary in preference to Dublin'.[15] Powerscourt soon came to hear about Franks' desire to have the reliquary and reacted strongly, writing to express his

indignation, as an Irishman as when a piece of work so distinctively Irish as the reliquary now at Christie's comes for sale and when there is an Institution in Dublin which devotes itself almost entirely to the antiquities and ancient history of Ireland, as does the Royal Irish Academy, one of the oldest and most learned bodies in the United Kingdom, that the larger, richer bodies of the same kind in England should not have the generosity to [allow] such a work ought to go to Ireland ... [Irishmen] wish to see a rarity of this kind go to the country which either produced it or at any rate where it was located in ancient times.[16]

Powerscourt rejected Franks' contention that

Ireland would be as well served by this work of art in the British Museum. But what Irishman would have a chance of seeing it or appreciating it there in comparison with what would be the case in Dublin! I am afraid it is the old story, that Irishmen are never to have a chance, & that it will go, if he has it, to an Institution in which Ireland has no interest, being swallowed up in its enormous extent, where it will be lost.[17]

The matter was referred to Carlingford and his Department of Science and Art (DSA) officials. The decision that the DSA would bid for the reliquary with the intention of sending it to Ireland was reached in a meeting which took place on Sunday 15 June at Carlingford's London home.[18] Carlingford had attended the

14 BM FC, no. 5, Franks to Gregory, 13 June 1884 (draft), strikethrough and emphasis in the original. Unfortunately the report Franks prepared dated 12 June 1884 detailing his desiderata at the sale seems not to have survived.   **15** BM FC, no. 6b, Gregory to Franks, 13 June 1884.   **16** BM FC, no. 10, Powerscourt to Franks, 14 June 1884.   **17** VAA, RP29943, Powerscourt to Childers, 14 June 1884.   **18** London, British Library, Add MS

private view of the sale on 12 June and had lunched immediately afterwards with Gregory, who may then have lobbied him with regard to the plan he and Powerscourt were hatching.[19] Gregory and Powerscourt knew that it required a political decision to buy the reliquary at public expense and that, as Lord President, Carlingford's power trumped that of the BM's trustees and curators, much to Franks' undisguised resentment.[20] To sum up Powerscourt's and Gregory's arguments: the reliquary deserved to be returned to Ireland; it would be out of context elsewhere, and it would not be expensive. The reliquary was bought for 410 guineas (£420 10s.) for the DSA. This was less than half the sum Powerscourt thought it might reach and he believed it to be moderate 'for an object of such rarity' – the DSA had been authorized to bid up to £1500 if necessary.[21] Gregory on the other hand thought that while it might reach £400, 'if there is only one Govt agency in the market it will not fetch £150', hence his disapproval of the price paid: 'I think the Reliquary was extremely dear'.[22] These comments show how hard it was to value such a rarity as the reliquary.

The reliquary was offered first to the Dublin SAM, leaving Ball in the uncomfortable position of staking the Museum's claim while admitting that it lacked the wherewithal:

> If we are to pay £420 out of our grant we shall be terribly crippled and the least we may claim is that the Museum should have all the advantage and eclat connected with the possession. To have it would be the means of shewing people what we are doing and what we are capable of undertaking. Placed in the Academy, it would be seen by comparatively few of the public.[23]

A few days later he added that

> If the Academy can raise the money for the purchase of the Reliquary, by any means, I would certainly prefer that they should have it than that it should come out of our [grant] ... If the reliquary goes to the Academy it will ultimately come here ... so that to avoid insolvency it would perhaps be best if the RIA should get the Reliquary.

Ball ended this realistic assessment of the situation – because the SAM was agreed to be the long-term resting place of the RIA's collection – with a dash of sour grapes:

63692, Carlingford's diary for 1884, fo. 167v: 'Under pressure all day: Donnelly and Armstrong came at 11, about Fountaine Sale ...'. Thomas Armstrong was director of the art division of the Department of Science and Art. **19** Ibid., fo. 166. **20** London, British Museum Archives, Original Papers, microfilm 179 (vols 80–1), no. 2738, Franks' report, 25 June 1884. **21** BL AP, Powerscourt to Spencer, 12 June 1884; Lord Powerscourt, 'The reliquary of St Lachteen', Letter to the Editor, *Freeman's Journal*, 23 June 1884, p. 5; VAA, RP5827, A.J. Mundella MP (Carlingford's deputy) to Donnelly, 17 June 1884. **22** BM FC, no. 6a, Gregory to Franks, 13 June 1884; no. 23, Gregory to Franks, 19 June 1884. **23** VAA, RP29807, Ball to Donnelly, 24 June 1884.

'I am told that as a mere work of art it is of no great merit'.[24] That final comment
echoes Powerscourt's revealing confession to Spencer that the reliquary was a 'thing
of not much interest to private buyers as it is not very ornamental, it is merely an
antiquarian curiosity'.[25] His unspoken conclusion seems to be that it was better
suited to an Irish public museum for its historic significance, than to an antiquarian's
private collection (such as Fountaine's), given its lack of aesthetic appeal. It might be
thought that curiosity value is exactly what would have endeared the reliquary to an
antiquarian. The comment does not fit well with the views expressed by
Powerscourt and Gregory in their letters to the press that the reliquary was 'most
remarkable' and of 'exquisite workmanship'. The DSA eventually agreed that the
RIA was the right location for the reliquary, 'with which collection it is more
cognate in character'.[26] The RIA was asked if it would pay the costs involved, which
had risen to £452 3s. 6d., including commission, but it could not. It may have been
the Lord Lieutenant who eventually convinced Childers to cover the cost of the reliquary from the Treasury's Civil Contingencies Fund, meaning that the reliquary
could come to Ireland at no cost to the DSA, or the Dublin SAM or the RIA.[27]

The reliquary was shown at a general meeting of the RIA at the end of
November 1884, when the President, Sir Samuel Ferguson, was eager to puff the role
of the RIA.[28] The arrival of the reliquary in Dublin would have been especially satisfactory to Ferguson who, as long before as 1843, had written that the government
would prefer Irish antiquities to go into the British Museum or else that it feared to
'foster the growing Irish feeling that has lately shown itself here, among other mani-
festations, in the purchase of a rich collection of Irish antiquities',[29] that is the
Dawson collection. For this reason, Ferguson thought, the government had kept the
RIA poor; nevertheless, by the 1880s, it had amassed the nucleus of the national
collection (fig. 3.2). Many of the objects of national significance in the possession of
the RIA by the end of 1884 had been purchased with the aid of full or partial government grants; those grants had been made by both Liberal and Tory governments, and
governments of both hues had been prepared to sanction purchases for Ireland to the
disgruntlement of the BM, as was the case with the reliquary. The RIA and therefore Ireland seems rarely to have 'lost' any object it really wanted.

The belief that important items of Irish heritage should be preserved was one that
had been gaining ground since the 1820s if not earlier. It is found for example in
Thomas Davis' essays such as 'Irish Antiquities', in which he deplored the destruction
of buildings and the exploitation of historic metalwork for its scrap value.[30] The idea
that moveable items should be located in Ireland was of more recent emergence and
was capitalized upon by the RIA. When composing its memorial to the Lord

24 VAA, RP29969, Ball to Donnelly, 27 June 1884.   25 BL AP, Powerscourt to Spencer, 13
June 1884.   26 VAA, RP29969, draft by Donnelly, 2 July 1884 and Donnelly to the Treasury,
12 July 1884.   27 VAA, RP49341, Ralph Lingen, Treasury, to Donnelly, 4 Nov. 1884.
28 'The reliquary of St Lachteen', *Irish Builder*, 1 Dec. 1884, p. 351.   29 E. Patten, *Samuel
Ferguson and the culture of nineteenth-century Ireland* (Dublin, 2004), p. 173 note 61.   30 T.
Davis, *Literary and historical essays* (Dublin, 1846), pp 46–53.

3.2 View in the Long Room of the Royal Irish Academy Museum, *c.*1884–90. The objects visible are (from the top of each case): (left) the Ardagh Chalice; the Breac Maodhóg and satchel; the reliquary of St Lachtin's arm; (centre, left) St Patrick's Bell; the Shrine of St Patrick's Bell; the Tara Brooch; (centre) electrotype copy of St Manchan's Shrine; the Cross of Cong; (centre, right) the Soiscéal Molaise Shrine (original or replica); the Shrine of St Patrick's Tooth; the Soiscéal Molaise Shrine (original or replica); (right) the Shrine of the Domnach Airgid; the Shrine of the Stowe Missal (side visible); the Shrine of the Cathach and the Corp Naomh on the extreme right (photograph © National Museum of Ireland).

Lieutenant on 20 June, the special committee of the RIA strongly advocated that the reliquary be placed 'among the other objects which [the RIA] has agreed to transfer ultimately to the New National Museum ... amid the suitable surroundings of the unequalled collections now in the Academy's Museum', the natural depository where

> it would take due place amid such famous ecclesiastical relics as the Cross of Cong, St Patrick's Bell and its shrine, the *Fiacail Padraig*, the *Domnach Airgid*, the *Cahah* [sic], the Stowe Missal shrine, the shrine of St Medog &c. among which it can scarcely be doubted that it would be more fitly placed than amongst a comparatively miscellaneous Collection made for the general illus-

tration of art ... [it] ought not to be separated from the other objects of
similar kind now in the Academy's Museum but should form with them a
portion of the special collection to which the Irish people will hereafter look
for Evidences of their ancient civilization.[31]

This echoes the position adopted by the RIA in 1867, when it stated that 'Celtic
archaeology' and its collection of antiquities 'can be best studied and appreciated in
Ireland, where alone there exists such traditional and manuscript information as is
essential to illustrate its historical and scientific value'.[32] Thus, the location of the reliquary in Ireland was not simply an issue of Irish possessiveness, but rather the rightful
location of an object of Irish manufacture alongside comparable objects where it
could best be appreciated, and in the context of the historical sources necessary to
understand and interpret it fully. Although the RIA was making its plea on behalf of
the Irish people, its museum was by no means public. Even the precise times at which
its museum was open are vague; there was no general admission and public attendance was low, leading the Academy to offer the excuse that its collections were 'not
of a nature to attract very numerous visitors'.[33]

There was an expectation that the state should have a financial role in ensuring
that objects, for which a claim of sufficient importance could be made, should be
bought out of commercial circulation and private ownership and placed in perpe-
tuity in national institutions. In 1867, the RIA stated that it was 'entitled to expect
from parliament the funds required to secure for permanent custody in their
Museum such important illustrations of our National History, which ought not to be
removed from this country, and could not with much propriety be deposited elsewhere'.[34] The notion that governments had a duty to protect and preserve objects on
the grounds that the historic evidence they embodied made them part of the
common inheritance of the people, was first advanced in revolutionary France.[35]
Then, action was required to prevent politically inspired iconoclasm; in the case of St
Lachtin's arm, intervention was required to permit an act of cultural recuperation. To
that end, it was asserted that the reliquary belonged in Ireland; that is, it belonged to
the Irish nation as part of its common inheritance and as a statement of historic
cultural achievement. There are echoes in this opinion of comments by John Ruskin
in *The Seven Lamps of Architecture* (1849), which had been employed by Sir John
Lubbock MP in the promulgation of his Ancient Monuments Protection Act (1882).
Although Ruskin and Lubbock had buildings in mind, their fundamental idea that
national history may be embodied in artefacts that are entrusted to the stewardship

31 RIA, Council Minute Book, 20, pp 351–58, memorial of the Council to the Lord
Lieutenant, 20 June 1884. A copy of the memorial as sent is VAA, RP30245.   32 RIA, SR
23 Q 23 (a scrapbook compiled by E.A. Conwell), 'Statement of the requirements of the
RIA adopted by the Council, February 18, 1867'.   33 RIA, Minutes of the Committee of
Polite Literature and Antiquities, 6, pp 431–2, 17 Apr. 1884.   34 RIA, 'Statement of the
Requirements ...'   35 J. Sax, 'Heritage preservation as a public duty: the Abbé Grégoire
and the origins of an idea' *Michigan Law Review*, 88 (1990), pp 1142–69.

of present authorities for posterity, is also applicable to moveable antiquities.[36] The concept was employed in 1864 by the Revd Charles Graves, president of the RIA who, in answer to the question 'Do you consider the collections in the charge of your Academy as national property?', told the Parliamentary Select Committee on Scientific Institutions, of which Gregory was the chair, that 'I regard ourselves as being simply trustees for the national benefit'. This was reiterated by his successor, the Revd J.H. Jellett, who told the RIA in 1870 that the Academy held archaeological treasures 'in trust ... for the benefit of archaeological science'.[37] That these arguments had already been successfully advanced must have been advantageous to Powerscourt and Gregory.

Yet Powerscourt admitted privately that judgments of the importance of an object should be made not only on the immediate, aesthetic merits of the object, but also on historic grounds. Powerscourt may have presented an inconsistent view of the visual qualities of the reliquary, choosing his words to suit his purpose, but the embryonic National Museum would have wanted the reliquary for either reason, aesthetic or historic, such institutions being interested in collecting examples of material culture both for, and irrespective of, their workmanship, materials or function. Powerscourt occupied an ambiguous position: on the one hand he sought actively to ensure the public possession in Ireland of an item of Irish historical significance while on the other he had a qualified view of its merits as an art object. Powerscourt saw himself as acting as an Irishman in patriotic defence of the Irish patrimony; alternatively, it may be thought that he was showing the instincts of his caste to lay claim to artefacts and knowledge as part of a project 'to enter into the study of the Irish past in order to set the rules of its discourse'.[38] Never did he doubt his authority to promote the purchase, the successful outcome of which was an endorsement of his decision-making power and cultural leadership.

ACKNOWLEDGMENT

My thanks to Stephanie Clarke (Central Archive, British Museum), Matthew Harvey (Department of Europe and Prehistory, British Museum), Rachel Moss (TRIARC – Trinity Irish Art Research Centre, Trinity College, Dublin), Raghnall Ó Floinn (National Museum of Ireland) and James Sutton (Victoria and Albert Museum Archive), for their help in the preparation of this article.

36 J. Sax, 'Is anyone minding Stonehenge? The origins of cultural property protection in England', *California Law Review*, 78 (1990), pp 1543–67. **37** *Report from the Select Committee on scientific institutions (Dublin)*, Parliamentary Papers 1864 (13), para. 5255. Crooke, *Politics, archaeology*, p. 104. **38** Patten, *Samuel Ferguson*, p. 11, citing D. Cairns and S. Richards, *Writing Ireland: colonialism, nationalism and culture* (Manchester, 1988), p. 31.

From the Comerford Crown to the Repeal Cap: fusing the Irish harp symbol with eastern promise in the nineteenth century

EMILY CULLEN

After the shamrock, the harp emblem was the second most widely invoked graphic representation of Irish identity in nineteenth-century Ireland.[1] Whether situated in the aristocratic drawing rooms of Thomas Moore's ilk or in the sublime landscapes of Thomas Gray's bard, the malleability of the harp symbol ensured its easy insertion into a variety of iconic discourses. While it now stands alone, historically the harp was fused with the imperial crown of England, the cap of liberty, the sunburst and the Comerford or Milesian Crown,[2] among other emblems. This article will examine the cultural functions of the Milesian Crown symbol and the fusion of the harp with this emblem on the frontispiece to Edward Bunting's third edition of *The Ancient Music of Ireland* of 1840 and also on the third and most ornate membership card of Daniel O'Connell's Repeal Association of 1844. I have chosen to examine these two images because they were seminal tableaux that foregrounded the harp image; they were viewed by thousands of Irish people in the 1840s; and they interacted with the political and cultural climate of the period in important ways. Throughout this article I will demonstrate that, because the harp was not a monolithic signifier, its meaning was frequently controlled by its visual contexts, and, in particular, through juxtaposition with other symbols.

THE USE OF THE HARP INSIGNIA IN THE NINETEENTH CENTURY: SOME CONTEXTS

Throughout the nineteenth century, the Irish harp continued to be recognized as evidence of a 'golden age' of pre-Christian Gaelic civility, while it also accrued new meanings and a wider visibility among the Irish population. Barra Boydell has noted that 'from the 1840s, the harp alongside round towers, wolfhounds, shamrocks and other devices becomes widespread in all areas of Irish life, and this harp was now

1 See Jeanne Sheehy, *The rediscovery of Ireland's past: the Celtic Revival, 1830–1930* (London, 1980), p. 12. 2 The Milesian Crown was the more popular term, in the nineteenth century, for the symbol that was based on the Comerford Crown. This crown is sometimes referred to by archaeologists as the 'Devil's Bit Mountain gold cap.'

almost exclusively based on the true Irish harp'.[3] He argues that as the harp grew in popularity as a symbol of nationalist, independent Ireland, it increasingly took on more realistic forms.[4] It is important to note, however, that some fifty years earlier, in the 1790s, the masthead of *The Northern Star* newspaper featured a realistic looking representation of an Irish harp.[5]

Peter Alter remarks that 'the harp is the only Irish symbol of the nineteenth century with a twofold function: it serves as a dynastic symbol and at the same time as a symbol of constitutional nationalism'.[6] I would argue that its semiotic functions were manifold, as the harp was crucially implicated in the processes of historical remembrance and of 'nationalization' that were continuous throughout the century. For example, the harp was recognized as an icon of the regeneration of antiquarian scholarship, as the personification of Ireland in the melodies of Thomas Moore, as the crucial *accoutrement* of the ancient bard as depicted on the cover of Thomas Davis' *Spirit of the Nation*, as a central symbol of O'Connell's Repeal Movement and of a certain demographic within the temperance movement. As well as the Young Irelanders, the Fenians deployed it along with a sunburst in the middle of a green flag. The harp was also centrally implicated in the creation of a new city flag for Dublin in 1885, which displayed a harp on a green background and three white castles in one quarter.[7] In addition, it was invoked, in the 1870s and 1880s and as a principal symbol of the Irish Parliamentary Party. L.P. Curtis, who has interpreted the graphic images of Erin and Hibernia that flourished in the late nineteenth century, has identified a variety of representations of Ireland that featured in *The Weekly Freeman* and *United Ireland*.[8] When we inspect a number of these cartoons from the weekly supplements, it becomes apparent that the condition of the harp within this iconography became a visual shorthand for the state of the Irish nation. Readers of the *Weekly Freeman* and *United Ireland* were expected to be able to interpret with ease the state of the country from depictions of the harp. For example, it could be fully/newly strung and therefore 'healthy', or unstrung and/or broken and therefore 'weak', 'ambiguous' or 'under threat'. While it is difficult to ascertain the full import or value of the harp symbol for the viewer at any given period, it is clear that certain inherited meanings based upon the harp's semiology were widely accessible by the public. The various subtexts, of nationalism and imperial power, surrounding the display of the harp image were easily interpreted among a greater audience of both literate and illiterate consumers.[9]

3 Barra Boydell, 'The iconography of the Irish Harp as a national symbol', *Irish Musical Studies* (Dublin, 1996), pp 131–45 at pp 142–4.   **4** See Barra Boydell, 'The United Irishmen, music, harps, national identity', *Eighteenth-Century Ireland*, 13 (1998), 44–51 at 51.   **5** Note that the harp on the seal of the Confederation of Kilkenny in the 1640s was also less fanciful and more realistic looking than the multiple images of harps that abounded in that era. The harmonic curve and heavy soundbox distinguished these images as truer representations of Irish harps than, for example, the Anglicised winged maiden harp of the seventeenth and eighteenth centuries, which was not based on any extant model of an Irish harp.   **6** Peter Alter, 'Symbols of Irish Nationalism', *Studia Hibernica*, 14 (1974), 104–123 at 108.   **7** Ibid., 118.   **8** See Curtis, *Images of Erin in the age of Parnell* (Dublin, 2000).   **9** Other traditionally

THE FRONT-COVER IMAGE OF EDWARD BUNTING'S 'ANCIENT MUSIC OF IRELAND'

Leith Davis has aptly remarked that the importance of Edward Bunting's three collections of music (of 1796, 1809 and 1840), based on the music played at the Belfast Harp Festival of 1792, are notable in the development of the iconography of the Irish harp. The first image I would like to consider here is the frontispiece from Bunting's third and final edition of the *Ancient Music of Ireland*, published in Dublin in 1840.[10] This field of signs unites images of Irish culture and British imperialism in a syntagmatic arch,[11] connected by a network of shamrocks. The harps flanking the title are linked to illustrations of two harpers who performed at the Belfast harp festival: Denis Hempson and Arthur O'Neill. A focal image on the page is the British lion and unicorn, which appear at the top under the British royal crown. Another symbol given prominence at the bottom centre of the image is the harp surrounded by a sunburst and now capped with the Comerford Crown (often referred to as the 'Milesian Crown').[12] Paradoxically, while Bunting dedicated this collection to the queen, he inserted the Milesian Crown above the harp with the symbol of awakened nationalism, the sunburst, as a declaration of a separate Irish feudal tradition. Instead of ambiguously employing the radiated 'Irish crown' above the harp,[13] as O'Connell did on one of his early Repeal cards, Bunting purposefully differentiated the provincial Irish crown from that of the British one, via its distinctive design. These symbols, arranged together, then, articulate a separate tradition, suggesting an Irish Golden Age and Milesian royalty. I would argue that this act of conversion was a covert counter-

textual significations, political or otherwise, have a limited audience due to the requirement of literacy to extract their messages. **10** Bunting, *The ancient music of Ireland* (Dublin, 1840). See also ch. 4 of Leith Davis, *Music, postcolonialism and gender: the construction of national identity, 1724–1874* (Notre Dame, IN, 2005). **11** My use of the term 'syntagmatic' here derives from the work of Roland Barthes. In his essay, 'The Imagination of the Sign' Barthes states that 'sometimes we "see" the sign in its symbolic aspect, sometimes in its systematic aspect, sometimes in its syntagmatic aspect.' He continues: 'the syntagmatic consciousness is a consciousness of the relations which unite signs on the level of discourse itself, i.e., essentially a consciousness of the constraints, tolerances, and liberties of the sign's associations.' See Barthes, 'The imagination of the sign', *Critical essays* (Chicago, 1972), pp 205–12. **12** See G.A. Hayes McCoy, *A history of Irish flags from earliest times* (Dublin, 1979), pp 132–3. **13** For further information on the radiated Irish crown see Breandán Ó Buachalla's insightful monograph, *The Crown of Ireland* (Galway, 2006). Note also that the concept of the 'kingship of Ireland' was inscribed into the Crown of Ireland Act of 1541 during the reign of Henry VIII. This act was created to reinforce the legal claim of the crown to Ireland and to bring all the inhabitants of Ireland within its dominion. In this context, the King's authority in Ireland was seen as independent of his authority in England and Henry VIII's 'Lordship of Ireland' now became a 'Kingship' for him and his successors.

4.1 Detail of harp capped with the Milesian Crown from the frontispiece of Dermod O'Connor's translation of Geoffrey Keating's *Foras Feasa ar Eirinn* (Dublin, 1723).

statement on the part of Bunting: he wished to show that the harp was no longer a token of colonial subordination by weaving in the concept of a separate Irish identity whose distinctive civilization must be acknowledged. By placing two crowned harps at the zenith of each side of the page, he managed to observe a level of diplomacy that distracted attention away from his invocation of the Milesian Crown. Further, since the latter was not a radiated crown, its status as a signifier of a separate Gaelic royalty was not immediately obvious or threatening to the colonial viewer.

ICONOGRAPHIC HISTORY OF THE MILESIAN CROWN

The emblem of the so-called 'Milesian Crown', used here by Bunting, made its iconographic debut in 1723 on the fanciful frontispiece to Dermod O'Connor's translation of Geoffrey Keating's *Foras Feasa ar Eirinn*.[14] Based on a golden crown –

14 See Dermod O'Connor's translation of Geoffrey Keating's *Foras Feasa ar Eirinn* (Dublin, 1723). Note also that the notion of an indigenous Irish crown was attached to the history of Brian Boru as many sources such as William Camden's landmark *Britannia* (1586) and John Gunn's later *Historical Enquiry respecting the Performance on the Harp in the Highlands of Scotland* (1807) tell us that 'The harp of Brian Boru was taken by his son, Donagh, together

later believed to be a Bronze-Age vessel – which was discovered by peat diggers on Joseph Comerford's land in Co. Tipperary in 1692 – the icon was used to represent the crown of the provincial kings of Ireland.[15] Elizabeth FitzPatrick observes that 'The fact that the Devil's Bit Mountain gold cap was found in Munster obviously inspired the eighteenth-century illustrator of Brian Bóruma to add it to the Munster king's royal paraphernalia'.[16] However, FitzPatrick calls attention to the anachronistic falsity behind this image by noting that, in reality, the Comerford Crown 'has no more place with this Early Medieval king than does his sixteenth-century-style armour, pointed crown or ornamental scepter and baroque shield'.[17] O'Connor's well-known schematization popularized the image of the Comerford Crown and spawned sporadic curiosity about the artefact on the pages of journals in the nineteenth century. In 1843, this same 'Comerford Crown' formed the basis for the design of Daniel O'Connell's green velvet Repeal cap, which played a crucial iconic role in the construction of his public image. According to Gary Owens:

> The most well-known item of clothing associated with O'Connell was his celebrated green velvet 'Milesian cap' or 'cap of liberty' that the artists John Hogan and Henry MacManus specially designed and that they presented to him at the famous 'monster meeting' held on the rath of Mullaghmast in 1843.[18]

As an advertisement in *The Nation* for a copy of the cap, which was mass-produced for sale, pointed out, it was modelled upon 'the old Milesian Crown of Gold, dug up AD1692, at Barnanely, of the Devil's Bit, County Tipperary, and brought to France by Joseph Comerford, Esq., afterward Marquis of Anglure in Champagne'.[19] Evidence suggests that many of O'Connell's followers were deeply moved by the idea of an indigenous Milesian Crown or repeal cap. As Owens has noted, 'To his [O'Connell's] critics, the Milesian cap represented nothing less than a modern-day Irish crown and was symptomatic of its wearer's brazen audacity. His followers, on the other hand, drew inspiration from the cap's suggestion of Irish royalty'.[20] It would

with his father's crown and other regalia, to Rome, where he fled, after having murdered his brother Teighe; and were all presented to the Pope, in order to obtain absolution.' This myth flourished among antiquarians until its authoritative deconstruction as a 'clumsy forgery' by George Petrie, who devoted a substantial section of his 1840 essay on the Trinity College harp to the story. See George Petrie, 'Memoir of Ancient Irish Harp Preserved in Trinity College' in Bunting, *The ancient music of Ireland* (Dublin, 1840), pp 40–2. **15** See Hayes-McCoy, pp 132–3. Joseph Comerford is thought to have brought the crown with him to the Château d'Anglure in France in the late seventeenth century. **16** It is notable that the Comerford Crown, and not the British crown, was positioned above the harp in this image. This was a deliberate conflation which, as we have seen, Bunting later took up in his frontispiece for his 1840 edition. **17** Elizabeth FitzPatrick, *Royal inauguration in Gaelic Ireland c.1100–1600: a cultural landscape Study* (Woodbridge, 2004), p. 3. **18** Gary Owens, 'Visualizing the Liberator: self-fashioning, dramaturgy, and the construction of Daniel O'Connell', *Eire/Ireland*, 33–4 (1998), 103–30. **19** *The Nation*, 7 Oct. 1843. **20** Owens, 'Visualizing the Liberator', 113.

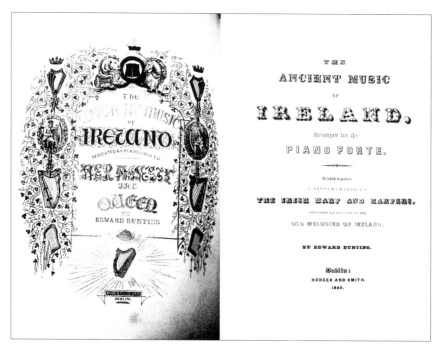

4.2 Frontispiece and title-page of Edward Bunting's 1840 edition of *The Ancient Music of Ireland* (Dublin), featuring the Milesian Crown and sunburst above the harp.

appear that Bunting's frontispiece for his 1840 edition of *The Ancient Music of Ireland* consolidated the iconic appeal of the Milesian Crown, which had provoked anti-quarian interest in such publications as *The Dublin Penny Journal* and *The Irish Penny Journal* since its first appearance. For example, the 'crown' is exoticized in the former as 'perfectly eastern' in its 'style and workmanship' and 'unlike every thing of the kind used in Europe within historic times'.[21] In England, the illustrators of *Punch* maga-zine were also alert to the comic potential of the Repeal cap, and O'Connell was frequently depicted, throughout the mid-late 1840s, donning his Milesian Crown in a mock, burlesque fashion.[22] Anti-O'Connell sentiment prompted his representation in English newspapers, at a time of Famine in Ireland, as 'The Real Potato Blight of Ireland'.[23] Leslie Williams has commented on this portrayal, noting that 'O'Connell-as-potato wears the Repeal cap, whose crown-like brim signalled disloyalty if not

21 See *The Dublin Penny Journal*, 1:9 (25 Aug. 1832). Note also that l'Abbé James Mac-Geoghegan created a strong case for the eastern origin of the Milesian Crown in his *Histoire de l'Irlande ancienne et moderne* (1758). **22** See, for example, 'A disturber of the public peace', *Punch*, 8 (1845), 185, 'The uncrowned monarch's next leave', *Punch*, 9 (1845), 6, '"Rint" v. potatoes: the Irish Jeremy Diddler', Punch, 9 (1845), 213, 'The bad boy who didn't care', *Punch*, 10 (1846), 221. **23** See William Newman, 'The real potato blight of Ireland', *Punch*, 9 (1845), 255.

treason for chauvinist *Punch*.[24] This demonstrates that the significance of the Repeal cap was taken up in different ways by English commentators. We will shortly observe how the Milesian Crown symbol reappears in the field of signs that constitutes Daniel O'Connell's third membership card of the Repeal Association.

Bunting's front cover image has provoked little scholarly discussion, yet it provides the only instance, to my knowledge, in which the harp is capped with both the Milesian Crown and the sunburst.[25] One possible reason for the general lack of discussion is the scant information available about the Milesian Crown symbol and the lack of awareness of its provenance and important link to O'Connell's Repeal cap. It is striking that Bronze-Age headdresses found in Spain, Germany and Sweden, similar to the Comerford Crown, have been assumed by archaeologists such as Sabine Gerloff to have had calendrical and celestial marking purposes, and were likely utilized or even worn by Bronze Age 'King priests'.[26] The distinctive markings on the crown, which have previously been interpreted as having a purely ornamental, diadem function, may have been used to determine the movements of the sun, moon and stars for agricultural and religious purposes. If the wearer of the 'crown' with such 'calendrical and celestial markings' had a greater understanding of seasons, their role in a community would most likely have been elevated. It is clear from studies by scholars such as Elizabeth FitzPatrick that Gaelic inaugurations took place in the open air, at symbolic sites such as Tulach Óg in Co. Tyrone,[27] and that Irish kings and chieftains did not wear an actual crown. Instead, they possessed a *slat na Rí* (Kingship rod), or a *slat tiarnais* (Lordship rod), and a king's shoe was utilized in the inauguration ceremony. The shoe was held above the head of the incoming lord or king and, subsequently, the newly titled monarch placed the king's shoe on his foot.[28] This

---

24 Leslie Williams, '"Bad press": Thomas Campbell Foster and British reportage on the Irish Famine, 1845–1849' in Laurel Brake, Bill Bell and David Finkelstein (eds), *Nineteenth-century media and the construction of identities* (London, 2000), pp 295–309 at p. 302.   25 Leith Davis, who has written about other images on this frontispiece has, however, omitted to comment on this icon. In a similar manner, Ó Buachalla's discussion of *The Crown of Ireland* relegates the Comerford Crown to a small footnote at the end of his monograph. Hayes-McCoy is the only scholar to provide substantial information on the Comerford Crown in his *A history of Irish flags from earliest times.*   26 See Sabine Gerloff, '1995: Bronzezeitliche Goldblechkronen aus Westeuropa. Betrachtungen zur Funktion der Goldblechkegel vom Typ Schifferstadt und der atlantischen ,Goldschalen' der Form Devil's Bit und Atroxi' in A. Jockenhövel (ed.), *Festschrift für Hermann Müller-Karpe zum 70. Geburtstag* (Bonn, 1995), pp 161–88, and Gerloff's essay, 'Reinecke's ABC and the chronology of the British Bronze Age' in C. Burgess, P. Topping and F. Lynch (eds), *Beyond Stonehenge: essays on the Bronze Age in honour of Colin Burgess* (Oxford, 2007), pp 117–61. Gerloff notes that the cone shape and ornamentation on the Comerford Crown is similar to other crowns found in Europe such as the Schifferstadt, Avanaton and Ezelsdorf crowns, and the Berlin cone. She proposes that, in the Bronze Age, ecclesiastical and secular functions were combined in one person ('state' and 'church' had the same head). A division probably only took place in latter half of first millennium BC (Greece). This information was supported in personal correspondence with the author in Dec. 2008.   27 See FitzPatrick, *Royal inauguration in Gaelic Ireland*, p. 139. 28 Ó Buachalla also states that 'Irish kings were never crowned ... nor was an artefact such

evidence serves to remind us of the mythologizing impulses of Irish antiquarians with regard to Irish artefacts such as the Milesian Crown. It also reinforces the fact that the harp was juxtaposed with unstable symbols and, thereby, implicated in narratives of questionable accuracy, while its own status and authority as an icon also helped to bestow legitimacy on more volatile images.

THE MILESIAN CROWN AND THE
EASTERN IRISHNESS OF THE HARP

A particularly notable feature of Bunting's frontispiece is the manner in which it suggests the pure lineage of the Irish harp from the classical lyre: the harp appears to derive from the lyre. Among the most important assertions contained in his *Ancient Music of Ireland* is Samuel Ferguson's declaration that the harp is more than likely descended from the Egyptian lyre. He postulates that 'the Irish have had their harp originally out of Egypt.[29] In making this statement, Ferguson glories in refuting Edward Ledwich's theory of the harp's Gothic origin, as related in his *Antiquities of Ireland* and in his appendix 1 of Joseph Cooper Walker's *Historical Memoirs of the Irish Bards*. Ferguson inverts the Scytho-Celtic speculations of Ledwich and Beauford, proffering instead an Eastern theory of origin for the Irish harp. He contends that 'It is impossible to look at a side view of the old *testudo*, without at once perceiving the similarity between it, taken in that aspect, and the one-armed Egyptian harp'.[30] He continues, 'Now, the transition from the Theban harp to that at present in use is by no means difficult to be traced'.[31] His final statement on the synthesis between an 'Eastern' origin and a Northern development of the harp confidently renounces Ledwich's hypothesis:

> Should these grounds appear sufficient for the surmise that the harp is really a variety of the *cithara* or *testudo*, derived through an Egyptian channel, the importance of our bardic tradition of the progress of the early colonists of Ireland from Egypt through Scythia, will at once be apparent.[32]

It is possible, therefore, to locate an affiliation with the 'Phoenician' school of thought in Ferguson's assertion. According to this theoretical position, 'the Celts or Milesians had first colonized Ireland via Spain and Egypt and were related to various 'ancient' Eastern cultures: Egyptian, Carthaginian, Etruscan, Phoenician, Armenian, Hebrew,

as a crown ever associated with their regal ordination. In the traditional accounts of the inauguration of Irish kings that have come down to us, the cultural artefacts utilised in the ceremony were a wand and a single shoe' (Ó Buachalla, *The crown of Ireland*, p. 25).   **29** Ferguson, 'Of the antiquity of the harp and bagpipe in Ireland' in Bunting, *The ancient music of Ireland: an edition comprising the three collections by Edward Bunting originally published in 1796, 1809 and 1840* (Dublin, 1969), pp 37–59 at p. 48. Speculation about the Scandinavian or Eastern provenance of the Irish harp was a feature of the antiquarian debates of the

Chinese, Indian, and others'.[33] We might hypothesize, then, that the iconography of Bunting's frontispiece is, effectively, an externalization of Ferguson's theory of the harp's eastern provenance.

The theory of origins was the most popular subject in the sphere of cultural discourse in the eighteenth century. Irish antiquarians incorporated the harp into a debate about the origins of the Celts that had been raging since the seventeenth century. The Phoenician argument supported the view that they had come from the Middle East, via Carthage and Spain to the islands off north-west Europe (the view that the Milesian sea-warriors from Spain were the original Celts was also tied to this position). The opposing Scytho-Celtic explanation held that the Celts had come from northern and eastern Europe. Scholars who favoured the notion of original Irish civility leaned towards the Phoenician side; those who favoured the view that the English had civilized the barbaric Gaels, to the Scytho-Celtic.[34] The harp was, thus, centrally implicated in the conquest myths that found support among both camps of opposing ideologues. The evolution of the Irish harp from the Egyptian lyre is underlined here by Bunting and reflects the popular Phoenician, Orientalist position. The iconic employment of both lyre and Milesian Crown now serves to underline Bunting's own 'Eastern' ideological stance. This cover image is, therefore, a visual articulation of the viewpoint contained within Bunting's text; namely, that the harp was not introduced to Ireland by rude and barbarous Scythians of the north, but that it came to us via the highly civilized Egyptians. Bunting's careful assembly of images was a powerful mnemonic device that instantly called to mind a sense of 'Eastern Irishness' and a host of cultural meanings. It thus constituted a figurative literalization of one of the main arguments in the preface of his book.

Eileen Reilly has observed that illustration 'modifies the response of the reader to the text'. She maintains that

> It both amplifies and simplifies the concepts and themes of the narrative by providing a parallel symbolic text . . . Images and symbols which have assigned

eighteenth century. See, for example, Edward Ledwich's 'Inquiries concerning the ancient Irish harp', Appendix 1 in Joseph Cooper Walker's *Historical memoirs of the Irish bards* (Dublin, 1786). **30** Bunting, *The ancient music of Ireland*, p. 50. **31** Ibid. **32** Ibid. **33** Joseph Lennon, 'Irish Orientalism: an overview' in Clare Carroll and Patricia King (eds), *Ireland and post-colonial theory* (Cork, 2003), pp 129–57 at p. 130. For wider reading on the Scytho-Celtic and Phoenician debates of the antiquarians, see Clare O'Halloran's authoritative study *Golden ages and barbarous nations: antiquarian debate and cultural politics in Ireland, 1750–1800* (Cork, 2004); Elizabeth Butler Cullingford, 'British Romans and Irish Carthaginians: anticolonial metaphor in Heaney, Friel and McGuinness', *PMLA*, 111:2 (March 1996), 222–39. **34** See J.H. Murphy, *Ireland: a social, cultural and literary history, 1791–1891* (Dublin, 2003). Note also that Diarmuid Gavin's documentary series for RTE, entitled *Blood of the Irish* (2009), featured ground-breaking genetic research, undertaken at Trinity College, Dublin, into the DNA and origins of Irish people. Gavin takes up the perceived Irish connection to the Spanish sea-warriors, the Milesians.

and accepted meanings can be presented in ways which emphasize, challenge or change those meanings.[35]

It would appear that Bunting wished to challenge, albeit in a subtle way, since his volume still inscribed a royal dedication. Ferguson appears to have had the final, authoritative word on the subject of the harp's Eastern origins and, sixty-five years later, successive musicologists, such as W.H. Grattan Flood, were still concerned to reaffirm his theory. For example, Flood wrote in 1905 that

> Perhaps the strongest proof of the affinity between the Egyptian and Irish harp is the still preserved sculptured harp on the stone cross at Ullard, Co. Kilkenny – wherein the fore-pillar is absent [...] thus corroborating the bardic tradition of the Milesians, as, according to the Irish annalists, 'the Milesians in their expedition from Spain to Ireland *were accompanied by a harper.*[36]

This front image must, therefore, be situated in its wider ideological environment. Not only were antiquarians speculating on the origin of our national instrument, but the sphere of Irish literature was also energized by this debate. An important influence on ideological developments was exercised by literary texts, such as Sydney Owenson's novels and Thomas Moore's *Melodies*. Over two decades earlier, Owenson reflected this contest on the origin of the harp in a defining scene from *The Wild Irish Girl: a National Tale* (1806), which simultaneously repudiated Ledwich's Gothic theory.[37] In so doing, Owenson, too, invoked the notion of the 'the national Lyre of Erin' to reinforce the distance between the Irish harp and the rude barbarians of the north. It is noteworthy that, in invoking the figure of the lyre in an Irish context, both Owenson and Bunting not only intimated their affiliations for a Milesian myth of origins, but they also assimilated the rich Pindaric associations of neoclassical literature into an Irish context, thus paving the way for Thomas Moore's application of the Sensibility register to the ancient Irish music repertory.

---

35 Eileen Reilly, 'Beyond gilt shamrock: symbolism and realism in the cover art of Irish historical and political fiction, 1880–1914' in Lawrence McBride (ed.), *Images, icons and the Irish nationalist imagination* (Dublin, 1999), pp 95–112 at p. 112.   **36** W.H. Grattan Flood, *The story of the harp* (London, 1905), pp 12–13.   **37** Glorvina, the heroine, tells her suitor, Horatio of the Irish harp's eastern provenance: 'this is another collateral proof of the antiquity of its origin, which I never before heard adduced, and which sanctions that universally received tradition among us, by which we learn, that we are indebted to the first Milesian colony that settled here, for this charming instrument, although some modern historians suppose that we obtained it from Scandinavia'. Sydney Owenson, *The wild Irish girl: a national tale* (1806) (New York, 1999), p. 71. See also Owenson's footnote on the same page which refutes Edward Ledwich on the subject of the harp's possible Scandinavian origins.

Third membership card of the Repeal Association of Ireland (1844). Note the Milesian Crown among the group of objects in the centre. Also, *Ollamh Fodhla* (bottom right) is depicted wearing the Milesian Crown, thus O'Connell makes a specific connection here between the crown and the Ollamh.

THE MEMBERSHIP CARD OF THE REPEAL ASSOCIATION

If the Milesian Crown was employed as the inspiration for Daniel O'Connell's Repeal Cap, it is also striking that the symbol featured clearly and prominently on the third membership card of his Repeal Association. From early on in his career, O'Connell understood the value of the motifs associated with the Celtic past in cultivating national identity. O'Connell's public character was intimately bound up with the symbolism of the Irish harp, and this association was to flourish during the era of the Repeal movement. During the Repeal era, O'Connell's use of emblems became even more pronounced and the harp symbol enjoyed a new degree of ubiquity.

On the third membership card of O'Connell's Repeal Association, the harp is installed in the foreground as a proud, shining emblem, surrounded by the sunburst and a geometric pantheon of the glorious men of Irish history. Its ornate Gothic frame is composed of portraits of Henry Grattan and Henry Flood in the central arch, and unites O'Connell with figures from ancient and modern history (including Sarsfield, Owen Roe O'Neill, Brian Bóruma and Ollamh Fodhla). A cache of iconic Irish treasures in the centre shows a harp against a sunburst, a sword, a shield, a horn in a wreath of shamrock and a Milesian Crown. St Patrick's head forms the stem of the device, while a smaller shamrock appears above it inscribed with the motto, 'Remember 1782'. The fact that Ollamh Fodhla, reputedly the first Milesian king of Ireland, wears the Comerford or Milesian Crown (the same crown that is represented beneath the harp in the central image), is especially significant and, once again, reflects the ways in which this crown's meaning was understood as connoting a sepa-rate and distinctive Irish royalty.

Seán Ryder has remarked upon the notable absence of revolutionary figures such as Tone, Fitzgerald, Russell and Emmet, and he has also shed light upon O'Connell's distancing of the Repeal movement from the politics of the United Irishmen.[38] According to Luke Gibbons, 'The imagining of the nation as a panorama of heroes unfolding in continuous time from antiquity is a pervasive narrative device in visionary nationalism'.[39] This schematization was arranged to evoke another great period of Irish history, when Ireland had an independent parliament in Dublin. The syntagmatic layout of this field of signs evokes a sense of religious iconicity and, thus, the portraits represented seem to be invested with a certain sense of sacrality. The previous membership cards of the Repeal Association also aimed to evoke Ireland's former parliament and they included the eighteenth-century Parliament House in College Green, and portraits of the eighteenth-century statesmen Grattan and Flood. The cards were thus concerned with the expression of a distinctive Irish identity, and were devoid of British imperialist symbolism.

Gibbons has called our attention to the fact that this image was an important item of evidence in the government's prosecution of Daniel O'Connell for sedition in 1844.[40] In a detailed iconographic analysis of its symbolism, the Crown prosecution sought to establish that 'the real design was concealed under the pretext of founding' the Repeal Association on the constitutional precedent and legal authority of Grattan's parliament in 1782. O'Connell's defence, in response, invoked the patriotic reputation of Grattan and Flood, and made fun, in particular, of the supposed subver-sive implications of Ollamh Fodhla and King 'Daithí'.[41] As Seán Ryder notes, O'Connell 'reminded the court *ad nauseum* of his many public condemnations of violent methods and oath-bound organizations'.[42] The solicitor general attempted to drive home his case, drawing attention to the inflammatory connotations of the images of the harp and the sunburst, and to the fact that O'Connell's defence had

---

38 Seán Ryder, 'Young Ireland and the 1798 rebellion' in L.M. Geary (ed.), *Rebellion and remembrance in modern Ireland* (Dublin, 2001), pp 135–47 at p. 141.   **39** Luke Gibbons, 'Republicanism and radical memory: the O'Conors, O'Carolan and the United Irishmen' in Jim Smyth (ed.), *Revolution and counter-revolution* (Cambridge, 2001), pp 235–6.   **40** Ibid. **41** The lore of King Daithí was 'popularized' in a ballad contained in *The spirit of the nation* entitled 'The fate of King Daithí'. Notably, the harp is depicted in a more aggressive manner in this ballad, for example, 'Fiercely their harpers sang, / Led by their gallant king, / They will to Erin bring / Beauty and treasure', 104–7 at 105. A footnote to this song demonstrates that much of the historical detail concerning King Daithí derives from Sylvester O'Halloran's *History of Ireland* (Dublin, 1772).   **42** Ryder, 'Young Ireland and the 1798 Rebellion', p. 137.

conveniently overlooked the inclusion of Patrick Sarsfield, the O'Neills and Brian Bóruma in the image.[43]

Unlike the first membership card of the Repeal Association of 1842, which stated 'God save the Queen' with the words 'Loyal National Repeal Association of Ireland' beneath, this third card did not depict a crowned harp. It did, however, give central prominence to the crownless harp, and this may reflect the fact that, by 1844, O'Connell had observed that many diverse groups of Repeal supporters identified themselves through the uncrowned harp insignia on their flags and banners. The statement of the prosecution illustrates that there was public discourse regarding the mobilization of the harp image in a particular register. There was a perceived need to make O'Connell accountable for the dissemination of this image, not only because it was communicating nationalistic ideas to the masses, but also because it had become an icon of national veneration. In defence of the Repeal card iconography, O'Connell declared that 'The object of the design for that card has been *the concentration of such national emblems* with statistical and historical circumstances as to render it, as far as possible, a manual of our reasons for demanding legislative independence.'[44] His declaration shows that, once again, the suggestion of the illustrious history of both the Irish harp and the Milesian Crown was directly linked to the validity of the case for Irish sovereignty. The success of the cards lay in their ability to manipulate the symbol of the harp in such a way as to win popular support under a common, unifying symbol.

CONCLUSION

The pairing of the Irish harp emblem with the Milesian Crown is a distinctive and neglected development in nineteenth-century iconic discourses. It calls to mind the fact that the harp was centrally positioned within the heated antiquarian debates about Irish origin myths. It also reflects the fever of antiquarians for evidence of an ancient classical antiquity and pre-Christian Irish civility. While the harp was perceived as a powerful, authoritative symbol, there was a push to identify other emblems that might carry the ideological weight of nationalism. This historical 'digging', combined with actual, archaeological excavation of a Bronze-Age artefact from a Tipperary bog in 1692, attempted to produce evidence that would support a particular political direction. It is important, however, to update the Comerford Crown story for a variety of reasons, not least because the authority of this crown was challenged by some as just a decorative vessel.[45] These arguments have been countered by archaeological evidence which suggests that, in this instance, the anti-

---

43 Ibid.   **44** *Shaw's authenticated report of the Irish state trials*, 1844, p. 566.   **45** See, for example, Sir William Wilde, *A descriptive catalogue of the antiquities of gold in the museum of the Royal Irish Academy* (Dublin, 1862), p. 8; George Eogan, *The accomplished art: gold and gold-working in Britain and Ireland during the Bronze Age* (Oxford, 1994), pp 6–7.

quarians may have got it right, or at least the fact that it was a headdress worn by a person of status with particular social functions. The application of the Comerford Crown, as a symbol to stand in for the history of a provincial Irish king, represented an attempted transfer of authority to an indigenous Irish crown, a separate icono-graphic tradition and, ultimately, the dilution of authority of the British Crown. The Milesian Crown also gained additional force as a symbol when combined with the semiotic power of the Irish harp. The fact that there is still a degree of uncertainty about the functions of the Comerford Crown underlines the fact that the harp was juxtaposed with equivocal symbols and, thereby, implicated in speculative narratives that were rendered no less powerful for their ambivalence. Unlike, however, the 'missing' Comerford Crown, long transferred to Anglure in France, the Irish harp retains its symbolic authority to the present day.

Margaret Stokes (1832–1900) and the study of medieval Irish art in the nineteenth century

ELIZABETH BOYLE

In late nineteenth-century Dublin, Margaret Stokes was widely considered to be the pre-eminent authority on medieval Irish art and archaeology.[1] However, despite a wealth of scholarship in recent decades on female writers and historians in nineteenth-century Ireland, Stokes' contribution has been almost entirely neglected.[2] The purpose of this paper is twofold: first to draw attention to Stokes as a significant scholar of medieval Irish culture, providing some historical and cultural context for her scholarly achievements; and second to illustrate briefly the ways in which Stokes visually re-imagined the medieval Irish past for a nineteenth-century audience in her role as an early exponent and practitioner of what is now termed Celtic Revival art.

READING MARGARET STOKES IN CONTEXT

Margaret M'Nair Stokes was born into one of nineteenth-century Ireland's most prominent academic families.[3] Her father and grandfather were both professors of medicine at Trinity College Dublin; her younger brother, William (1839–1900), was a renowned surgeon; and an older brother, Whitley (1830–1909), is still widely regarded as one of the most significant scholars of medieval Celtic languages and

---

1 See, for example, Henry Bradshaw, *Collected papers* (Cambridge, 1889), p. 479; W.F. Wakeman, *Catalogue of the Petrie collection* (Dublin, 1874), p. 3: 'To Miss Stokes, our rising authority (if not *the* authority) on subjects connected with early Celtic art and ornamentation ...' (emphasis in the annotated copy in the National Museum of Ireland). I am grateful to Dr Denis Casey for this latter reference. **2** For example, Anne Colman, 'Far from silent: nineteenth-century Irish women writers' in M. Kelleher and J.H. Murphy (eds), *Gender perspectives in nineteenth-century Ireland* (Dublin, 1997), pp 203–11; Mary O'Dowd, 'From Morgan to MacCurtain: women historians in Ireland from the 1790s to the 1990s' in M.G. Valiulis and M. O'Dowd (eds), *Women and Irish history: essays in honour of Margaret MacCurtain* (Dublin, 1997), pp 38–58; Nadia Clare Smith, *A 'manly study'? Irish women historians, 1868–1949* (Basingstoke, 2006). **3** For a biographical overview, see C.L. Falkiner, 'Stokes, Margaret M'Nair (1832–1900)', rev. Marie-Louise Legg, *Oxford Dictionary of National Biography* (Oxford, 2004), www.oxforddnb.com/view/article/26558, accessed 11 Dec. 2008; J. Stokes, 'Margaret McNair Stokes', *Irish Arts Review*, 9 (1993), 217–19. I am very grateful to Dr Joseph McBrinn for alerting me to this latter article.

literatures. The Stokes family's social circle included many scholars and antiquarians who made important contributions to the study of medieval Irish literary and visual culture, such as Eugene O'Curry (1794–1862), John O'Donovan (1806–61), George Petrie (1790–1866) and Sir William Wilde (1815–76).

The only recent article to engage with Margaret Stokes' scholarship in any detail is a review of one of her books by Simon Young, published in *Peritia* in 2002. The purpose of Young's short article was to review two early works on evidence for the cults of medieval Irish saints in Italy: namely, Margaret Stokes' *Six months in the Apennines, or a Pilgrimage in Search of Vestiges of the Irish Saints in Italy*, published in 1892, and Anselmo Tommasini's *I santi irlandesi*, published in 1932, and in English as *Irish Saints in Italy*, translated by J.F. Scanlan, in 1937. Young describes Stokes' work as 'a remarkable period piece that evokes not the age of migrations nor that of ascetic monks but modern costume dramas about late Victorian Britain and Ireland'.[4] He states further that the book contains 'pages that could have come out of an E.M. Forster novel' and that 'Stokes' considerable energy is too much for the remains of the Irish *peregrini*, and when they bore her or do not yield the information she seeks, she turns to Shelley and finishes the chapter on a high note'.[5] Having thus dismissed Stokes' work – and, indeed, Stokes herself – in two paragraphs, Young devotes the rest of his article to a more in depth analysis of Anselmo Tomassini's study. His article leaves us with the sense that Stokes was a rather silly woman, whose flighty mind – more concerned with picturesque picnics than rigorous research – failed to make any contribution to the study of the Irish monastic presence in early medieval Europe.

Something which Young failed to take account of (or deliberately chose to ignore) is the fact that he was not comparing like with like. Between the publication of Stokes' book in the 1890s and Tomassini's in the 1930s, there had been seismic shifts in approaches to, and methods of, historical enquiry; 'History' had become professionalized and had developed as a distinct academic discipline, with separate departments of history being established in European and American universities. Furthermore, Stokes was a woman who was writing at a time when access to formal university training was generally denied to members of her sex. This study argues that works such as hers demand more subtle criticism than that offered by Young if their value as scholarship is to be assessed in any meaningful way.

Stokes' *Six months in the Apennines* is composed in the form of letters to her sister; the results of her scholarly observations are encased within a multiplicity of short narratives that describe each stage of her journey through northern Italy. Young's negative view of Stokes' work is probably shaped by its hybrid form. Young finds the epistolary travel narrative to be a distraction from Stokes' scholarship; in fact, the narrative and the historical scholarship are inextricably linked. This epistolary style was by no means unique to Stokes; the publication, just five years after Stokes' book, of Bram Stoker's *Dracula* (1897), marks what is probably the best-known use of the

---

4 Simon Young, 'On the Irish *peregrini* in Italy', *Peritia*, 16 (2002), 250–5 at 250.   **5** Ibid., 251.

epistolary device in popular literary culture. More significantly for our purposes, Stokes' use of the letter-collection and travel narrative forms, within which she artic-ulates the results of her scholarly research, was in conformity with the work of other nineteenth-century female art historians. As Maria Frawley has noted, the work of women such as Anna Jameson (1794–1860) and Elizabeth Eastlake (1809–93) ranged across genres from fictionalized travel biography and 'visits and sketches' to major reference works, review articles and handbooks for public and private galleries.[6] Throughout the nineteenth century, female art historians continued to experiment with hybrid forms.[7]

An examination of Margaret Stokes' published output shows a similar variety of forms, from travel accounts, monographs published under the auspices of local educa-tional societies or galleries, works by other historians that were posthumously edited or completed by Stokes, and articles in prominent periodicals.[8] In her use of the epistolary travel narrative, Stokes was a practitioner of a popular contemporary genre and, importantly, a recognized form in which women could acceptably publish schol-arly discourse. The fact that Stokes did not begin in earnest to publish her own research until after the death of her parents further implies that she was constrained by the social expectations of her gender; indeed, the death of her father in 1878 may also have provided her with the financial means to pursue her independent research interests.

Three years after the publication of *Six Months in the Apennines*, Stokes published her second volume on evidence for the cults of Irish saints in continental Europe, *Three Months in the Forests of France: a Pilgrimage in Search of Vestiges of the Irish Saints in France* (London, 1895). In the latter work, Stokes was addressing a similar topic to that of the former, namely evidence for the cults of medieval Irish *peregrini*, those men who had exiled themselves from Ireland for religious purposes. However, *Three Months in the Forests of France* is far more highly regarded as a scholarly production than Stokes' earlier work.[9] Although she retained the epistolary travel narrative form as her primary structuring device, a comparison of the two books reveals that, in the later work, she had toned down some of the picturesque elements of her prose and focused more emphatically (though still not entirely) on the historical evidence. We should read this maturation of Stokes' style as evidence of her growing confidence in her ability to operate within a more scholarly framework. She was learning on the job, so to speak.

In this connection, there is another aspect of *Six Months in the Apennines* that is

---

6 Dublin-born Anna Jameson was one of the most influential female art historians of the nineteenth century, and author of, among other works, *Sacred and legendary art* (London, 1848). In addition to her publications in scholarly journals and her translation work, Elizabeth Eastlake also published an epistolary travel narrative, *Letters from the shores of the Baltic* (London, 1844). **7** M.H. Frawley, *A wider range: travel writing by women in Victorian England* (London and Toronto, 1994), p. 73. **8** A preliminary bibliography of Stokes' work is included as an appendix to this article. **9** For example, Young, 'On the Irish *peregrini*', 255.

mocked by Young, but is of central importance in understanding the intellectual context within which Stokes was working, and that is her dedication of her book to her sister, Elizabeth, and 'her friends who form her Church History class in the literary society of Alexandra College, Dublin'.[10] Young seems to view this dedication as further evidence of Stokes' frivolity: the reality is quite the contrary. Alexandra College was founded with a view to providing formal education to mainly middle class, Church of Ireland women, although even from its earliest days there were also Roman Catholics, Jews and Nonconformists on the College's roll call.[11] As Anne O'Connor notes in her history of the college, 'Alexandra's major contribution to women's education in Ireland was to open university education and public examinations to women, it being the first educational institution for girls in Ireland that aspired to university education for its pupils'.[12] Furthermore, 'it was in the vanguard of the movement to persuade Dublin University to open its degrees to women', something that finally occurred three years after Margaret Stokes' death.[13] Thus, its classes were not simply diverting pastimes for middle class ladies; the college produced many exceptional female scholars, including the eminent scholar of medieval Irish literature, Eleanor Hull (1860–1935).

Margaret Stokes may herself have attended Alexandra College in her late thirties, and she subsequently taught art history at the College in 1877: her course materials, published in 1880, bear titles such as 'The transfiguration of Our Lord in art' or 'Readings in art and archaeology: Hades in art'. It is clear from the dedication page of *Six Months in the Apennines* that her sister Elizabeth was making a similar contribution in the teaching of ecclesiastical history. Alexandra College recognized the significance of their former pupil's contribution to the study of medieval Irish art and archaeology, and a Margaret Stokes Lecture was endowed in her memory in 1902: speakers included such distinguished scholars as Kuno Meyer (1858–1919) and the folklorist and future President of Ireland, Douglas Hyde (1860–1949).[14]

Before we can critically assess Margaret Stokes' scholarship, it is vital that we place her in her proper historical, social and intellectual context. By taking Stokes' work out of context, Young did not allow for the fact that Stokes had encoded her scholarship according to the accepted norms of her day. Having placed Stokes' work within the wider historical and cultural context of the female art historian and autodidact in the late nineteenth century, the present study will now look more specifically at Stokes' re-imaginings of the Irish past; that is, in her role as an intercessor between the medieval Irish past and her nineteenth-century audience.

10 Stokes, *Six months*, dedication page.   11 A.V. O'Connor and S.M. Parkes, *Gladly learn and gladly teach: Alexandra College and School, 1866–1966* (Dublin, 1984), p. 2.   12 Ibid., p. 1.   13 Ibid.   14 Ibid., p. 57.

(RE)CONSTRUCTING A MEDIEVAL IRISH PAST

Stokes' audience was primarily middle class and Anglophone. Many of her books were published in London, and yet her subject matter ensured that her work was of greatest interest to readers in Ireland, or to people of Irish extraction living in Britain. In other words, her readership largely consisted of that complex hyphenated group, the so-called 'Anglo-Irish'. It can be argued that following the 1800 Act of Union, and the social trauma of the mid-nineteenth-century Famine, this was an audience that was receptive to a narrative of medieval Irish history that was more positive and inclusive than the dominant paradigm of preceding centuries, which saw Irish vernacular art as indicative of a primitive and barbarian society in need of Anglo-Norman civilization. However, one need not conclude that Stokes was pursuing a conscious political agenda; rather, Stokes' starting point was an assumption that medieval Irish visual culture was inherently interesting, worthy of study and deserving of inclusion in the mainstream art historical canon.

In her recent study of female Irish historians, Nadia Clare Smith drew a distinction between 'Unionist women historians' and 'Nationalist women historians'.[15] Stokes' relationship with Alexandra College would imply that she belonged to the former category. However, as Smith herself acknowledges, this is not necessarily a useful distinction to draw, in the sense that the scholarship of so-called 'Unionist historians' included positive assessments of the pre-Anglo-Norman Irish past that 'often expanded the possibilities for writing Irish history within a more nationalist framework'.[16] The politics of the Stokes family as a whole is difficult to define by such simplistic dichotomies. Stokes' grandfather had been a close friend of Wolfe Tone, and a supporter of the United Irishmen until they advocated the use of violence. Indeed, following the rebellion of 1798, Whitley Stokes Snr was suspended from his post as professor of medicine at TCD for two years as a result of his support for the United Irishmen's cause.[17] Margaret Stokes' father, William Stokes, was a supporter of Catholic emancipation, a close friend to many prominent Catholic intellectuals and renowned for his willingness to extend his medical expertise to the treatment of the starving poor during the Famine of the 1840s. William Stokes spoke out vehemently against both the Young Ireland movement and Isaac Butt's espousal of Home Rule, and yet he maintained a warm friendship with Butt and held Thomas Davis in high regard. The Stokes family seems to have adopted a broadly Unionist outlook, or at least their social and religious liberalism was tempered by a moderate political conservatism throughout the nineteenth century.[18]

---

15 Smith, *A 'manly study'?*, chs 1 and 2. **16** Ibid., pp 7, 15. **17** Some biographical information about Whitley Stokes Snr can be found in the *ODNB* entry for his son (and Margaret Stokes' father), William: L. Perry Curtis, 'Stokes, William (1804–1878)', *Oxford Dictionary of National Biography* (Oxford, 2004), www.oxforddnb.com/view/article/26561, accessed 11 May 2009. **18** Margaret's brother, William, wrote a biography of their father, and dedicated it to Margaret: W. Stokes, *Wiliam Stokes: his life and work, 1804–1878* (London, 1898), p. 100 on Catholic emancipation; pp 105–6 on Thomas Davis; pp 106–7 on

It is difficult to accurately pinpoint Margaret Stokes' political views, beyond the fact that she seems to have been a moderate Unionist, because her scholarship is not driven by any conscious political agenda. She approached her source material as fairly and objectively as possible and, as Smith has noted of Stokes' friend and contemporary Mary Ferguson (1823–1905), she shared 'a desire to counter anti-Irish prejudice in historical scholarship [which] was not incompatible with the patriotic unionist political stance she shared with many of the leading antiquarians'.[19] As we shall see, however, Stokes' objectives were cultural rather than political.

Jeanne Sheehy has argued that, unlike the Dutch or the English, for example, by the nineteenth century, Irish artists had not developed a distinctive 'national style'.[20] As a result, artists tended to make their art distinctively Irish through two methods: first, through the use of common motifs such as harps, shamrocks, Irish wolfhounds and the like; and, second, through imitation of much older Irish artistic and architectural models. This latter approach was driven by the work of antiquarians, archaeologists and art historians, who explicated the material culture of medieval Ireland, acting as mediators between Ireland's medieval past and those artists who wished to incorporate its visual culture into their own work, as a marker of cultural (though not always political) independence from Britain. As one of the foremost authorities on medieval Irish art in the nineteenth century, Margaret Stokes thus played a central role in explicating and rehabilitating Ireland's artistic past. Furthermore, aside from her numerous publications on medieval Irish art and architecture, she also played a more pro-active role in promoting new architectural and artistic idioms based on Ireland's cultural past.[21]

To give an example, then, we might look at some of Stokes' work on Irish Romanesque architecture. In her *Early Christian Art in Ireland*, Stokes begins her section on the Irish Romanesque style by stating that

> The introduction of Romanesque architecture into England is marked by the erection of Westminster Abbey by Edward the Confessor, in 1066, portions of which original building may still be seen in the Canon's Garden of the Abbey. Fifty years before this date, the little church of St Caimin of Iniscealtra was built by King Brian Bóruma, and this building marks the transition to the enriched round-arch style of Ireland. It appears that at this period in England a primitive Romanesque style already prevailed, which, though it has been termed Anglo-Saxon, was of purely Italian origin. This early style modified the character of that which in the reign of Edward the Confessor came as a fresh importation from Normandy, and to this source may be traced whatever distinctive features separate English Norman from that of Normandy itself. In

Isaac Butt; pp 110–11 on the Famine. **19** Smith, *A 'manly study'?*, p. 14. **20** Jeanne Sheehy, *The rediscovery of Ireland's past: the Celtic Revival, 1830–1930* (London, 1980). **21** This should be viewed within a wider European context. See, for example, the essays in Nicola Gordon Bowe (ed.), *Art and the national dream: the search for vernacular expression in turn-of-the-century design* (Dublin, 1993).

Ireland, as we learn from such buildings as the churches of Maghera, Banagher and Temple Martin, a distinct style also prevailed at the time in which the Romanesque of Normandy was introduced there.[22]

For Stokes, the typically 'Celtic' designs used in the ornamentation of round-arch doorways was an aspect of Irish Romanesque which she deemed to be a distinctive, native feature. However, Stokes also took care to note that this 'Celtic' style was common to both 'Britain and Ireland before the Roman occupation of Britain'.[23] Throughout, Stokes portrayed the corpus of Irish Romanesque churches as equal to the English, and subject to the same foreign influences. This is consonant with her overall portrayal of medieval Irish visual culture as being outward-looking, and participating in a shared European literary and artistic heritage. It is important to note that this is a characterization of medieval Irish culture that would be familiar to scholars working in Celtic Studies today. It is also significant that, unlike the early nineteenth-century scholars who coined the term 'Romanesque', Stokes did not see Romanesque art as a vulgarized or degenerate form of a classical ideal, but rather as a sophisticated vernacular style which, in its Hiberno-Romanesque incarnation, combined shared aspects of European visual culture with distinctive Irish elements.[24]

Stokes' work was not confined to explicating medieval Irish visual culture. She also played a dynamic role in reinterpreting that culture as part of the movement known as the Celtic Revival. For example, Stokes acted as a consultant on numerous architectural projects in the so-called 'Hiberno-Romanesque' style, such as the James Franklin Fuller-designed St Michael and All Angels in Clane, Co. Kildare, which was consecrated in 1883.[25] Furthermore, Fuller stated that his design was indebted to the Earl of Dunraven's *Notes on Irish architecture*, a work on medieval Irish architecture that was edited by Margaret Stokes. Stokes' commitment to the Hiberno-Romanesque style is interesting, given her close association and longstanding friendship with a leading Irish proponent of Gothic Revival architecture, Benjamin Woodward.[26] In this regard, it should be remembered that the 'rediscovery' of the medieval Irish past should be viewed in terms of a wider European neo-medievalist aesthetic, which encompassed the ideals of the Gothic Revivalists, Celtic Revivalists, Pre-Raphaelites and Arts and Crafts movement alike.[27]

In addition to her role as a consultant, Stokes' own contribution as an early practitioner of what is now termed Celtic Revival art is of great interest. For example, her illustrations for Sir Samuel Ferguson's *The Cromlech on Howth* (1861) include impressive reworkings of illuminated initials from the Books of Kells and of Durrow

22 Margaret Stokes, *Early Christian art in Ireland* (London, 1887), part II, pp 63–4. **23** Ibid., p. 67. **24** For a recent, comprehensive survey of Irish Romanesque architecture see Tadhg O'Keeffe, *Romanesque Ireland: architecture and ideology in the twelfth century* (Dublin, 2003). **25** Sheehy, *The rediscovery*, p. 128. **26** Frederick O'Dwyer, *The architecture of Deane and Woodward* (Cork, 1997), pp 285, 364. **27** See Elizabeth Boyle, 'Whitley Stokes's *immram*: evolution, Ireland and Empire' in J. Strachan and A. O'Malley-Younger (eds), *Ireland: revolution and evolution* (Oxford, 2009), pp 101–15 at p. 113.

(fig. 5.1). Ferguson's poem was illuminated by Stokes, and accompanied by her draw-ings – landscapes populated with the physical remnants of Ireland's ancient and medieval past – and was published together with 'notes on Celtic ornamental art, revised by George Petrie, LL.D.'[28] Thus, Ferguson's modern composition was accorded the scholarly accoutrements normally reserved for editions and translations of medieval Irish texts, suggesting that Ferguson wished to invest his poem with a kind of pseudo-historical legitimacy. Stokes' illuminated initials derived directly from her research on medieval Irish manuscripts and we can observe the same initials used in *The Cromlech* appearing as scholarly illustrations in her *Early Christian Art*.

Indeed, we can see the interconnectedness of Stokes' historical research and her creative agenda in her chapter on manuscript illumination in her *Early Christian Art*, in which she stated:

> Presenting the following manual of the archaeology of Ireland, the writer's object is to indicate how far the knowledge of her native arts in the past may subserve to their higher development in the future. It is only by adherence to a certain system of study and method of treatment that this result can be looked for. The object is not to present a guide to the antiquities of Ireland, but rather to indicate how these antiquities should be approached, so as to draw forth whatever elements of instruction may lie hidden in them for workers in the present day.[29]

This clearly marks Margaret Stokes out as a woman who, while having a scholar's eye in her study and interpretation of medieval Irish art and architecture, ultimately saw herself as a medium through which the visual culture of the medieval Irish past could be channelled to a new audience, receptive to the idea of a medieval Ireland that combined the native and the foreign, and eager to use Ireland's past as a means to create a distinctive modern artistic identity.

That Stokes was herself an artist should not be forgotten; she was tutored in art by George Petrie who, while best remembered as an antiquary, was first and foremost a landscape painter.[30] Furthermore, on an ethnographical research trip to the Aran Islands undertaken by members of the British Association, the 25-year-old Stokes, who had accompanied her father and brother, painted extensively alongside Sir Frederic Burton (1816–1900), one of nineteenth-century Ireland's most important artists, and eventually director of the National Gallery in London. Margaret Stokes' sketches, paintings and etchings could easily be overlooked, considered only as a form of scholarly apparatus whose sole function is to illustrate her investigations into

---

28 Samuel Ferguson, *The cromlech on Howth* (London, 1861), title page. **29** Stokes, *Early Christian art*, part I, p. 6. **30** After Petrie's death, Stokes was responsible for the arrangement of the collection of his drawings at the Royal Irish Academy: Siobhán O'Rafferty, 'Gilbert and the Royal Irish Academy' in M. Clark, Y. Desmond and N.P. Hardiman (eds), *Sir John T. Gilbert, 1829–1898: historian, archivist and librarian* (Dublin, 1999), pp 45–58 at p. 50.

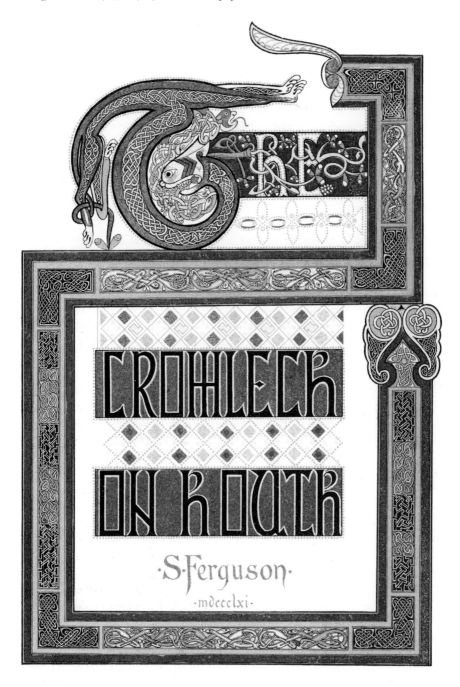

5.1 *The Cromlech on Howth* (1861), illustrated by Margaret Stokes.

medieval art, but I suggest that they also need to be evaluated as artistic products in their own right.

CONCLUSION

It should be acknowledged that not all of Stokes' works were universally well-received. One reviewer, writing in the *Pall Mall Gazette*, criticized Stokes' 'heavy and pedantic' style, describing her prose as not 'attractive or pleasing'.[31] That said, the reviewer in question was a certain Oscar Wilde, and if one has to be criticized for having an unattractive writing style, it would be hard to find a worthier critic; even Wilde praised Stokes' illustrations for her *Early Christian Art*, and described the work as a 'useful volume'.

Margaret Stokes was highly regarded in her day, and it is unfortunate that she has been overlooked by modern scholars – this perhaps in some degree due to the prominence of a later female historian of medieval Irish art, Françoise Henry (1902–82). Stokes' scholarship deserves to be revisited by scholars of medieval Irish culture and nineteenth-century Irish history alike. She was part of a small, interconnected group of scholars – Catholic and Protestant – who collectively uncovered a medieval Irish past that was outward-looking, receptive to foreign influences, engaging with and contributing to European culture; a history that is manifested in medieval Ireland's rich corpus of literature – both in Latin and in Irish – and its visual culture – art, architecture and metalwork. Although the historiography of medieval Ireland was dominated for most of the twentieth century by the idea of a culture that was conservative, wilfully unorthodox, and characterized by 'the backward look', this paradigm has been steadily demolished over the past decade, as historians have re-engaged with the multi-faceted relationships between early medieval Ireland, England and Europe, and, in this, we can see that Margaret Stokes was a true scholarly pioneer, one worthy of more attention than she has been accorded thus far.[32]

---

31 Oscar Wilde, review of Margaret Stokes, *Early Christian art in Ireland*, in *Pall Mall Gazette*, 17 Dec. 1887.   **32** Some of the ideas discussed here were first presented to the History of Art Seminar at the University of Glasgow and to the Sixth Annual Conference of the North East Irish Cultural Network at the University of Sunderland, and I am grateful to the organisers and participants for their valuable comments. The title page from Samuel Ferguson's *The Cromlech on Howth* is reproduced by kind permission of the Syndics of Cambridge University Library.

APPENDIX: A PRELIMINARY BIBLIOGRAPHY OF
THE WORKS OF MARGARET M'NAIR STOKES[33]

Didron, Adolphe Napoléon, *Christian iconography: or, the history of Christian art in the Middle Ages*, trans. E.J. Millington, 2nd vol. completed with additions and appendices by Margaret Stokes (London, 1851–86).

Ferguson, Samuel, *The cromlech at Howth* (London, 1861), illustrated by Margaret Stokes.

Stokes, Margaret, 'Irish art in Bavaria', *Journal of the Royal Historical and Archaeological Association of Ireland*, 4th series, 1 (1870), 352–9.

——, 'On two works of ancient Irish art known as the *breac Moedog* (or shrine of St Moedog), and the *Soiscel Molaise* (or gospel of St Molaise)', *Archaeologia* 43 (1871), 131–50.

Petrie, George, *Christian inscriptions in the Irish language*, ed. Margaret Stokes, 2 vols (Dublin, 1872–8).

Wyndham-Quin, Edwin R.W., third earl of Dunraven, *Notes on Irish architecture*, ed. Margaret Stokes, 2 vols (London, 1875–7).

Stokes, Margaret, *Early Christian architecture in Ireland* (London, 1878).

——, *Alexandra College Literary Society art readings for 1880. 1: the transfiguration of Our Lord in art* (Dublin, 1880).

——, *Alexandra College Literary Society art readings for 1880. 2: the radiated crown of the Roman emperor* (Dublin, 1880).

——, *Alexandra College Literary Society art readings for 1880. 5: a key to the Sistine Chapel painted by Michael Angelo* (Dublin, 1880).

——, *On two bronze fragments of an unknown object, portions of the Petrie collection in the museum of the Royal Irish Academy* (London, 1882).

——, *Readings on archaeology and art: Hades in art* (Dublin, 1883).

——, 'Sir Samuel Ferguson', *Blackwood's Magazine* 140 (July 1886), 624–36.

——, *Early Christian art in Ireland* (London, 1887).

——, 'Inquiry as to the probable date of the Tara Brooch and chalice found near Ardagh with a chronological table of those examples of Irish architecture, sculpture, metalwork and manuscripts, the dates of which can approximately be fixed', *Proceedings of the Royal Irish Academy*, 2nd series, 2 (1888), 451–5.

——, *Six months in the Apennines, or a pilgrimage in search of vestiges of the Irish saints in Italy* (London, 1892).

——, 'St Beoc of Wexford and Lan Veoc in Brittany', *Journal of the Royal Society of Antiquaries of Ireland*, 5th series, 3 (1893), 380–5.

——, 'Celtic crosses at Castledermot', *Journal of the County Kildare Archaeological and Historical Society* 1 (1894), 281–5.

33 My original preliminary bibliography has been greatly supplemented following consultation of Janette Stokes, 'Margaret Stokes (1832–1900) and her intellectual circle', M.Litt., TCD, 2004. I am extremely grateful to Ms Stokes for granting me permission to incorporate her bibliographical research into my own.

——, *Three months in the forests of France: a pilgrimage in search of vestiges of the Irish saints in France* (London, 1895).

——, *Notes on the cross of Cong* (Dublin, 1895).

——, *The high crosses of Castledermot and Durrow* (Dublin, 1898).

——, *The high crosses of Ireland* (Dublin, 1898).

——, 'The instruments of the Passion with an illustration of the tomb of William Fitzgerald, Kildare', *Journal of the Royal Society of Antiquaries of Ireland*, 5th series, 8 (1898), 137–40.

——, 'Notes on the high crosses of Moone, Drumcliff, Termonfechin and Killameny', *Transactions of the Royal Irish Academy* 31:13 (1901), 541–78.

Devotion and representation
in nineteenth-century Ireland

CATHERINE LAWLESS

INTRODUCTION

In 1858, on the occasion of a visit to the new cathedral of St Patrick's in Dundalk, Cardinal Wiseman (1802–65) wrote of how astonished he was at 'the advance of religious progress in Ireland, manifest in the grand and magnificent scale on which all her religious edifices are now constructed'. The profound changes that had occurred in the built landscape of Ireland since the cardinal's youth struck him forcibly.[1] Churches were not only sacral places; they were also sites of memory and identity. In the aftermath of the famine, the devotional mentality of Irish Catholicism was transformed from an impoverished, itinerant and spatially unspecific set of ritual practices to one which took place in richly decorated, sensually rich consecrated sites, furnished with stained glass, statues, mosaics and other decorative and liturgical objects. Regardless of the artistic quality of these objects, many of which were mass-produced, an aesthetic revolution can be said to have taken place as a result of the 'devotional revolution'.[2]

AESTHETIC AWARENESS

The literate laity was kept aware of and thereby included in the process of church design and building by reports, often lengthy, in newspapers such as the *Freeman's Journal* and the *Nation*, as well as by advertisements seeking funds for the completion of various churches and notices of consecration ceremonies or the laying of foundation stones. Architects were named and designs discussed, suggesting that the readership of these papers had at least passing knowledge of the architectural trends of their day. In 1855, the *Nation*, carrying a report from the *Freeman*, reported on the opening of the new cathedral of Killarney, pointing out that it was 'was designed by

1 Cardinal Wiseman, *The sermons, lectures and speeches delivered by His Eminence Cardinal Wiseman, Archbishop of Westminster, during his tour in Ireland in August and September, 1858, with his lecture delivered in London on the 'impressions' of his tour.* Revised by His Eminence (Dublin, 1859), p. 124. **2** Emmet Larkin, 'The devotional revolution in Ireland, 1850–75', *American Historical Review*, 77:3 (1972), 625–52. See Connolly on the physical change in the Irish devotional landscape: S.J. Connolly, *Priests and people in pre-famine Ireland, 1780–1845* (Dublin, 2001), p. 111.

the celebrated Pugin, and we need not, therefore, add that it belongs to the most beautiful and picturesque style of Gothic architecture'.[3] On the opening of the church of Our Lady of Refuge in Rathmines, the correspondent wrote of how the building, 'in the form of a Greek Cross, the style purely Grecian' reminded him strongly of the Madeleine in Paris.[4] The same year, the *Nation* reported on the revival of medieval style in painting, adopted by all 'Protestant rectors of Puseyite tendencies' and its delight that it was being practiced in Ireland, using as an example the work in the Catholic church in Crossmaglen by Mr Bernard Finegan.[5] In 1859, the *Cork Examiner* reported on the building of the church of SS Peter and Paul in Cork, designed by E.W. Pugin (1834–75). It highlighted how it had been furnished with a copy of the design and was 'a church that will combine, in an extraordinary degree, commodiousness for worshippers, great beauty and harmony of proportion, with singular richness of details'.[6] Justification for the expense of building such churches was answered in an 1876 report on the consecration of a new altar in the Church of the Immaculate Conception, Coole, Castleisland, Co. Kerry, by the Right Revd Dr Moriarty, bishop of the diocese, who pointed to the great support of the large majority of priests and parishioners, but noted the very few 'who gave no cooperation, because they thought the wretched old hovel, now a thing of the past, good enough for the service of the Almighty God'.[7] Another motive in the decoration of churches can be glimpsed in a report on the portico of St Audoen's Roman Catholic church in Dublin, in 1878. The *Nation* accounted for the large degree of cooperation between the parish priest and the laity in raising funds to renovate its façade. It observed the strategic location of St Audoen's and its 'glaring defects' compared to the newly renovated Christ Church.[8]

FIRMS SPECIALIZING IN ECCLESIASTICAL DECORATION

Such a discourse in popular newspapers shows considerable interest in the visual arts and their application to Roman Catholicism, as well as a significant degree of awareness of contemporary artistic developments. The newspapers also carried advertisements for ecclesiastical warehouses and suppliers and stained glass manufacturers. Arguably the most significant of these was the Hardman company of Birmingham, whose founder, John Hardman (1811–67) worked with A.W.N. Pugin (1812–52) in producing ecclesiastical furnishings and stained glass.[9] By 1854, John Hardman and Co. were advertising in the *Nation* that they had premises in 48 Grafton Street. The advertisement described various liturgical objects and ecclesias-

3 *Nation*, 4 Aug. 1855; the paper frequently referred to Pugin and his designs, for instance, 9 Oct. 1852, on his last drawing; 27 Sept. 1856, on Loreto abbey, Gorey. 4 *Nation*, 28 June 1856. 5 *Nation*, 20 Dec. 1856, carried from the *Newry Examiner*. 6 *Nation*, 20 Aug. 1859. 7 *Nation*, 23 Dec. 1876. 8 *Nation*, 24 Aug. 1878. 9 Ann Eatwell and Ruth Gosling, 'Hardman family (*per. c.*1820–1935)', *Oxford Dictionary of National Biography* (Oxford, 2004), online ed. Jan. 2008, www.oxforddnb.com, accessed 30 Dec. 2008.

tical decorations, vestments, religious prints, and vases for altars and oratories 'richly decorated with the monographs of our Blessed Lady in blue and gold'. The Irish linen surplices were made 'according to the Roman shape'. The agent was Mr Thompson, who was also agent for the Düsseldorf Christian Art Union.[10] Thomas Earley (1819–93) was born in Birmingham of Irish parents, and was an apprentice of Hardman & Co. under John Hardman and Pugin.[11] An advertisement for the newly formed company of Earley & Powells[12] in December 1864 promoted the fact that he was 'the only church decorator living who was taught his profession by the late A. Welby Pugin', and solicited the clergy and gentry of Ireland for patronage. Their business was located at Camden Street, Dublin.[13] Earley was not only trained by Pugin, but had seen contemporary French design, as he had visited France in 1847, according to the letters of Pugin.[14] Edward Powell (1833–76) and Henry Powell (1835–82) were nephews of John Hardman.[15]

In 1871, an *Irish Times* article entitled 'The revival of ancient stained glass in Ireland', fourth in a series on Irish arts, manufactures and resources, discussed, as the title suggests, stained glass art in Ireland. It mentioned no other firm in Ireland but Earley & Powells, whose 'splendid specimens are sent out, which vie with the choicest pieces of the old masters, and cannot be surpassed by any of the revived modern schools, either in England or the Continent'. It bemoaned the lack of awareness of such Irish crafts and noted how so much revenue, which could create employment, was lost to foreign competitors. The article goes on to single out for praise the windows of the Chapel Royal and the parish church in Enniskerry.[16] Earley tragically committed suicide in 1893.[17] His nephews, John Bishop Earley (1865–1935) and William Earley (1872–1956) continued the family business, the latter having studied at the Dublin Metropolitan School, where he won a prize for stained glass in 1891.[18]

Another Dublin firm, Messrs Barff and Co., and Mr G.B. Star advertised 'Statuary, stained glass, furniture etc.' in 1857 and, in 1858, the advertisement stated that there was, in fact, a 'depot for religious statuary' at Mr G.B. Star's, 27 Lower Ormond Quay.[19] In December 1858, an advertisement appeared announcing the separate enterprises of Messrs Barff and Co., 'Artists and church decorators' at 5 Lower

10 *Nation*, 1 Apr. 1854. **11** Christine Casey, *The buildings of Ireland: Dublin. The city within the Grand and Royal canals and the Circular Road* (London and New Haven, 2005), p. 630. **12** A vast number of drawings and designs by Earley & Powells, and later Earley & Co. were donated to the National Irish Visual Arts Library (henceforth NIVAL) at the National College of Art and Design, Dublin (henceforth NCAD), available in an online database at http://nival.ncad.ie/about_earley.htm. The drawings were digitized by Eneclann and are an invaluable resource. The Irish Architectural Archive, Dublin, also holds material from the firm (IAA Acc.99/95 to 99/100) and information about the firm is found on the database at www.dia.ie. **13** *Nation*, 10 Dec. 1864. **14** Margaret Belcher (ed.), *The collected letters of A.W.N. Pugin, vol. 3: 1846–1848* (Oxford, 2009), p. 189. **15** Eatwell and Gosling, 'Hardman family'. **16** *Irish Times and Daily Advertiser*, 3 Oct. 1871. **17** *Irish Times*, 29 June 1893. **18** http://nival.ncad.ie/about_earley.htm, accessed 12 Dec. 2008. For William Earley's prize, see *Irish Times*, 26 Dec., 1891. **19** *Nation*, 12 Dec. 1857; *Nation*, 31 July 1858.

Ormond Quay, and Mr George R. Star, 'Decorator, house painter, and gilder', at 7 Lower Ormond Quay. Messrs Barff and Co. took care to point out that their business was located 'immediately opposite Mr Duffy's, the publisher'.[20] A year later, Barff and Co. were able to state that they had an agent in Limerick, Mr James Kennedy.[21] In 1862, the company advertised that it had 'executed the Rossmore Testimonial Window in Monaghan Church' and that they were engaged on the stained glass windows for 'St Patrick's Cathedral, Dublin'.[22] Unfortunately, by 1864, it appears that the company was bankrupt, perhaps overstretched by taking on considerably larger premises that they could not afford to maintain.[23] Cavanagh's Mosaic Altars were advertised 'To the Catholic clergy', to be had 'only at the manufacturers, 77 Marlborough Street, Dublin' in 1859.[24] Donegan's 'Ecclesiastical Warerooms' of Dame Street, Miss Fleming's Vestment and Church Ornament Warerooms of Essex Quay and Miss Pentland's Church Vestment Warerooms of Lower Sackville Street were among the advertisements of the *Catholic Directory* of 1865. G. Nannetti, of Dublin and Glasgow, drew attention to his 'rare collection of religious and other figures, both ancient and modern',[25] while Del Vecchio's Studio, F. Barnet, of Edinburgh and Dublin, included among its wares 'Beautiful statues of the Immaculate Virgin, with serpent under foot' in three different sizes, 'Two fine statues SS Peter and Paul, five feet six inches. The Blessed Virgin and Child, and St Joseph … the Twelve Apostles … a most splendid Crucifixion … St Francis Xavier, and the Virgin and Child, St Dominick, St John the Baptist', all with various sizes given.[26]

Much was mass-produced and imported. Miss Dowling 'respectfully' used the *Catholic Directory* to solicit the attention of the Catholic prelates, clergy and gentry to her 'present magnificent stock of church ornaments'. Having just returned from continental travels, she assured her clients of wide-ranging stock from altar paintings replicating the works of the Masters as well as the latest in framed Stations of the Way of the Cross, from 30s. to £10 per set; ditto in rich gilt frames, with fourteen crosses, from £12 to £21.[27] Dowling's competitor, Miss Cahill, reassured the clergy that she was 'at present supplied with a rare assortment of altar requisites from Paris and elsewhere'.[28] H.P. Kearney's of North Earl Street described themselves as having an 'Altar and church furniture manufactory by steam power and machinery.'[29] In 1878, the *Nation* issued a pictorial supplement, a 'beautiful chromo-lithograph from a design by J.F. O'Hea' of St Patrick.[30]

Business was competitive, and Irish craftsmen and suppliers had to compete with British and continental firms. The taste of much of the higher clergy was Italianate and classical, as exemplified in the early letters of Cullen. In 1821, he sent four 'pretty

---

20 *Nation*, 18 Dec. 1858.   **21** *Nation*, 10 Dec. 1859.   **22** *Irish Times and Daily Advertiser*, 19 Dec. 1862.   **23** *Irish Times and Daily Advertiser*, 9 Nov. 1864; 5 July 1866. For their property transactions, see Michael Wynne, 'Stained glass in Ireland: principally Irish stained glass, 1760–1963' (PhD, TCD, 1975), p. 130.   **24** *Nation*, 17 Dec. 1859.   **25** *Nation*, 22 July 1854.   **26** *Catholic Directory*, 1865.   **27** *Catholic Directory*, 1865.   **28** *Nation*, 25 June 1870.   **29** *Nation*, 13 May 1871.   **30** *Nation*, 2 Mar. 1878, advertised, to be issued in the *Nation* of 16 Mar.

Italian pictures' to his father; two representing the Virgin, one St Mary Magdalen and one the Last Supper.[31] In 1844, he wrote of a 'little marble statue of the Blessed Virgin' that he had sent from Leghorn to his brother Michael, so that, if his 'little god-daughter Margaret ever thinks of becoming a nun you must give it to her to bring with her to the convent'. He also mentioned a picture of the Martyrdom of St Andrew.[32] In 1823, he described the funeral of the neoclassical sculptor Antonio Canova, which was 'worthy of Rome and so great a man'.[33] Crookshank and Glin have written of the wasted opportunities of Catholic emancipation on Irish religious art, stating that oleograph and copies of Nazarene paintings were generally preferred.[34] In 1876, the *Drogheda Argus* was 'gratified to learn' that the Dominicans in Louth had purchased a copy of Fra Bartolomeo's *Magdalen* in Lucca.[35] The Church of the Holy Cross, Clonliffe, was decorated with a painting by Gagliardi, 'the distinguished Roman artist to whom was entrusted the painting of all of the Vatican Council'.[36] The Italian sculptor Giovanni Benzoni was given the commission of sculpting in marble the Immaculate Conception for Kilkenny Cathedral,[37] despite the availability of his friend, the Irish classical sculptor John Hogan (1800–58).[38]

Stained glass windows, altars and ecclesiastical decorations were frequently purchased from Mayer of Munich, who exhibited in the Dublin International Exhibition of 1865.[39] Stained glass was also purchased from firms such as Lobin of Tours.[40] British firms were also used, as in the St Laurence window of 1869 in St Peter's Catholic church of Dungourney, Co. Cork, inscribed 'Edinburgh 1869'.[41] In 1856, Paulius Sutorius and Co., from Amsterdam, advertised their arrival in Dublin with a variety of designs.[42] The same year, Mons. L. Leman, from Paris, begged to inform his patrons that he had just arrived from Lyons and Paris with vestments, 'Ready made, in the Roman, Pitren and French fashions', and various other objects including prayer beads, crucifixes, bronzes, pictures, prints and medals.[43]

Such foreign competition did not go unchallenged. In 1856, an advertisement

31 Peader MacSuibhne (ed.), *Paul Cullen and his contemporaries, with their letters, from 1820–1902*, 5 vols (Naas, 1961–77), I, p. 91. **32** Ibid., p. 252. **33** Ibid., p. 117. **34** Anne Crookshank and the Knight of Glin, *Ireland's painters, 1600–1940* (New Haven and London, 2002), p. 228. **35** *Drogheda Argus* carried by *Nation*, 16 Sept. 1876. **36** *Nation*, 16 Sept. 1876. **37** *Revue de l'art chrétien*, I (1857), 94. **38** *Irish Quarterly Review* (1858), 576. See also John Turpin, 'John Hogan and the catholic religious revival', *Maynooth Review*, 5:1 (1979), 64–70. On the Italian decoration of St Francis Xavier, Gardiner Street, see Maureen Ryan, 'Roman opulence in a Dublin church: the high altar of St Francis Xavier's', *Irish Arts Review Yearbook*, 14 (1998), 33–9. **39** *Official catalogue: Dublin International Exhibition* (Dublin, 1865), p. 94. Mayer & Co. glass was ubiquitous in the nineteenth century throughout Europe and the USA. **40** Casey, *Dublin*, pp 278, 629; Casey and Rowan, *The buildings of Ireland: north Leinster* (New Haven and London, 1993), p. 240. St Francis of Assisi, Wexford (www.buildingsofireland.ie, accessed 26 Sept. 2008). Lobin exhibited at the Palais de l'Industrie in 1855, reviewed by the *Ecclesiologist*, 16 (1855), 285, and his obituary was given in the *Civil Engineer and Architect's Journal*, 28 (1865), 64. **41** www.buildingsofireland.ie/niah/ accessed 22 Nov. 2009. **42** *Nation*, 31 May 1856. Further advertisements appeared on 7, 21 and 28 June. **43** *Nation*, 8 Nov. 1856.

appeared in the *Nation* entitled 'Justice to Ireland', for the Guild of St Luke's Society of Operative House Painters of Dublin, to the 'Hierarchy, clergy, and heads of religious houses in Ireland'. The Society wished to call attention to the fact that 'for some time past, a successful attempt has been made to persuade the public that, in order to have the revived MEDIAEVAL style of CHURCH DECORATION correctly executed, it is necessary to import Englishmen for the purpose, on the assumption that Irishmen cannot be had in Ireland who understand this branch of the painting business'. The Society wished to draw the attention of prospective patrons to Irish talent by pointing out the statues of St Lawrence O'Toole in St Vincent's Hospital, a figure of the Blessed Virgin for Lady Bellew, Barmeath, and figure of the Virgin for the chapel in Clarendon Street as showing no need for importing painted statues for churches 'from Germany and elsewhere'.[44]

In 1860, Hubert Maguire & Son claimed to be the 'first Irishmen at home to make this sacred branch of painting their peculiar study', and were confident that 'whilst employing *native hands*', they were 'able to compete with any contractor from any country'.[45] In this context, it is perhaps no accident that, while showing a correspondent the Irish cross for the Rock of Cashel being sculpted at Earley & Powells for the Scully family, Edward Powell took the opportunity to discuss the manufacture of stained glass in Ireland and pointed out at least two articles that made Irish produce superior:

> Irish peat is used in the process of vitrefaction (which burns in the stain), and while in English works the sulphur of the coal impairs the brilliancy of the glass, and in Continental manufactories the firewood used gives out a heat that is neither condensed nor steady, our Dublin friends procure from Irish peat a great and peculiar benefit ... The lead that is used in binding the glass comes from the Wicklow mines, and it is regarded as quite superior to any specimens of the foreign product.[46]

By the later nineteenth century, the importation of foreign religious items and the awarding of contracts to foreign firms was the subject of much criticism. In 1886, the Irish Industrial League expressed its concern that the windows of the Pro-Cathedral were being embellished with 'stained glass of foreign manufacture'.[47] The Roman Catholic hierarchy was attacked again, in 1895, when the Earl of Mayo delivered a lecture on the 'forthcoming Arts and Crafts Exhibition' and stated that while he had heard that there were several firms in Dublin who claimed to manufacture stained glass, he would really like to hear if the glass was truly made in Dublin. Calling on the reverend gentlemen present, he insisted that there should be enough orders from the Roman Catholic churches to ensure that such industries could be started and

44 *Nation*, 1 Mar. 1856. It reappeared 15 Mar.   **45** *Catholic Directory*, 1860, p. 62, referred to in Lisa Godson, 'Catholicism and material culture in Ireland, 1840–1880', *Circa*, 103 (2003), 38–45 at 45.   **46** *Nation*, 23 July 1870.   **47** *Irish Times*, 1 Sept. 1886.

maintained.[48] Charles MacCarthy, City Architect, at a meeting of the Architectural Association of Ireland, went further and pointed out that although it was regrettable that, under the influence of Pugin, the English parish church model had been used for Irish Catholic church-building instead of buildings such as Cashel or Holy Cross, it had to be admitted that the leaders of the Gothic revival were earnest and sincere, and questioned whether the same could be admitted in his own time, stating that contemporary church architecture was 'absolutely without interest' and suggesting that in future designers should leave out the Carrara marble altar, with its bristling reredos, the vulgar stained-glass from Germany, and that impertinent carved oak pulpit from Belgium ...'[49] In 1893, 'Free Lance' conducted an interview with the stained glass artist Joshua Clarke (d. 1921) (father of the better known Harry) under the heading 'An almost lost Irish industry'.[50] Clarke agreed with 'Free Lance', 'why, you are nearly right in saying there is hardly any stained glass windows manufactured in the city. But I can speak for myself anyhow, and assure you that *I* manufacture them.' He also agreed that there was a pernicious practice of stamping continental windows in Dublin, thus obscuring their true origin.[51]

Perhaps the most successful retailer of mass-produced religious items was J.J. Lalor. In 1877, J.J. Lalor, of 52 Phibsborough Road, Dublin, advertised the 'Medal of the Sacred Heart Association', giving a detailed description (although not an image) of the design of the medal and the inscription.[52] By 1880, J.J. Lalor, still in Phibsborough Road, had enterprisingly brought out medals of the Knock apparitions as well as a 'well-executed lithograph ... drawn from the description given by Miss Brigid Hough in the *Weekly News* of 24th April'.[53] Premises in North Earl Street were established in 1883,[54] and by 1890 the 'Irish Catholic Repository', run by J.J. Lalor, was established in Middle Abbey Street, where the business is still located.[55] Lalor sold religious books, often translated from French, pictures for prayer books, pictures for framing, pictures printed on silk, linen or porcelain, rosaries, medallions, medals and statues 'coloured and plain', and furnished 'estimates for special sized statues for churches, private oratories &c.'[56] Also on sale were packets of 'beautifully coloured lithographed cards' of various saints, 'admirably adapted for use in prayer-books' and containing printed prayers on the back in English'.[57] Even note-paper provided the opportunity for imagery, with Lalor advertising one quire of extra supervine note-paper, 'beautifully stamped in colour with the following religious devices artistically designed as a note-heading: "The Sacred Heart of Jesus, the Immaculate Conception, the Ecce Homo, the Crucifixion and Cross with Dove"'.[58]

48 *Irish Times*, 6 Mar. 1895.   **49** *Irish Times*, 9 Oct. 1901.   **50** For Clarke, see Nicola Gordon Bowe, *The life and work of Harry Clarke* (Dublin, 1994), p. 11.   **51** *Weekly Irish Times*, 2 Sept. 1893.   **52** *Nation*, 26 May 1877.   **53** *Nation*, 1 May 1880 and 22 May 1880.   **54** www.jjlalor/Main/Home.htm, accessed 11 Oct. 2009.   **55** *Nation*, 13 Dec. 1890.   **56** *Nation*, 4 Jan. 1890.   **57** *Nation*, 19 July 1890.   **58** *Nation*, 4 Jan. 1890.

REPRESENTATION

Traditional continental virgin martyrs, such as St Catherine of Alexandria, St Agatha and St Lucy, were certainly represented, but such representations were in the minority compared to saints affiliated to the religious orders – and in particular the Post-Tridentine orders, such as St Alphonsus Liguori, St Charles Borromeo, St Philip Neri and St Ignatius of Loyola – and old Irish saints such as Patrick, Brigid and Columba. Most popular religious representations, however, concentrated on cults associated with the Virgin or Christ, such as the Immaculate Conception, the Sacred Heart and the Holy Family – the latter linked to the rising cult of St Joseph. Two of these cults, the Immaculate Conception and the Sacred Heart, shall be considered here.

The Immaculate Conception of the Virgin Mary was declared as dogma 8 December 1854. The doctrine, that the Virgin Mary was conceived without sin, was long accepted within orthodox Catholicism, although its early history was controversial. The role of the archbishop of Dublin, Paul Cullen, and his support of the doctrine is well known. In 1854, Cullen issued as a Jubilee to begin 24 September 'to enable our Holy Father, the pope, to decide on the question of the Immaculate Conception'.[59] Lest any should doubt as to what outcome Cullen desired, he added that indulgences were to be given to those who visited various churches, one of which was the 'Church of the Immaculate Conception in Marlborough Street' (the Pro-Cathedral).

Imagery of the Immaculate Conception spread, as elsewhere, through the use of the Miraculous Medal. This was struck between 1830 and 1831 at the command of an apparition of the Virgin to a French sister of Charity, Catherine Labouré (d. 1875), and a sodality was formed to promote it – the Children of Mary. According to Carroll, it was decided by the church authorities to base the image of the Virgin on the well-known image of the Immaculata, as Labouré's description of the Virgin differed with each apparition.[60] This image showed the Virgin Mary crowned with stars, standing on a crescent moon and crushing the serpent beneath her feet. The apparition was explicit about the words to be carved on the medal: 'O Mary, conceived without sin, pray for us who have recourse to you'.[61]

In Ireland, sculptures of the Immaculate Conception included the one by Giovanni Benzoni for the Cathedral in Kilkenny (1857),[62] one which was inaugurated as a gift of the recently deceased Countess of Shrewsbury and her sister, Miss Talbot, in the Church of the Assumption in Wexford (1858), an inauguration that was accompanied by a sermon from the fiery Redemptorist Father Petcherine and witnessed by the Children of Mary,[63] a statue which was consecrated by Dr Dixon

59 *Nation*, 30 Sept. 1854. **60** M.P. Carroll, 'The Virgin Mary at LaSalette and Lourdes: whom did the children see?', *Journal for the Scientific Study of Religion*, 24:1 (1985), 56–75 at 70. **61** Hilda Graef, *Mary: a history of doctrine and devotion*, 2 vols (New York, 1965), 2, p. 86. **62** *Revue de l'art chrétien*, 1 (1857), 94. **63** *Nation*, 31 July 1858.

in the Convent of St Vincent de Paul in North William Street, Dublin.[64] In London, there was a 'votive offering of a statue of the Immaculate Conception' in St Mary's church, Romeny terrace, Westminster.[65] A 'splendid statue of the "Immaculate Conception"' was carried by a youth as part of the feast of the Assumption in the eponymous church in Wexford, in 1859.[66] Del Vecchio's studio in Great Brunswick Street offered a 'beautiful Statue of the Immaculate Virgin, with serpent under foot, five feet six inches, three feet six inches, and one foot six inches',[67] while the Capuchin fathers 'gratefully acknowledged' among the prizes for their bazaar 'a beautiful statue of the Immaculate Conception, three feet in height, the gift of a friend'.[68]

Devotion to the Immaculate Conception grew even more after the apparitions of the Virgin identifying herself as the Immaculate Conception to Bernadette Soubirous (1844–79) in Lourdes in 1858.[69] In 1866, a railway station was opened at Lourdes, facilitating pilgrimage to the shrine,[70] and by the early 1880s the Irish Oblates of Mary Immaculate went there frequently.[71] By 1876, a pulpit had been presented to the Augustinian Order in Drogheda as a thanksgiving to the Blessed Virgin of Lourdes by 'a friend'.[72] The same year, the newspaper also reported on the offering by Clonfert of a banner to the shrine itself. The banner was made of green poplin and bore images of the harp and the Celtic Cross, the whole surrounded by shamrocks. Brought by Father Coon to Lourdes, he found it difficult to find a place to hang it, so crowded with banners was the shrine. The superior of the shrine eventually displaced one from France in order to accommodate the Irish banner, beside one from Canada and opposite one from Trinidad, 'the great empire of the English-speaking family of the Church'.[73] Also in 1876, an Irish celebration was held at Lourdes and a rich lamp of silver presented, 'procured through the unwearying exertions of the Revd Thomas Kinane, the respected Administrator of Thurles, and author of the edifying work, "The Dove of the Tabernacle"'. The offices of the *Nation* and *Weekly News* sold a copy of a book entitled *Our Blessed Lady of Lourdes* for one and sixpence.[74]

Churches throughout Ireland were furnished with representations of the Blessed Virgin of Lourdes, or with Lourdes grottoes. In 1877, a statue of the Virgin of Lourdes, inscribed with 'I am the Immaculate Conception', was presented to the church of St James in Cappagh, in memory of Mrs White of Nantenan. The sculp-

---

64 *Nation*, 21 Aug. 1858. **65** *Nation*, 27 Aug. 1859. **66** *Nation*, 27 Aug. 1859. **67** *Catholic Directory*, 1865. **68** *Nation*, 26 May 1877. **69** Marina Warner, *Alone of all her sex: the myth and cult of the Virgin Mary* (London, 1990), p. 249. On the links between nineteenth-century apparitions of the Immaculate Conception and folk piety, see Miri Rubin, *Mother of God: a history of the Virgin Mary* (London, 2009), pp 417–19. On how Bernadette was influenced by the imagery of the Miraculous Medal, see Carroll, 'The Virgin Mary at LaSalette and Lourdes', 56–74. **70** Mary Heimann, *Catholic devotion in Victorian England* (Oxford, 1995), p. 140. **71** John Turpin, 'Visual Marianism and national identity in Ireland, 1920–1960' in Tricia Cusack and Síghle Bhreathnach-Lynch (eds), *Art, nation and gender* (Aldershot, 2000), pp 67–78 at p. 73. **72** *Nation*, 20 May 1876, carried from the *Drogheda Argus*. **73** *Nation*, 16 Sept. 1876. **74** *Nation*, 12 Aug. 1876.

6.1 Earley & Co. pencil and wash design for stained glass window (reproduced by kind permission of the National Irish Visual Arts Library, NIVAL/EC/60).

ture shows the Virgin standing with a crown of stars, her hands joined, and clothed in white with a blue sash.[75] The designs usually showed a woman in white, with a blue sash, standing in a grotto with her hands joined, looking down on the young Bernadette, as in the design for stained glass by Earley & Co., Dublin, possibly for a site in Dunsany, Co. Meath (fig. 6.1).[76] So ubiquitous did the cult of the Immaculate Virgin become, that an *Irish Times* correspondent aroused the good natured reproach of a Church of Ireland clergyman by describing the figure of the Blessed Virgin painted by Joshua Clarke in the stained glass windows of Ballywalter parish church as the Immaculate Conception.[77]

Closely related to the cult of the Immaculate Conception was that of the Sacred Heart of Jesus, whose images are, perhaps, even more ubiquitous than the Immaculata. The 1883 painting by Aloysius O'Kelly, *Mass in a Connemara Cottage*, now on loan to the National Gallery of Ireland, shows a young priest, clothed in white, saying mass in a large, reasonably well-furnished cottage. On the otherwise bare wall in the background of the painting, a coloured print of Christ displaying his sacred heart is shown. Devotion to the Sacred Heart arose from the visions of the seventeenth-century nun, Margaret Mary Alacoque (1647–90) at Paray-le-Monial in France.[78] In Ireland, Nano Nagle founded the Sisters of the Charitable Instruction of the Sacred Heart of Jesus, thus furthering the devotion through her active order.[79] In 1846, the Sacred Heart of Jesus received further devotion when a Sister of Charity, Apolline Andreveau, was the recipient of a vision of the Virgin, who came with a red scapular with the instruments of the Passion and the Sacred Heart on it, and the legend 'Holy Hearts of Jesus and Mary, pray for us'.[80] The feast of the Sacred Heart was extended to the universal church in 1856, and Alacoque was beatified in 1864.[81]

That same year, the church in Donnybrook claimed to be the first Irish church dedicated to the Sacred Heart.[82] By 1876, J.J. Lalor was advertising the sale of medals of the Sacred Heart in the *Nation* and other newspapers.[83] In 1877, a description of the medal of the Sacred Heart Medal Association was placed in the advertisement, which gave a detailed description of the design and inscription and said that it had been sanctioned by the Vincentian Fathers.[84]

The same year, the Capuchin fathers held a bazaar in which some of the prizes were 'Two beautiful oleographs of the Sacred Hearts of Jesus and Mary, and a large one of his Holiness Pope Pius IX'.[85] The pageantry and spectacle offered by the many

75 Matthew Tobin and Lisa O'Connor, www.limerickdioceseheritage.org, accessed 28 Nov. 2009. **76** NCAD, NIVAL EC/60. The word 'Dunsany' is erased on the drawing. **77** *Irish Times*, 15 Apr. 1899, and the letter from J.A. Greer LL.D. of the Vicarage, Ballywalter, Co. Down, *Irish Times*, 18 Apr. 1899. **78** Mary Lee Nolan and Sidney Nolan, *Christian pilgrimage in modern Western Europe* (Chapel Hill, NC, and London, 1989), p. 103. **79** Caitriona Clear, 'Nagle, Nano' in S.J. Connolly (ed.), *Oxford companion to Irish history* (Oxford, 2007), p. 395. **80** Nicholas Perry and Loreto Echeverría, *Under the heel of Mary* (London, 1988), p. 95. **81** Frank Leslie Cross (ed.), *Oxford Dictionary of the Christian Church* (London, 1957), p. 856. She was canonized in 1920. **82** *Nation*, 27 Aug. 1864. **83** *Nation*, 5 May 1877. **84** *Nation*, 26 May 1877. **85** *Nation*, 26 May 1877.

6.2 Earley & Powells, stained glass window. Apparition of the Sacred Heart to Margaret Mary Alacoque, Roman Catholic Church, Arles, Co. Laois, *c.*1868.

confraternities of the Sacred Heart can be seen in the description of the arrival of the Sodality of the Sacred Heart from Balindangan to Knock in 1880, 'carrying several banners, among which was one remarkably splendid, bearing a portrait of our Blessed Lady in an attitude of prayer, and surmounted by a richly gilt cross. This was brought as a present to our Lady of Knock'.[86]

Stained glass windows depicting the Sacred Heart were extremely popular. Often they depicted Christ gesturing to the glowing heart in his chest, flanked in neighbouring windows by the Blessed Virgin and St Joseph, thus making a type of holy family, as in a design for Cashel by Earley & Powells in a book of designs dated 1864–9,[87] or in the *c.*1900 window attributed to Mayer of Munich in Rathowen, Co. Westmeath.[88] Sometimes the apparition to Margaret Mary Alacoque was shown, as in the windows in Arles, Co. Laois, by Earley & Powells, contributed by a Mrs Grace *c.*1868 (fig. 6.2),[89] or in the 1883–8 window by Mayer of Munich in Waterford Cathedral, where the design is almost baroque in its sense of movement and its

86 *Nation*, 22 May 1880.   **87** NCAD, NIVAL EC/137.17.   **88** Casey and Rowan, *North Leinster*, p. 460.   **89** *Irish Builder*, 10:203 (1 June 1868), 143. The windows can be seen at http://freepages.family.rootsweb.ancestry.com/~mjbrennan/arles057.jpg, accessed 2 Dec. 2009.

glowing colour.[90] In Fews, Co. Waterford, the nun kneels in front of an altar, above which appears Christ of the Sacred Heart, while Gothic vaulting indicates an ecclesiastical space, a design echoed by the similar window at Ballylaneen, Co. Waterford.[91] The Sacred Heart also appeared in sculptures, such as the one outside Dublin's St Francis Xavier, by Terence Farrell (c.1877–94)[92] and the sculptures by Messrs Patrick J. O'Neill in the cathedral at Thurles, Co. Tipperary (1879).[93]

By the late nineteenth and early twentieth centuries, criticism grew of both the mass-produced Catholic items discussed above, and stained glass windows, so that even those produced in Ireland by Irish firms were seen as inadequate in design, and those imported from Germany – predominantly from Munich – were seen as crass imitations of oil paintings by some art critics.[94] The extraordinary talent of Harry Clarke and the artists of *An Túr Gloine* demonstrated the potential for high quality, individualistic design in church decoration. However, nineteenth-century devotional art – much of it of a higher quality than its turn-of-the-century critics allowed – can show how devotions and cults were spread, how individuals and groups participated in collective decisions of design and iconography, and how mass-production facilitated the growth of instrumental Catholicism, and even the growth of cults themselves. Windows – even the worst of them allowing light to be diffused through different hues and colours into, usually, a neo-medieval interior – altars and statues – ranging from those executed by well-known sculptors to mass-produced cheap plaster images – show how commemorative choices were made and identities perpetuated. In his study of stained glass, Michael Wynne warned that nineteenth-century windows could not be studied without a systematic church inventory and better photographic conditions.[95] With the work of the NIAH nearing completion, perhaps this an ideal time for a comprehensive study of nineteenth-century Roman Catholic church art.

90 www.waterford-cathedral.com/pictures07.html, accessed 29 Nov. 2009. **91** www. buildingsofireland.ie/niah, accessed 22 Nov. 2009. **92** Casey, *Dublin*, pp 131–2. **93** *Irish Times*, 23 June 1879. **94** Robert Elliott, *Art and Ireland*, with a preface by Edward Martyn (Dublin, 1902), passim, but in particular pp 173–4, 214, 217. **95** Wynne, 'Stained glass in Ireland', p. 119.

Rome and Kenmare: Margaret Cusack and Ultramontane print culture[1]

PATRICK MAUME

Margaret Anna Cusack ('The nun of Kenmare') (1829–99) has attracted considerable recent attention. Short biographies have appeared, and a book on Irish women historians discusses Cusack,[2] but there is no comprehensive survey. Many commentators, emphasizing two autobiographies written after leaving the Catholic Church, see Cusack as a persecuted proto-feminist social reformer,[3] while Sister Philomena McCarthy (representing the Kenmare Poor Clares – with whom Cusack quarrelled)[4] and James Donnelly (discussing the Knock shrine)[5] call her a self-aggrandizing neurotic. The author of the most recent study, taking her retrospective statements in the autobiographies at face value, suggests that she was always at heart a Protestant who 'never truly embraced the Catholic faith'.[6] This view, it will be shown here, is highly debatable.

This paper emphasizes Catholic apologetic works that Cusack published at Kenmare – when she maintained that one could not be too ultramontane[7] and that 'liberal Catholic' and 'bad Catholic' were synonyms[8] – as exemplifying the apocalypticism surrounding Pope Pius IX and use of popular media by nineteenth-century ultramontanism. Ultramontanism developed in the era of the French Revolution, intensifying under Pius IX (Papacy 1846–78). It reacted against perceived eighteenth-century theological corruptions, including rationalism, which downplayed miracles and discouraged emotional devotionalism, and Gallicanism (autonomy of local

1 Thanks to Paul Bew, Derval Fitzgerald and James McGuire. All cited works by Cusack unless otherwise stated. Although entitled 'Kenmare Publications', Cusack's works were usually printed and published in Dublin and/or London. For copyright reasons, some books were published simultaneously in Dublin, London, Melbourne and New York or Boston – e.g. the title page of *Book of the blessed ones* has four imprints; Burns, Oates (London); J. Duffy and M'Glashan and Gill (Dublin); J. Swayne (USA); G. Elwood (Melbourne). Place of publication for Cusack's works cited here should be assumed to be 'Dublin and London' unless otherwise stated. 2 Nadia Clare Smith, *A 'Manly Study'? Irish women historians, 1868–1949* (London, 2006), pp 31–7. 3 Irene ffrench Eagar, *The Nun of Kenmare* (Cork, 1970); Margaret Rose O'Neill, *The life of Mother Clare: out from the shadow of the Upas tree* (Seattle, WA, 1990). 4 Sr Philomena McCarthy, *The Nun of Kenmare: the true facts* (Killarney, 1989). 5 James Donnelly, 'The Marian shrine at Knock: the first decade', *Éire–Ireland*, i, 28:2 (1993), 54–99. 6 Catherine Ferguson CSJP, *Margaret Anna Cusack (The Nun of Kenmare), Knock, November 1881–December 1883* (Warrenpoint, Co. Down, 2008), pp 8, 93. This book appeared too late to be fully used in this paper. 7 *Book of the blessed ones* (1874), p. 48. 8 *Jesus and Jerusalem* (3rd ed., 1872), p. 56.

churches from the Pope and subordination to national rulers). Ultramontanes glori-
fied the Middle Ages as the era of faith, and sought a revived Christendom with the
Papacy as moral guide. Ultramontanism was populist-authoritarian, contrasting
simple folk piety with aristocratic scepticism and reviving (remodelled to suit
modern decorum) devotional practices that Enlightenment-influenced clerics had
condemned as superstitious. Ultramontanes deployed modern technology; railway
systems facilitated mass pilgrimages, stereotype printing and durable steel engraving
plates disseminated devotional literature and images.[9]

One of Cusack's role-models was the populist French journalist Louis Veuillot
(1813–83), editor of the Catholic weekly *L'Univers*. Detested by Liberal Catholics for
anti-intellectualism and authoritarianism, Veuillot commanded a large audience,
publicized the Lourdes apparitions, and was long praised as a model Catholic journalist.[10] Cusack praised Veuillot for his divinely given gift of exposing shams,[11] and
occasionally wrote for *L'Univers*.[12]

For Veuillot, and many other Catholic commentators, Pius IX exemplified the
papal mission. Pius was initially a reformer, but after limited constitutionalism within
the Papal States produced further demands and his refusal to totally identify the
church with Italian nationalism brought republican revolution (suppressed by French
troops), he left his secular domains in the hands of his reactionary Secretary of State,
Cardinal Antonelli.[13] Pius believed the alliance of throne and altar to be necessary for
civilization, and that without the Papal States the Papacy could not function properly. He was a Marian devotee, proclaiming the Immaculate Conception of the
Virgin Mary Catholic dogma and endorsing contemporary Marian apparitions such
as Lourdes and La Salette.[14] He promoted devotion to the Sacred Heart (associated
with the seventeenth-century apparition of Jesus to Margaret Mary Alacoque, whom
Pius beatified, at Paray-le-Monial in central France).[15] For admirers, including
Irishmen who joined Papal forces resisting Italian unification, Pius embodied an
apocalyptic struggle between good and evil and re-enacted the sufferings of Jesus.[16]
His longevity, the growth of Roman pilgrimages, and dissemination of his image
attracted devotion to the Pope as an individual (rather than as the abstract embodi-
ment of an office).[17] Some believed themselves to be in the Last Days, with Pius as
the last Pope. Cusack popularized continental Catholic devotions; her connection

---

9 *Pius IX* (1878), pp 39–41. **10** Owen Chadwick, *A history of the popes, 1830–1914* (Oxford,
1998), pp 323–7; Ruth Harris, *Lourdes: body and spirit in the secular age* (London, 1999), pp
118–28. **11** *Pius IX*, pp 568–9, 650. **12** *The case of Ireland stated: a plea for my people and my
race* (1880), p. 18; *The story of my life* (1891), p. 343. For Veuillot's praise of Cusack see ffrench
Eagar, *Nun*, p. 83 (misreading it as criticism). **13** Chadwick, *Popes*, pp 92–4. **14** *Pius IX*,
pp 154, 168–9. **15** Chadwick, *Popes*, p. 557. For Cusack's promotion of Sacred Heart
devotion (including recently founded French sodalities), see *Jesus and Jerusalem*, pp 264–78,
403–8, 409–11. **16** Patrick Maume, 'Fenianism as a global phenomenon: Thomas O'Malley
Baines, papal soldier and Fenian convict' in Leon Litvack and Colin Graham (eds), *Ireland
and Europe in the nineteenth century* (Dublin, 2006), pp 148–59. **17** Sheridan Gilley, *Newman
and his age* (2nd ed. London, 2003, 1st 1990), p. 375.

VIEW OF ROME FROM THE TIBER.

7.1 Rome from the Tiber, from Cusack's *Life of Pius IX*, with decorative border combining shamrocks and liturgical instruments and mottoes highlighting Ireland's fidelity to the papacy. New means of communication, and new technology allowing the mass-reproduction of high-quality images, brought Rome closer to nineteenth-century Ireland (reproduced by permission of Special Collections, Boole Library, UCC).

with Knock reflected her long-standing emphasis on the proximity of material and supernatural worlds and her belief that contemporary Irish Catholicism possessed many uncanonized saints and unnoticed miracles. This unrealistically exalted mindset brought disillusion and a return to Protestantism, but later publications display similar preoccupations, though reversing the objects of hero-worship and denunciation.

Cusack was born on 6 May 1829 in a middle-class Co. Dublin evangelical household. She learned Italian, French and Latin from her brother's tutors, becoming an ardent reader with literary ambitions. Her father developed heart trouble and the family became dependent on wealthy relatives. The parents separated when Margaret was 14. Mrs Cusack took the children to relatives in Exeter; she favoured her son over Margaret. In Cusack's 1872 novel *Hornehurst Rectory*, where Cusack became two characters, Kate Rossmore and Gertrude Helmer, Kate's treatment by her ultra-evangelical mother, Lady Rossmore, resembles Dives' neglect of Lazarus[18] and exemplifies how not to raise children;[19] Lady Rossmore's evangelical associates such as 'Signor

---

18 *Hornehurst Rectory* (New York, 1872), pp 52–3, 136.   **19** Ibid., pp 52–3.

Marchetti', modelled on Newman's adversary, the louche ex-Dominican Giacinto Achilli,[20] and fortune-hunting Dr Thundertone, who publicly ridicules a consecrated Host,[21] are excoriated. *Hornehurst Rectory* also features an anti-Catholic Fleet Street newspaper, the *Morning Slanderer*, edited by an ex-priest,[22] reflecting Cusack's lifelong preoccupation with the media as disseminators of religious controversy.

Cusack came to the Oxford Movement through the writings of John Keble and E.B. Pusey, reacting against Calvinist-inspired fears of damnation which gave her a two-year neurotic collapse.[23] After the death of her fiancé, she joined a London-based Anglican sisterhood, later merged with another Puseyite order under Lydia Sellon.[24] *Hornehurst Rectory* portrayed Sellon as a self-indulgent, manipulative tyrant, living luxuriously while driving sisters to death through fasting and overwork; her convent resembled hostile Evangelical images of Catholic convents.[25] Cusack noted that while Sellon had genuine health problems, her illnesses generally suited her own convenience.[26] After reverting to evangelical Protestantism, Cusack reiterated these criticisms.[27]

Cusack decided that if the doctrines professed by Puseyites were true, certainty lay in the Roman church, which she joined on 2 July 1858. *Hornehurst Rectory* emphasized Pusey's arrogance (especially towards women).[28] Pusey ('Dr Humbletone') bowdlerized Catholic texts for followers' devotional use.[29] After reversion, Cusack claimed that Rome similarly bowdlerized patristic texts to conceal departures from the early church.[30] Cusack accused Pusey of wishing to be a little pope over his followers;[31] his good and bad angels (literally) struggled unequally as he told a follower to forcibly prevent a dying daughter from converting;[32] he would be damned for keeping others from the true church through pride.[33]

Cusack later claimed that Cardinal Wiseman advised her to undertake Catholic literary work.[34] On 2 July 1859, Cusack entered the Poor Clare convent in Newry, whose superior was Mary O'Hagan, sister of Thomas O'Hagan, subsequently Lord Chancellor of Ireland. Cusack was professed in 1860 as Sister Mary Francis Clare

20 Ibid., pp 167–72; Sheridan Gilley, 'Achilli (Giovanni) Giacinto', *Oxford DNB*, www.oxforddnb.com/view/article/55519 accessed 28 July 2009. **21** *Hornehurst*, pp 325–7, 330–1; see also pp 153–4, 187–8, 443, 568–77. The Evangelical Thundertone, as his name suggests, is a loudmouthed bully. By portraying the Anglo-Catholic Pusey as a manipulative hypocrite under a similar name (Humbletone), Cusack insinuates that however much Anglican Ritualists and Evangelicals dislike one another, they share a Protestant 'tone', which outweighs their differences. **22** Ibid., pp 426–36. **23** [M.F. Cusack], *Five years in a Protestant sisterhood and ten years in a Catholic convent* (London, 1869), pp 8–10. **24** Sean Gill, 'The power of Christian ladyhood: Priscilla Lydia Sellon and the creation of Anglican sisterhoods' in Stuart Mews (ed.), *Modern religious rebels: presented to John Kent* (London, 1993), pp 144–65. **25** *Hornehurst*, pp 227, 239–42, 383, 405, 513; *Five years*, pp 52, 79–82, 100–3, 105–7. **26** *Five years*, pp 112–13. **27** *Life inside the church of Rome* (London, 1889), pp 257–9; *Story*, pp 57–81, 88–9. **28** *Hornehurst*, pp 92–3, 101, 192, 341–2. **29** Ibid., pp 349, 427–4, 515–17, 639–40. **30** *Life inside*, pp 87–9, 107–8, 126, 129–32ff. **31** *Hornehurst*, pp 210–13, 345–6; *Story*, p. 63. **32** Ibid., pp 353–6. **33** Ibid., pp 99, 318, 685–7. **34** *Five years*, pp 209–21; *Story*, p. 100; McCarthy, *Nun*, pp 9, 18–19.

(many of her books were published under the name M.F. Cusack). She had received an inheritance from relatives; a 'dowry' of £500 was invested on her behalf, the remainder was donated to the convent.[35] In October 1861, Cusack joined O'Hagan in a Kenmare foundation sponsored by the parish priest, Father John O'Sullivan. Cusack was horrified by the poverty of Kerry. The nuns established a school and convent in spartan conditions; the first Benediction service in the town was celebrated at Christmas 1861, and the consecration of their church in 1863 saw the first Pontifical High Mass in Kenmare.[36]

At first, Cusack taught in the convent school (she advocated gentleness towards delicate and sensitive children),[37] but after she published a *Life of St Francis*, other devotional works rapidly followed from Kenmare Publications. Her 1862 translation from German of *The Life and Revelations of St Gertrude the Great* (combined with a Life of this mystic and locutionist by Cusack herself) characteristically linked Franciscan and Benedictine traditions,[38] praised the French Benedictine abbot of Solesmes, Dom Prosper Guéranger, for encouraging French dioceses to replace local liturgical forms with the Roman rite,[39] and criticized Catholics sceptical of private revelations – Jesus spoke to His chosen brides as to His apostles.[40] Cusack corresponded with Guéranger through English Benedictines, reflecting this enclosed nun's literary networking;[41] her literary activities brought exemption from the rule that correspondence be scrutinized by superiors. The medieval *Life of St Gertrude* – compiled by an anonymous religious within the saint's convent – served as a literary model for Cusack's life of O'Hagan, published after the abbess' death in 1876 by the sisters of the Kenmare convent.

Cusack composed several 'faith and fatherland' histories, corresponding with scholars such as the poet Denis Florence McCarthy (a translator from Spanish with a cousin in the Kenmare convent), the Lansdownes' agent Townsend Trench, Canon Ulick Bourke of Tuam and Dr John McCarthy (vice-president of Maynooth; Bishop of Kerry, 1878–81), borrowing books from gentry families, Maynooth and the Royal Irish Academy.[42] Some antiquarian works were published by subscription.

Cusack's writings for popular audiences might have shocked gentry subscribers. Her novel *Ned Rusheen, or who fired the first shot?*, in which a tenant is accused of murdering a landlord (killed by his dissipated eldest son) was a viscerally angry treatment of upper-class Protestant family dynamics. The simple faith of the Catholic poor and the pastoral work of nuns were contrasted with upper-class amorality, inspired by Satan. A father-son quarrel, driven by evil spirits hovering beside them,

35 McCarthy, *Nun*, pp 5–6. **36** *In memoriam Mary O'Hagan: abbess and foundress of the convent of Poor Clares, Kenmare* (Dublin and London, 1876), pp 258, 303. **37** *Jesus and Jerusalem*, pp 251–2; *Good reading for girls* (1877), pp 207–9. The latter is addressed to former pupils – 'you are all my children', p. 215. **38** [M.F. Cusack], *The life and revelations of St Gertrude the Great*, translated by the Poor Clares of Kenmare (first published 1862: repr. by Tan Books, Rockford, IL, 2002 – all page references to this ed.), pp xxvii–xxviii, 14n. **39** *Gertrude*, p. xxix. **40** Ibid., p. xxx. **41** Ibid., pp xxxviiii–xxxix, 266n. **42** McCarthy, *Nun*, pp 14, 61.

is described and illustrated.[43] *Tim O'Halloran's choice, or from Killarney to New York* was dedicated to the committee of a Catholic orphanage. Commissioned by an American publisher, it depicted a dying Kerry peasant resisting a mercenary Protestant missionary's attempts to secure his son, then traced the son's fortunes; he almost committed theft, but repented when a Marian statue looked at him,[44] and was adopted by a converted American banker. Soupers were the devil's agents,[45] driven by spite and greed and plotting further persecution of Catholics; an appendix listed souper misdeeds in Ireland, quoting Cardinal Cullen's description of them as disappointed spinsters making others as miserable as themselves, and advocated disseminating cheap Catholic tracts.[46] Protestant missions 'everywhere' were frauds spreading atheism.[47]

Cusack skilfully marketed her books to Catholic schools and American audiences. She countered American non-recognition of European copyrights by working with American Catholic publishers. Nevertheless, she suffered considerable losses through fires, plagiarism and embezzlement. She circulated extensive catalogues of Kenmare publications. By 1872, she claimed to have sold over 200,000 copies of her works.[48] Even a hostile biographer notes their good-quality print and paper.[49] Cusack, declaring that 'the press is now what the pulpit was in former times . . . We must meet the propagandism of evil with the propagandism of good',[50] denounced Catholics who read works by Protestants and unbelievers or wrote for Protestant publications.[51] Her 'Kenmare Series' of devotional writings had an appendix on promoting Catholic literature, claiming to have inspired over a hundred circulating libraries.[52]

In 1869, Cusack published her first autobiography, *Five Years in a Protestant Sisterhood and Ten Years in a Catholic Convent*. This responded to the Saurin case, where a discontented English ex-nun sued her superiors; although she had not been retained against her will, descriptions of authoritarian convent discipline and the fact that nuns of gentle birth performed menial labour unfavourably impressed British opinion.[53] Cusack glowingly contrasted her Catholic and Protestant conventual experiences, declaring that labour and voluntary poverty inspired the nuns' care for the poor[54] and emphasizing that the right of a Catholic nun to appeal to her bishop provided a safeguard absent in Puseyite sisterhoods (Irish convents were under the jurisdiction of diocesan bishops rather than provincial superiors – a point of importance for Cusack's later career.) McCarthy cites *Five Years* as proof that Cusack was

---

43 *Ned Rusheen* (New York, 1871), frontispiece, p. 62. Compare the insistence on diabolic power and intervention in *Jesus and Jerusalem*, pp 52, 66. **44** *Tim O'Halloran's choice* (Dublin, 1877), pp 225–30. **45** Ibid., pp xiii, 80n. **46** Ibid., pp xxxix. **47** Ibid., pp 178–80, 259–62. **48** Note to Sadlier edition (New York, 1872) of *Hornehurst Rectory*. **49** McCarthy, *Nun*, p. 25. **50** *Good reading*, p. v. **51** *Life of the Most Revd Joseph Dixon D.D., primate of all Ireland* (1878), pp 84–5, 109; *Good reading*, pp vi–viii. **52** *Jesus and Jerusalem*, p. 469. **53** W.L. Arnstein, *Protestant versus Catholic in mid-Victorian England: Mr Newdegate and the nuns* (Columbia, MO, and London, 1982), pp 108–27. **54** *Five years*, pp xvi, 221–2, 230–4.

7.2 The frontispiece of Cusack's 1871 novel *Ned Rusheen* shows devils inspiring a
murderous quarrel between a landlord and his son, while their guardian angels flee,
rendered powerless by the sins of their charges. Cusack's work portrays a universe
interpenetrated by countless direct supernatural interventions (reproduced by permission
of the National Library of Ireland).

more contented than she later maintained, but its extreme idealization is discon-
certing. Cusack denied that any nuns were unhappy.[55] Discussing miracles within
convents (including the recent cure at Assisi of a nun driven from the cloister by the
Italian government),[56] she mentioned sisters who saw visions of Purgatory and a
sister miraculously cured of spinal disease, hinting that she was the anonymous
visionary and invalid.[57]

Cusack's writings were important to the convent's finances (though they were
not, as she claimed, its principal source of income).[58] With the bishop's permission,
she acquired her own bank account for publishing expenses.[59] She had a room of her
own (normally only granted to elderly and infirm nuns) to write undisturbed; as her
handwriting grew illegible, she employed a secretary. Her writing was littered with
easily correctible errors, suggesting haste and lack of editing; in her life of Daniel
O'Connell, Edmund Burke's son Richard was called his brother;[60] in *Pius IX*, the seat
of Italian government in the years before 1870 is placed at Naples rather than
Florence.[61] Cusack suffered recurrent health problems (rheumatism and neuras-
thenia); she described illness and over-work as divine blessings, a sign that every nun
was a Christ, sent to saint and sinner, and hated by the world.[62] She mentioned being
routinely dispensed from fasting because of ill-health.[63] Some devotional works
presented depressive episodes (implicitly denied in *Five Years*) as signs of divine favour
and spiritual growth.[64] Oral tradition in the Kenmare convent (derived from hostile
nuns, but supported by passing remarks in Cusack's books) claimed that O'Hagan let
Cusack absent herself from communal prayers and remain awake, writing until 4am,
and that sensitivity to noise led Cusack to physically attack sisters.[65] There must have
been serious questions about the wisdom of admitting to a religious order someone
who could not function without far-ranging exemptions from its Rule, necessarily
isolating her from communal life. These exemptions might have been withdrawn if
a superior hostile to Cusack were supported by the bishop.

Cusack's 1878 biography of Archbishop Joseph Dixon of Armagh claimed that
'favours' (miracles) were obtained through prayer at his tomb and quoted correspondents who desired his beatification; the book may have imitated dossiers submitted
to the Congregation for Saints as the first step towards canonization.[66] Dixon was
compared to Jean-Marie Vianney, Curé d'Ars (1786–1859), the nineteenth-century
French parish priest famous for austerity, simplicity and skill as preacher and
confessor[67] (and for harassment by demons). The struggle of the post-Revolutionary

55 Ibid., p. 251.   **56** Ibid., pp 291–5.   **57** Ibid., pp 287–91.   **58** McCarthy, *Nun*, pp 30–1,
42; *The Nun of Kenmare: an autobiography* (1888), pp 126–30, 132, 134–5, 159–60, 218; *Story*, pp
161–2.   **59** *Autobiography*, pp 35, 61, 136–7.   **60** *Life of the Liberator, Daniel O'Connell* (1877
ed.), pp 116–17.   **61** *Pius IX*, p. 636.   **62** *Mary O'Hagan*, pp xi–xix, 199–202.   **63**
Autobiography, p. 27; *Story*, pp 125–6.   **64** *The pilgrim's way to heaven* (2nd ed., 1873), pp 5–7,
11, 31–2; *Jesus and Jerusalem*, pp 182–5, 214–18, 464.   **65** McCarthy, *Nun*, pp 28–30, 53–4.
66 *Dixon*, pp 192–3, 502–3; K.L. Woodward, *Making saints: how the Catholic Church determines
who becomes a saint, who doesn't, and why* (New York, 1991), pp 68–9.   **67** *Dixon*, pp xxvi, 179,
511; Robert Gildea, *Children of the Revolution: the French, 1799–1914* (London, 2008), pp

French church to rebuild its infrastructure and re-evangelize the population, which Vianney symbolized, paralleled disciplinary and devotional changes orchestrated by Irish bishops; Cusack emphasized Dixon's implementation of ecclesiastical reforms at a provincial synod,[68] and his successful campaign against ribbonism.[69] This view of French Catholic revival as a model for Ireland had devotional as well as pastoral aspects. The Newry and Kenmare convents fostered devotions to the French Marian apparitions at La Salette (1846) and Lourdes (1858); Cusack claimed that miraculous cures through Lourdes water occurred in Kenmare.[70]

Like Vianney, Dixon was presented as the ideal priest. Cusack rhapsodized on the need to honour the priesthood; criticism of priests emanated from the devil,[71] Dixon, always retaining his baptismal innocence,[72] was devoted to Marian shrines such as La Salette,[73] received spiritual favours through St Catherine of Siena and St Joseph, as Vianney did through St Philomena,[74] and prophetically declared that Napoleon III's acquiescence in the loss of papal territory (1859) would bring the Emperor's downfall.[75] A.M. Sullivan, often seen as embodying 'faith and fatherland' nationalism, was found wanting by comparison. Cusack attacked Sullivan's memoir *New Ireland* (an 'amusing work' resembling William Stuart Trench's *Realities of Irish Life*) for ignoring Dixon's role in recruiting papal soldiers, and denounced Sullivan's claim that home rule election victories against clerical opposition showed the declining political influence of Irish priests.[76] Cusack was probably reacting to the defeat of Bishop Moriarty's candidate in the 1872 Kerry by-election.[77] Cusack's comparison of Dixon to Vianney reflects her regular complaint that Irish and English Catholics hailed miracles elsewhere while ignoring innumerable miracles which, she believed, occurred unnoticed in Ireland.[78]

In 1878, Cusack also published *The Life and Times of His Holiness Pope Pius IX: Faithful Pastor, Loving Father, Patient Cross-Bearer* (1878) in six parts, with engravings of scenes from the Pope's life imitating medieval manuscript illustrations.[79] Each page was bordered by one of four patterns. One bore the motto 'Father of the Poor, Great in Meekness' accompanied by angels carrying the instruments of the Passion, symbolizing Pius as martyr. Another declared 'Farewell, Great Pontiff, True Lover of Faithful Ireland' and showed incense-burners and candles (symbolizing prayer) decorated with shamrocks. The third – 'Ave Maria Gratia Plena', decorated with roses in honour of the Marian title 'Mystic Rose' – showed Marian symbols associated with the revelation of the Miraculous Medal to Catherine Labouré (1830) and Pius' defi-

118–22; *Blessed ones*, pp 337–9. **68** *Dixon*, pp 253–360. **69** Ibid., pp 224–8, 238–42, 354–5. **70** *Mary O'Hagan*, pp 137–8. **71** *Dixon*, pp x–xvii, xix, 19–26. **72** Ibid., p. 5. **73** Ibid., pp 175–7, 181–2. **74** Ibid., pp xxvi, 122–4, 178–9, 184–5, 373–4. **75** Ibid., pp 421–2, 455–6, 468–9. See also *Pius IX*, pp 514, 516. **76** *Dixon*, pp 489–90; *Pius IX*, pp 308–9. **77** The 1877 edition of Cusack's *Life of the Liberator, Daniel O'Connell* (first pub. Kenmare, 1872) contained an essay on Ireland's future, arguing that personal moral reform must precede national freedom (pp 791–805). **78** *Dixon*, pp xx xxv; *Pius IX*, p. 552. **79** For this style of publishing see the opening page of the large edition of Henri Lasserre, *Notre-Dame de Lourdes* (1878) reproduced as illustration in Harris, *Lourdes*, p. 181.

nition of the Immaculate Conception (1854). A fourth commemorated 'St Joseph, Patriarch of the Universal Church' – to whom Cusack had a personal devotion – with lilies symbolizing his chastity.

The *Life of Dixon* described the Roman population as universally pious;[80] here, Cusack proclaimed that nothing was alleged against the moral character of the Italian clergy,[81] and claimed that the Roman people – except for criminal 'scum' – supported Pius.[82] She attributed the hostile British view of Pius IX to dishonest newspapers;[83] his only fault was leniency.[84] Like other apologists, Cusack emphasized Pius' introduction of gas, piped water and railways to Rome.[85] The Mortara case, where a Jewish boy was baptized by a Catholic servant and taken from his parents by papal authorities, was met by complaining that its denouncers ignored child-stealing Protestant proselytizers in Ireland; Cusack claimed that Roman Jews were 'greatly favoured by Pius IX'.[86] Cusack said that there were no mercenaries in the Papal army; its foreign soldiers did their duty as Catholics.[87] Italian opposition to Pius was attributed to the special endeavours of the Devil against Rome, possibly indicating the Last Days.[88] Cusack claimed that Britain endangered itself by harbouring Italian political refugees;[89] those who stole church property endangered all property rights.[90] The growth of Italian radicalism after unification and German socialism during the Kulturkampf (anti-Catholic persecution, 1871–8) proved that 'no religion means no government ... To-day the altars are flung down; tomorrow the throne'.[91] She defended Pius' denunciations of free speech and freedom of religion by noting the circulation of 'bad books' by revolutionaries and Biblical instances of blasphemers struck dead by God.[92] Catholics converted to Protestantism, such as the Garibaldian ex-priest and Protestant missionary Alessandro Gavazzi, drew particular scorn: 'No man works so hard for the devil. As an apostate, he has flung the grace of God utterly from him, and he is at the mercy of the fiend'.[93] The refusal of the German cleric and scholar Döllinger to accept Infallibility was attributed to disappointed ambition and limited intellect.[94]

Cusack echoed Pius IX's self-image as 'Mary's child and prince',[95] foretold by prophets,[96] and man of sorrows renewing the sufferings of Jesus, with Napoleon III as Judas, the fall of Rome as Calvary,[97] the hypocrite Cavour[98] and Garibaldi (accused of cowardice)[99] as Pilate and Herod, Mazzini as principal instrument of Satan.[1] She

80 *Dixon,* pp 151–2.   **81** *Pius IX,* p. 256.   **82** Ibid., pp xxix.   **83** Ibid., pp xii–xix, 69–70, 379–80, 619–29.   **84** Ibid., p. 493.   **85** Ibid., pp 505–7, 538–40.   **86** Ibid., pp 288, 542–4, 548–9; David Kertzer, *The kidnapping of Edgardo Mortara* (New York, 1998).   **87** *Pius IX,* pp 569–70.   **88** Ibid., pp 3–4, 67–8, 232–3, 501.   **89** *Dixon,* pp 141–2; *Pius IX,* p. 528.   **90** *Pius IX,* pp 380–3.   **91** Ibid., pp xxix, 583–6.   **92** *Pius IX,* pp 341–2, 387–8, 593–4; contrast *Black pope: a history of the Jesuits* (London, 1896), pp 211–12.   **93** Ibid., p. 290.   **94** Ibid., p. 609.   **95** Ibid., pp 214, 429, 443–4.   **96** Ibid., pp 16–23.   **97** Ibid., pp 36–7, 40–1, 92, 273, 604, 640–2, 652.   **98** Ibid., pp 515–16, 565. The Herod comparison is also used for the Italian government's introduction of civil marriage, with Pius (baptised Giovanni) as John the Baptist defending sacred matrimony (pp 111–12, 390–3, 673–4).   **99** Ibid., pp 420, 603–4.   **1** Ibid., pp 240, 255–6, 304–5.

ARCHBISHOP MASTAI RESCUES LOUIS NAPOLEON BONAPARTE.

7.3 The future Pius IX, as archbishop of Spoleto, shelters the future Napoleon III, a
fugitive from justice, after the future emperor participated in an uprising against the Papal
government – from Cusack's *Life of Pius IX*. The border, with angels carrying the
instruments of the Passion, symbolizes Cusack's view (shared by Pius himself) that the
attacks on the Papal States re-enacted the passion of Jesus, with Pius as Christ-figure; in
this drama, Cusack casts Napoleon III as Judas betraying his benefactor (reproduced by
permission of Special Collections, Boole Library, UCC).

claimed that Pius worked miraculous cures.[2] She predicted his future canonization as St Pius the Great.[3]

During the near famine of 1879–80, Cusack used her organizational skills, extensive contacts, and international reputation to develop a network of relief committees in Kerry and other western areas. She became involved in public controversy over the treatment of tenants on the Lansdowne estates. The American Land League publicist, James Redpath, highlighted her activities on the Lansdowne estates in Kerry, which he had been invited to visit by Cusack.[4] Cusack wrote pro-Parnell articles in the *Daily Chronicle*; her *Case of Ireland stated* (1880) denounced absentee landlordism.

Meanwhile, her position at the convent grew insecure following the deaths of Father O'Sullivan, Mother O'Hagan (whose successor, Teresa Lowry, proved unsympathetic) and Bishop David Moriarty (d. 1877) and his successor Dr John McCarthy (d. 1881), who had encouraged her work. Cusack had clashed with Andrew Higgins when he was parish priest of Kenmare, after she had described him in 1876 as 'the Father whom God sent in the hour of need', comparable to the Curé d'Ars'.[5] Faced with the prospect of Andrew Higgins as bishop of Kerry, Cusack turned her attention to Knock. Her *Life of the Blessed Virgin Mary* (1880) discussed the 1879 Marian apparition as a divine favour to the famine-stricken west, and in 1880 she published *The 'Irish Lourdes': the Apparition of the Blessed Virgin at Knock, Co. Mayo*. This declared the apparition as a sign of Mary's maternal care for the suffering Irish. Cusack combined this with a fierce attack on Protestant disbelief in non-Biblical miracles, 'which God reserves for His Church'.[6]

On 16 November 1881, Cusack left Kenmare, ostensibly to return to Newry. She went to Knock, announcing her intention to found a convent and Industrial Training House for girls. After acrimonious financial negotiations, she secured canonical release from the Poor Clares, and received conditional permission from Archbishop John MacEvilly to found a convent. An 1882 pamphlet, *Three Visits to Knock*, promoted Knock as an Irish Lourdes.[7] Cusack published medical certificates of miraculous cures modelled on those already issued at Lourdes,[8] and described several different apparitions – as distinct from the single canonical apparition in later accounts.[9] Cusack described cures of Protestants as well as Catholics, claiming to have witnessed the miraculous cure of a 7-year-old by conditional baptism, and to have experienced a miraculous cure herself.[10] Cusack criticized those who refused to

2 Ibid., pp 275, 478–83, 486–9.   **3** Ibid., pp 456, 485, 665.   **4** *Irish World*, 4 Sept. 1880 (repr. from *New York Tribune*); *Case of Ireland*, pp 76–7, 103.   **5** *Mary O'Hagan*, pp vi (dedication), 339–40.   **6** Continuing ecclesiastical miracles were a major point of contention between nineteenth-century Catholics and Protestants – Gilley, *Newman*, pp 335–7, 342.   **7** *Three visits*, pp 1–2.   **8** Harris, *Lourdes*, pp 288–331. The Medical Bureau associated with the French shrine was not established until 1883; for Knock certificates, see *Three visits*, pp 81–87. **9** Cusack seemed unaware that the Lourdes apparitions underwent a winnowing process, with several alleged visionaries dismissed as fraudulent or deceived by the devil – Harris, *Lourdes*, pp 91–109.   **10** *Three visits*, pp vi–vii, 84–5. Cusack later attributed it to

accept the authenticity of the La Salette and Lourdes apparitions, arguing that France might have been saved had sufficient attention been paid to them.[11]

MacEvilly and Cusack soon fell out over the question of how conditional his permission had been; Cusack privately told a dismayed MacEvilly that she was a prophet who received Marian apparitions.[12] MacEvilly later described this claim as 'all bosh', and expressed fear that she might revert to Protestantism.[13] He was scandalized by her habitual disregard for the rules of enclosure, though some local priests defended her as 'someone having a special mission who is not bound by the ordinary rules that guide others'.[14] *Three Visits to Knock* praised Father Bartholomew Cavanagh, the parish priest of Knock, as another Curé d'Ars,[15] but their relationship broke down over his attempts to control her convent – her later writings claimed that Kavanagh was so eager to believe in miracles that he persuaded himself that certain occurrences were miraculous, even when natural explanations were available, and that this self-deception was so extreme as to raise suspicions that he was deliberately dishonest.[16] In November 1883, Cusack and her novices went to England.

In February–March 1884, Cusack travelled to Rome to secure approval for the rule of her new order, St Joseph's Sisters of Peace, with the twin objectives of helping the poor and circulating good books (the latter aspect may have been inspired by the Assumptionist Fathers, the order in charge of the Lourdes shrine, who emphasized the apostolate of the printing press to the extent of running a daily newspaper). The rule was formally approved on 18 May 1884.

On returning to England, Cusack discovered that the priest in a parish where her nuns were assigned had seduced four successive schoolmistresses. She was horrified that after the scandal became public the priest simply moved to another diocese because there was a shortage of priests, and disciplining him would spread scandal. She saw this complicity as more disturbing than the original sin.[17] Such cases – most disturbingly her realization at Rome that Cardinal Antonelli, eulogized in *Pius IX*, had been financially and sexually corrupt[18] – combined with her quarrels to undermine her idealized view of the priesthood. She later recalled a visit to Paray-le-Monial en route to Rome, when she wondered why, after such an epochal revelation as the Sacred Heart, the present-day convent had so few nuns and the surrounding population was indifferent. The poverty of Naples, as blatant as anything she had seen in London and coexisting with flamboyant displays of Catholicism, shocked her,[19] and at Assisi she realised that a miracle-story which she had copied uncritically from a mediaeval life of St Clare was fabricated because the events

---

autosuggestion – *Story*, pp 236–7. See Ferguson, *Cusack*, pp 13–14, 18, 28. **11** *Three visits*, pp 5, 18–21. **12** Donnelly, 'Marian shrine', pp 83–8. **13** Ferguson, *Cusack*, pp 81–2. **14** Canon Ulick Bourke in Ferguson, *Cusack*, pp 78–81; Ferguson reprints much significant correspondence relating to Cusack's stay at Knock. **15** *Three visits*, pp 50–6, 67–80. **16** *Story*, pp 259–62, 276–7, 283–4, 291–3, 315–16, 320–2. **17** *Life inside*, pp 14–15, 19–26; *Story*, pp 337–8. **18** *Autobiography*, pp 28–9; *Life inside*, pp x–xi; *Pius IX*, pp 354, 416–47, 646. **19** Ibid., pp 299–300.

CARDINAL ANTONELLI.

7·4 This illustration from Cusack's *Life of Pius IX* juxtaposes the pope's chief minister, Cardinal Giacomo Antonelli, with a border of Marian symbols celebrating the Marian devotions promoted by Pius IX and by Cusack ('1830' refers to the revelation of the Miraculous Medal to Catherine Anne Labouré; 8 December 1854 was the date of Pius IX's proclamation of the Immaculate Conception of Mary as Catholic dogma). Cusack's subsequent realization that Antonelli had not been a pattern of personal piety, as she had assumed, influenced her defection from Catholicism (reproduced by permission of Special Collections, Boole Library, UCC).

described could not have been seen from the point where they were supposedly viewed.[20]

In October 1884, Cusack left for the USA, opening an American mother-house in Jersey City in May 1885. Cusack's difficulties with American bishops were compounded by her intervention concerning Father Edward McGlynn, excommunicated by Archbishop Corrigan of New York in 1887 for advocating the radical economic theories of Henry George. Although Cusack denounced McGlynn's economic theories,[21] she antagonized Corrigan by complaining that many church dignitaries neglected the poor[22] and by suggesting that McGlynn should have been treated more considerately.[23] After episcopal retaliation threatened the order with extinction, Cusack left her convent for a Protestant Episcopalian refuge on 10 July 1888. The order's property was held in her name, but she signed it over in expectation of receiving financial provision. Instead, the order even retained her dowry; she wrote bitterly of being penniless after a lifetime's work.[24]

The Nun of Kenmare: an Autobiography (1888), ostensibly written as a Catholic, showed deep bitterness against the church and expressly attacked papal infallibility (defended in *Pius IX*). It commented on the tendency of religious orders to begin by serving the poor and end by serving the rich, snobbery and class divisions within convents, and the tendency of English and Irish Catholic authorities to value a few upper-class English converts more than the multitudinous Irish poor – although the Irish were denounced for ingratitude, and many of her criticisms of the Kenmare nuns and certain priests concerned allegedly uncouth and plebeian behaviour.[25]

Cusack returned to Britain, announced her conversion to Methodism, became an anti-Catholic lecturer and author, and published a second autobiography, *The Story of My Life* (1891). Both books released a host of injuries, doubts and painful petty experiences pent up by her former idealization of Catholicism.

Cusack's Protestant writings contain some striking assertions, fuelled by the conviction that she had been deceived and had wasted her life. She lamented that her belief in Pius IX as a persecuted saint reflected ignorance induced by church authorities.[26] The former enemy of 'Jesuitphobia'[27] called St Ignatius Loyola a secret Buddhist,[28] and claimed that the Jesuits gave Leo XIII an occasional dose of poison to keep him obedient.[29] She proclaimed that Catholic hostility to souperism represented attacks by a church that extorted money from its poorer members on Protestant institutions trying to help the poor, adding that Italy would benefit from Methodist missionaries[30] and advising Protestant house-holders to make Catholic

20 *Story*, pp 347–8.   **21** *The question of today: anti-poverty and progress* (New York, 1887), pp 43, 45, 80n. Cusack wrote in similar vein for the conservative *New York Sun* at the behest of the Irish-born journalist William Mackay Laffan (McCarthy, *Nun*, p. 77; *Story*, p. 382). **22** *Anti-poverty*, p. 110.   **23** Hugh McLeod, 'Edward McGlynn: a rebel against the Archbishop of New York' in Mews (ed.), *Modern religious rebels*, pp 166–84; *Anti-poverty*, pp 140–55.   **24** *Story*, p. 132; *Life inside*, p. xxi.   **25** *Autobiography*, pp 298–300; *Story*, pp 221–4; *Life inside*, pp 254–6.   **26** *Life inside*, pp ix–x.   **27** *Liberator*, p. 502n; *Pius IX*, pp 243–4, 613.   **28** *Black pope*, pp 37, 106–11.   **29** Ibid., pp 364–7.   **30** *Life inside*, p. 273.

servants join family prayers.[31] Denouncing Catholic martyrs executed in the Elizabethan era as traitors, she called the Manchester Martyrs equally deserving of canonization.[32] Attacks by Irish-American dynamiters on Parliament were equated with the 1605 Gunpowder Plot as Catholic conspiracies,[33] and the Invincibles were called tools of priests.[34] Patrick Ford was a 'monster of outrage';[35] Archbishop Corrigan's willingness to work with Ford showed that he thought dynamite attacks were less sinful than denouncing the archbishop's luxurious lifestyle (as McGlynn did).[36] She quoted Cardinal Newman as comparing her former hero Veuillot to the anti-Catholic lecturer William Murphy (notorious for ribald parodies of the confessional);[37] Cusack called Murphy a 'victim of Romanist rage and hatred for the crime of telling the truth'.[38] Cusack quoted Newman slightly out of context; he said that by presenting exaggerated and unsustainable accounts of authentic Catholic doctrines, Veuillot might produce as much scandal as Murphy.[39]

In fact, Cusack's Protestant writings displayed characteristic preoccupations, albeit now directed against Catholicism. She cited a declaration by the La Salette visionary Melanie Calvet that immoral priests were the source of France's misfortunes,[40] and predicted that religious orders would annex Knock, as they took Lourdes from the parish priest who promoted the cult.[41] She still admired St Francis of Assisi, declaring that in later times he would have been an Evangelical,[42] and expressed continued respect for the *Imitation of Christ* and St Francis de Sales.[43]

Cusack formerly claimed that when Catholicism failed to disseminate its message, anti-Catholic media poisoned public opinion and brought renewed anti-Catholic persecution;[44] now she purveyed an apocalyptic belief that Jesuit infiltration of the print industries stifled exposure of the evils of Rome and facilitated papal assumption of temporal as well as spiritual power over Britain and America.[45] Denouncing Rome as the mystery of iniquity – the antichrist whose worldwide empire marks the Last Days[46] – she declared that tolerating Catholicism led to persecution by it.[47] She predicted an Inquisition in America; that Trinity College Dublin would be confiscated by Italian cardinals and that Ireland would be placed under Papal rule.[48]

In a letter to Lecky, she lamented that while Protestants were very ready to shout 'No Popery', they were slow to help anyone who left Rome.[49] After brief residence in Bournemouth and Brighton, Cusack's last years were spent at Leamington Spa, Warwickshire, with Methodist friends who watched her to guard against possible relapse into Catholicism or Catholic harassment. She was visited by local nuns, and displayed affection for them, which they believed, possibly mistakenly, indicated a

31 *Story*, pp 395–6.   **32** *Black pope*, pp 329–30.   **33** Ibid., pp 337–8.   **34** Ibid., pp 343–4.   **35** *Life inside*, pp 168–76.   **36** Ibid., pp 100–1, 342–4, 349–53, 363–5.   **37** Arnstein, *Newdegate*, pp 88–107; *Oxford DNB*.   **38** *Black pope*, pp 405–6.   **39** Gilley, *Newman*, pp 377–8.   **40** *Life inside*, p. 377.   **41** See Harris, *Lourdes*, pp 191–3.   **42** *Story*, p. 113.   **43** Ibid., pp 87–8; for de Sales, see also *Jesus and Jerusalem*, pp 348–50.   **44** Dixon, pp 369–70; *Pius IX*, p. 112.   **45** *Black pope*, p. 271n; *Life inside*, pp xiii, xix, 70–2, 150–1, 307–9.   **46** *Life inside*, pp xi–xii.   **47** Ibid., pp xiv–xv, 95.   **48** *Black pope*, p. 227.   **49** Cusack to Lecky, 19 May 1892, cited in Clark Smith, 'Manly Study'?, p. 172, n4.

desire for reconciliation with Rome.[50] From second-hand testimony many years afterwards, the Kenmare Poor Clares believed that she received the last sacraments before her death on 5 June 1899;[51] however, contemporary Protestant papers published an account of her deathbed by a Methodist minister, Revd Gregory, who was present.[52]

Cusack was airbrushed from the history of her order until officially reinstated as foundress in 1970. Her *Illustrated History of Ireland* was reprinted in 1995; some late works are available from ultra-Protestant websites, while an Illinois-based reprint house catering for traditionalist Catholics reprinted her *Life and Revelations of Gertrude the Great*. Indeed, Cusack had much in common with the sub-culture of 'angry visionaries', professing loyalty to pope and church in principle, while despising and rejecting their authority in practice, and rejoicing in private revelations of looming chastisement.[53] This persistent apocalyptic sub-culture within Catholic devotionalism was invigorated by the upheavals following Vatican II, as by the conflicts surrounding Pius IX.[54]

50 McCarthy, *Nun*, pp 59, 77–8; but note *Story*, p. 400.   **51** McCarthy, *Nun*, pp 78–9. **52** *The Catholic* (Dublin), Oct. 1899. Cusack corresponded with the editor of *The Catholic*, Thomas Connellan, an ex-priest turned Protestant missionary (*Catholic*, July 1899). Ferguson, *Cusack*, p. 95, publishes a contemporary account by a nun who visited her in her last days, which states that she did express an ungratified wish to revert to Catholicism at the end, but also that she suffered extreme mental confusion.   **53** Fr Benedict J. Groeschel, *A still small voice: a practical guide on reported revelations* (San Francisco, 1993), pp 43–5, 84–90. **54** M.W. Cuneo, *The smoke of Satan: conservative and traditionalist dissent in contemporary American Catholicism* (Baltimore, MD, 1999).

Pictures of piety and impropriety: Irish religious periodicals of the 1830s

ROBIN J. KAVANAGH

Whether in the form of a painting, a sculpture or a photograph or as a printed image, a depiction, we know, is never merely an illustration.[1] It is a product of a process of work that is imbued with the weight of material culture. Toby Barnard describes this as 'having a value unrelated to monetary worth'.[2] Inanimate objects or images may possess intangible qualities, such as civility, respectability, decency and piety, and all of the possible antitheses of these.

Peter Burke suggests that religious images fall into four categories of purpose. They are images that are a means of religious instruction and indoctrination, images that become devotional icons or objects of cults, images that stimulate meditation, and images that become weapons of controversy and propaganda.[3] All of these vari-ations of religious iconography provide historians with evidence of religious beliefs and commonly held views of life, death and afterlife in the localities in the period of their creation. John Miller judges that in many cases the ideas for printed images that appeared in the press were influenced by political crises in which religion played a part and so were intended to serve an immediate polemical purpose.[4] In light of Burke's four-part categorization approach, this paper reveals how the editors of the *Catholic Penny Magazine* chose images, they hoped, would emphasize a renewed sense of self-confidence in the Catholic Church. However, their passive stance helped to hasten the demise of the publication against the radically dissimilar stance of its coun-terpart, the *Protestant Penny Magazine*.

From the papers of Archbishop Daniel Murray emerges evidence to support the claim that the *CPM* came into existence in the 1830s at the urging of influential French Catholics, who judged that there was a real need in Ireland for Catholics to develop a more prominent presence in their national press.

There were many religious periodicals of all denominations in Ireland and Britain during this decade, although the vast majority of them were not illustrated. Most publications included a visual display on their masthead or frontispiece that symbol-ized, or was a pronouncement of, their faith or affiliation. These were publications purposefully created, published and circulated to members of their particular reli-gious group and parishes. For example, a Catholic publication, *Annals of the*

1 Gordon Fyfe and John Law (eds), *Picturing power* (London, 1988), p. 1.   **2** Toby Barnard, *A guide to the sources for the history of material culture in Ireland, 1500–2000* (Dublin, 2005), p. 11.   **3** Peter Burke, *Eyewitnessing* (London, 2001), p. 48.   **4** John Miller, *Religion in the popular prints, 1600–1832* (Cambridge, 1986), p. 14.

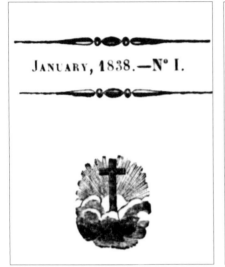

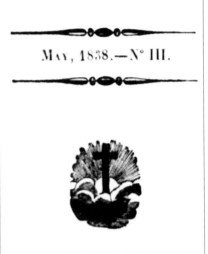

8.1 *Annals of the Propagation of the Faith* (Dublin, 1838). This insignia on the frontispiece changed over the course of a six-month period in 1838. The illustrations show a marked progression in the size of the crucifix from January to July. The image began as a small crucifix in the clouds in front of the sun. It became a much larger one that appears to be radiating over the whole earth. This is clearly a reference to the extensive growth of international Catholic missionary activity during this period (images courtesy of the Russell Library, NUI Maynooth).

Propagation of the Faith,[5] began publishing in Paris in 1838 and then in Dublin in 1839. This periodical's frontispiece image reflected the progression and continued advancement of Catholicism in Ireland and around the world (fig. 8.1).

    As technological advancements in print stereotype casting and lithography were introduced, illustrated religious publications became routine. The images that adorned the pages of many of the religious periodicals served a multiplicity of purposes. They served as an adjunct to the clergymen in their role as religious instructors. Along with accompanying text, the illustrations reflected Christian liturgical and scriptural knowledge. Stories from the New and Old Testaments with accompanying images helped carry along the narratives and assisted in revealing the underlying doctrinal messages. They were instrumental in the inculcation of particular sets of morals and beliefs and were highly influential in setting a tone for normalcy or deviancy on a variety of subjects. Some images were chosen for their ability to convey accepted Christian behaviour and values by depicting role models or by showing negative examples.

Images can afford, in many instances, a more privileged insight into the mentalities of their contemporaries than written sources alone can. They typically hint at the theological, social and political controversies of the age. Confessional division and religious intolerance persistently convulsed the Catholic and Protestant communities in Ireland. Evangelical fervour beginning in the early 1820s helped to heighten a very volatile situation that prompted interdenominational feuding. Irish Catholics and Protestants in the farming community displayed unprecedented resistance in seeking a reprieve from tithe payments to the established church. During the post-emancipation decade, Irish Catholics gained a newly acquired sense of importance and self-esteem through their religion.[6] Concerns over Irish church reform and municipal reform were hotly debated issues in parliament. All of these controversies of the 1830s prompted the beginning of a war of words in pictures and print between ecclesiastical leaders that lasted well into the mid-century.[7]

The *Catholic Penny Magazine* (*CPM*) was under the inspection of 'Catholic Divines'. This term refers to the full title: the *Catholic Penny Magazine: published weekly under the inspection of the Catholic Divines*, which signifies a council or synod of bishops that held regular meetings to discuss the magazine and other religious matters. These members of the Catholic hierarchy employed the engraver, Benjamin Clayton II, to create a suitably striking image for the frontispiece of the first number of the *CPM*. Clayton, a prominent engraver in Dublin, was the chief engraver for the popular *Dublin Penny Journal* and other works published in Dublin. His father, Benjamin Clayton the elder, was the engraver for the *Sentimental and Masonic Magazine* and his plates were used on corporation seals and many other Irish and English publications. His three sons, Samuel, Benjamin and Robert, followed him into the trade.[8]

The illustration commissioned for the opening number of *CPM* depicted St Peter's Basilica in Rome perched on a rock in a hellishly stormy sea with a threatening sky (fig. 8. 2). The image conveys the impression of the Catholic Church as a besieged or 'persecuted church'.[9] Metaphorically, this depiction seeks to establish, in

---

5 *Annals of the propagation of the faith*, Jan. 1838.   **6** Jacqueline Hill, *From patriots to unionists* (Oxford, 1997), p. 347.   **7** For a more comprehensive study on the origins of the Evangelical 'Second Reformation', see Irene Whelan, *The bible war in Ireland: the 'Second Reformation' and the polarization of Protestant-Catholic relations, 1800–1840* (Dublin, 2005); Thomas McGrath, *Politics, interdenominational relations and education in the public ministry of Bishop James Doyle of Kildare and Leighlin, 1786–1834* (Dublin, 1999), pp 134–56.   **8** W.G. Strickland, *A dictionary of Irish artists*, ii (Dublin, 1969), p. 181.   **9** Desmond Keenan, *The Catholic church in nineteenth-century Ireland: a sociological study* (Dublin, 1983), p. 25.

8.2 Frontispiece, Benjamin Clayton II, *Catholic Penny Magazine* (Dublin, 15 Feb. 1834)
(courtesy of the Russell Library, NUI Maynooth)

visual terms, the invulnerability of the Roman Catholic Church and axiomatically the Catholic religion as having withstood the ravages of persecution under the Penal Laws and continuing to remain stalwart against the contemporary challenge of the evangelical campaign. The caption quotes from the gospel of Matthew 16:18 and emphatically states 'Upon this rock I will build my church and the gates of hell shall not prevail against it'.[10] The forceful character of this illustration appears to confirm Jacqueline Hill's assessment that 'Irish Catholics were beginning to shed their customary deference and were openly challenging the Church of Ireland on spiritual, historical and utilitarian grounds'.[11] Although the stance of this illustration is confrontational and seems to conform to Burke's category of controversial or propaganda images,[12] subsequent illustrations took a considerably softer approach remaining true to the *CPM*s 'spiritual and educational' intent:[13]

> It is our desire to show religion in its native grandeur; to prove that nothing is so pleasing as piety; so pure as virtue; so lasting as truth; or so happy as serving God in spirit and in truth . . . Whilst religion shall be our main object, we will introduce every thing consonant to it. Arts, Science and Literature shall thus be made tributary to virtue; and human knowledge lead to that which is divine. Matter interesting to the husbandman and housekeeper will not be neglected. With what is useful we shall insert what is agreeable; and by combining piety with instruction – poetry with prose, and moderation with strict adherence to truth, we shall endeavor to connect all things with that never-failing link of faith and morals, which unites the throne of God.[14]

The appearance of the *Catholic Penny Magazine* in 1834 was due to the conflation of several factors. Communications between Irish Catholic church leaders and their French counterparts reveal the likely catalyst for the introduction of the *CPM* in 1834. From the papers of Archbishop Daniel Murray emerges evidence to support the claim that this publication came into existence at the urging of French Catholics, who judged that there was a real need in Ireland for Catholics to develop a more prominent presence in their national press. Leading Catholic thinkers of Restoration France were actively involved in the publishing industry and they aggressively urged the Irish Catholics to be more assertive in the publishing arena. They included Hugues-Felicité Robert de Lamennais, a liberal-minded priest who, along with Henri-Baptiste Lacordaire and the Comte de Montalembert, launched a newspaper called *L'Avenir* in 1830 to promote freedom of conscience, press and religion. This newspaper was an advocate for an independent Catholic church and called upon Catholics to lead a movement for political democracy and economic justice.[15]

The *CPM* was conceived as an effort to fortify the Irish Catholic sense of community. However, this periodical, as was the case with most of the devotional

---

10 Frontispiece of *Catholic Penny Magazine*, 1:1 (15 Feb. 1834). 11 Hill, *From patriots to unionists*, p. 333. 12 Burke, *Eyewitnessing*, p. 48. 13 *CPM*, 15 Feb. 1834, p. 1. 14 Ibid., p. 1. 15 www.fiu.edu/~mirandas/bios1824-iii.htm, accessed 12 May 2005.

literature produced by the religious institutions for mass consumption, reflected the ideals and attitudes of the Catholic Church leadership rather than the everyday attitudes and beliefs of its adherents.[16] The Catholic hierarchy embraced the illustrated 'penny' periodical format in order to communicate a forceful and urgent sense of spiritual renewal and affirmation of faith to the 'people of Ireland'.[17] The hierarchy of the Irish Catholic Church felt an obligation, or urgency, to address in print the affront they had received in 1832 in the first number of the *Dublin Penny Journal*. The Protestant editors of the *DPJ* chose to describe their contributors as 'the best possible instructors of the day' for the people of Ireland.[18] The Catholic Archbishop of Dublin, Revd Daniel Murray, decided that there was an urgent need in 1834 for a Catholic penny periodical, as who but the Catholic Church should be the 'best possible instructors' of its adherents? His address to the people, which appeared in the first number of the *CPM*, makes this supremely clear:

> On presenting the people of Ireland with the first number of the *Catholic Penny Magazine*, we wish to ask: – 1st. Is such a work necessary? 2nd. Are the people able to purchase it? 3rd. What should it contain? As friends of the arts and lovers of science, we do not wish to lessen the demand for either; but still we think, that there is much against good sense in the present flying sheets, and more sound than substance in the 'best possible instructors' of the day … '2nd. Can the people purchase a Catholic penny magazine? Whilst London has three catholic magazines, Birmingham one and Glasgow another, cannot all Ireland, with six millions of Catholics support one? Nay whilst we have in Dublin five or six weekly and monthly literary journals, with many others imported from the sister country, can we not secure the success of one more immediately deserving our attention?' 3rd. What should it contain? Every thing fit to be read by all, and nothing unfit to be read by any … Whilst religion shall be our main object, we will introduce every thing consonant to it. Arts, science and literature shall thus be made tributary to virtue; and human knowledge lead to that which is divine … With what is useful we shall insert what is agreeable; and by combining piety with instruction.[19]

Each week, the periodical carried a frontispiece illustration purposely chosen to contribute to and promote feelings of Catholic religious devotion, and further to provide some useful information about the progress of the Catholic Church. The Catholic hierarchy challenged the Established Church in this illustrated periodical by utilizing images that visually portrayed its dignified and renewed sense of self-confidence. Some of the illustrations reinforce Comerford's suggestion that morals and customs attached to this new Catholic ethos were attempting to imitate contemporary Protestantism (fig. 8.3).[20]

16 Niall Ó Ciosáin, *Print and popular culture in Ireland, 1750–1850* (London, 1997), p. 118. **17** *CPM*, 15 Feb. 1834, p. 1. **18** *DPJ*, 30 June 1832, p. 1. **19** *CPM*, 15 Feb. 1834, p. 1. **20** R.V. Comerford, *Ireland* (London, 2003), p. 113.

THE

Catholic Penny Magazine

PUBLISHED WEEKLY,

UNDER THE INSPECTION OF CATHOLIC DIVINES.

No. 59.   DUBLIN, SATURDAY, MARCH 28, 1835.   Vol.

THE SACRAMENTS ILLUSTRATED.—No. 1

THE MANNER OF ADMINISTERING THE SACRAMENT
OF BAPTISM IN THE CATHOLIC CHURCH.

[BY THE RIGHT REV. DR. CHALLONER.]

THE church makes use of many ceremonies in baptism.   1st,

8.3 Frontispiece, *Catholic Penny Magazine*, 'The Manner of Administering the Sacrament of Baptism in the Catholic Church', 28 March 1835. This illustration depicts the way in which the Catholic Church statutes of 1831 recommended the Sacrament of Baptism to be administered. The text that accompanies this surprising image explains that 'regularly speaking, and excepting the case of necessity, the church does not allow baptism to be administered anywhere but in the churches which have fonts' (*CPM*, 28 Mar. 1835, p. 1). The *CPM* began a proposed pictorial series of images entitled 'The Sacraments Illustrated', but after the initial appearance of the above illustration on 28 March 1835, the series was discontinued without explanation (image courtesy of the Russell Library, NUI Maynooth).

The large majority of Irish Catholics in the 1830s may have had difficulty identifying themselves with this elegantly attired Irish Catholic family in this idealized
vision of the baptismal sacrament. Dublin Catholic provincial statutes of 1831
strongly recommended that the sacraments be held in the church,[21] but it was not
made obligatory until 1850, following the Synod of Thurles.[22] Local parish priests
were greatly challenged to administer the sacraments in accordance with the ideal
manners set down by the provincial statutes. Out of sheer necessity, in many of the
rural parishes, clergymen regularly performed baptism, marriage and other sacraments in the homes of their parishioners. This practice continued well into the latter
part of the nineteenth century, as evidenced by Aloysius O'Kelly's painting, *Mass in a
Connemara Cabin*, 1883.[23] The editors of the magazine seem anxious to project an
image of respectability and propriety among their congregation.

Other carefully chosen illustrations took many different approaches and covered
a variety of subject matter. During the course of its short publication life of fourteen
months from 15 February 1834 to 25 April 1835, *CPM* featured forty-three engravings. Seventeen of the illustrations are inspirational depictions of newly built,
renovated or extant Catholic churches, cathedrals, colleges, schools and convents in
Ireland, England and the USA. Eight portraits of eminent Catholic ecclesiastics
appear in the periodical with accompanying biographical and church career information, among them, Revd Dr Oliver Kelly, Archbishop of Tuam (1815–34), Revd
Dr James Doyle, Bishop of Kildare and Leighlin (1819–34) and Revd Charles
Gobinet (1613–90), author and Doctor of Divinity at the Sorbonne. Scriptural illustrations such as 'The Creation', 'The Expulsion' and 'The Resurrection' featured
regularly along with engravings of the Blessed Virgin Mary, St Patrick and St Brigit
along with other subjects that reinforced Irish Catholic teaching.

There existed, for some time, strong links between the French and Irish Catholic
church due to the great number of Irish clergymen who had received their theological education in France. Catholic proponents of Restoration France, Lamennais
and Montalembert, urged the Irish Catholic hierarchy to be more assertive in the
publishing arena. Montalembert had travelled extensively in Ireland and met with
Daniel O'Connell in 1830. Montalembert, a strong supporter of Irish Catholic civil
liberty, was a regular contributor to *Le Correspondant*, a semi-weekly Parisian newspaper founded by Carné Cazalès and Augustin de Meaux in 1829. The motto of *Le
Correspondant* was copied from George Canning's words: 'Civil and religious liberty
throughout the world' and its object was to reconcile Catholicism and modern
ideas.[24] Unlike the situation in Ireland, French Catholics used their newspapers and
periodicals to generate support not only for French causes, but also for causes bene-

21 Patrick Corish, *The Irish Catholic experience* (Dublin, 1985), p. 179. **22** Nigel Yates,
Religious condition of Ireland, 1770–1850 (Oxford, 2006), pp 114–15. **23** As evidenced by the
painting, *Mass in a Connemara Cabin* by Aloysius O'Kelly, 1883. See Niamh O'Sullivan, 'The
mystery of the lost painting', *Irish Times*, Weekend Review, 2 Nov. 2002. **24** Catholic
Encyclopedia: 'Comte de Montalembert', available at *www.newadvent.org*, accessed 18 June
2006.

ficial to all Catholics. This was unlike the situation in Ireland in the early 1830s. The correspondence between Archbishop Daniel Murray and the Comte de Montalembert establishes a strong connection between the Irish Catholic hierarchy and leading French Catholics. Their relationship generated a very moving and successful appeal by the editors of *L'Avenir* to the Catholics of France on behalf of the famine sufferers in the western dioceses of Ireland during the period 1832–6. During this period, Austin Bourke documents an 'unmistakeable epidemic' that attacked the potato crops, causing the 'first potato disease to cause serious alarm in Ireland'.[25] The monetary success of the *L'Avenir* appeal reached 46,000 francs, with the exact figures documented in the correspondence of Archbishop Daniel Murray.[26] On behalf of Murray, Archdeacon Fr Hamilton wrote a series of letters to the Comte de Montalembert, thanking the editors and the people of France for their generosity. In the letter dated 27 August 1831, Hamilton informed de Montalembert that the urgent level of distress was over and the poor who had benefited from their aid would pray for them. He also judged that 'the aid from French Catholics not only met temporal needs but also prevented the poor accepting the aid proffered by proselytizers; not only life, but faith was preserved'. In response, de Montalembert wrote back that 'They would be recompensed if the Catholic press in Ireland informed its readers of the sympathy their French co-religionists felt for them and how they expressed that sympathy'. Hamilton acknowledges this request and verifies that he will inform Murray of de Montalembert's wishes: 'but even though the Catholic press in Ireland cannot compare with the energy and talent Catholic needs require, he will do his utmost to pay just tribute to what *L'Avenir*, its editors and the Catholics of France have done'.[27] This statement corroborates the theory that the Irish Catholic leaders felt a deep sense of dissatisfaction at that time with the Irish press and its ability to be an effective and influential voice for the Catholic church.

It is clear from Murray's papers that there was a desire by the Catholic hierarchy to capitalize on the newly developed distribution network of the Catholic Book Society set up by W.J. Battersby. A cursory account of *The Catholic Penny Magazine* by Irene Whelan, that relied upon previous T. Wall and B. Hayley publications, denigrated this publication as 'rather mean and shabby in appearance',[28] and inaccurately portrayed it as one of 'Battersby's projects'.[29] This type of portrayal fails to comprehend the merit of this periodical as a key to the emergence of the Catholic press in Ireland.

Members of confraternities, sodalities, libraries and book societies were relied upon to take copies for themselves, and also to promote the circulation of the publication and to distribute copies 'at the cheapest premiums amongst the poor children or scholars of their parish'. The belief was that it would be possible to reach a

25 Austin Bourke, *The visitation of God? The potato and the Great Irish Famine* (Dublin, 1993), pp 31–2.   **26** Mary Purcell, 'Dublin Diocesan Archives: Murray Papers, file 31/3:1831 and 1832', *Archivium Hibernicum*, 37 (1982), 31–3.   **27** Ibid., 33.   **28** Whelan, *The bible war in Ireland*, p. 224.   **29** Ibid.

THE

Protestant Penny Magazine.

PUBLISHED MONTHLY.

EDITED BY THE REV. EDWARD NANGLE, A.B.

No. XVI.   DUBLIN, OCTOBER, 1835.   Vol. II.

NOVEL METHOD OF CATCHING FISH.

8.4 (*opposite*) Frontispiece, anon., 'A novel method of catching fish', *Protestant Penny Magazine* (Dublin, Oct. 1835). This illustration depicts a priest in a fishing boat celebrating the age-old tradition of the blessing of Galway Bay while the villagers look on from the cliffs. The accompanying text offers a disparaging view of this Catholic tradition: '... a debasing superstition has stopped the one only right channel of devotional feeling, and turned the current of their affections into many wild and devious extravagancies ... He proposes to bless the bay; and he professed the fullest assurance that the fish, happy of enjoying the privilege of swimming in sanctified water, would speedily return to their former resort, even at the hazard of frying on the village gridirons' (*PPM*, Oct. 1835, p. xvi) (image courtesy of the National Library of Ireland).

circulation of 7,000 to 10,000 for each number and so 'defray the expense of paper, print, stereotype, cuts'.[30] This was a good plan, but it did not go exactly as they wished. Parishes at home and abroad in England and Scotland were receiving the *Catholic Penny Magazine*, but in low numbers. Events in Ireland, however, ultimately worked against the success of the *CPM*.

During the early decades of the nineteenth century, the British evangelical societies targeted Ireland's Catholic population with what is described by David Hempton as their 'conversionist zeal'.[31] The *CPM* soon found itself embroiled in a weekly clash of ideologies when the *Protestant Penny Magazine* was launched in Dublin on 28 June 1834, four months after the introduction of the *Catholic Penny Magazine*.

Nangle, a firm believer in the power of the illustrated press, used illustrations to adopt a firm adversarial stance towards the *CPM*.[32] Nangle was a firm believer in the power of the illustrated press, and through the *PPM* he forthrightly adopted its adversarial attitude. In its very first number, the *PPM* reproduced an illustration from the famous *Foxe's Book of Martyrs*.[33] As a record of injustice, this book has been a storehouse of controversy and fodder for debate in the Christian faith since the sixteenth century. Irene Whelan judges that not only were Revd Nangle and his Achill Mission the 'most visible aspect of the westward thrust of the evangelical movement', but that this mission created more 'controversy and sectarian conflict' than any other project in the campaign to evangelize the west of Ireland.[34]

While editor of *PPM*, Nangle used a combination of didactic prose with satirical caricatures, morality cartoons, and highly selective historical depictions, all of which were specifically chosen to foster an anti-popery discourse and to summon a controversy of ecclesiastical disputation. In subsequent issues of *PPM*, an assortment of frontispiece illustrations appeared that depicted scenes of torture during the period of the Inquisition (fig. 8.5), and other images that attempted to debase, humiliate or equate Catholicism with the superstitions of 'Pagan Ireland' (fig. 8.4).

30 *CPM*, 17 May 1834. **31** David Hempton, *Religion and political culture in Britain and Ireland* (Cambridge, 1996), p. 101. **32** Ibid., p. 261. **33** John Foxe, *Actes and monuments of these latter and perillous dayes touching matters of the church, wherein ar comprehended and decribed the great persecutions ...* (London, 1563). **34** Whelan, *The bible war in Ireland*, pp 260–1.

THE

Protestant Penny Magazine.

PUBLISHED MONTHLY.

No. III.   DUBLIN, SATURDAY, AUG. 30, 1834.   Vol. I.

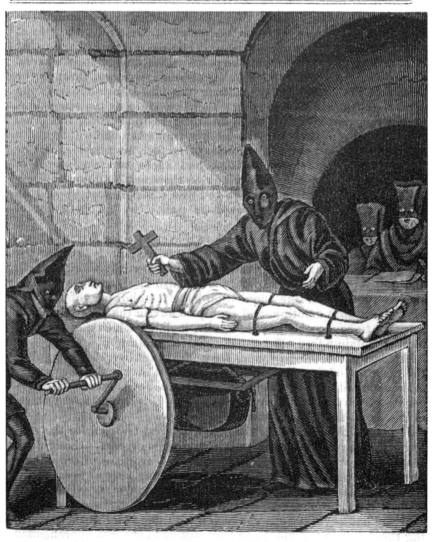

THE INQUISITION.

8.5 (*opposite*) 'The Inquisition', *Protestant Penny Magazine* (Dublin, 30 Aug. 1834). 'As we purpose to give an account in some subsequent numbers, of the origin, constitution and proceedings of the Inquisition, we have here prefixed a representation of one species of torture inflicted by that merciless tribunal on its hapless victims, whose only crime consists in their refusal to believe those monstrous fables and blasphemous absurdities, which the pope endeavours to palm on the credulity of mankind for divine truths. We have further dragged the atrocities of the Inquisition into the light of public observation, because the disgusting detail shews that the pretension of the Romish church to infallibility has no support but that which it derives from a most unblushing impudence. It is difficult even to write on such a subject with the calmness of temper becoming a Christian' (*PPM*, 30 Aug. 1834) (image courtesy of the National Library of Ireland).

Revd Nangle delighted in 'religious warfare',[35] and by the time he settled at the Achill Mission he was already proficient at using the printing press to the advantage of the evangelical movement. Upon the cessation of the *PPM* in 1836, Nangle turned his attention to printing again. He began the publication of the *Achill Missionary Herald and Western Witness*[36] to keep his benefactors in Ireland and England informed of the progress and religious advances made at the Achill Mssion.

The proprietors of the *Protestant Penny Magazine* reported that they achieved large circulation runs numbering in excess of 19,000 copies per issue.[37] At the same time, the *Catholic Penny Magazine* had great difficulty achieving a circulation of 5,000 copies.[38] Despite the enthusiastic support and encouragement of two major Dublin independent newspapers, the *Freeman's Journal* and *The Register*, CPM after one year in publication was unable to achieve circulation figures sufficient to make the publication financially viable.[39]

There is ample evidence to suggest that the Catholic hierarchy had lost the will or desire to keep this periodical going, due to its having become a weekly source of provocation for the rival publication, the *Protestant Penny Magazine*. By allowing its demise to occur, it removed any possibility of it continuing to be a proverbial 'red rag to a bull', an object to provoke critique. This attitude of passivity in the face of adversity, while admirable, angered and frustrated some of the *CPM*'s supporters. W.J. Battersby became the voice of the Irish Catholics when he initiated and became publisher and editor of *A Complete Catholic Registry* in 1836. This publication documented all the general matters connected with the life and progress of the Catholic religion until Battersby's death in 1873.[40] Battersby's Catholic registry is considered to be the forerunner of the modern *Irish Catholic Directory*.

35 Theresa McDonald, *Achill: 5000BC to 1900AD* (Dublin, 1992), p. 79. **36** *Achill Missionary Herald and Western Witness* (1837–64). **37** *Protestant Penny Magazine*, Dublin, 1836, preface to vols 1 and 2. **38** Battersby to Murray, 11 Feb. 1835 (DDA, Murray Papers, file 1834–5/122). **39** Battersby to Murray, 11 Feb. 1835 (DDA, Murray papers, file 1834–5/122). **40** From 1836 until W.J. Battersby's death in 1873, this work continued to be published with various name changes: *Battersby's Complete Catholic Registry*; *Battersby's Catholic Directory*; *Almanac and Registry of the Whole Catholic World*; and *Battersby's Registry for the Whole Catholic World*.

The Irish Catholic Church appears to have followed the lead from the French Catholics, who were well positioned in terms of participation in the popular press. The process of resurgence and renewal for Catholics had been occurring on the continent for some time. The *CPM*, under the supervision of the Catholic hierarchy, proved to be an abject failure in terms of its poor circulation and its lack of support from the clergy and laity in the parishes. Its scriptural and devotional illustrations failed to excite interest or add to its allure with the masses. However, the periodical provided a first important step towards establishing a truly Catholic press in Ireland. Mass illiteracy and severe poverty were, certainly, major obstacles to all sales of any printed reading matter, even illustrated ones. The *Catholic Penny Magazine* found itself, in 1834, having to assume a demeanour more akin to performing 'damage control' and avoiding serious confrontation against its rival. The *Catholic Penny Magazine* may have lost the battle in the printing industry of the 1830s, but in terms of its contribution to resurgent Catholicism in Ireland, it merits special recognition.

Text and illustrations in
Samuel Lover's *Handy Andy*

MAXIME LEROY

The first decades of the nineteenth century witnessed dramatic breakthroughs in printing techniques. In Ireland, mass-production of books was greatly enhanced by the introduction of stereotype printing in Dublin in 1813 (*The New Testament*, G. Grierson, Dublin, 1813). From the mid-1820s onward, the development of steel engraving made it possible to print illustrated books on a much wider scale than ever before. The first book printed in Ireland and illustrated in its first, as opposed to a later, edition was William Carleton's *Father Butler*, published in Dublin by W. Curry in 1829. Combined with higher literacy, these technical improvements had a specific impact on literature. A growing number of people could *read* novels as well as *look at* them in illustrated magazines or editions. Literary fiction could now be 'visualized and promoted from within a given fictional plot'.[1]

Although technically English, *Handy Andy* is an Irish novel by its setting and characters, and by its author's self-presentation as 'an Irishman'.[2] It was serialized in *Bentley's Miscellany* and appeared in book form in London in 1842. The title page advertises 'twenty-four illustrations by the author'. The number is not arbitrary – folding sheets of paper for quartos made it cost-effective to keep the number of plates under twenty-five. Bibliographic research though, shows the existence of editions with twenty-six plates. Howes bookstore mention in their catalogue: 'Sadleir 1451. Wolff 4192. First edition. Both these eminent collectors had copies of *Handy Andy* in original cloth; Sadleir with 24 plates … Wolff with 26'.[3] Although Samuel Lover had to take account of this publishing imperative, being an author-illustrator gave him the rare opportunity to enjoy a 'one-person control situation'[4] over an essential aspect: the relations between the text and its visual representations. This paper is an attempt to explore the relevance of a systemic approach to self-illustration. It studies Lover's drawings in their interaction with text, paratext and painting. It also shows how they interact with one another within the book and how the complex system of visual, verbal and symbolic representation that Lover devised promotes a new vision of Ireland's history.

---

1 G. Stewart, 'Reading figures: the legible image of Victorian textuality' in C.T. Christ and J.O. Jordan (eds), *Victorian literature and the visual imagination* (Berkeley, 1995), p. 345. **2** S. Lover, *Handy Andy* (London, 1842), p. vii. **3** www.howes.co.uk/295–17.htm. **4** L. Alloway, 'Artists as writers, part two: the realm of language', *Artforum*, 12:8 (1974), 14.

p. 1   p. 440

Table 9.1 The distribution of illustrations through the novel.
Each black square represents an illustration.

RELATING ILLUSTRATIONS TO NARRATIVE

As the graph shows, Lover distributed his plates quite evenly throughout the book. The reason is simple – the illustrations follow the storyline. Verbal and visual narratives are running parallel and their semantic contents overlap. Plate 15 for example shows the hero on his disastrous first wedding night; the next two plates show Tom Loftus, a minor character appearing in the corresponding chapter; plate 18 shows Andy again as the narrator takes us back to the main plot. For the reader, this means enjoying 'the pleasure of repetition with variation'[5] (seeing what one has just read or reading what one has just seen). One of the narrational impulses of comicality in the story (Andy's succession of blunders) is thus coupled with a visual counterpart.

However, the illustrations can be resented for breaking up the text as well as the reading. They are pauses both in space and time, especially as they are full plates; that is, unnumbered pages printed on one side only. There are no pictorial capitals in *Handy Andy*, nor any smaller pictures dropped mid-text, as woodcut permitted. Unlike Thackeray, Lover chose to keep text and images separate. One reason is that his drawings all show action scenes, which require more space (the one exception being Fanny Dawson's portrait). They correspond to key scenes in the narrative and can usually be tied in with specific sentences, as in the following example: 'M'Garry ... turned on the bed and opened his eyes. There he saw a parcel of people standing round him, with candles in their hands, and countenances of drunken wonder and horror.'[6]

The illustrations thus select and give a visual rendition of the most expressive moments in the chain of events told in the narrative. The *ut pictura poesis* debate had just been revived in Britain by Ross' 1836 translation of Lessing's *Laocoön* and Lover seems to have partly taken in Lessing's concept of pregnant moments[7] in that his pictures isolate one instant in the temporal sequence of the story, sometimes condensing a whole page of description as in the road accident episode introducing Furlong, a distrustful English official from Dublin Castle:

> Before [Furlong] could discharge a second pistol, Andy had screened himself under the horse's head ... Now, Micky's care were quite enough engaged on his own account; for the first pistol-shot made the horses plunge violently and the second time Furlong blazed away set the saddle-horse kicking and he

5 L. Hutcheon, *A theory of adaptation* (New York, 2006), p. 4.   6 Lover, *Handy Andy*, p. 58.

9.1 'An Irish Inquest', between p. 48 and p. 49 (Samuel Lover, *Handy Andy* (London, 1845)).

9.2 'The Reward of Humanity', between p. 82 and p. 83 (Samuel Lover, *Handy Andy* (London, 1845)).

crouched low on the grey's neck, holding fast by the mane and shouting for mercy as well as Andy, who … held his hat above him, in the fashion of a shield, as if that would have proved any protection against a bullet.[8]

However, differing from Lessing's view of painting as a spatial art versus poetry as a temporal art, Lover never used pictures to show simultaneous events which the text describes in their temporal sequence. The example above shows that the relation between text and illustration is rather one of reversed ekphrasis: illustration literally re-presents the text (presents it again), highlighting through its narrative graphicness what is happening, and thereby enhancing the effect of the story.

Another connection with Lessing though, is that the picture bears significance through the anticipation of what will happen *after* the instant it represents, just like the marble group showing Laocoön and his sons: will Andy be run over by the coach? Will Micky be shot? What will happen to the wounded man on the road? Plate 17 uses the same device. It captures the moment *just before* Tom realizes that Sir Arthur has been watching him for a while doing his musical number in a ministerial office. The clerk's face announces the ensuing scene of reprimand (fig. 9.3).

Obviously, the suspense is purely comical: both in their textual and visual variants, the two examples (the second one especially) remind us of Evanthius' description of comedy as a world in which 'the dangers [that the characters] run into are neither serious nor pressing and their actions conclude happily'.[9] But the role played by the reader's emotions is evidence for a threefold semiotic system involving text, illustration and reader's mental image. The illustrations will inevitably compete with the reader's own mental representations of the scenes – what in the vocabulary of systemics would be called negative feedback and which paradoxically undermines the author's attempt to orientate the reception of the text through illustration.

Numerous feedback loops (positive and negative) can thus be seen within the book: the illustrations proceed from the text, but by giving *one* rendering of it they shape its meaning; the reader will approve or not of the author's representation but will inevitably be influenced by it. Furthermore, two other paratextual elements, an 'Address' and a 'Notice' to the reader, show the author's willingness to listen to his audience and respond – even proleptically – to their criticism. A dialogue that commenced with serial publication through reviews and letters to the editor is being continued: 'The present volume, I hope, will disarm any cavil from old quarters … Frequent inquiries have been made "Why *Handy Andy* was not continued?" and the frequency of the demand has proceeded the supply.'[10]

These remarks are mixed with a metaphor describing writer as painter ('I have been accused of giving flattering portraits of my countrymen'; 'to paint one's country') and Lover reminds us that he was 'a portrait-painter by profession'.[11] The

7 G.E. Lessing, *Laocoön: or, the limits of poetry and painting*, trans. W. Ross (London, 1836).
8 Lover, *Handy Andy*, p. 94. 9 J.A. Cuddon, *Dictionary of literary terms and literary history* (London, 1991), p. 160. 10 Lover, *Handy Andy*, pp v–vi. 11 Ibid.

9.3 'Tom Organ Loftus and the Duke', between p. 258 and p. 259 (Samuel Lover, *Handy Andy* (London, 1845)).

9.4 'The Widow Flanagan's Party', between p. 178 and p. 179 (Samuel Lover, *Handy Andy* (London, 1845)).

traditional 'telling versus showing' dichotomy should therefore be complexified into a telling/showing/interacting system in which looking for auctorial intentions may seem increasingly irrelevant and confronting images to narrative may not be sufficient to grasp their full significance.

ICONOGRAPHICAL REFERENCES IN 'HANDY ANDY'S ILLUSTRATIONS

One assumption in a systemic approach to illustrations is that they also acquire meaning from their relation to other pictures. Lover was primarily known for his marine paintings and miniature portraits. He had been a member of the Royal Hibernian Academy of Art since 1828. His knowledge of painting was wide.

Handy Andy is a comical novel. In what way are the illustrations comical? Two pictorial devices are used – caricature and parody. Caricature is mainly used in group portraits, because it provides material for social satire. The style is similar to the one found in contemporary illustrated magazines like *Punch*, for example the pianist's and singer's features in 'The Widow Flanagan's Party' (fig. 9.4).

Parody is used with different purposes. 'The Abduction' parodies a serious pictorial theme. The title refers to an impressive line of neoclassical paintings, all inspired by Greek mythology: *The Abduction of Europa*, *The Abduction of Persephone*, *The Abduction of Psyche*, *The Abduction of Ganymede*, *The Abduction of the Sabine Women* to name but a few. Here though, farcical elements debunk the tragedy. Comparing the picture to, say, Romanelli's *The Abduction of Helen*, shows double-edged swords turned into fighting sticks and the beautiful Helen of Troy replaced by a stage-Irishman dressed up as a girl (fig. 9.5).

Also taking off an ancient theme, 'The Challenge' shows a revengeful woman dressed in black and about to commit murder – a kind of nineteenth-century Medea. This time, parody lies in the situation: instead of killing her children, the lunatic grandmother wants to fight a duel with Furlong, who, following some farcical misunderstanding, has been accused of dishonouring her granddaughter (fig. 9.6).

These references to paintings or art history do not emerge from the reading of the corresponding passages. They are clear only to the person looking at the illustration. In other words, there is dissociation between reader and looker. The illustrations construct their own comicality, separately from the text. The novel is not a closed-in system in which text and illustrations are brought into dialogue with each other only; exogenous images interact with them as well. However, illustration and text do share common signification. Some drawings are not comic, like Fanny Dawson's portrait or the final scene entitled 'The Party at Killarney'. Again this can be explained by the relation of each plate to one of the novel's intricate plots. Fanny is part of a strictly sentimental plot. Her picture is unique in that it is not related to one scene in particular but it is very much in keeping with the tradition of girls posing for portraits or women reading. Greuze's *Lady Reading Eloise and Abélard* (1759), Fragonard's *The Reader* (1772), and Reynolds' *Theophilia Palmer Reading Clarissa Harlow* (*c*.1775) may

9.5 'The Abduction', between p. 280 and p. 281 (Samuel Lover, *Handy Andy* (London, 1845)).

9.6 'The Challenge', between p. 326 and p. 327 (Samuel Lover, *Handy Andy* (London, 1845)).

have inspired Lover. The window and curtains in 'Fanny Dawson' are reminiscent of Vermeer's *A Girl Reading a Letter by an Open Window* (1657), while the chair and the girl's posture recall Boucher's *Madame Pompadour* (1750) (fig. 9.7).

The final scene, 'The Party at Killarney', has a functional conclusive purpose. It shows all the main characters happily reunited. The references are obvious, from Greek symposium scenes to Brueghel's *Wedding Feast* (fig. 9.8).

What clearly appears is that interactions occur not only between textual–visual but also between visual–visual elements. The caption that accompanies each plate is a referential index functioning like a painting's title. Two questions can then be raised: what are the limits to a system not only representing itself but encompassing, in a coded way, the whole history of art? What purpose can be seen in it?

WHAT THE PICTURES DO NOT SHOW:
'HANDY ANDY'S INVISIBLE ICONS

Paradoxically, existing illustrations highlight what they do *not* show. For example, Egan never appears in them. Most of all, only one picture shows Edward O'Connor, arguably the real main character in the novel. In his 'Address', Lover gives as much importance to him as to Andy Rooney. Edward is described as 'a gentleman and a patriot'; he stands for the 'honest, intelligent, and noble spirits' of 'the land that bore him'.[12] He is therefore strongly linked with the image of Ireland that the narrator wants to convey. This fact can be used to explain the paradoxical scarcity of images about him.

Edward O'Connor is patterned on real contemporary figures. Like Thomas Davis, he is a Protestant and the author of emotional nationalist ballads that emphasize Ireland's past and oppressed history. His name is also a near homophone to Daniel O'Connell's, whose pacifism he shares. On the day of the election, he prevents bloodshed by persuading English troops not to open fire on the crowd of Egan's supporters. The scene is not represented, though it potentially has the most dramatic visual effect:

> [The] long file of bright muskets flashed in the sun ... when a young and handsome man, mounted on a noble horse, came plunging and ploughing his way through the crowd ... [And] as his dark clustering hair streamed about his noble face, pale from excitement, and with flashing eyes, he was a model worthy of the best days of Grecian art – ay, and he had a soul worthy of the most glorious times of Grecian liberty!
> It was Edward O'Connor.[13]

There are two reasons at least for not representing the scene. First, because the scene is being told with so many words describing visual effects ('bright', 'flashed', 'light',

12 Ibid., p. vi.   13 Ibid., p. 203.

9.7 'Fanny Dawson', between
p. 70 and p. 71 (Samuel Lover,
Handy Andy (London, 1845)).

9.8 'The Party at Killarney',
between p. 378 and p. 379
(Samuel Lover, *Handy Andy*
(London, 1845)).

'dark', 'pale', 'flashing') and verbs of movement ('wheeling', 'rushing', 'advancing', 'waving'), any pictures would have been redundant, if not disappointing. Second, because as a writer of Irish novels for a primarily English audience, Lover always carefully avoided touchy political issues. Yet, the passage is full of clear allusions to Edward's ideals. This is where the Greek sub-text reappears, but as historical model, not as parody:

> Why should the ancient glories of Greece and Rome form a large portion of the academic studies of our youth? Why should the evidence of their arts and their arms be held precious in museums, and similar evidences of ancient cultivation be despised because they pertain to another nation? Is it because they are Irish they are held in contempt? Alas! in many cases it is so − ay, and even (shame to say) within her own shores. But never may the day arrive when Ireland shall be without enough of true and fond hearts to cherish the memory of her ancient glories.[14]

Such a heart Edward certainly has, and as such he is the counterpart of Andy, whose simple-mindedness trivializes Irish character. The only picture of him shows him in a gallant posture as he gets into the barn where O'Grady's supposed coffin lies (fig. 9.9).

The links between text and illustrations are therefore highly complex: the serious historical references in the former are counterparts to the parodical references in the latter. The meaning of text and illustrations therefore depends on the model generated by the reader-looker. Multiple sub-systems can be worked out, each of them producing idiosyncratic signification:

> i. [comic story + caricatures] ⇒ novel as farce
>
> ii. [comic story + caricatures] + [love story + sentimental portrait] ⇒ farce as comic relief in a truly sentimental novel
>
> iii. [Greece as parody (illustrations) + Greece as model (text)] ⇒ novel as proposed rewriting of Irish history etc.

All depends on the chosen point of focus. A key scene in the novel is when Edward takes the young O'Grady to '"his den"', as he called a room which was appropriated to his own particular use'. Over three pages we discover in it 'a law library', 'works bearing on Irish history', 'old parchment covers', 'various ornaments', a 'sword', other 'weapons', a 'frontlet of gold', a 'harp', a 'crosier', a 'trinket', and a 'golden bodkin'. Gusty shows surprise: 'why have you a bishop's staff, and swords, and spears, hung up together?' What the young boy fails to see of course is precisely the point of focus, the fact that all the objects in the room are 'national relics', 'the mute evidences …

---

14 Ibid., pp 362–3.

9.9 'The Barn', between p. 300 and p. 301 (Samuel Lover, *Handy Andy* (London, 1845)).

of [Ireland's] former glory and civilization'[15]. Since Walter Scott's *The Antiquary* (1816), collectors of antiques have been numerous in literary fiction. Edward O'Connor's collection of objects is also typical of 'the 1840s Ascendancy fashion for antiquities and archaeology'.[16] As such, it partakes in the new vision of Irish history that developed in the early 1840s and whose purpose for the narrator is 'to cherish the memories of [Ireland's] ancient glories [and] to give to her future sons the evidences of her earliest western civilization'.[17]

   What clearly emerges from this scene is that along with the narratives (either history writing or songs and ballads which abound in the novel), symbolic icons play an essential part in the forging of national mental representations. The minute description of some of the objects, especially the crosier, is again an example of ekphrasis, this time in a more traditional sense, recalling for example the description of Achilles' shield in the Iliad:

> But beyond all these [objects], was a relic exciting deeper interest – it was an ancient crosier, of curious workmanship, wrought in the precious metals and partly studded with jewels; but few of the latter remained, though the empty collets showed it had once been costly in such ornaments. Could this be seen

15 Ibid., pp 361–3.   **16** R. Foster (ed.), *The Oxford illustrated history of Ireland* (Oxford, 2000), p. 189.   **17** Lover, *Handy Andy*, p. 363.

without remembering that the light of Christianity first dawned over the western isles *in Ireland*?[18]

Visual rendering would be counter-productive here. The crosier is what semiologists describe as the index or trace left behind by a symbol that can only point at some reality but never fully embody it. Its main value lies in the *missing* stones that allow remembrance, that is individual and collective mental (re)construction, to invest it with emotional and ideological meaning. Active participation is demanded by Edward from Gusty, and by the narrator from the reader. The illustrator stops drawing and the narrator confesses to the failure of language to grasp the deep significance of the objects: they are but 'mute evidences'.[19] This reminds us of what Vogler describes as 'the aspect where words fail' or what Miller calls 'the ineliminable residue of all articulation, the foreclosed element, which may be approached, but never grasped: the umbilical cord of the symbolic'.[20] The crosier acts as symbol linking the Irish people to its past. Andy, abundantly shown in the pictures, is a caricature, whereas Edward is the symbol of a regenerative vision of Ireland's past: a farewell to stage-Irishness, as Andy's transformation in the final chapters illustrates, to be filled in with new meaning.

In conclusion, we can say that in *Handy Andy*, Lover emphasizes the importance of indigenous visual, verbal and mental imagery in the construction of national consciousness. The literary-political construction is by no means anti-unionist: Andy can only shake off his stage-Irish character by becoming a lord. But the complex system of interaction between numerous elements (text, illustration, painting, paratextual address to the reader and ultimately the reader's consciousness) points to the necessity, albeit in a comical way, for a new frame of historical reference and representation.

18 Ibid., p. 362. **19** Ibid. **20** Cited by A. Loos, 'Symbolic, real, imaginary', http://csmt.uchicago.edu/glossary2004.

From painting to photograph: James Robinson's *The Death of Chatterton*

LEON LITVACK

The history of photography in Ireland takes in some interesting figures and historical moments; but this narrative is relatively under-researched and undervalued. Indeed Luke Gibbons notes 'the absence of a visual tradition ... equal in stature to [Ireland's] literary counterpart'.[1] Aside from Slattery's PhD thesis of 1992 (which is by no means comprehensive),[2] Chandler's illustrated volume (which, while well illustrated, has infelicities of prose and is not well referenced)[3] and Kelly's sourcebook,[4] there have been few attempts to provide a comprehensive analysis of the development in nineteenth-century Ireland of one of the most significant technological innovations of the modern age, and one which continues to fascinate and to exercise powerful influences over us all.[5] One of the most interesting moments in this narrative concerns a prominent Dublin photographic artist named James Robinson (fig. 10.1), whose career began shortly after the introduction of photography to this island, and extended until late in the nineteenth century. As a businessman, he took advantage of new technological developments to enhance trade, and carefully observed trends and fashions in order to provide his customers with the very latest photographic applications. Though he was one of the most successful Irish photographers of the nineteenth century, he produced a particular series of images which caused controversy, and had far-reaching consequences, raising interesting questions about the intersection between photography and other arts, and the ownership and sales of images – questions which we are still concerned with today.

Robinson opened his premises at 65 Grafton Street in 1846, at which time the Daguerreotype, along with Fox Talbot's Calotype process, were the two established methods for capturing images. The Daguerreotype, invented in 1839, was the world's

I would like to thank Justin Carville, Eddie Chandler, Robert Clark, Gillian Greenham Hannum, and Richard and Leonee Ormond for their assistance with this research. **1** Luke Gibbons, 'Alien eye: photography and Ireland', *Circa*, 12 (1986), 10–11. **2** Peadar Slattery, 'The uses of photography in Ireland, 1839–1900' (PhD, TCD, 1992). **3** Edward Chandler, *Photography in Ireland: the nineteenth century* (Dublin, 2001). **4** Liam Kelly, *Photographs and photography in Irish local history* (Dublin, 2008). This indispensable volume features a short general history of photography, brief biographical sketches of the major Irish figures, locations of significant Irish photographic collections, and chapters on reading photographs and photographic evidence. **5** Specialist studies on particular aspects of 19th-century Irish photography are included in Ciara Breathnach (ed.), *Framing the West: images of rural Ireland, 1891–1920* (Dublin, 2007).

10.1 James Robinson, reproduced by
kind permission of the National Media
Museum, Bradford/SSPL.

first photographic process, and involved the capturing of a positive image on a metal plate; the sitter had to remain still for between ten and twenty minutes, which, though a disadvantage, produced a sharp, distinct image. The Calotype was produced by exposing a photo-sensitive paper to light, in order to produce a negative, which was then laid on top of another sheet of photo-sensitive paper, and exposed to light, thereby producing a positive image. This process improved over the years and expo-sure times decreased.[6] Robinson advertised frequently in *Saunders's News Letter*, and the evolution of the notices over time documents some of the changes in photo-graphic technology. They also indicate the changing nature of business practices as, in the early years, many traders came to photography from other specialities, or added it to existing businesses. Examples include opticians who were familiar with lenses, and chemists who dealt on a daily basis with powerful – indeed dangerous – substances required in the chemical processes that lay at the heart of image repro-duction. The market was fiercely competitive, and the majority of the Dublin studios had premises along 'the Photographers' Mile', which took in Upper Sackville Street, Lower Sackville Street, Westmoreland Street, College Green, Grafton Street, and to a lesser extent St Stephen's Green.[7] *Thom's Almanac* for 1846 describes Robinson as a

6 See Helmut Gernsheim, *The origins of photography* (London, 1982).   **7** See Chandler, 'philosophical artist and optician', and his premises as a 'polytechnic museum and gallery of curiosities'.[8] By 1850, he had clearly included the sale of cameras – though not the taking of portraits – as part of his business. His advertisement of 9 July, which almost resembles a handbill for a circus, reads as follows:

> James Robinson invites the attention of the nobility, gentry and strangers in Dublin to his exposition of novelties just received from Paris, consisting of microscopes, telescopes, opera glasses, Daguerreotype and Calotype cameras, electric telegraphs, electro-magnetic machines, and every description of philosophical and chemical apparatus; patent portable soda water machines, French cafetieres, portable gas lamps, Moderateur oil lamps, and various other applications of science to domestic purposes, curious scientific and amusing toys, Fantocinni figures, mechanical pictures, optical deceptions, phantascopes, dissolving views, panoramas, enchanted spy glasses, polyoramas, &c., &c. Fireworks of every description – polytechnic museum, 65 Grafton-street.[9]

This sensational listing, with a range reminiscent of a department store, highlighted objects which appeal to the eye; it also promoted scientific innovation, and sought to produce a sense of wonderment in metropolitan readers, who were also mass-consumers. The advertisement also raises interesting issues of class, as Robinson invites the well-to-do – though not the working classes – to visit his premises.

By 1853, when the first Dublin Exhibition was in progress, Robinson produced an advertisement offering opera glasses for hire to visitors.[10] By 1854, he had adopted the newly available Collodion process, which, he claimed, was 'much cheaper' than other methods, and could produce 'indestructible' photographs 'in a few seconds'.[11] This up-to-date photographic technique, introduced in 1851, involved spreading a viscous, light-sensitive liquid onto a plate; when this was exposed to light an image was captured. The wet plate was then developed, and the image fixed. When a paper negative was placed against the glass and exposed, an image was produced. Unlike the Calotype, this process was never patented, so that the art of photography became more widely practised, and the cost was reduced to one-tenth of what it was formerly.

By August 1854, Robinson was selling photographs of Donnybrook Fair, together with other 'Photographic Views',[12] which made their way not only into albums, but also into frames to serve as items of domestic decoration. In 1855, he began selling copies of paintings, engravings and statues, suitable, he said, for display in the

Photography in Ireland, pp 97–8, where the author provides names and addresses of individual practitioners. Chandler erroneously gives Robinson's dates at 65 Grafton Street as 1850–1900 (p. 98). **8** *Thom's Irish almanac and official directory for 1846* (Dublin, 1846), pp 850, 1001. **9** *Saunders's News Letter*, 9 July 1850. **10** Ibid., 6 July 1853. Robinson also contributed examples of his own work to the Exhibition, in the form of stereoscopic photographs, as well as cameras for Daguerreotype, Calotype and Collodion. **11** Ibid., 2 May 1854. **12** Ibid., 26 Aug. 1854.

'Drawingroom [sic], the Scrap Book or the Study'[13] – an interesting application, because nowadays it would be assumed that the capturing of such images might be seen as an infringement of copyright, if permission had not been obtained from the artist or owner.[14] In the early days of photography, however, such issues were less clearly understood.

Robinson's efforts ensured that the taking of photographs became a more democratic pursuit, accessible to the general public as well as to dedicated professionals. In an extended advertisement of June 1855, he catalogued the photographic equipment available at his premises, which included a wide range of cameras, lenses and chemicals. He offered instruction without charge to customers, 'without limitation', he said, 'as to the number of lessons'. As proof of the results that could be obtained, he covered the walls of his gallery with the work of many amateur photographers. As evidence of the esteem in which he was held, he noted that he was 'Optician to his Excellency the Lord Lieutenant'.[15]

Robinson made available to his customers another interesting innovation: stereoscopic, or three-dimensional, photographs. In May 1856, he announced the 'arrival of an immense number of stereoscopes and stereoscopic pictures on glass, paper and plate, including groups, objects of art, statuary, views of Italian, Swiss and other foreign and home scenery, at very moderate terms'.[16] The stereoscope took off in a big way in 1851, when Queen Victoria and Prince Albert examined the device at the Crystal Palace in London, and were presented with a stereoscope by its inventor, Sir David Brewster (1781–1868). It allowed the viewer to see a double image of the same subject; when viewed through the device, the image appeared to be one three-dimensional photograph. The image is made by a single camera with two lenses, set about two and a half inches apart: about the same distance as that between the eyes. In terms of layout, many stereographs are interesting, because they feature so many planes: there are often objects of interest in the foreground, mid-ground and background, all of which stand out prominently when viewed through a stereoscope.[17] It is estimated that by the mid-1850s, over a million households in Britain and Ireland owned a stereoscope, either a simple viewer, or a more elaborate cabinet-type, which could hold up to fifty or so positives.

Robinson was also a member of the Dublin Photographic Society, and served on its council in the period 1854–7. This body was originally formed in 1854 by a group

---

13 Ibid., 13 Mar. 1855.   **14** The current complexities of copyright law and its problems in the UK are dealt with in Kevin Garnett, Gillian Davies and Gwilym Harbottle (eds), *Copinger and Skone James on copyright* (15th ed., London, 2005). In Ireland, the authoritative texts are Robert Clark and Shane Smyth, *Intellectual property law in Ireland* (2nd ed., Dublin, 2005) and Robert Clark (ed.), *Irish copyright and design law* (Dublin, 2001).   **15** *Saunders's News Letter*, 6 June 1855.   **16** Ibid., 6 May 1856.   **17** For considerations of the differences between conventional photographs and stereographs, see Jonathan Crary, *Techniques of the observer: on vision and modernity in the nineteenth century* (Cambridge, MA, 1991); Rosalind Krauss, 'Photography's discursive spaces' in Rosalind Krauss (ed.), *The originality of the avant-garde and other modernist myths* (Cambridge, MA, 1986), pp 131–50.

of amateurs, though professionals later joined their ranks. The meetings consisted of talks by members on their experiences of new processes, demonstrations of technique and displays of new apparatus.[18] It is interesting that among the original members were the sculptor Joseph Kirk, and the painter Michael Angelo Hayes, who apparently did take photographs, though none has survived. In 1856, the Society held an exhibition (the first of its kind in Ireland), in which Robinson's 'excellent productions', consisting of large paper portraits, were praised by *Saunders's News Letter*. The event largely featured contributions by Irish photographic firms such as Yeates and Son (opticians), Bewley and Evans (apothecaries), and Robinson (photographers and photographic retailers). The report in *Saunders's News Letter* spoke of the connection between painting and photography, and between art and science:

> It is scarcely too much to say that photography marks an era in pictorial art between which and physical science it seems to be a sort of link. The marvellous truthfulness of its phantom creations in point of form cannot be surpassed; and should future science find some way of catching the bright colours of nature by a kindred process, its triumph will be complete. That the photographic apparatus can give great assistance at present to painters of portraits and landscapes is undoubted; and the enthusiasm with which the votaries of the photographic art at present cultivate it, affords a guarantee as to its continued progress.[19]

Thus far, it is apparent that Robinson availed of – and profited from – the culture of mass consumerism which photography helped to engender in mid-nineteenth-century Ireland. He positioned himself as a sensationalist and entertainer, attracting custom by exciting a sense of wonder and curiosity in potential clients. He relied on their modern sensibilities, wishing to save time in having portraits taken, and exercising thrift by having photography done cheaply. He allowed them to experience scenes domestic and foreign, and to appreciate works of art by bringing them into their immediate surroundings. Indeed he made them more vivid through three-dimensional stereoscopic effects, and encouraged his public to try photography for themselves. The interest photography was gaining in the public mind meant that he had a ready client base, who were interested in seeing things more vividly and honestly than was possible before.

18 See Oscar Merne, *The story of the Photographic Society of Ireland, 1854–1954* (Dublin, 1954). There is a fuller account in Slattery's 'Photography in Dublin, 1839–1861, with special reference to the Dublin Photographic Society, 1854–8 and the Photographic Society of Ireland, 1858–60'. This unpublished work was used as part of an associateship submission for the Royal Photographic Society Dublin in 1982. It is held at the National Media Museum, Bradford. **19** 'Exhibition of the Photographic Society', *Saunders's News Letter*, 12 May 1856. A second exhibition was held in 1858 at the Royal Dublin Society, in conjunction with an 'Exhibition of Decorative Art'; about 150 photographs were put on display. See Slattery, 'Photography in Dublin', p. 36.

In 1856, the young painter Henry Wallis (1830–1916), then an adherent of the Pre-Raphaelites, completed his first work, entitled *Chatterton* (fig. 10.2), which created a sensation when it was exhibited at the Royal Academy.[20] It concerned the young poet Thomas Chatterton (1752–70), who was bewitched by the medieval, and wrote on parchment a collection of poems in the name of Thomas Rowley (*c.*1400–70), a fifteenth-century monk, and attempted to pass them off as original. He was condemned as a forger by influential figures, among them Horace Walpole (1717–97), but nevertheless rode the tide of success until he died from an accidental overdose of laudanum. A myth, however, arose that this proto-Romantic had committed suicide, ending his life as a starving poet in a friendless garret, his genius cruelly unrecognized.[21] This death of a purportedly unfulfilled youth has been memorialized and profoundly embroidered by elegists, eulogists, poets, musicians, artists and sculptors for more than two centuries.

The painting is quite striking in its effect. Wallis adheres to the few details that are known, including the phial of poison on the floor, torn up manuscripts and the details of the garret room. He got the young George Meredith (whom he knew) to pose as the dead poet.[22] The painting imagines the poet as a martyr, prone and almost Christ-like, with the light of dawn illuminating Chatterton's serene features; emotional impact is heightened by the vibrant colours (particularly reds, blues and greens) contrasting with the lifeless form. The dome of St Paul's is visible in the background; the motif of the open window is repeated in paintings and photographs of this period, depicting a contrast between life and light outside, and death or sleep within.[23] There is also a contrast between the birth of the new day, and the stretching of a flower on the window-ledge towards the sun, and the dead boy on the bed. On the original frame were inscribed words from Marlowe's *Doctor Faustus* (1590):

> Cut is the branch that might have grown full straight
> And burned is Apollo's laurel bough.

20 Wallis was noted as a historical genre painter, in oil and watercolour. He studied in London and Paris, and during the 1850s was influenced by the Pre-Raphaelites. Aside from *Chatterton*, his most notable work is *The Stonebreaker* (1857, now at the Birmingham City Art Gallery). In 1859, he came into an inheritance from his stepfather, and his work declined, though he remained a Royal Academy exhibitor until 1877. He maintained a passionate interest in archaeology, ceramics and Renaissance art, and became a noted expert on pottery. See Christopher Wood, *Victorian painters*, 2 vols (Woodbridge, 1995), 1, p. 549, and Robyn Hamlyn's entry in the *Oxford Dictionary of National Biography*. There are two studies for *Chatterton* at the Tate; there are two other versions of the painting by Wallis: one at the Yale Centre for British Art, and another in the Birmingham City Art Gallery.   **21** For a full account of Chatterton's life, see E.H.W. Meyerstein, *A life of Thomas Chatterton* (London, 1930), and Richard Holmes, 'Thomas Chatterton: the case reopened', *Cornhill Magazine*, 178 (1970), 200–51.   **22** Two years after the painting was completed Wallis ran away with Meredith's wife. See Diane Johnson, *The true history of the first Mrs Meredith and other lesser lives* (London, 1973), p. 104.   **23** See, for example, Henry Peach Robinson's *Sleep* (1867) and *Fading Away* (1858).

10.2 Henry Wallis, *Chatterton* (1856) (© Tate London 2009).

In addition to having direct relevance to Chatterton, the painting may also be read as a critique of society's harsh, unfeeling treatment of artists.

During its London viewing, accolades were showered upon the painting, not least from John Ruskin, who deemed it

> Faultless and wonderful: a most noble example of the great school. Examine it well inch by inch: it is one of the pictures which intend, and accomplish, the entire placing before your eyes of an actual fact – and that a solemn one. Give it much time.[24]

When it was sent to Manchester in 1857 to appear in the 'Art Treasures of the United Kingdom' exhibition in the section dedicated to 'Paintings by Modern Masters', it received further acclaim, and was called 'a sensation'.[25] In April 1859, it was sent to Ireland, where it was seen by James Robinson.

Wallis had sold his painting to fellow artist Augustus Egg (1816–63), who rose to fame with such works as *Past and Present* (1858). Egg, while maintaining ownership of the painting, sold the copyright (for a fixed period) to Robert Turner, a publisher from Newcastle-upon-Tyne. The agreement between Egg and Turner, dated 18

24 'Academy Notes, 1856' in E.T. Cook and Alexander Wedderburn (eds), *The works of John Ruskin* (London, 1904), 14, p. 60. See also *Saturday Review*, 17 May 1856, p. 58; *Art-Journal*, n.s. 2 (1 June 1856), p. 169, which remarks on the 'marvellous power' of the picture; and *Spectator*, 24 May 1856, p. 570. 25 *Morning Star*, 5 May 1858, p. 6. See *Catalogue of the art treasures of the United Kingdom, collected at Manchester in 1857* (London, 1857).

March 1859, stated that Turner had, from that point onward, sole right to publish and profit from an engraving of the picture, and could exhibit the original oil for up to two years in pursuance of that aim. The subject of *Chatterton* readily lent itself to Victorian engraving, the first criterion for which was that the work displayed human interest.[26] Engen confirms the Victorian public's huge appetite for reproductive prints, which provided an ideal outlet for expressions of political opinion, religious teachings and artistic taste.[27] The engraving industry was very important to the profits to be derived from a work of art; indeed a painter's reputation was often decided by the popularity of the engraving rather than the success of the painting alone.[28] Engravers' studios grew into large 'factories', employing numerous apprentices in order to increase the speed and volume of production.[29] The Printsellers' Association (founded in 1847 to register and control the publication of fine art prints) attached monetary values to prints, and published lists in which the prices and print-runs were advertised. In the Prefatory Note to the Association's *Alphabetical List of Engravings*, it was noted that in their first year of operation they stamped seventy-five works, embracing 15,332 proofs, or an average of 204 proofs per plate, including artist's proofs, proofs before letters and lettered proofs, the publishing value of which was £72,000. In 1892, the publishing value of such plates was £214,016.[30] Such listings enhanced the desirability of owning fine art prints, and some artists, like Edward Burne-Jones, had plates destroyed after only 250 or 300 prints had been taken. Another initiative designed to enhance marketability was instigated by the Art Unions (the first of which was formed in London in 1836); they organized lotteries which offered prints as prizes, and commissioned well-known engravers to produce these works. They assisted in shaping uniform public attitudes towards the arts, and raised sums so large (up to £50,000) that the government attempted to intervene in stopping what it considered a veiled form of gambling.[31]

---

26 R.K. Engen, *Victorian engravings*, ed. Hilary Beck (London, 1975), p. 5. **27** Engen cites the popularity of engraved portraits of the Duke of Wellington, Disraeli and Queen Victoria; prints depicting military achievements and the Great Exhibition; and engravers' contributions to illustrated editions of the Bible, *Victorian engravings*, p. 6. **28** An artist could produce multiple versions of a painting in order to enhance profits; but engravings were far more lucrative. In the case of Edwin Landseer (1802–73), for example, his painting *Peace and War* sold for £1,260, while the copyright for engraving the same painting was sold for £3,150; see D[elabere] Roberton Blaine, *Suggestions on the Copyright (Works of Art) Bill* (London, 1861), p. 8. Less famous artists used engraving rights to establish their reputations and develop a wider audience. **29** There was a variety of tasks to be performed in engravers' studios: the 'facsimile man' copied the artist's design onto a plate; the 'tint man' applied colour to the plate before printing; other individuals were involved in 'grounding' plates for mezzotint, grinding the ink, etching or engraving a plate, and the final hand-colouring of the print if it had not been printed in colour by the 'tint man'. See Engen, *Victorian engravings*, p. 7. **30** G[eorge] W[illiam] Friend, *An alphabetical list of engravings declared at the Office of the Printsellers' Association, London ... since its establishment in 1847 to the end of 1891*, 2 vols (London, 1892–4), 1, prefatory note. The provision of information to the list by publishers was voluntary. **31** See Engen, *Victorian engravings*, p. 8.

CHATTERTON.—On View for a few days only, At Mr. CRANFIELD'S GALLERY, GRAFTON-STREET, Dublin, The Extraordinary Picture of " THE DEATH OF CHATTERTON," (" The Marvellous Boy,") The property of Augustus Leopold Egg, Esq., A.R.A. " This faultless and wonderful Picture" will be remembered by all visitors to the Royal Academy and the Manchester Exhibition, where it was daily besieged by crowds of anxious visitors. THOMAS CRANFIELD, 115 GRAFTON-STREET.

CAUTION TO PHOTOGRAPHERS. Mr. TURNER hereby intimates to Photographic Artists and others, that Proceedings at Law will be immediately instituted against any one Infringing upon his Copyrights by means of Photography or otherwise. 82 Grey-street, Newcastle, April 1st, 1859.

10.3 Announcement of the exhibition of Wallis's *Chatterton* in Dublin, and Robert Turner's 'Caution to Photographers', *Saunders's News Letter*, 2 April 1859.

Such considerations confirm the importance to such temporary copyright-holders as Turner of the potential profits to be derived from commissioning an engraving of Wallis' *Chatterton*. An announcement was made in *Saunders's News Letter* and in other Dublin papers, on 2 April 1859, to inform the public of the upcoming exhibition at the gallery of Thomas Cranfield on Grafton Street; the notice featured brief quotations from both Wordsworth and Ruskin. On the same day, in the same paper, Turner published a warning to all photographers, that 'Proceedings of the Law will be immediately instituted against any one infringing upon his copyrights by means of photography or otherwise' (fig. 10.3).[32]

On 22 April, James Robinson, as well as issuing an advertisement for photographic supplies, produced a notice that he would be offering for sale 'Stereoscopic pictures of the last moments and death of the poet Chatterton'.[33] He in fact wished to produce a series of four images documenting 'The Life and Death of the Poet, Chatterton'; these were to include *Chatterton in the Muniment Room at Bristol*, *Chatterton Writing his Last Letter to Walpole*, *Chatterton Contemplating Suicide* and *The Death of Chatterton* (fig. 10.4).[34] All were completed, except *Chatterton in the Muniment Room*. None of the images Robinson produced was a photograph of the Wallis painting, copies of which were specifically warned against by Turner, in a newspaper

32 *Saunders's News Letter*, 2 Apr. 1859. 33 Ibid. 34 The case was reviewed in great detail, complete with full texts of both published and unpublished documents, by a barrister, C.H. Foot, in his pamphlet *The death of Chatterton case: Turner v. Robinson. Containing a full report of all the proceedings – the evidence – the judgment of His Honour the Master of the Rolls – and the judgments of the Lord Chancellor and the Lord Justice of Appeal in Chancery* (Dublin, 1860).

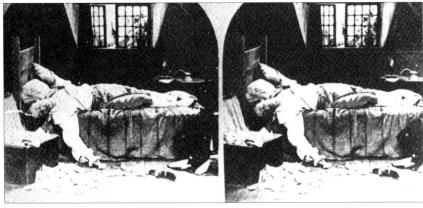

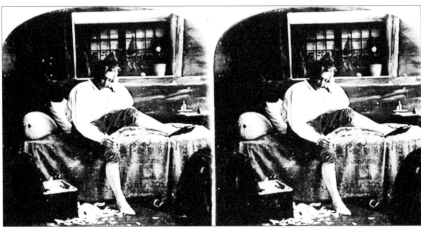

10.4 James Robinson, *The Death of Chatterton* (*above*) and *Chatterton Contemplating Suicide* (*below*) (stereoscopic photographs, both 1859). Reproduced by kind permission of Special Collections, University of Pennsylvania (Henisch Collection), and Edward Chandler.

which Robinson presumably read, since his own advertisements regularly appeared in it.

A comparison between the painting and the stereograph (which was offered in both monochrome and hand-tinted colour versions) demonstrates that there are significant similarities: the attitude of the central figures, sporting flowing locks, dressed in similar loose-fitting shirts, with one shoe on and the other off; the box of manuscripts on the left; the cushions on the bed; the phial on the floor; the dormer windows of similar shape, with flowers on the ledge and curtain opened to the left; and the tables (albeit of different shapes) with the burnt out candles. Robinson had been to see the painting, and had studied several biographical works about Chatterton. He arranged a set in his studio, as he said, 'with a pallet, table and box, and formed the back-ground scene outside the window, by a view of London, painted by a scenic artist, on a canvas screen'.[35] He then used his young assistant, Isaac Murray, as a model for Chatterton. The details in the two images are very close; if the stereograph can be imagined in vivid colour (particularly the red hair and purple/blue breeches), then the resemblance is closer still. Yet it must be remembered that Robinson's image was not a photograph of the painting, but rather one based on the painting.

Turner felt aggrieved; his first response to the challenge came a week later, in the form of a letter dated 27 April, which his solicitors addressed to Robinson, telling him that they would 'commence legal proceedings against you forthwith, for pirating said work, and publishing same'. They cautioned him 'against making any further copies of said work, or sales of same, as immediate proceedings will be taken to hold you responsible for the injury Mr Turner has, or may incur by such your act in this behalf'.[36]

Robinson did not respond directly to this letter; instead he published a revised advertisement (fig. 10.5), which appeared on 29 April (the last day on which the painting was exhibited); in addition to advising once again that his photographs were for sale, he added:

> J.R. begs most emphatically to deny having copied or pirated his stereoscopic slides from any picture exhibited in Dublin; and it must be obvious to any one that has the slightest knowledge of the principle of the stereoscope that pictures such as he has produced could not be obtained from the flat surface of any painting or engraving.[37]

That evening, there was a meeting of the Dublin Photographic Society, at which the President, Sir Jocelyn Coghill, produced a copy of Robinson's photograph, and 'claimed for photography the title of being a sister not a handmaid [sic] of art'.[38] Robinson (who was also present) then explained that despite the 'startling resemblance', it was no copy, but rather a stereoscopic photograph. He acknowledged that he had been threatened with legal proceedings for alleged piracy, 'but', the report said, 'he was to maintain his own right'. The Society approved of its member's actions, and responded 'hear'.[39]

Turner then filed a petition in the Court of Chancery, stating that he was about to publish an engraving of the picture, and that the publication issued by Robinson would greatly prejudice the sale and lessen his profits. His claim was upheld, and an injunction was granted on 11 May 1859, which prevented Robinson from exhibiting, publishing or selling any of his Chatterton images without the permission of Turner.[40]

35 Quoted in Foot, *The death of Chatterton case*, p. 13.   **36** Letter of 27 Apr. 1859, from Messrs Kiernan and McCreight, solicitors for Turner; quoted in Foot, *The death of Chatterton case*, pp 9–10.   **37** *Saunders's News Letter*, 29 Apr. 1859.   **38** Coghill also delivered to the Dublin Photographic Society a lecture 'On the mutual relations of photography and art', *Royal Dublin Society Journal*, 2 (Jan. 1860), 380–8.   **39** 'Photographic Society', *Freeman's Journal*, 30 Apr. 1859.   **40** Details of the legal proceedings are described in G.B. Greenhill,

THE DEATH OF CHATTERTON.—
JAMES ROBINSON begs to announce that he has now ready
for Sale the most wonderfully effective and beautiful Stereoscopic
Pictures ever yet produced, Photographed by him from the living
model, representing
THE LAST MOMENT AND DEATH OF THE POET CHATTERTON,
1s. 6d. each plain, 2s. 6d. coloured.
J. R. begs most emphatically to deny having copied or pirated his
Stereoscopic Slides from any Picture exhibited in Dublin ; and it
must be obvious to any one that has the slightest knowledge of the
principle of the stereoscope that pictures such as he has produced
could not be obtained from the flat surface of any painting or engraving.   Polytechnic Museum and Photographic Galleries,
65 GRAFTON-STREET.

10.5 Robinson's revised advertisement, *Saunders's News Letter*, 29 April 1859.

Robinson countered by filing an affidavit on 16 May 1859, in which he claimed
that stereoscopic photographs (consisting of 'two photographic pictures of the same
object, differing slightly from each other'), and the effect obtained by looking
through a stereoscope, was 'unattainable by any artist in one picture or engraving'.[41]
He produced a large number of stereoscopic pictures in his studio, and explained that
he made preparation for the four stereographic scenes in March 1859 – that is, before
he had seen Wallis' painting. He then raised some interesting issues concerning prece-
dence, and their implications for copyright. He emphasized the three occasions on
which the work was 'publicly exhibited', and he also mentioned an engraving of 1794
by Edward Orme (1775–1848), itself based on a painting by Henry Singleton (1766–
1839), from which he believed that Wallis might have taken the idea for his painting.
Several details are common to all the works, including the prone position on the bed,
the phial, the box, scraps of paper strewn on the floor, and the latticed dormer
window in the garret room. Robinson submitted that, owing to the depiction of the
subject in Orme's engraving, the Wallis painting was 'not original in its design'.
Robinson also denied that Turner would have suffered any damage by publication of
the stereoscopic photograph 'and submitted that he has a perfect right to make and
sell such pictures, and that under any circumstances Mr Turner had no right or title
to interfere with him'.[42] There then followed a series of additional affidavits,
including one from Turner, stating that he believed Robinson did not contemplate
producing a series of pictures until after he received the letter of 27 April; Robinson
responded with evidence that he had prepared images before then. There was
another from Wallis, stating that his design for the picture was original. Yet another,

'The Death of Chatterton, or photography and the law', *History of Photography*, 5.3 (1981), 199–
205. The events recounted here are summarised from Foot.   **41** Quoted in Foot, *The death
of Chatterton case*, pp 12–13.   **42** Quoted in Foot, *The death of Chatterton case*, p. 14.

from an assistant at Cranfield's gallery, stated that the express purpose of the exhibition was to get subscribers for the engraving, which Turner commissioned from the noted engraver Thomas Barlow (1824–99).

The case came up for hearing before Master of the Rolls in November 1859. Turner argued that Robinson had printed, published and sold 'piratical imitations' and 'copies of the design' of the painting whose copying rights had been acquitted by Turner. Turner's solicitors requested an injunction preventing Robinson from exhibiting, publishing or selling the photographs. The case was based on the principle that under Common Law an unpublished work remains the sole property of the artist, or of the individual to whom the artist grants copyright, and despite being exhibited in London, Manchester and Dublin, the painting remained 'unpublished'. At the time of the hearing, no specific statute dealt with the copying of painting (although engravings had enjoyed copyright protection from 1735);[43] instead, counsel drew examples from manuscripts, as well as the copying of books, plays and sculpture.[44] In order to help the Master adjudicate in the particular case of *Chatterton*, he sent letters to the Royal Academy and to the organizers of the Manchester exhibition, asking whether the copying of exhibited pictures was allowed or not; in each case the answer was in the negative.[45] Thus, in this particular case, the judge observed, Wallis' painting was not 'published'. He added:

> I apprehend that it is clear that by the common law, copyright or protection exists in favour of works of literature, art or science, to this limited extent only, that while they remain unpublished no person can pirate them, but that after publication they are by the common law unprotected.[46]

Robinson contended that the picture was published by Wallis, who parted with it; he also permitted a wood engraving, which was published in the *National Magazine* in November 1856, in a series of 'Specimens from Recent Exhibitions' (that is, the display in Manchester);[47] but the judge countered by saying that 'In the case of a literary work, whether it is in manuscript or in print, it is the same work'; but an engraving is not. What the judge particularly objected to in the case of Robinson was the 'pirating of the colouring' of Wallis' painting 'in all its minutest details';[48] this, he said, made it much more like the painting than an engraving, and so the injunction was continued.

Robinson appealed the decision early in 1860, and it was heard before the Court

43 The Engravers' Copyright Act (commonly referred to as the 'Hogarth Act', after the famous engraver) was passed in 1735. **44** The copyright of plays was secured by the Dramatic Copyright Act (1833); copyright of sculpture was assured by the International Copyright Act (1844). **45** Sir Charles Eastlake, however, in reply to a letter from Master of the Rolls, said that no such rules existed at the National Gallery in London, and copying was indeed permitted. See Foot, *The death of Chatterton case*, pp 26–7. **46** Ibid., p. 22. **47** *National Magazine*, I (Nov. 1856), p. 33. **48** Quoted in Foot, *The death of Chatterton case*, p. 24.

of Appeal on 9 May. The Lord Chancellor gave his decision on 7 June 1860. He believed that Turner, who owned the copyright to Wallis' *Chatterton*, and temporarily took possession of it from Egg, expressly exhibited the painting at Thomas Cranfield's in Dublin in order to obtain subscriptions for an engraving. He noted that 'any person who entered the room to see it, must have known that he was admitted in the expectation of his becoming a subscriber to the engraving … In all fairness of reasoning, this express and reasonable limitation would have excluded the idea that the public could acquire any other right or privilege'[49] – in other words, Robinson would have known that it was not permitted to copy the picture. As further proof of Robinson's understanding of the situation, the judge cited his altered advertisement of 29 April (fig. 10.5), which appeared after the letter sent by Turner to Robinson, warning him not to sell his photographs. The Lord Chancellor upheld the injunction, and Robinson was ordered to pay costs.

There were certain long-term effects of this complicated Chancery case. A summary was published in July 1860, by the barrister Charles Foot. The title page included a quotation from John Ruskin's *The Political Economy of Art*; it read, 'All copies are bad … Whenever you buy a copy, you buy so much misunderstanding of the original … besides increasing, ultimately, chances of mistake and imposture'.[50] In the preface, Foot stated that

> I have been induced to publish this case by the fact that it is one of first impression, and decides questions of vital interest to the Artist, as well as to the purchaser of the right to engrave his works. If *Turner v. Robinson* had been decided other than it was, the perfection to which the art of photography has attained has almost imperilled the copyright of every painting. It has obtained, in a great measure, for works of Painting, that protection, which has been given by statute, to every novelty or improvement in every other production of mind or hand.[51]

It had important consequences for the relationship in law between photography and painting.[52] The judgment established that a photographic mock-up of a painting (easily enough achieved at a time when artists painted photographically) was equiv-

---

49 Ibid., p. 63.   **50** Foot, *The death of Chatterton case*, title page.   **51** Ibid., preface.   **52** *The Art-Journal*, commenting on this case in July 1859, noted that it was 'indeed high time that the question concerning copyright should be settled by the legislature' ('Art at Law', *Art-Journal*, n.s. 5 [1 July 1859], 227). Yet, in terms of the quality of the picture, the journal commented the following month: 'We confess we cannot see what injury could have been sustained by the publisher of the intended print; we believe, on the contrary, the photograph might have been its best advertisement. The picture, although a work of singular ability, is not calculated to make a popular engraving; the subject is grievously painful; the "marvellous boy", dead from poison administered by his own hand, is surely not an incident to be contemplated with pleasure, although it may be a necessary adjunct to a pictured history of his mournful life' ('The Photograph of Chatterton', *Art-Journal*, n.s. 5 [1 Aug. 1859], 259).

alent in copyright terms to an engraving (or indeed a photograph) of the painting itself. This judgment contributed in interesting ways to the Fine Art Copyright Act of 1862, which, for the first time, extended copyright protection to paintings, drawings and photographs for the term of life of the artist plus seven years.[53] It took so long to extend copyright to painting because many painters had not felt the need for bespoke legal protection, on account of the protection afforded to engravings by the 1735 Engravers' Copyright Act: if an engraving is commissioned before the painting is put on public display, then the design of the picture, as reflected in the engraving, is entitled to copyright.[54] There was considerable parliamentary debate concerning the inclusion of photography in the copyright provisions. For example, on 20 March 1862, an MP named Harvey Lewis argued that photography was 'not a fine art but a mechanical process'. The Solicitor General, Roundell Palmer, responded that 'while strictly and technically speaking, a photograph was not in one sense to be treated as a work of fine art, yet very considerable expense was frequently incurred in obtaining good photographs'. He continued by outlining the fine work that had been done in the field of travel photography.[55] The Bill received Royal Assent on 29 July 1862. To obtain protection, photographers had to register images at Stationers' Hall, London, and pay a fee. Over 250,000 items were registered during the act's lifetime (1862–1912). Most were commercial pictures, including royal and celebrity portraits, views and genre scenes, advertising images and photos of floods, shipwrecks and other newsworthy events. One irony of the wording of the act was that copyright could be lost altogether if the artist, upon the first occasion of the first sale of his work, failed to make an agreement in writing reserving the copyright to himself.[56]

It is also interesting to consider what happened to Robinson and Turner as a consequence of the case. Turner did commission an engraving, which was produced by Thomas Barlow in 1860,[57] and was probably published. There is some question

53 A useful 'Commentary on the Fine Art Copyright Act 1862' by Ronan Deazley appears in *Primary sources on copyright (1450–1900)*, ed. Lionel Bently and Martin Kretschmer (www.copyrighthistory.org, 29 Sept. 2008). The Act was given impetus by lobbying from the Society of Arts, and by the staging in London of the International Exhibition of 1862, for which many works of art were brought to the United Kingdom from abroad, and so required copyright protection while in the country. Interestingly photographs were excluded from the fine art section. **54** See D[elabere] Roberton Blaine, *On the laws of artistic copyright and their defects* (London, 1853), p. 26. **55** *Hansard*, 3rd series, 165 (1862), 1890–1. **56** See Egerton Beck, 'Copyright in artistic works', *Burlington Magazine*, 56 (1930), 107–13. **57** Thomas Oldham Barlow (1824–89; ARA 1873) was a popular mezzotint engraver and etcher, who engraved paintings by John Philip (for which he is best known), John Everett Millais, William Holman Hunt, William Powell Frith, Richard Ansdell and Sir Edwin Landseer. His completed prints were exhibited at the Royal Academy, and were published by the most prominent Victorian publishers. They sold for as much as £10 for limited editions, and were often produced in a variety of 'states', including 'Artist Proof' (high quality, without letterpress), Before Letters, Vellum, India, Presentation, Japan, Prints, and Plain Impressions. For a complete listing of Barlow's engravings see Rodney K. Engen, *Dictionary of Victorian engravers, print publishers and their works* (Cambridge, 1979), pp 23–4.

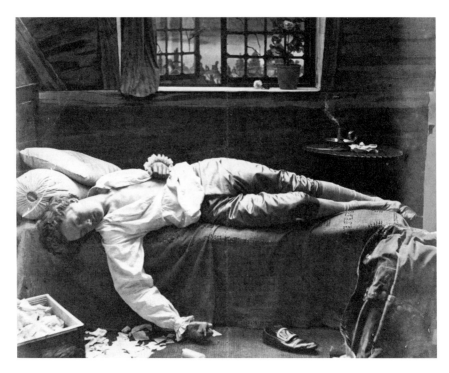

10.6 James Robinson, *The Death of Chatterton* (flat collodion print, 1859). Reproduced by kind permission of the National Media Museum, Bradford/SSPL.

over whether the engraving entered the public domain, because it was never registered with the Printsellers' Association; while this procedure was never obligatory,
other Barlow engravings were registered. Nevertheless, there exists the record of a
copy, signed by Barlow and bearing the publisher's blind stamp, having been sold by
the Maas Gallery, London, in 1997 for £3560.[58] If Turner profited from Barlow's
engraving, then partial consolation was achieved. Turner continued to show Wallis'
Chatterton in England, in centres like Birmingham and his native Newcastle-upon-
Tyne; it eventually made its way back to Egg. Today, little is known of the Tyneside
printer who owned the copyright to a highly evocative painting. Robinson also
produced a flat print (fig. 10.6) at the same time as the stereograph, though he did
not offer it for sale in Dublin at the time of the Wallis exhibition at Thomas
Cranfield's. It is of larger format than the stereograph, and so it is useful for
comparing to the painting. It uses the same studio set, but appears much more vivid
than the stereograph. Today, it is a highly prized item; the one in the plate comes from
an Irish album of 1862, currently in the National Media Museum in Bradford, which
also contains images by Oscar Rejlander, and was valued at £14,000.[59]

58 See 'After Henry Wallis, *The death of Chatterton*: mixed method engraving by Thomas O.
Barlow' in *Victorian and Pre-Raphaelite engraving* (London, 1997), plate no. 109. **59** Murphy

Robinson continued to trade in Dublin, and advertisements that appeared shortly after the Chancery case made no reference to it: it seemed to be business as usual. He maintained his premises along the photographers' 'Golden Mile', and took his sons into the business. The firm of James Robinson & Sons traded on Grafton Street until just before the outbreak of the First World War. He was a leading figure in the development of photography in Ireland, and the *Death of Chatterton* case, while perhaps personally difficult and expensive for Robinson, helped to mark the important contribution that this evolving art form made to the meeting of art and science, and to an expansion of visual aesthetics in the nineteenth century.

Album, Inventory nos 1991–5027, National Media Museum, Bradford. This album dates from 1862, and contains 275 photographs, assembled by an M. Murphy. It was purchased by the Museum in 1989.

Resisting vision: photography, anthropology and the production of race in Ireland

JUSTIN CARVILLE

In 1986, the National Library of Ireland produced a small, illustrated booklet, *The Irish Face*, to accompany an exhibition of the same title.[1] Part of a series of educational publications designed to function as guides and departmental catalogues to the library's collections of historical documents, prints, drawings and printed ephemera, *The Irish Face* marked a departure in terms of both the content and the scope of the library's previous publications. Going beyond the library's own catalogue of holdings, the booklet and associated exhibition drew on a range of private and institutional collections to illustrate a generic theme – the physical characteristics of the Irish face – rather than a specific set of historical objects. In the words of the author of the introduction, the booklet 'illustrates the faces of a selection of Irish people, anonymous or celebrated, from various periods through the ages, and it reviews the artists and the techniques and media employed in their portrayal. It also gives some indications of the 'look' in fashion at different times, and how the Irish liked to present themselves to the world'.[2] From prehistoric ceremonial maceheads and stone carvings, Celtic idols, illuminated manuscripts and sixteenth-century portraits, to carved busts, Victorian caricature, photography and 'modern painting', the publication drew on an eclectic range of media and material artefacts to illustrate the visualization of the Irish as a race from the third century BC right through to the 1980s.[3]

Much discourse on race since the 1859 publication of Charles Darwin's *Origin of the Species*, emphasized evolutionary theories of racial hierarchy and cultural identity, in *The Irish Face*, however, evolutionism of a different order emerges.[4] As the representation of the Irish face is traced from prehistoric times to the present day, progress is identified in the fidelity and modality of the medium utilized to depict the physical characteristics of the Irish as race. As the 'vagueness of the portrayal' of the ceremonial macehead is superseded by the 'lack of personality' and 'vacant mask-like quality' of Christian metalwork, to the rejection of the 'photographic style' by modern painters in favour of expressing 'the nature of the subject by concentrating on selected aspects', the aesthetic and material primitivism of prehistoric stone carving is placed at the bottom end of an evolutionary spectrum of visual representation that ends with the rational, scientific use of the photographic image in physical

---

1 *The Irish face* (Dublin, 1986). 2 Ibid., p. 7. 3 An obvious omission in the taxonomy of media utilized would appear to be cinema, both indigenous and foreign productions. 4 Charles Darwin, *The origin of the species* [1859] (Oxford, 1982).

anthropology.[5] This essay is concerned with a specific example of this far end of the evolutionary scale of visual representation, the use of photography in Victorian anthropology, but it is equally concerned with its role in the formation of what *The Irish Face* as both an exhibition and a publication contributed to, the 'visual economy' of Irish identity. Discussing specific examples from a series of studies on the ethnology of the islands along the western seaboard during the early 1890s by Alfred Cort Haddon and Charles R. Browne, the essay examines the representation of Irish identity within the context of ethnographic inquiry. Exploring the incorporation of photography into late Victorian anthropological methods, the essay analyses the emergence of the photographic image and anthropological discourse into an already circulating set of visual representations and discourses that constructed Irish identity in the Victorian public imagination. Of particular concern is the role of the photographic image in the production of ethnographic data, the social relations between the photographers and subject, and what this may contribute to our understanding of the formation of Irish visual culture.

PHOTOGRAPHY, RACE AND THE VISUAL ECONOMY OF IRISH IDENTITY

In the 1881 New Year's Eve edition of *Punch, or the London Charivari*, an illustration of Mr Punch being guided by Fr Time along an exhibition of colonial 'types' appeared with the title 'Time's Waxworks'.[6] Under the title in brackets, the text reads '1881 *just added to the collection*', followed by Mr Punch's statement 'Ha! You'll have to put him in the chamber of horrors!' Punch's remarks are in response to Fr Time's introduction of the latest annual edition to his waxworks collection, a simianized, and it must be noted, fenianized Celt. Alongside other annual imperial problems, is the simianized figure of the Celt with a flint-lock gun under one arm, and a sack of dynamite under the other. As if to remove any possible ambiguity of the intended message of the image, the illustration also includes the word 'anarchy' across the cap of the simianized, waxwork figure.

There are obvious historical references in the illustration to imperial relations and England's position in global colonial politics and conflict. Alongside the 1881 figure of the simianized Fenian is what appears to be an African warrior, an obvious reference to the 1879 conquest over the Bantu-speaking Zulu people of Natal, and further along are what appear to be Egyptian and Eastern imperial specimens. Discussing such illustrations in the chapter 'Victorian Comic Art' in his study of the graphic reinforcement of cultural stereotypes, L. Perry Curtis, noting that 'physiognomy is as inseparable from caricature as the stereotype is indispensible to any form of prejudice', has observed that illustrators frequently collapsed physical appearance into

5 *The Irish face*, pp 8, 14, 49.   **6** The illustration is reproduced in L. Perry Curtis, *Apes and angels: the Irishman in Victorian caricature*, rev. and expanded ed. (Washington, DC, 1997), p. 24.

cultural behaviour in their visual depictions of the Irish. Discussing the work of George Cruikshank and John Tenniel, two of the most prolific illustrators of Irish subject matter throughout the nineteenth century, he states that both 'relied constantly on the physiognomical equation of prognathism and savagery, if not bestiality, when they sought to epitomize Irish rebels and republicans'.[7] Curtis' assessment of the role of Victorian caricature in establishing Irish cultural stereotypes is not, of course, without its critics, most notably Roy Foster. Taking to task Curtis' claims that *Punch* reflected anti-Irish bigotry in England by discussing a range of examples that supposedly demonstrate that the publication could be supportive and sympathetic to the cause and plight of the Irish, Foster explains away Curtis' thesis by suggesting that much of the satirical jibes at the Irish were fair comment and genuinely funny.[8] Suggesting that *Punch*'s treatment of the Irish was not markedly different than its representation of other groups, he remarks 'Nor were its representations of the Irish very pronouncedly different in physiognomy from the representations of English plebeians'.[9]

Leaving to one side Foster's problematic observation that the similarity in physiognomic depiction between the simianized Irish and English under-class in the pages of *Punch* was equitable, both Curtis' thesis of anti-Irish stereotyping, and Foster's criticism of his over-determined reading of *Punch*'s political satire, overlook the significance of such imagery in visualizing the popular imaginary of Irish identity. Such imagery established a visual code and grammar of the Irish face through the utilization of not only popular conceptions of race and cultural behaviour, but also theories drawn from the social and human sciences to render their illustrations immediately legible and familiar to the Victorian public. What is significant about *Punch*'s 'Time's Waxworks' illustration, for example, is that it draws not only on Darwinian theories of evolution in its visual presentation of the simianized, Fenian Irish alongside other racially categorized peoples, but also on anthropological exhibitionary practices familiar to the Victorian public from the 1870s through the industrial and imperial exhibitions that were increasingly held throughout Europe in the closing decades of the nineteenth century.

Such exhibitions, in their formation of the modern state through the combination of spectacle and surveillance — what Tony Bennett terms the 'exhibitionary complex' — opened up the body of the colonized to the unrelenting scrutiny of the Anglo-Saxon gaze.[10] As is apparent in the waxworks illustration, the body, whether presented as an inanimate waxwork figure or a living tableau, was rendered a mute ethnographic spectacle for the curious gaze of the British public. Such practices of staging ethnographic spectacle grew out of a growing demand by the public in imperial centres for spectacular displays and presentations of the indigenous races of the

---

7 Ibid. p. 26.   **8** Roy Foster, *Paddy & Mr Punch: connections in Irish and English history* (London, 1993), pp 171–94.   **9** Ibid., pp 173–4.   **10** Tony Bennett, 'The exhibitionary complex' in David Boswell and Jessica Evans (eds), *Representing the nation: a reader* (London, 1995).

new imperial world order. Anne Maxwell has observed that in their display of colonized peoples through taxonomies of hierarchical classification, the organizers of such imperial ethnographic displays utilized a familiar lexicon of stark oppositions to reinforce the racial difference between the white Anglo-Saxon viewer and the colonial specimens silently exhibited for visual consumption.[11] The visualization of this language of stark oppositions, whether through illustrations such as 'Time's Waxworks', the spectacular displays of staged ethnography in imperial exhibitions, textual descriptions of racial physiognomy, popular prints, paintings and photographic images, increasingly drew on the scientific discourse of anthropology in its formation of a visual economy of Irish identity throughout the nineteenth century. In the closing decades of the century, the racial distinction between the Irish and the Anglo-Saxon was scientifically quantified through the metrics of physical anthropology, a development that sought to remove once and for all any ambiguity of racial distinction that arose through the similarity in skin colour between the races. While the visual and visualized racial differences between Anglo-Saxons, Africans and Asians could be emphasized through differences in skin pigmentation, colour alone could not distinguish between Anglo-Saxons and Celts. The development of the 'type concept' within anthropological discourse aimed to identify through empirical methods the visible characteristics of a race that distinguish it from all other races.[12] Thus, to the circulating imagery that exaggerated the physiognomy of the Irish to monstrous dimensions to emphasize their racial difference, was added a supplementary category of images whose uniformity, dullness and deliberate lack of aesthetic codification masked their visual rhetoric of racial difference. By the closing decade of the century, the popular and scientific anthropological visualization of race combined to project what this essay terms, a 'visual economy' of the Irish face that traversed the public and disciplinary boundaries of popular culture and the social sciences.

Although it has become fashionable within the academy to describe the everyday role and use of images within societies as 'visual culture', the term visual economy is more appropriate to describe the circulation of images between the spheres of public culture and scientific institutions with which this essay is concerned. As Raymond Williams and Chris Jenks have both demonstrated, the term 'culture' has complex and contested meanings in its usage within different disciplinary paradigms.[13] History, literary and cultural studies tend to emphasize culture as a system of signifying practices and symbolic meanings that bind people into communities. While this remains a significant approach to examining the role of images within specific historical contexts, it frequently conceals the complexities of the relationship between the producer and consumer of images, and the subjects represented in them. Additionally,

11 Anne Maxwell, *Colonial photography and exhibitions: representations of the 'Native' and the making of European identities* (Leicester, 1999), p. 2.   **12** George W. Stocking, Jr., *Race, culture and evolution: essays in the history of Anthropology* (Chicago, IL, 1982), p. 56.   **13** Raymond Williams, *Keywords* (London, 1976); Chris Jenks, *Culture* (2nd ed., London, 2005).

the term 'visual culture' does not adequately account for the continued presence and circulation of both 'images' and image objects across and between diverse social, ethnic and racial groups of peoples, and geographical and historical contexts. To paraphrase Deborah Poole, while it is possible to conceive of the British public, and indeed the Irish metropolitan elite, as participating in the same economy as the rural Irish peasantry who were the subject of much ethnographic inquiry during the last two decades of the nineteenth century, it is much more difficult to identify them as having a shared culture.[14] Exploring the visual economy of Irish identity not only allows for an examination of vision as socially and systematically organized, but also for the questioning of the production of images and image meanings within different contexts, the circulation of these images and meanings within and across diverse groups of peoples, and the discourses through which such images are assessed, evaluated and put to use. These are important areas of inquiry in the context of anthropology, which increasingly became an ocularcentric discipline as it sought to professionalize its activities through the incorporation of 'scientific' methods of participant-observation, and the production, accumulation and use of visual material as 'objective' data.[15] They are especially salient to the ethnographic survey of the western seaboard by Haddon and Browne, as not only did the photographic image function as a 'scientific' method of data-collection and as 'objective' anthropological evidence, it also formed what Mary Louise Pratt describes as 'the contact zone' between the ethnographic observer and the ethnographically observed.[16] As the discussion of the use of photography in their published reports demonstrates, this contact with ethnographic subject brought into question the very reliability of photography to function as ethnographic data.

UNRAVELLING THE 'TANGLED SKEIN OF THE SO-CALLED IRISH RACE'

More recognized for his conception and leadership of the seven-month multi-disciplinary Cambridge University expedition to the Torres Strait of 1898, an expedition initiated by a visit a decade earlier during which he first used photography as an ethnographic tool,[17] Haddon was appointed Chair of Zoology in the Royal College of Science, Dublin, in December 1880. He later became Assistant Naturalist at the Science and Art Museum.[18] During a dredging expedition as part of his zoological

14 Deborah Poole, *Vision, race and modernity: a visual economy of the Andeán image world* (Princeton, NJ, 1997), p. 8.   15 On the history of the use of images within the construction of scientific objectivity, see Lorraine Daston and Peter Galison, 'The image of objectivity', *Representations*, 40 (1992), 81–128.   16 Mary Louise Pratt, *Imperial eyes: travel writing and transculturation* (London, 1992), pp 6–7.   17 Elizabeth Edwards 'Performing science: still photography and the Torres Strait Expedition' in Anita Herle and Sandra Rouse (eds), *Cambridge and the Torres Strait* (Cambridge, 1998), pp 106–135 at 122.   18 A. Hingston Quiggin, *Haddon the Head-Hunter: a short sketch of the life of A.C. Haddon* (Cambridge, 1942),

research funded by the Fisheries Board in 1890, Haddon encountered for the first time the indigenous populations of the western seaboard and expressed his interest in the ethnology and physical anthropology of the islanders.[19] During the same voyage, he remarked of his experiences of stopping along the coast of Connemara that

> I enjoyed it immensely as it was a peep into another world and many of the ways of looking at things were very different from what I have been accustomed to. It is becoming more and more evident to me that the ordinary Saxon is incapable of understanding the typical Irish. How much less is he capable of governing him! Cut-and-dried rules and methods of procedure are useless. Theory is all very fine; the facts of Irish idiosyncrasies refuse to be treated in a logical manner and they are stubborn facts too.[20]

Although Greta Jones has stressed that Haddon's awareness of the political tensions in Ireland was tempered by his unwillingness to make any comment that may be deemed controversial within the emerging discipline of anthropology, his remarks on the governance of the Irish demonstrate the prevailing colonial discourse surrounding debates of Home Rule.[21] Despite his reservations about the Saxon's ability to comprehend and govern the Irish, and of the use of logical and reasoned methods to do so, however, the use of rigorous anthropological methods was precisely how he sought to proceed to 'unravel the tangled skein of the so called Irish race'.[22]

In 1891, in co-operation with D.J. Cunningham, professor of anatomy at Trinity College Dublin, Haddon established an Anthropometric Laboratory. The seriousness of the scientific endeavour was not in doubt, although it was paradoxically expressed in jocular terms during the official opening of the Laboratory. In his speech at the opening, the Revd Dr Houghton remarked that its work was no penny in the slot enterprise, a clear derogatory reference to the populism of Francis Galton's London Anthropometric Laboratory first established at the *International Health Exposition* of 1884, at which the public were measured and provided with a copy of their physical anthropometric details for a fee of 3*d*.[23] Despite the jibe at the populist pursuit of his scientific theories, Galton's methods and ideas cast a long shadow over the surveys of

pp 54–6. For a brief overview of the Torres Straits expedition, see Anita Herle and Sandra Rouse, 'Introduction: Cambridge and the Torres Strait' in *Cambridge and the Torres Strait*, pp 1–22.   **19** Quiggin, *Haddon the Head-Hunter*, pp 67–8.   **20** Quoted in Quiggin, *Haddon the Head-Hunter*, p. 72.   **21** Greta Jones, 'Contested territories: Alfred Cort Haddon, progressive evolutionism and Ireland', *History of European Ideas*, 24:3 (1998), 205–6.   **22** D.J. Cunningham and A.C. Haddon, 'The Anthropometric Laboratory of Ireland', *Journal of the Anthropological Institute*, 21 (1891), 35–9 at 36.   **23** Revd Dr Haughton quoted in 'The Anthropometric Laboratory Trinity College', *Irish Times*, Friday 26 June 1891, p. 4; J.S. Jones, 'The Galton Laboratory, University College London' in Milo Keynes (ed.), *Sir Francis Galton, FRS: the legacy of his ideas* (London, 1993), pp 190–4 at p. 190.

Irish race carried out under the auspices of the Dublin laboratory. Galton, the first chairman of the Ethnographic Survey of the United Kingdom, of which the Dublin laboratory was part, advised on the technical aspects of physical anthropology, and the use of photographic portraiture in the production and presentation of anthropometric data.[24] Galton's theories of hereditary faculties were largely directed towards differences in class and maintaining class formations, his theories only occasionally being mobilized towards racial difference in relation to policies of immigration, and middle-class anxieties of miscegenation.[25] Despite Galton's own lack of interest in race, his theories of the permanency and fixity of type, combined with his utilization and development of photographic methods to visually reconstruct various degenerate types was instrumental in the role of photography in the Ethnographic surveys. Galton's theories were particularly suitable to Haddon's conception of photography as an emerging method of physical anthropology.

Photographic anthropometry was well established within anthropological fieldwork by the time Haddon and Browne undertook their surveys. In 1869, both Thomas Henry Huxley and John Lamprey developed photometric methods designed to establish the photograph as a document from which quantifiable, comparative data could later be retrieved by anthropologists who never had physical contact with the subjects they were studying.[26] In Lamprey's system, the photographic image was transformed into a geometric space through the use of thread and a wooden frame to construct a vertical and horizontal grid of two-inch squares. Placing the camera a fixed distance from the wooden grid, each subject was photographed in front and side profile, so that exact measurements of body morphology could easily be calculated without having to use any additional measuring apparatus in the field. In theory, the photograph was transformed into a self-contained Cartesian space for repetitive and replicable corporeal calibration of human specimens. The photograph provided a silent and purely visual ethnographic epistemology for comparative analysis of the human races.

Galton provided fewer metric options in his instructions to the Ethnological Survey Committee reproduced by Haddon in his contribution to the photography section of *Notes and Queries*. Haddon's description of photography as an ethnographic method in this handbook of anthropology as well as in his introduction to ethnology, *The Study of Man*, demonstrate a more sophisticated approach to the use of photography within ethnographic field-work than his earlier uses of the medium in Ireland.[27] Somewhat ironically, given the static rigid poses required for photo-

24 James Urry, 'Englishmen, Celts and Iberians: the Ethnographic Survey of the United Kingdom, 1892–1899' in George W. Stocking, Jr. (ed.), *Functionalism historicized: essays on British social anthropology* (Madison, WI, 1984), p. 91.   **25** David Green, 'Veins of resemblance: photography & eugenics' in Patricia Holland, Jo Spence and Simon Watney (eds), *Photography/politics two* (London, 1986), pp 9–21 at p. 14.   **26** Frank Spencer, 'Some notes on the attempt to apply photography to anthropometry during the second half of the nineteenth century' in Edwards, *Anthropology and photography*, pp 99–107.   **27** Alfred Cort Haddon, *The study of man: an introduction to ethnology* (London and New York, 1898), pp

graphic types, he remarked that the arrangement of groups 'should be taken instantaneously so as to get perfectly natural attitudes, for it must never be forgotten that when a native is posed for photography he unconsciously becomes set and rigid and the delicate play of the limbs lost'.[28] Through a strange reversal, the body of the colonial native is inscribed as naturally predisposed to the static authority and social control embedded in the process of producing anthropological type portraits. Central to the function of the type photograph were two interwoven assumptions about the technical and discursive utility of photography to physical anthropology. One positioning the mechanical objectivity of the camera as erasing any sense of social encounter between photographer and subject turned object, despite the obvious close proximity required for the production of portraits. The second incorporating photography into existing, if somewhat fractured, relations of social power already embedded within colonial and anthropological discourse. Photography conformed seamlessly, or so it was envisaged, with the wider technical and discursive apparatus of visibility of state institutions that subjected the colonized, the poor and the dispossessed to a pervasive and scrutinizing gaze. It was through such technical and discursive practices of visibility that, as Michel Foucault observed, 'the techniques that make it possible to see induce effects of power, and in which, conversely, the means of coercion make those on whom they are applied clearly visible'.[29] The reconstruction of types through photography was thus not only positioned as the objective, dispassionate optics of modern anthropological methods, but through photography's mechanical erasure of social encounter, the racial specimens of the type photograph became mute, static figures whose epistemological value was confined to the geometric space of the photographic document.

'UNGOVERNABLE EYES': ANTHROPOLOGY AND THE PRODUCTION OF PHOTOGRAPHIC TYPES

As Christopher Pinney suggests, the histories of photography and anthropology appear to have followed similar chronological, epistemological and philosophical trajectories.[30] More astutely, he has observed that there are two possible accounts of this parallel history. The first emphasized photography's conquest of the 'world as picture', positively celebrating its unfettered transcription of reality and supposed verisimilitude in authoritatively and transparently reproducing the world presented to the camera's lens. The second acknowledged that photography's authority and position within western culture as visual knowledge and scientific 'evidence', has always been subject to contestation, its history littered with episodes in which faith

464–7. *Notes and queries in anthropology* (3rd ed., London, 1899).   **28** *Notes and queries*, p. 239. **29** Michael Foucault, *Discipline and punish* (London, 1977), pp 170–1.   **30** Christopher Pinney, 'The parallel histories of Anthropology and Photography' in Elizabeth Edwards (ed.), *Anthropology & photography, 1860–1920* (New Haven, 1992), pp 74–95 at p. 74.

in its inscriptive power has been undermined. For Pinney, similar questions of disruption and circumscribed meanings exist within the history of anthropology. The second history will be returned to momentarily, but an examination of the role of photography within Haddon and Browne's published series of articles suggests, on the surface at least, that the first narrative of photography and anthropology was predominant in their aspirations for its role in visualizing and quantifying the physical characteristics of the Irish face.

In the third section of their first published study of the ethnography of the Aran Islands, 'Anthropography', Haddon and Browne outlined in detail the methods and instrumentation used to survey the physical anthropology of the islanders.[31] This included measuring hair and eye colour to calculate the Index of Nigrescence (the degrees of melanin pigmentation in the face), a quantitative method that its inventor John Beddoe believed to reveal the ethnic and racial origins of those subjected to its calculations. This involved subtracting the number of red and fair-haired persons from that of dark haired and twice the number of black-haired, expressed by the formula $D+2N-R-F=Index$. In addition the cranial, facial and bodily measurements of the islanders were recorded to ascertain the Cephalic Index, distinguishing between *dolichocephalic* (long-headed), *mesaticephalic* (medium-headed) and *brachycephalic* (short-headed) subjects. Scientific instruments such as the 'Traveller's Anthropometer' and 'Flower's Craniometer' as well as other measuring apparatus were employed to reduce the islanders to a set of numerical figures. The peoples encountered in their journey were thus subjected to a process of calibration as they became systematically and numerically spacialized as a set of quantifiable figures, vertically and horizontally displayed for scientific scrutiny in tables and charts. This aspect of their ethnographic survey demonstrated an unwavering faith in numbers, a devotion to rigorous measurement and quantification as the guarantee of 'scientific' anthropological evidence. Significantly, photography was incorporated into this faith in measurement and quantification, not only as an instrument of calibration in its own right, but also as an anthropographic method. Calibration and photography were combined, for example, in the collection of data for the calculation of the Index of Nigrescence, as 'one of the most valuable means of obtaining the colours was the getting together of groups to be photographed or measured, and the noting both of them and of the members of the knot of spectators which was sure to assemble'.[32] In the section outlining the use of photography within the survey's methods and instrumentation of anthropography, they note the taking of thirteen full-face and side-view portraits of the subjects measured, and the promise of a photograph being a reward for 'undergoing the trouble of being measured and photographed'.[33]

Within the discursive positioning of photography among the social and physical sciences, the type photograph, in theory, was passive empirical evidence of the

---

31 Alfred Cort Haddon and Charles R. Browne, 'The ethnography of the Aran Islands, County Galway', *Proceedings of the Royal Irish Academy*, 3rd ser. (1893), 768–830.   32 Ibid., 773.   33 Ibid., 778.

outward visual appearance of social and racial character. Despite the faith demonstrated by Haddon and Browne in the photographic image as a form of pure visual epistemology, its perceived ability to depict anthropological knowledge of race through the physiognomy of the body and in particular the face, was, in fact, tied to a network of existing discourses. These discourses were not only those associated with the abstraction of the subject into a series of atomized and calibrated measurements – themselves presented as tables and charts – but also of the anthropology of racial type itself, and of the photographic image as objective, anthropological evidence.

Yet it was the significance of these very discourses to the purchase of the 'type photograph' as the visual manifestation of quantifiable, anthropological data, which in part made them so problematic.[34] The very concept of the racial 'type' within Victorian anthropology was itself a theory replete with contradictions and scientific conjecture. As George Stocking has observed, 'despite its apparently rigorously scientific approach and its constantly mounting accumulation of systematic measurement, physical anthropology carried within itself a framework of assumption rooted in the polygenist tradition' of correlating physical difference with differences in culture, intelligence and moral norms.[35] Theories of racial type were founded on the *interpretation* of the numbers generated by the qualitative methods of physical anthropology, rather than on what the numerical calibration of races revealed in themselves.[36] Although the polygenist concepts of pure race were premised on the belief that hereditary racial essence was manifest in particular parts of the body, most notably the face, the racial 'type', as a concept, functioned to define the 'parameters of race' rather than the presence of definable hereditary features in all specimens.[37] The concept of a uniquely identifiable racial type was so problematic that when American anthropologist William Ripley requested a photograph of a 'pure Alpine type of the Black Forest' from a correspondent, he was unable to acquire one, despite thousands of specimens being subjected to anthropometric measurements.[38] The concept of hereditary racial 'types', devised to overcome the impossibility of identifying individual subjects who displayed all the characteristics of racial purity, was no more successful in its endeavours, to the extent that its biggest proponent, Paul Topinard, admitted that it was at best a hypothesis, 'convenient for study, but impossible to demonstrate'.[39]

Although photography was mobilized within anthropology to visually demonstrate the persistence of hereditary racial types, it too only served to raise questions about the viability of the very science and theory that underpinned its claims to transparently present ethnographic facts. More problematic was their utilization of

34 Elizabeth Edwards, 'Photographic "Types": the pursuit of method', *Visual Anthropology*, 3 (1990), 235–58 at 256.   **35** George W. Stocking, *Race, culture and evolution*, p. 55.   **36** Stephen Jay Gould, *The mismeasure of man* (New York, 1996), p. 106.   **37** Edwards, 'Photographic "Types"', 240.   **38** Stocking, *Race, culture and evolution*, p. 58.   **39** Cited in Stocking, *Race, culture and evolution*, p. 59.

the 'type photograph' as an ethnographic method for both the collation of anthropometric data, and as the visual manifestation of quantitative anthropological methods, which contributed to the rupturing of the projected narrative in identifying distinct racial types. In their 'pursuit' of photography as anthropological method, Haddon and Browne did not so much 'present' examples of racial types as *reproduce* 'photographic types', a series of photographs that attempt to duplicate the codes and conventions of the anthropological 'type' photograph.[40] This is not to suggest that they should be categorized as examples of a proto-postmodernism, of images referencing an endless procession of other images, there is in fact more depth to their representation of the surface appearance of the Irish face. Rather, their methodological pursuit of the type photograph was designed to display the technical signs of visual ethnographic methods for a viewer who knew exactly how to read the technical information depicted within the frame of the photograph. It was this pursuit and faith in the type photograph as anthropological method that ultimately created fissures in their attempts to visualize the Irish face.

In Browne's series of ethnographic studies throughout the 1890s, the complexities of the social encounters between the observer and the observed subject in the collation of physical measurements and the visualization of the face as the visible marker of racial type, became so interwoven and contested that the series warranted increased commentary in the discussion of anthropometric methods. The series also required the use of surreptitious methods to collate ethnographic data, and necessitated the acquisition of alternative technological apparatus to visualize racial type. In the *Ethnography of Inishbofin and Inishshark*, for example, Browne notes the difficulty in obtaining data for the Index of Nigrescence as the usual gathering of spectators which assembled when photographs were taken did not occur (figs 11.1 & 11.2).[41] Despite Haddon and Browne's earlier suggestion that one of the most valuable means of collecting data on hair and eye colour was to observe the assembled group of islanders who congregated to watch the taking of photographs,[42] this example demonstrated 'the opposite effect, as the people have a strong dislike to having their portraits taken'.[43] Despite this difficulty, Browne's brother, J.M. Browne, succeeded in obtaining type portraits as well as 'a considerable number of typical groups' and views of 'modes of life and environment'.[44] In the *Ethnography of the Mullet*, Browne introduced the 'hand camera' to the repertoire of apparatus, which 'proved to be a great advantage, enabling portraits of unwilling subjects to be taken, and adding to the value of the photographs of occupations by admitting to their being taken when the performers were in motion. It could also be used on occasions when high winds would not allow the setting up of a tripod stand' (fig. 11.3).[45] The benefits of the

40 Edwards, 'Photographic "Types"', 237–43.   **41** Charles R. Browne, 'The ethnography of Inishbofin and Inishshark, Co. Galway', *Proceedings of the Royal Irish Academy*, 3rd ser. (1893), 317–70 at 322.   **42** Haddon and Browne 'Ethnography of the Aran Islands', 773. **43** Browne, 'The ethnography of Inishbofin', 322.   **44** Ibid.   **45** Charles R. Browne, 'The ethnography of the Mullet, Inishkea Islands and Portacloy, County Mayo', *Proceedings of the Royal Irish Academy*, 3rd ser. (1895), 591–2.

11.1 'The Ethnography of Inishbofin and Inishshark' (from *PRIA*, 3 (1893),
courtesy of the National Library of Ireland).

11.2 'The Ethnography of Inishbofin and Inishshark' (from *PRIA*, 3 (1893), courtesy of the National Library of Ireland).

11.3 'The Ethnography of the Mullet, Inishkea Islands and Portacaloy'
(from *PRIA*, 3 (1895), courtesy of the National Library of Ireland).

industrialization of photography, reducing, as Walter Benjamin observed, to 'one abrupt movement of the hand [. . .] a process of many steps', was further elaborated in Browne's discussion of anthropographic methods the following year.[46] Noting the addition of a half-plate Trinity tripod camera made by *Curtis Bros.* to the selection of instrumentation employed, Browne remarked that

> The value of a hand camera for field-work, as an aid to, or substitute for the heavier more slow tripod stand-camera can hardly be overrarated, as it can be employed for taking the portraits of persons who cannot be induced to get photographed by the other instruments, and it can also be used on very rough ground or in high winds, where the other camera could not be kept steady; for objects in motion, and local customs or occupations, it is invaluable.[47]

More associated with the snap-shot photography of the industrial and urban middle-class, the hand-held camera, utilized by the playwright John Millington Synge in his ethnographic travelogue *The Aran Islands*, engendered furtive scopic practices that enabled the production of photographic types without the consent of the ethno-graphic subject.[48] Technology and surreptitiousness increasingly combined in Browne's ethnographic methods to gather metric data and suitable examples of photographic types. As early as 1885, Beddoe condoned the use of elaborate ruses to measure subjects. Recounting staged debates among fieldworkers about the size and shape of their heads to be settled with his callipers: 'The unsuspecting Irishmen usually entered keenly into the debate, and before the little drama had been finished were eagerly betting on the size of their own heads, and begging to have their wagers determined in the same manner'.[49] Haddon recounts a similar episode in *The Study of Man*, when he furtively takes side and front views of a man from the west of Ireland who had never been photographed and refused to have his portrait taken (despite encouragement from his family), while he was seated in a chair being meas-ured.[50] These are likely to be the series of photographs of Tom Connelly taken

46 Walter Benjamin, 'On some motifs in Baudelaire' in Hannah Arendt (ed.), *Illuminations*, trans. Harry Zohn (London, 1992), pp 152–96 at 171.   **47** Charles R. Browne, 'The ethnography of Ballycroy, County Mayo', *Proceedings of the Royal Irish Academy*, 3rd ser. (1893–6), 76. The company to which he refers is probably Curtis Bros., 'Opticians, electrical engineers, scientific instrument makers, 10 Suffolk Street, Dublin'. Haddon's papers at Cambridge University Library contain an invoice from this company to RIA dated 30 Apr. 1894 for 1 Pullman Camera & Legs, 1/2 dozen 1/4 plates, Frames and 1 'Lunky' Camera. **48** John Millington Synge, *The Aran Islands* (Dublin, 1907). On Synge's photographs of the Aran Islands, see Justin Carville, '"My wallet of photographs": photography, ethnography and visual hegemony in John Millington Synge's *The Aran Islands*', *Irish Journal of Anthropology*, 10.1 (2007), 5–11; Justin Carville, 'Visible others: photography and romantic ethnography in Ireland' in Maria McGarrity and Claire E. Culleton (eds), *Irish modernism and the global primitive* (New York, 2008), pp 93–114.   **49** John Beddoe, *The races of Britain: a contribution to the anthropology of Western Europe* (London, 1885), p. 8.   **50** Haddon, *The study of man*, p. 463.

11.4 Haddon Collection P.7466.ACH1 (courtesy of Museum of
Archaeology and Anthropology, University of Cambridge).

during Haddon's visit to the Aran Islands and later included in his lantern slide
collection of Irish ethnology (figs 11.4 and 11.5). According to Haddon, once the
man had found out he was very pleased, and such devices became necessary to
induce country folk to submit to the technical calibration of their bodies. Such ruses
and surreptitious ethnographic methods did not, however, always prove productive.
Despite the combined furtive ocular practices of snap-shot photography and ethnographic observation, Browne expressed his frustration at only being able to obtain
measurements of thirty-eight men at Carna. The men who were obviously afraid to
'subject themselves to examination' as a result of a the connection made between
their visit and a rumour of impending war and conscription to the militia, were also
dissuaded by a local man's claims that a fairy acquaintance complained that allowing
oneself to be measured was unlucky.[51]

Haddon was perhaps correct in his observation that the Saxon was incapable of
understanding the Irish, 'much less govern him'.[52] Yet what emerges through the
resistance, intervention and subversion of the ocular practices of anthropology
detailed in Browne's reports, which Homi Bhabha might describe as 'the natives'
refusal to satisfy the colonizer's narrative demand', were what Synge identified in his
description of the primitive character as the natives 'ungovernable eyes'.[53] The groups

51 Charles R. Browne, 'The ethnography of Carna and Mweenish, in the parish of Moyruss,
Connemara', *Proceedings of the Royal Irish Academy*, 3rd ser. (1900), 505–6. **52** Quoted in
Quiggin, *Haddon the Head-Hunter*, p. 72. **53** Homi K. Bhabha, *The location of culture*
(London, 2004), p. 141; Synge's brief description of the primitive physiognomy of the Irish

11.5 Haddon Collection P.7467.ACH1 (courtesy of Museum
of Archaeology and Anthropology, University of Cambridge).

of men and women gathered to watch the metric calibration of bodies and projected
an 'oppositional gaze' and, by the silent corporeality of their look, changed the reality
of encounter between anthropologist and anthropological specimen.[54] Through their
refusal to conform to the performances of social power in front of the cameras lens,
and in their insistence in re-negotiating the visual methods of anthropology, the
subjects exhibit more active agency in the process of identify formation than the
rigorous methods of producing racial types had envisaged. The disciplined gaze of
surveillance was reflected back as the 'the displacing gaze of disciplined', the observer,
however fractured and fragmented, becoming transformed into the observed.[55]

CONCLUSION

Haddon and Browne's utilization of the 'type' photograph contributed to a visualized economy of Irish identity that continued to circulate well into the twentieth
century. Such images dominated both scientific and popular visual representations of
Ireland and the Irish, and increasingly came to equate the visual depiction of the face
with the physiognomic and cultural characteristics of race. In some cases, such as the
Ireland entry to H.N. Hutchinson's popular illustrated ethnographic encyclopaedia,

is in *The Aran Islands*, p. 92.   **54** bell hooks, *Black looks: race and representation* (Boston, MA,
1992), pp 115–31.   **55** Bhabha, *The location of culture*, p. 127.

the facial photographic portrait functioned both 'honorifically and repressively',[56] with images of rural Irish peasants combined with the commercial studio portrait of a 'type of Irish beauty'.[57] Within the colonial context of Haddon and Browne's visualization of 'photographic types', the combination of photography and practices of calibration functioned repressively as both a means of representation and as the site of social relations between the ethnographic observer and what they referred to as ethnographic 'specimens'. Yet, in their discussion of the methods of anthropography, their furtive ocular practices through new technologies of photographic production and surreptitious methods of ethnographic observation, reveal that the visible and calibrated bodies resisted the conformity and uniformity so desired by anthropological method. The attempt to turn the subject into mute object through the conflation of calibration and visualization continually interrupted by resistance to the disciplined and disciplining vision of the anthropological construction of race.

56 Allan Sekula, 'The body and the archive', *Oct.*, 39 (winter 1986), 3–64. **57** H.N. Hutchinson, *The living races of mankind: a popular illustrated account of the customs, habits, pursuits, feasts & ceremonies of the races of mankind throughout the world*, 2 vols (London, 1900).

Two visions of Irish republicanism drawn up in captivity: John Mitchel's *Jail Journal* and Michael Davitt's *Leaves From a Prison Diary*

OLIVIER COQUELIN

Writing a diary, a journal or letters while in jail for political reasons is quite a common feature of modern and contemporary times.[1] In Ireland, such phenomena manifested themselves notably through the republican movement – and most recently through some of the IRA prisoners in the Maze prison from the 1970s onwards. But the two most prominent cases undoubtedly date back to the nineteenth century; the most prominent because they paved the way for the two main leanings within modern Irish republicanism – orthodox republicanism and republican socialism, most recently epitomized in the 'provisional' and 'official' movements. These two cases actually take the form of a journal and of a diary, written in captivity by John Mitchel and Michael Davitt respectively and entitled *Jail Journal* and *Leaves From a Prison Diary*.

The goal of the present article is therefore to explain, through an ideological analysis, why these nineteenth-century political works can be regarded as major pieces of writing in modern and contemporary Irish history, and to discuss the extent to which they symbolize the inception of a culture of prison writings in the Irish republican movement. But before tackling these issues, it seems necessary to define and describe succinctly both orthodox republicanism and republican socialism.

The political doctrine of modern Irish republicanism[2] was born with the Irish

---

1 This theme was developed as part of several conferences held notably in the University of York ('Prison Writings in Early Britain', schedule available at www.york.ac.uk/crems/downloads/Prison%20Writings/conference_report.pdf accessed 3 June 2008, and in the University of Angers, France ('Récits de prison et d'enfermement [Prison and Confinement Narratives]', schedule available at www.univ-angers.fr/images/documents/Lettres/MSH/programme_colloque_prison.pdf accessed 5–7 June 2008. 2 As opposed to 'original Irish republicanism', which flourished in the 1790s through the Society of United Irishmen, who were mainly inspired by the contractual and secular dimension of the Enlightenment when fighting against what they regarded as a corrupt and illegal power held by a vast majority of Anglican landlords. The original Irish republicans had therefore a political, irenic and economic conception of national liberation based on the conquest of the Irish government for the middle classes of every religious persuasion, with the support of the lower classes, in order to liberate the Irish economy from the restrictions imposed by Britain. For a thorough

Republican Brotherhood (IRB), also known as the Fenian movement, throughout the latter half of the nineteenth century. The orthodox version of Irish republicanism aimed to establish an independent Irish republic, ideally by a strategy of 'physical force' that was a constituent part of the Irish republican tradition[3] – even though the development undertaken by the Fenians over time had led them, in certain circumstances, to consider other means to achieve their objective, at least until the 1910s.[4] In the socio-economic field, on the other hand, the orthodox Irish republicans had but a vague idea of how they would build independent Ireland. Thus, for example, while peasant proprietorship was sometimes advocated in the nineteenth century, the welfare of the peasantry, or of the people as a whole, was nonetheless subservient to national freedom. For, according to the Irish separatists, the settlement of the social and economic questions depended on the political emancipation of Ireland. This close connection between political liberation and socio-economic prosperity was in line with one of the ideological mainstays on which Irish nationalism, whether constitutional or revolutionary, had rested since the passing of the Act of Union in 1800.[5]

By contrast, as a counterpoint to this republican orthodoxy emerged fringe leftist groups standing for socio-economic upheavals within the framework of a politically liberated Ireland, a goal which they expected to achieve by combining social and political struggles of whatever nature on a revolutionary basis. Their nationalism, therefore, took on a class character, in accordance with their social conception of an Irish nation mainly embodied in the proletariat and peasantry. Hence, the name 'republican socialism' used to refer to this current of thought combining Irish republicanism with socialism,[6] the first key figure of which was undoubtedly James Connolly.[7] But, before the advent of the orthodox Fenians and the republican social-

analysis of early republicanism in Ireland, see for example Nancy Curtin, *The United Irishmen: popular politics in Ulster and Dublin, 1791–8* (Oxford, 1994); Stephen Small, *Political thought in Ireland, 1776–98: republicanism, patriotism, and radicalism* (Oxford, 2002). **3** R.V. Comerford, *The Fenians in context: Irish politics and society, 1848–82* (Dublin, 1998), pp 227, 239. **4** On the different stages of the IRB's ideological development, from the origins to the Easter Rising of 1916, see notably Owen McGee, *The IRB: the Irish Republican Brotherhood, from the Land League to Sinn Féin* (Dublin, 2005); M.J. Kelly, *The Fenian ideal and Irish nationalism, 1882–1916* (Woodbridge, 2006). **5** On this topic, see for example Olivier Coquelin, 'La Révolution conservatrice: genèse idéologique de l'Irlande politique et sociale, 1800–1923 [The Conservative Revolution: ideological genesis of political and social Ireland, 1800–1923]' (PhD, University of Rennes 2, France, 2004), pp 50–304. **6** The term 'socialism' as used here refers to those various nineteenth-century theories and doctrines aiming at collective ownership and management of the means of production, capital, land, property, etc., in the interest of the community as a whole. **7** On the origins and ideological foundations of republican socialism, see notably Richard English, 'Green on red: two case studies in early twentieth-century Irish republican thought' in D. George Boyce et al. (eds), *Political thought in Ireland since the seventeenth century* (London, 1993), pp 161–89; Olivier Coquelin, 'Lalor, Davitt et Connolly, ou l'avènement de l'aile gauche du mouvement révolutionnaire irlandais, 1846–1916 [Lalor, Davitt and Connolly, or the advent of the left wing of the Irish revolutionary movement, 1846–1916]' *LISA (Littérature, histoire des idées,*

ists on the Irish political scene, the doctrinal foundations on which their respective goals were based had been laid by two historical figures, John Mitchel and Michael Davitt, through the journal and diary they had drafted while in prison, as shall be seen below.

Mitchel was born to Presbyterian parents in Camnish, near Dungiven (Co. Derry), in 1815. A lawyer by training, he practised as a solicitor between 1840 and 1845. Meanwhile, he had engaged in political activities, as he joined Daniel O'Connell's Repeal Association in 1843. Two years later, he became associated with the Young Ireland movement and its newspaper, the *Nation*, for which he was to write a number of articles before he resigned his position as a journalist in 1847, owing to political differences. In fact, Mitchel differed from the other Young Irelanders in that he pronounced himself for radical courses of action such as armed insurrection, at least as a last resort, so as to reach Irish independence. He therefore launched his own newspaper, the *United Irishman*, in February 1848. However, the French Revolution of February 1848 contributed to the radicalization of the Young Ireland movement henceforth won over to Mitchel's goal of an independent Irish republic established by force of arms. The attempted achievement of this goal took place in July 1848 without Mitchel, due to his arrest on a charge of seditious libels, about two months before the outbreak of the abortive rebellion. He was sentenced to transportation for a fourteen year term, but escaped from the penal colony of Tasmania in 1853 and took refuge in the USA, where he was to embrace the cause of the South in the Civil War as well as that of the Fenians from 1865. He returned to Ireland in 1875 and died just a few days after he had won a by-election to become a Member of Parliament, with the support of the IRB.[8]

It was during his five years of captivity that Mitchel drafted what was to become his major piece of work, which was first published as a book in 1854 under the title of *Jail Journal*. This work can be regarded as a classic of Irish republican literature in that, in addition to the detailed accounts of Mitchel's prison life and opinions on events and individuals, it emphasizes at least three of the main doctrinal mainstays on which the orthodox version of modern Irish republicanism is based: the establishment of Irish independence by force of arms; the establishment of Irish independence under a republican form of government; and the subservience of social issues to the political and national question. These doctrinal mainstays remain features of modern Irish republicanism having nonetheless undergone development throughout its history.[9] And while they had already imbued Mitchel's political

images, sociétés du monde anglophone), Culture and society (2006), available at www.unicaen.fr/ mrsh/lisa/publications/enCours/coquelin01.pdf accessed 4 June 2008. **8** Although seven biographies of Mitchel had been published between 1888 and 1947 – see, for example, William Dillon, *The life of John Mitchel*, 2 vols (London, 1888) – it was not until the early 2000s that a new biography was written. Aidan Hegarty, *Mitchel: a cause too many* (Belfast, 2005). But the latest publication on Mitchel's life was the work of James Quinn for the Historical Association's Life and Times New Series, in 2008. James Quinn, *John Mitchel* (Dublin, 2008). **9** See note 4.

writings in both the *Nation* and the *United Irishman*, they were to take on a genuine literary dimension through his *Jail Journal*. As Arthur Griffith puts it in his preface written in the 1913 edition, 'In the political literature of Ireland it [Mitchel's *Jail Journal*] has no peer outside Swift. In the literature of the prison it has no equal.'[10]

Thus, the insurrectional aspect of Mitchel's political ideology is highlighted notably by the recurrent use of words having violent connotations towards British rule in Ireland. Words such as 'cruel', 'crime', 'criminal', 'chastise', 'punish', 'punishment', 'vengeance', 'avenge' etc., referring to a British government which, in Mitchel's language, symbolizes tyranny and injustice, as opposed to a British nation or people the best friend of whom 'is simply he who approves himself the bitterest enemy to their government, and to all their institutions, in church and state'.[11] In so doing, he quite clearly intimates that British sway in Ireland can be overthrown but by 'physical force', especially as 'to this condition [of Great Famine] had forty years of "moral and peaceful agitation" brought Ireland'.[12] This last point means that the inefficiency of constitutional agitation, as Mitchel sees it, can be regarded as a vindication of the use of arms to achieve independence, which is explicitly confirmed in the following passages:

> And, as if that were not enough, all the influence of the constitutional agitators, and, in a great measure, of the priests also, has been exerted to make the use of arms appear a sin against God. They have not been taught that it is the prerogative of man to bear arms – that beasts alone go without them … Before there can be any general arming, or aptitude to insurrection, there must first be sound manly doctrine preached and embraced. And next, there must be many desultory collisions with British troops, both in town and country … If Ireland, in '82, instead of winning her independence from the coward foe by the mere flesh of unbloody swords, had, like America, waded through carnage to her freedom, like America she had been free this day. A disastrous war even, had been better than a triumphant parade.[13]

But this is above all hatred of British supremacy, conveyed in a number of particular terms, which vindicates the use of arms in Mitchel's mind. Hatred which also stimulates the 'sound manly doctrine' that he contemplates preaching, starting with a republican principle having supposedly inspired his revolutionary designs. Except that Mitchel's republicanism, notably owing to his *a priori* inegalitarian vision of humanity,[14] quite clearly had its roots less in the political theories of the eighteenth-century philosophers than in his visceral hatred of England and her institutions. To this last point bears testimony the following extract from a dialogue between Mitchel, alias The Ego, and a fictional character called Doppelganger, who is none other than his double:

---

10 Arthur Griffith, 'Preface' in John Mitchel, *Jail journal: or, five years in British prisons* (Dublin, 1913), pp xv–xvi. 11 Ibid., p. 83. 12 Ibid., p. xlix. 13 Ibid., pp 146–7, 205. 14 On p. 84, Mitchel refers to 'the eternal inequalities of condition in human society'.

Doppelganger	I know well that you feel no antipathy to either a monarchical or an aristocratic government, as such; that, in fact, within your secret heart, you care very little about Republicanism in the abstract.
The Ego	Not a rush. What then?
Doppelganger	Then I am forced to conclude that your anxiety for the success of the French Republic[15] springs from something else than zeal for the welfare of the human race.
The Ego	A fig for the human race; to be sure it does.
Doppelganger	Yes; it is born of no love for mankind, or even French mankind, but of pure hatred to England, and a diseased longing for blood and carnage.[16]

And Mitchel, alias *The Ego*, further adds concerning aristocratic and monarchic institutions: 'I regard aristocratic and monarchic institutions … as being for the Western nations of Europe worn out … For England, for Ireland especially, I believe those institutions are far more than worn out'.[17] Mitchel's republicanism can therefore be considered more as a means to an end than as an end in itself, the end being to secede from the British Empire so as to establish an independent Irish state; an end which was to be that of the subsequent orthodox republican movement − although the original IRB was also, to quote Owen McGee, 'a revolutionary fraternal organization determined to instil into the Irish masses the ability to think and act as' citizens of a free nation,[18] '… an underground party that could accommodate diversity of political opinion',[19] provided that all members[20] shared the same supreme goal of an independent democratic republic in Ireland.

In the same vein, as early as autumn 1847, Mitchel had adopted the idea of social revolution, according to his contemporary, James Fintan Lalor − namely based on the abolition of landlordism so as to establish instead peasant proprietorship through a fair and equitable distribution of land among the Irish farmers, provided, nonetheless, that this social revolution should act as a catalyst for a mass uprising against imperial oppression. As Arthur Griffith points out in this respect, 'To Mitchel, the question of the land was a question to help Ireland to political independence. To Lalor, the political independence was a question to help the peasantry to regain the soil'.[21] But while Mitchel's idea of social revolution subservient to political revolution is not explicitly expressed in his *Jail Journal*, he alludes to it several times, as in the already quoted passage: 'Before there can be any general arming, or aptitude to

15 Mitchel refers to the French Second Republic established in Feb. 1848 as a result of an armed revolution. 16 Mitchel, *Jail journal*, p. 80. 17 Ibid. 18 McGee, *The IRB*, p. 15. 19 Ibid., p. 12. 20 And even such a major republican figure as John O'Leary, who was ideologically more inclined to foster the establishment of an Irish monarchy. Leon O'Broin, *Revolutionary underground: the story of the IRB, 1858–1914* (Dublin, 1976), p. 30. 21 Arthur Griffith, 'Preface' in James Fintan Lalor, *James Fintan Lalor: patriot and political essayist*, ed. L. Fogarty (Dublin, 1918), p. ix.

insurrection, there must first be sound manly doctrine preached and embraced. And next, there must be many desultory collisions with British troops . . .'. In addition to the principle of Irish independence under a republican form of government, we are entitled to believe that this 'sound manly doctrine' that Mitchel refers to, also includes the principle of social revolution, as he was to confirm, at least implicitly, in a letter of 1859: 'I am convinced and have long been, that the mass of the Irish people cannot be roused in any quarrel less than social revolution, destruction of landlordism, and denial of all title and tenure derived from English sovereigns'.[22] Here too, we may safely infer from all this that Mitchel's desire to destroy landlordism was motivated more by the British origins of landlordism than by any supposed endorsement of Enlightenment-inspired liberalism or socialism. Socialist doctrines and their advocates, which he utterly abhorred anyhow, were described in his *Jail Journal* as 'something worse than wild beasts'.[23] And it was notably on this last issue, relating to socialism, that Michael Davitt was to differ from the orthodox republicans in the late 1870s and early 1880s.

It was in Straide, Co. Mayo, that Michael Davitt was born into a Catholic family of small tenant farmers in 1846, the first year of the Great Famine. Evicted from their farm in 1850, the Davitts were compelled to emigrate to England, where they took up residence in the industrial town of Haslingden in Lancashire. While there, Michael Davitt largely educated himself and developed a political consciousness notably thanks to his contact with the local members of the IRB, which he joined in 1865. However, his various subversive activities eventually attracted police attention. He was arrested for illegal arms-dealing in 1870 and sentenced to fifteen years of labour servitude in Dartmoor Prison. Seven years later, he was released on ticket-of-leave, partly as a result of public pressure over his harsh treatment – especially as he had been one-armed since he was eleven, following an accident in the cotton mill of Haslingden where he had started work two years earlier.[24]

During his detention, Davitt had supposedly drawn the conclusion that the policy of 'physical force' hitherto carried out by the Fenian movement since its creation in 1858 had been in vain and inefficient. It was therefore necessary to change the republicans' strategic direction, through the creation of a mass national movement unified around the land question.[25] But while Davitt failed to convince the IRB

---

22 Quoted in Thomas Flanagan, 'Rebellion and style: John Mitchel and the *Jail journal*', *Irish University Review*, 1 (1970), 6. **23** Mitchel, *Jail journal*, p. 78. **24** T.W. Moody, *Davitt and Irish revolution, 1846–82* (Oxford, 1981), pp 3–180; T.W. Moody, 'Michael Davitt in penal servitude, 1870–77', *Studies*, 30:120 (1941), 517–30; T.W. Moody, 'Michael Davitt in penal servitude, 1870–77', *Studies*, 31:121 (1942), 16–30; Carla King, *Michael Davitt* (Dundalk, 1999), pp 10–14. **25** This is what Davitt asserted in interviews published in the *Irishman* on 14 Dec. 1878 and in the *Daily World* on 9 July 1882. It is important to note here that Davitt's assumption that he developed his new ideas while in jail is questioned notably by his contemporary, John Devoy. John Devoy, *Michael Davitt: from the Gaelic American*, eds Carla King and W.J. McCormack (Dublin, 2008, first published in instalments in the *Gaelic American* in 1906), p. 22.

Supreme Council of the merits of his designs, based on the combination of Irish self-government and land reform, Charles Parnell and his supporters in the Irish Parliamentary Party, together with some republican activists and leaders, were won over to Davitt's and John Devoy's 'new departure'.[26] As a result, the Irish National Land League was launched in October 1879 with Parnell as its president. Davitt recalled in his 1904 *Fall of feudalism*, that 'what was wanted was to link the land or social question to that of Home Rule, by making the ownership of the soil the basis of the fight for self-government'.[27] This ran counter to a republican orthodoxy relegating socio-economic issues to positions of secondary importance and seeing the English Parliament as, to quote the leading Fenian figure Charles Kickham, 'no place for an Irish patriot'.[28]

Armed with the slogan 'the Land for the People', the Land League waged a land war for over two and a half years: a land war against landlordism, to which the British government responded with a mixture of concession and coercion: concession with the adoption of the 1881 land act, which established the famous three Fs (fair rent, fixity of tenure, free sale of a tenant's interest in a property); coercion with the imprisonment of the Land League leaders, including Davitt between February 1881 and May 1882.[29]

During his second spell in prison, Davitt drafted his first major piece of work, entitled *Leaves From a Prison Diary* and published in 1885.[30] The book is composed of thirty-four lectures in which, in addition to the detailed accounts of his prison life and views on various social issues, Davitt puts forward a certain number of socio-economic proposals to be implemented in a system called 'state socialism'. In this

26 According to T.W. Moody, the real initiator of this second 'new departure' in Irish politics – the first one dating from 1873 with the Fenians' support to the Home Rule movement led by Isaac Butt – was not Davitt but John Devoy – one of the leaders of the American Fenian organization, *Clan na Gael* – who conceived it as follows: 'First, abandonment of the federal demand and substitution of a general declaration in favour of self-government; second, vigorous agitation of the land question on the basis of a peasant property, while accepting concessions tending to abolish arbitrary eviction; third, exclusion of all sectarian issues from the platform; fourth, Irish members to vote together on all imperial and home questions, adopt an aggressive policy and energetically resist coercive legislation; fifth, advocacy of all struggling nationalities in the British Empire or elsewhere'. Published in *Irishman*, 16 Nov. 1878. Also quoted in Michael Davitt, *The fall of feudalism in Ireland or the story of the Land League Revolution* (London, 1904), pp 125–6. See also T.W. Moody, 'The New Departure in Irish politics' in H.A. Cronne et al. (eds), *Essays in British and Irish history in honour of James Eadie Todd* (London, 1949), pp 303–33; Moody, *Davitt*, pp 122–3, 233–4, 249–53. **27** Davitt, *Fall*, p. 121. **28** *Irishman*, 9 Nov. 1878. **29** Moody, *Davitt*, pp 320–533; King, *Michael Davitt*, pp 22–37. **30** It is interesting to note here that, while in jail in 1881–2, Davitt had drafted another essay devoted to some of his reflections on subjects which differed, in many respects, from those developed in *Leaves*. Initially planned to be published after his release from prison, it was not until 2003 that Davitt's 'jottings' were edited for the first time by Carla King. Michael Davitt, *Jottings in solitary*, ed. Carla King (Dublin, 2003); Michael Davitt, *Leaves from a prison diary, or lectures to a 'solitary' audience* (London, 1885).

work, Davitt overtly espouses a socialist or socialistic doctrine, founded on at least three mainstays: state ownership of raw materials and railways; development of worker cooperatives regulated by the state; and land nationalization. Inspired by the American economist Henry George,[31] Davitt's project of land nationalization – whereby 'it is the annual value of the bare land, irrespective of improvements, which it is proposed to appropriate in the form of taxation'[32] – was motivated by the fact that the principle of peasant proprietorship which lay behind the Land League's slogan 'the Land for the People', actually did not concern the people as a whole, but only a portion of it – that is, the peasantry. Thus, under the system of state ownership of land, 'every individual worker would be in a position to command exactly that share of the wealth produced which he had by his labour created; while the community at large would be put in possession of that portion of the wealth produced of which it was the sole creator'.[33]

Davitt's collectivistic and socialistic designs were not to arouse great enthusiasm among the Irish people as a whole, however, and even less among an Irish peasantry eager to acquire private and individual property. As for the traditionally anti-socialist Irish nationalists, whether constitutionalist or revolutionary,[34] they disparaged Davitt's plans in particular because he conceived that they could be implemented by a British government, and therefore in a situation of national subservience to British rule. To this, Davitt was to respond in the *Times*, first, that 'I am convinced, however, that a calm consideration of the question will dissipate the idea that the nationalization of the land of Ireland is any more of a recognition of England's right to rule us than is involved in the payment of taxes or in calling upon its government to advance the necessary funds for the carrying out of a scheme of peasant proprietary'; and, second, that 'the only remedy (for the Anglo-Irish difficulty) is self-government for Ireland and the nationalization of the land under the administration of an Irish Parliament'.[35] This last point means that Davitt remained faithful to his aim based on the political and social liberation of the Irish people; a social liberation henceforward imbued with socialistic principles. Besides, this aim is quite explicitly expressed in *Leaves From a Prison Diary*, at least in the following sentence: 'Our grievance is national, as well as constitutional and social, and none but a national and constitutional remedy will suffice for its removal'.[36] As for his political objectives, while Davitt offers a pragmatic proposal for a constitution quite similar to that enjoyed by Canada at that time and likely to gain support from the nationalists of all shades of opinion,[37] he also alludes to the fact that he has not basically abandoned the idea of Irish legislative independence as 'the rational solution of the whole Irish question', as he was to write much

---

31 According to Carla King, the book that greatly influenced Davitt's writings on land nationalization, while in jail, was Henry George's *Progress and poverty*, first published in 1879. Davitt, *Jottings*, pp xxiv–xxv; Henry George, *Progress and poverty* (New York, 1998, orig. 1879). **32** Davitt, *Leaves*, p. 229. **33** Ibid. **34** There were nonetheless a few republicans with socialist leanings such as, for example, Thomas Fitzpatrick and Fred Allan who became affiliated to the IRB in 1880. McGee, *The IRB*, p. 68. **35** *Times*, 7 June 1882. **36** Davitt, *Leaves*, p. 341. **37** Ibid., pp 346–51.

later in his *Fall of feudalism*.[38] Even more unambiguous, in this respect, is the following extract from his will, which was made public shortly after his death in 1906: 'To all my friends I leave my kind thoughts, to my enemies the fullest possible forgiveness, and to Ireland my undying prayer for her absolute freedom and independence, which it was my life's ambition to try to obtain for her'.[39]

In the light of the preceding analysis, we are entitled to believe that Davitt's *Leaves From a Prison Diary* contains the doctrinal seeds of what was to be commonly called 'republican socialism' – particularly following the creation of James Connolly's Irish Socialist Republican Party (ISRP) in 1896 – the advocates of which aimed at the radical and progressive transformation of political and social Ireland, through courses of action of a pragmatic nature.[40] And this was confirmed, at least indirectly, by George Gilmore, one of the leaders of the republican socialist organization, the Republican Congress,[41] when he wrote in 1935: 'The Republican Congress was another attempt to do what Lalor and Davitt and Connolly had tried to do'.[42]

Both *Jail Journal* and *Leaves From a Prison Diary* are major pieces of writing in modern and contemporary Irish history, in that they embody some sort of ideological transition between two currents of thought within Irish republicanism – transition between original republicanism[43] and modern republicanism for Mitchel's *Jail Journal*; transition between orthodox republicanism and republican socialism for Davitt's *Leaves From a Prison Diary*. And the fact that they were drafted in jail also marked the inception of a culture of prison writings in the Irish republican movement, but a culture founded on the feature of ideological transition, as mentioned above. For this transitory phenomenon was to occur again with the 'provisional' prisoners in the Maze prison, after the 1981 hunger strikes. Thus, the ideological evolution undertaken by the IRA prisoners, whose written and oral accounts have been published in two books,[44] was to have an impact on the heterodox strategy adopted by the provisional movement in the resolution of the Northern Irish conflict from the 1990s.[45]

---

38 Davitt, *Fall*, p. 724. **39** Quoted in Devoy, *Michael Davitt*, p. 14. **40** Nowadays, republican socialism is embodied notably in the Irish Republican Socialist Party (IRSP), founded in 1974, which is guided by the belief 'that the class struggle and national liberation struggle cannot be separated . . .'. The IRSP's website is www.irsm.org/irsp/ accessed 5 June 2008. **41** The Republican Congress was a short-lived political party founded by left-wing republicans and communist activists in 1934. George Gilmore, *The Republican Congress* (Cork, 1986, orig. 1935). **42** Ibid., p. 4. Except that, in the socio-economic field, Fintan Lalor can be described more as either a radical reformer or a 'social revolutionary' – advocating a fair and equitable distribution of land among the Irish peasantry – than as a socialist, properly speaking. David N. Buckley, *James Fintan Lalor: radical* (Cork, 1990); Coquelin, 'Révolution conservatrice', pp 332–69. For a definition of socialism, see note 6. **43** See note 2. **44** Brian Campbell et al. (eds), *Nor meekly serve my time: the H-Block struggle, 1976–1981* (Belfast, 1994); Laurence McKeown, *Out of time: Irish republican prisoners, Long Kesh, 1972–2000* (Belfast, 2001). **45** This is what the former IRA volunteer and prisoner, Laurence McKeown, asserted, among other things, in the lecture he delivered during a conference held at Brest University, France, on 22–4 Nov. 2007 (schedule available at

It remains to be seen, as part of a future study, whether the letters and statements of the executed leaders of the 1916 Easter Rising, published as a book in 1971, belong to this culture of prison writings peculiar to the Irish republican movement.[46]

www.univ-brest.fr/Recherche/Laboratoire/CRBC/photo/Programme%20IRLANDE2. pdf, accessed 5 June 2008. Laurence McKeown, '"Casualties of war" or "agents of change": Irish republican prisoners, Maze/Long Kesh Prison, 1972–2000' in Olivier Coquelin et al. (eds), *Political ideology in Ireland: from the Enlightenment to the present* (Newcastle, 2009), pp 274–82. **46** Piaras F. Mac Lochlainn (ed.), *Last words: letters and statements of the leaders executed after the rising at Easter 1916* (Dublin, 2005, orig. 1971).

'Always with a pen in his hand …': Michael Davitt and the press[1]

CARLA KING

Funny, isn't it, that I am addressing the whole Irish race every week! Meetings in Ireland – letters to Canada, United States and Australia – with a word now and then to the Saxon in his own home. It is hard work.[2]

The born journalist who once tastes journalism will never, never give it up – until the knacker's day.[3]

This paper focuses on what Michael Davitt spent his adult life doing for a living – writing for the press. From 1880, when he began sending short pieces to the *Irish World*,[4] until his death in 1906, almost without a break, Davitt wrote continually, for Irish, British, American and Australian newspapers and periodicals and through his journalism, he exerted a considerable influence on public opinion at home, in Britain and among the Irish overseas.

The closing decades of the nineteenth century marked a particularly auspicious time to be a journalist and, as Davitt briefly was, an editor. The status of journalists had risen since earlier in the century, when they tended to be seen as hack writers, relaying the news and gossip of the day, to claim recognition as the 'fourth estate'.[5] There was an explosion of publishing toward the end of the century. The rise in real incomes and increased literacy, coupled with lower production costs for newspapers meant a much larger market and the number of papers produced rose to a peak in

1 I should like to thank the Board of Trinity College Dublin for permission to quote from the Davitt papers; the National Library of Ireland for permission to quote from the Mrs William O'Brien papers, the Michael McDonagh papers and correspondence between Davitt and Henry George Dixon; and the archbishop of Dublin for permission to quote from the Archbishop William Walsh papers. I am very grateful to Alan O'Day and Bill McCormack for reading and commenting on earlier versions of this article. **2** TCD MS 9521/5911, Davitt to McGhee, 18 Nov. 1883. **3** Dolf Wyllarde, *The pathway of the pioneer* (London, 1906), p. 35. **4** The *Irish World* (1870–8 and from 1878 until its closure in 1951, the *Irish World and American Industrial Liberator*) was a weekly newspaper, edited by Galway-born Patrick Ford (1837–1913) in New York. Ford, a campaigning journalist, who served his apprenticeship on William Lloyd Garrison's abolitionist newspaper, *The Liberator*, was an ardent home ruler and supporter of land nationalization. **5** George Boyce, 'The fourth estate: the reappraisal of a concept' in George Boyce, James Curran and Pauline Windgate (eds), *Newspaper history: from the 17th century to the present day* (London, 1978), pp 19–40.

1900, when 172 daily newspapers were published in Britain.[6] Each political party had its paper, some short-lived, others more enduring.

The role of the press in promoting the land and national movements in Ireland and among the Irish overseas can scarcely be overestimated. Benedict Anderson has pointed to the importance of newspapers in encouraging individuals to see themselves as part of an imagined national community, linked to people they never meet and yet whom they consider to be members of the same group.[7] In immediate terms, the press provided a means of informing their readership about the activities and aims of the Land League and National League, and the Irish Parliamentary Party.[8] Meetings were advertised and their proceedings reported at length, speeches were printed, often in full, disseminating the policies of the organization and its leaders to a local or national readership, and letters pages allowed exchange of views among readers. That modern type of social organization that Samuel Clark identified in the land war and characterized as national, associational, proactive and an 'active collectivity', is inconceivable without the press.[9] Moreover, the funding that flowed into Ireland in these years, whether for relief of distress or to help finance the land and national movements, was mostly gathered through the newspapers such as the New York *Irish World* or the Boston *Pilot*, with contributions being sent into the newspaper offices in response to appeals, and the donors and sums donated listed in its pages.

Davitt's interest in the press went back a long way. In his Fenian youth, he sent patriotic poems to an English Catholic paper, the *Universal News*, and he probably kept up with political developments by reading newspapers in the Haslingden Mechanics' Institute. Following his release from prison in 1877, he discovered his ability for public speaking but he does not appear, initially at least, to have considered journalism as a career. However, when he visited the USA on a lecturing tour in the summer of 1878, he was among newspaper men, such as James J. O'Kelly[10] and John Devoy,[11] then both on the staff of the New York *Herald*. With Devoy, he planned to establish a weekly newspaper, funded initially by the American body, Clan na Gael, to be circulated in Ireland. The proposal came to nothing and he returned to Ireland

---

6 Deian Hopkin, 'The socialist press in Britain, 1890–1910' in Boyce, Curran and Windgate (eds), *Newspaper History*, pp 294–306.   **7** Benedict Anderson, *Imagined communities: reflections on the origin and spread of nationalism* (2nd ed., London, 1991), pp 35–6, 92–4, 119–20.   **8** The Irish National Land League was inaugurated on 17 Oct. 1879 with the aim of securing a reduction in rents and establishing a peasant proprietary in Ireland. It was proclaimed in Oct. 1881. The Irish National League was established on 17 Oct. 1882 to provide popular support for the Irish Parliamentary Party, led by Charles Stewart Parnell. It was subsumed into the United Irish League following reunification of the Irish Parliamentary Party in 1900. The Irish Parliamentary Party was founded by Isaac Butt in 1874. From 1880, Parnell formed it into a formidable national phalanx in the House of Commons and the first recognizably modern political party in Britain or Ireland.   **9** Samuel Clark, *Social origins of the Irish Land War* (Princeton, NJ, 1979).   **10** James J. O'Kelly (1845–1916), war correspondent and Parnellite politician.   **11** John Devoy (1842–1928), Irish-born Fenian, he spent most of his adult live in the USA, where he was an influential figure and journalist among the Irish-American community.

where, from early in 1879, he was engaged in promoting the land movement, and while this work yielded no income, it put him in the centre of things, from which he contributed letters for the *Irish World* of New York. Thus was his career as a journalist launched almost accidentally, and yet Davitt had some of the instincts of a journalist. He hoarded impressions and ideas in journals and diaries, kept press-cuttings and was an avid reader of newspapers and periodicals.

This was an era of campaigning journalism, and Davitt's writing was in that style. There was no effort at objectivity, though there was concern to establish accuracy. His articles were in the form of letters, signed by him, providing accounts of events, but also his analyses and arguments. What editors sought from him is today referred to as the 'opinion piece'. Quite a few Irishmen of his day were making a name in journalism, including T.P. O'Connor and J.L. Garvin in Britain, and Patrick Ford, John Boyle O'Reilly and John Devoy in the USA, and it is striking how many among the figures of the Irish movement were journalists, either part-time or full-time: Justin McCarthy (1830–1912), William O'Brien (1852–1928), T.P. Gill (1868–1931), T.M. Healy (1855–1931), Tim Harrington (1851–1910), J.J. O'Kelly (1845–1916), Frank Hugh O'Donnell (1848–1916) and Arthur Griffith (1871–1922), among others. Moreover, there was quite a close connection between journalism and membership of parliament, with twenty-nine MPs in the House of Commons in 1892 listing their main occupation as 'journalist'.[12]

Once he had opted for a career in journalism, Davitt had to seek out work. It was poorly paid and labour intensive: one friend remembered him as always with a pen in his hand. His responsibility as secretary of the Land League was unpaid and his ceaseless lecturing around Ireland and Britain was generally on the basis that his expenses would be covered. Only when on lecture tours in the USA or Australia, would he earn part of the takings. But one gets the impression from his diaries that he much preferred writing to public speaking. Lecture tours were physically gruelling; he would be constantly on the move from one place to the next, addressing audiences every evening, or sometimes twice or three times a day, but also by the nature of this work he would be required to say much the same thing over and over, only tailoring some of each speech to the local audience. In his journalism, on the other hand, he could react to events and issues as they arose, and had much more scope for reflection and analysis.

In August 1882, he became correspondent to the *New York Daily News*, his first letter responding to the news of Fanny Parnell's death (he had visited her in Bordenstown the week before). His letters describe the situation in Ireland in the aftermath of the Land League, and recount efforts to establish a replacement organization, which finally bore fruit in the form of the Irish National League.[13] The articles ceased in December, however, when the editor tried to cut his fee. In any case, he was facing back into another prison term for a speech he made in Navan on

---

12 Alan J. Lee, *The origins of the popular press in England, 1855–1914* (London, 1976), p. 294, table 32.   **13** TCD MS 9602/62–82. Letters to the *New York Daily News*.

26 November 1882, for which he had been prosecuted under the Crimes Act. On his release, in June 1883, he fired off applications to the managing editors of ten different newspapers in the USA and Canada, offering a weekly letter on Irish affairs at the rate of $50 per four letters and calculating in his diary what his annual income would be if all or only some of them agreed to the arrangement.[14] Not all of them did, but by the end of August he wrote to a supporter that he had not been so hard worked since the Land League days.[15]

This was also insecure employment. While there were a large number of news-papers, they tended to come and go. In 1883, however, he began writing for the *Melbourne Advocate*, and his friendship with its editor, Joseph Winter, endured for the rest of his life. His contributions to the paper were fairly regular, even though the income from this too could fluctuate. In November 1885, he also commenced a series of weekly articles in the Dublin *Evening Telegraph*, the evening paper of the *Freeman's Journal*, entitled 'About Our Artisans and Their Industries'.[16] In the first of these, devoted to 'Dublin shipwrights', Davitt referred to complaints that over the previous years little attention had been paid to the plight of artisans, compared to the issue of tenant farmers. He addressed specific industries, such as 'Glass bottlemaking', 'Cork-cutting', 'Engineering, Shipbuilding &c.', but then he turned to more general issues, such as the rackrenting of city dwellers. He urged them to take matters into their own hands and organize along the lines of the Land League.[17] This was a modern style of journalism, including individual examples of hardship, in the pattern of W.T. Stead's famous 'muckraking' investigations. The articles provoked a lively debate in the letters pages of the *Evening Telegraph* and elsewhere, on the subjects of Dublin's industrial decline and housing conditions, and suggestions for remedies and probably prompted his election as a town councillor for Arran Quay Ward in Dublin.[18]

Despite his public prominence and immense popularity, it is quite striking that Davitt rarely had any regular work as a journalist with a British or an Irish paper. When Parnell launched the weekly *United Ireland*, edited by William O'Brien, there seems to have been no attempt to employ him. O'Brien's wife, Sophie, voiced what may have been an opinion shared by her husband, when she wrote '... [a]s to most of Davitt's writing it was dull and newspaper work was not in his line – especially when he took pains. It grew pedantic, but what he dashed off was often the most witty and amusing.'[19] Davitt's writing certainly wasn't in O'Brien's more florid style,

---

14 TCD MS 9538/28, Diary 16 June 1883. The newspapers were: *New York Daily News*, *Philadelphia Times*, *Cincinnati Commercial*, *Chicago Tribune*, *New Orleans Times*, *Denver Herald*, *St Paul Daily Globe*, *San Francisco Chronicle* and *Montreal Post*. **15** NLI, MS 9697/68. Davitt to H.G. Dixon, 30 Aug. 1883. **16** The *Evening Telegraph* was published from 1871 to 1924. It was attached to the *Freeman's Journal* and worked out of its office in Prince's Street, beside the General Post Office, in Dublin. **17** *Evening Telegraph*, 17 Dec. 1885; copy in TCD MS 9607/8–9. **18** Carla King, 'Michael Davitt, the *Evening Telegraph* and Dublin Corporation, 1885–6', *Dublin Historical Record*, 40:2 (autumn 2007), 196–207. **19** NLI 8507(3) fo. 9. Mrs William O'Brien papers.

but the real reason for his avoidance of him is more likely to have been political. The leaders of Parnell's movement were almost unanimous in their opposition to Davitt's support for Henry George's policy of land nationalization. The trajectory of the Irish National League from its foundation in October 1882 and of the Irish Parliamentary Party following the Kilmainham Treaty, was to the right, where as Davitt's politics were more radical.

Increasingly sidelined in Irish politics, Davitt began the year 1884 with a scheme to set up a weekly of his own, to be called *Land and Liberty*. His problem was how to raise the necessary finance to establish it. A meeting with contacts in Belfast yielded little but in October, Davitt's hopes were raised again, with plans for a weekly halfpenny paper, to be called *The Democrat* based in London, in collaboration with Helen Taylor (John Stuart Mill's stepdaughter), and William Saunders, both members of the Democratic Federation and an associate of theirs, Charles Durant, a London printer and later a Labour Party candidate. It eventually emerged that the other participants intended Saunders, not Davitt, to be the editor,[20] and he was not directly involved with the *Democrat*, launched in November 1884, although the paper remained sympathetic to him.[21] In undertaking a lecture tour in the USA in the autumn and winter of 1886, he hoped to raise funds for a newspaper, but he realized half way through that it would not provide sufficient money to make this possible.[22]

Apart from the *Democrat*, the British radical paper to which Davitt remained closest in the 1880s was the *Pall Mall Gazette*, edited from 1883 to 1889, by its campaigning editor, W.T. Stead. Davitt and Stead respected each other's social radicalism and commitment to reform, and developed a lasting friendship.

When the editor of the *Freeman's Journal*, Edward Dwyer Gray died in March 1888, Archbishop Thomas Croke wrote to Davitt, suggesting that he would like to see him succeed to the post, but warning that his ideas might be considered 'very advanced'.[23] Davitt immediately wrote to Archbishop Walsh, a member of the Board, seeking his endorsement, citing in support of his application the fact that he was a substantial shareholder in the company, that he was an experienced journalist who had also worked in his youth as a printer, and that he had 'a fair business training in connection with public companies'. He expressed himself willing to abandon the public platform if appointed and to run the paper along the 'present lines'.[24] He applied for the post but was later to discover that his way had been blocked by Parnell, who had indicated to the principal director of the paper, Alderman Kernan, that the candidate should enjoy the support of the Irish people as a whole, should 'commend himself to the class from whom the shareholders are largely taken' (not be too radical) and should possess sufficient journalistic experience and prudence for

20 TCD MS 9541/51 Diary, 9541/52, 14 Oct.; 10 Oct.; 9541/54, 28–9 Oct. 1884.   **21** Lee, *Origins of the popular press*, p. 139.   **22** TCD MS 9545, Diary, 25 Sept. 1886.   **23** TCD MS 9334/276, Croke to Davitt, 31 Mar. 1888.   **24** Dublin Diocesan Archives, Walsh Papers, Ref. 403/4–6, Shelf 360, 1888, Davitt to Walsh, 1 Apr. 1888.

the successful undertaking of the paper.[25] In the event, the directors decided to hold the job for Gray's son, who, it was hoped, would take over the post at a later date.[26]

Eventually, Davitt did get the opportunity to run his own paper, the *Labour World*, in the autumn of 1890. What may have strengthened his resolve to risk it at this time was an appreciation of the need for newspapers to press for a radical/Irish agenda. Following the split in the Liberal Party over the first home rule bill in 1886, most of the London newspapers were opposed to granting home rule for Ireland. Moreover, Davitt, who had played a crucial role in defending the Irish movement in the hearings of the Special Commission on Parnellism and Crime, would have been acutely conscious of the need for some pro-Irish voice in the London press. There is a parallel to be drawn here with T.P. O'Connor, who founded his evening newspaper, *The Star*, for cognate reasons and aimed at a similar readership in 1886. However, O'Connor had considerable political and some financial backing from within radical liberalism, whereas Davitt did not.[27]

Davitt had been planning to launch his paper since early in the year, jokingly referring to it as the *Weekly Earthquake*, and writing to John O'Connor Power that

> My friends here [in Ireland] are divided in opinion on the advisability of my project. The sagest of them thinks that Parnell & Co. will consider such an organ – although published in London – as a menace to their influence, and he believes they will try their best to ruin it. Others of my friends think I should go ahead, as the time is most favourable.[28]

The paper's political orientation was to be independent but, he wrote, 'its support will be freely given to the Liberal Party in such policy or legislation as shall have for object the social and industrial improvement of the working classes'.[29] However, when the radical MP, Charles Dilke, offered to buy shares in the paper, Davitt informed him that they had all been taken up.[30] This appears to have been untrue. Davitt himself owned 400 of the shares and took a further 200 when the share capital of the company was increased from £5,000 to £10,000 in September, a position that left him with a heavy liability when the paper ultimately failed. His refusal of assistance from Dilke may have arisen from a determination to preserve his paper's independence.

The *Labour World* was published in London, with an office on the Strand, the first edition appearing on Sunday, 21 September 1890. All Davitt's idealism, indeed naiveté, is evident in the paper – it was obviously the product of years of yearning to

25 Emmet Larkin, *The Roman Catholic church and the Plan of Campaign, 1886–1888* (Cork, 1978), pp 192–3. See also Laurence Marley, *Michael Davitt, freelance radical and frondeur* (Dublin, 2007), pp 100–1. **26** Felix M. Larkin, '"A great daily organ": the *Freeman's Journal*, 1763–1924', *History Ireland*, 14: 3 (2006), 44–9. **27** Ian Sheehy, 'T.P. O'Connor and *The Star*' in D. George Boyce and Alan O'Day (eds), *Ireland in transition, 1867–1921* (London, 2004), pp 76–91. **28** NLI MS 11,445, Davitt to O'Connor Power, 28 Feb. 1890. **29** Ibid. **30** British Library, Dilke Papers, Add. 43914, fo. 270, Davitt to Dilke, 19 Sept. 1890.

edit his own paper. It was extremely ambitious: sixteen packed pages – and attempted to cover a great deal, including items from overseas. In the first edition alone, there were such wide-ranging articles as 'The workmen in Rome', 'Anarchist riot in Genoa', 'Chinese colonists in Russia', 'The workers in Belgium', 'Canadian crops', 'Notes from the Far West' (of the USA), a piece about a grain and cotton store destroyed by fire in Alexandria and a report of rioting in Sydney. There were short entries on 'Labour in London' and 'Lancashire notes' and an article on labourers in Ulster. There were items translated from French newspapers, and Davitt drew on local information and articles submitted by a wide range of friends and associates. Apart from the week's news and political events, the paper included labour news, short stories, poems, historical essays, theatre reviews, book reviews, publishers' lists, notices of forthcoming meetings and a letters page. Women readers were addressed in a weekly column, 'Among women workers', by 'Edith', which catered to working women, and there was some sports coverage. Clearly, for the amount of reading provided, at a penny a week the paper was very good value. In terms of its focus, although Irish issues were covered, the *Labour World* was considerably more labour than Irish, and was aimed at a general working-class readership, rather than the Irish in Britain. He even succeeded in attracting a respectable amount of advertising. The paper was well received and in the second number, Davitt had to apologize to the large number of potential readers who had been unable to obtain copies and 60,000 copies of the second issue were printed.

Davitt had worked for American newspapers and was well aware of the new journalism and its innovative reporting, which he applied to some degree in his paper in the range of the items covered and more personal tone adopted. He could never have afforded the new technology of photographs but he did include drawings. The first issue of the paper publicized the programme of the Irish Labour Federation, the organization of agricultural labourers that Davitt had helped to launch in January 1890, alongside an obituary of John Boyle O'Reilly, editor of the Boston *Pilot* and an old friend of Davitt. Meetings of the Irish Labour Federation, British trade union activities and London radical and socialist gatherings were regularly covered in the paper. Keir Hardie pointed out that in 1890 the *Labour World* was one of only three Labour papers in existence, the other two being his own *Labour Leader*, which appeared monthly, and the *Labour Tribune*, a miners' paper.[31] Davitt's Russian biographer, Valeria E. Kunina, noted the importance of the paper in supporting the message of new unionism. She cited the example of James Sexton, a Liverpool Irish docker, originally an Irish nationalist, who transferred his support to trade unionism at the time of the Parnell crisis and later became a founder member of the Independent Labour Party. She quotes Sexton's memoirs, in which he recalled the influence of Davitt's *Labour World* on the development of his ideas.[32]

31 J. Keir Hardie, 'Michael Davitt I: the Democrat', *Socialist Review* (Aug. 1908), 410–17, reproduced in *Lives of Victorian political figures*, vol iii, ed. C. King (London, 2007), pp 380–7. **32** Valeria E. Kunina, *Maikl Devitt, syn irlandskogo naroda, 1846–1906* (Moscow, 1973), pp 132–3; James Sexton, *Sir James Sexton, Agitator* (London, 1936), pp 107, 127; Henry Pelling,

One senses Davitt's freedom in his ability to express his political opinions without worrying about what the editor might think. There was in the first issue an analysis of what Londoners were paying annually in ground rent (Davitt calculated it at £15 million). Politically, more potentially explosive was a series of articles examining the role of police *agents provocateurs*, written by Davitt, which ran from the second issue. Entitled 'Pigott and his patrons!', its subtitle, 'Unionism and crime' echoed that of *The Times*' attack on Parnell in 1887. The series traced the career of James 'Red Jim' McDermott of Brooklyn, who had organized dynamite plots in Cork and Liverpool in the spring of 1883, apparently using money provided by the British Consul-General of New York and officials of Dublin Castle. Davitt claimed that he had duped would-be conspirators, Featherstone, Deasy and others, and then handed them over to the police, and he demanded a public enquiry into the matter.[33]

Editing the paper was very hard work, and on the night the first edition was printed, Davitt complained to his friend, Richard McGhee that the anxiety associated with it was the most trying and troubling experience of his life.[34] Two weeks later, he confided to McGhee, 'I am ... worried almost to death by the infernal printers. It was only by the skin of the teeth, I got out my edition on Thursday night. There seems to be no help for it, but to grin and bear it. I am learning something of the tyranny of Trades Unionism.'[35] But these were essentially teething troubles, and on the whole, Davitt's relationship with the staff was good. So why was the paper so short-lived? – it only survived until May 1891. What seems to have caused its downfall was a piece of bad luck; Davitt firmly believed that he was dogged by it. The paper commenced publication in September. Less than three months later came the Parnell split. In fact, Davitt was the first to call publicly for Parnell's resignation, in an editorial entitled 'Mr Parnell's position'. Almost immediately came the Kilkenny by-election, and Davitt, having nailed his colours to the mast, took an important part in the fray. He also played an active (some might say scurrilous) role in the north Sligo by-election campaign in March-April 1891. By January, he was overcome by illness and put the newspaper in the hands of a manager, Charles Diamond, who somewhat blunted the radical edge of the paper. However, the combined effects of the alienation of readers by the paper's partisanship of the anti-Parnellite side, and the sheer demands on Davitt's time as a result of his participation in the battle resulted in its eventual demise. His health gave out again and this is the reason he gave for his resignation in his final editorial on 2 May. He handed over the editorship to Henry Massingham, a Fabian with an interest in Irish issues, but only three more editions of *Labour World* appeared before it folded at the end of May.[36]

Origins of the Labour Party (Oxford, 1965), p. 199.   **33** *Labour World*, 27 Sept. 1890, editorial, p. 3.   **34** TCD MS 9328/181/10, Davitt to McGhee, 18 Sept. 1890.   **35** TCD MS 9328/181/11, Davitt to McGhee, 4 Oct. 1890.   **36** Massingham went on to become editor of the *Daily Chronicle* and to build a career as a well-known, socially conscious editor and man of letters. See Alfred F. Havighurst, *Radical Journalist: H.W. Massingham, 1860–1924* (Cambridge, 1974); and H.W. Nevinson and A.J.A Morris, 'Henry William Massingham (1860–1924)' in H.C.G. Matthew and Brian Harrison (eds), *Oxford Dictionary of National*

The paper's failure meant that Davitt had to seek work as a journalist once more. He resumed his fortnightly letters to the *Melbourne Advocate* and contributed to a variety of other American and British Liberal newspapers, notably the London radical *Daily Chronicle* and the *Westminster Gazette*. The *Daily Chronicle*, edited by A.E. Fletcher, was noted for its campaigns for social reform, and was to the left of Liberal journalism, the most radical of the London morning papers,[37] Fletcher later becoming a parliamentary candidate for the Independent Labour Party in 1895. He was succeeded as editor by Henry Massingham, and Davitt's contributions to the paper continued. The *Westminster Gazette*, founded in 1892 as a heavyweight Liberal paper, was edited by J.A. Spender, nephew of William Saunders of the *Democrat*. Spender was somewhat less radical than his uncle and he and Davitt clashed in autumn 1897 over the *Westminster Gazette*'s criticisms of the McKinley government in the USA.[38] Nevertheless, Davitt contributed further articles to the paper at intervals. He also wrote a series for the New York *Sun* called 'Home Rule Notes', but had to abandon it in 1895 when he embarked on a ten-month lecture tour of Australia.

As his interest in overseas affairs grew, Davitt repeatedly challenged imperial policies in the House, his new focus partly reflected, to some extent, in his journalism. Shortly after the outbreak of the Boer War in October 1899, he resigned his seat in protest against its conduct and travelled to South Africa in February 1900 as a war correspondent for William Randolph Hearst's *New York American Journal* and the *Freeman's Journal*. He spent three months travelling around the Boer Republics, eventually publishing a book about the war, largely based on his articles.[39]

Another aspect of Davitt's writing for the press was his contribution to Liberal reviews. These published long articles and essays on topics of the day and provided a forum for debate of a more detailed and reflective kind than letters to the press. The years between 1865 and 1914 marked a peak of influence of the monthlies and quarterlies, and as John Mason points out, this era of political journalism saw 'the creation of a new, self-conscious intelligentsia'.[40] Between Davitt's first contribution to the *Contemporary Review* in August 1883 and his last, to the *Independent Review*, in April 1905, at least twenty-one articles in reviews were definitely authored by him, although there may have been more, as articles in nineteenth-century reviews were not always signed.[41] Of these, four were written for Percy Bunting's *Contemporary Review*, the first, on 'The punishment of penal servitude', was penned when he was actually in jail, this time in Richmond Prison in Dublin.[42] Under Bunting's editor-

Biography, 37 (Oxford, 2004).   **37** Lee, *Origins of the popular press*, p. 162.   **38** British Library, Spender Papers, Add. 46391, fos 18019, Davitt to Spender, 24 Aug. 1897 and TCD MS 9348/534, J.A. Spender to Davitt, 27 Aug. 1897.   **39** Michael Davitt, *The Boer fight for freedom from the beginning of hostilities to the Peace of Pretoria* (New York and London, 1902).   **40** John Mason, 'Monthly and quarterly reviews' in Boyce, Curran and Wingate (eds), *Newspaper History*, pp 281–93.   **41** For the text of Davitt's articles in reviews, see *Michael Davitt: Collected writings, 1868–1906*, ed. C. King (Bristol, 2001), vol. 1 'Pamphlets, speeches and articles, 1868–1888', and vol. 2, 'Pamphlets, speeches and articles, 1889–1906.   **42** Articles published in the *Contemporary Review* include 'The punishment of penal servitude'

ship, the journal offered a platform on social reform issues, and spanned the political space between radical liberalism and socialism. The largest number of Davitt's articles, however (eight in all) were submitted to the *Nineteenth Century*.[43] This journal, edited by James Knowles from its foundation in 1877 until 1908, was one of the most popular and prestigious of its day. Contributors varied widely in political outlook, but the main trend of what John Mason terms '[t]his famous Victorian debating society'[44] was moderate Liberal. One of Davitt's articles was published in *To-Day*, the monthly magazine of the Social Democratic Federation, edited by its secretary, H.H. Champion. Published in April 1884, it provided a detailed critique of the 1881 Land Act and the policy of land purchase.[45] Two articles appeared in *The Speaker*, a London-based political weekly, on which the nationalist historian R. Barry O'Brien served as assistant editor. One, 'Le Caron's (re-published) story', was a heavily sarcastic attack on the memoir of Thomas Miller Beach (alias Le Caron), a government spy.[46] The other, 'Home Rule and Labour Representation', defended the Irish Parliamentary Party's support of the Liberal Party against suggestions that it was neglecting the cause of labour.[47] In 1905, he came out with a fantasy account of 'The Irish National Assembly (session of 1910)', which appeared in the *Independent Review*, a British radical review, published by T. Fisher Unwin.[48] Two of Davitt's articles were published in French magazines: the *Review de Famille* and *Minerva*. In the first, 'La question d'Irlande', he set out to explain Ireland's case for home rule to French readers and went on to discuss the Parnell split and Ulster unionist opposition to home rule.[49] The second, 'Les États-Unis et l'Europe', expressed Davitt's opposition to Anglo-American rapprochement and what he saw as British domination of American foreign policy, urging that Europeans and Americans should pursue closer relations with each other. Only one long article appeared in an Irish journal: Davitt's response to an article by Standish O'Grady, entitled 'Irish conservatism and its outlooks', published in *Dublin University Review* in August 1885. O'Grady had chastised Irish landlords for failing in their role as reformers and natural leaders of society.[50] The editor, Charles Oldham, invited Davitt to respond, which he did in the

---

(Aug. 1883), 'Mr Giffen and the Irish question' (Apr. 1886), 'The Irish landlords' appeal for compensation' (Apr. 1888), and 'Remedies for Irish distress' (Nov. 1890). These and the other articles referred to are reprinted in *Michael Davitt: Collected writings, 1868–1906*, vols 1 and 2, ed. C. King.   **43** Articles published in the *Nineteenth Century* include 'The report of the Parnell Commission' (Mar. 1890), 'Retiring the landlord garrison' (May 1890), 'The latest Midlothian campaign' (Nov. 1890), 'Impressions of the Canadian North-West (Apr. 1892), 'The priest in politics' (Dec. 1893), 'Fabian fustian' (Dec. 1893) and 'The evicted tenants' problem' (Apr. 1894).   **44** Mason, 'Monthly and quarterly reviews', pp 281–93.   **45** 'The Irish social problem', *To-Day*, 1:4 (Apr. 1884), 241–55.   **46** Thomas Miller Beach, *Twenty-five years in the Secret Service; the recollections of a spy, by Major Henri le Caron* (London, 1892). Davitt's review was published in *The Speaker*, 29 Oct. 1892, 521–4.   **47** 'Home Rule and labour representation', *The Speaker*, 28 Apr. 1892, 465–6.   **48** 'The Irish National Assembly (Session of 1910)', *The Independent Review*, 5 (Apr. 1905), 284–98.   **49** 'La question d'Irlande', *Revue de Famille* (1 Sept. 1892), 394–409.   **50** Standish O'Grady, 'Irish conservatism and its outlooks', *Dublin University Review*, Aug. 1885, 4–15.

September edition. In his reply, also entitled 'Irish conservatism and its outlooks', Davitt argued that O'Grady's aim of saving Irish landlordism was a vain hope since they were a moribund class.[51]

Davitt's contributions to journals to a large degree reflect his political position, not only in their content, but also in the organs in which they were published. While recognizing that he probably contributed more to British journals than to Irish ones because they paid, it is clear that he functioned within a radical liberal milieu, with some leanings towards socialism, while his Irish nationalism and his interest in the broader world added important other dimensions.

Davitt's journalism never earned him a comfortable living, and he remained comparatively poor until the final years of his life. He picked up work where he could, as in 1900, when T.P. O'Connor passed to him an offer of employment on the American paper, the *Cosmographic*. O'Connor had been asking £10 for a 1,200-word fortnightly letter, and the paper's editor, Julius Chambers, would not offer more than five guineas, but Davitt was willing to work for this sum until May, when the paper was in arrears with even this payment and he stopped sending letters. In 1903, William Randolph Hearst (1863–1951), the American newspaper magnate, sent him to investigate the Kishinev pogrom that broke out in the town on Easter Sunday, amid scenes of great brutality in which fifty-one Jewish inhabitants were killed and at least 424 were injured.[52] His role in establishing what had happened and who was responsible, and his call for international assistance for the victims, were important in drawing attention to the issue, and he followed up his articles with a book, *Within the Pale: the True Story of Anti-Semitic Persecutions in Russia*.[53] The London editor of Hearst's *New York American Journal* tried to persuade him to travel to Bulgaria for a month later in 1903, but he declined, being anxious to finish his book.[54] In 1904 and 1905, he returned to Russia, again at Hearst's request, in the first instance to cover Russian responses to the Japanese war and to interview Leo Tolstoy, and in the second, to comment on Bloody Sunday and its aftermath.

Once the *Labour World* folded, it seemed as if Davitt was unlikely to run his own paper again. Yet, in the final months of his life he had planned to establish one. His conflict with the Irish Catholic hierarchy over the education question had deepened and he was denounced in Lenten pastorals in 1906, the *Freeman's Journal* refusing to publish his reply. He became convinced of the need for a paper that would provide a voice of opposition to both the official line of the Irish Parliamentary Party and the increasingly vociferous Irish-Irelandism of Griffith and Moran and he planned to establish a paper to be called the *Irish Democrat*, perhaps echoing the title of Saunders' *Democrat*. However, Davitt died before it could be launched.

51 'Irish conservatism and its outlooks', *Dublin University Review*, Sept. 1885, 94–108. 52 C. King, 'Michael Davitt and the Kishinev Pogrom, 1903', *Irish Slavonic Studies*, 17 (1996), 19–43. 53 Michael Davitt, *Within the Pale: the true story of anti-Semitic persecutions in Russia* (New York and London, 1903). 54 TCD MS 9480/4579–83, letters from E.F. Flynn to Davitt, Sept. 1903.

To conclude, it is worth asking what role Davitt's journalism played at the time. His writing was aimed at several distinct readerships: the Irish at home; the British working class; the Irish in America; the Irish in Australia; and the British and Irish intelligentsia. His letters and articles reflected preoccupations with issues of justice – for the poor, the exploited, prisoners' rights and questions of national self-determination, to name a few. These resonated with British radical circles increasingly concerned with great humanitarian issues of the day. To the British readerships, he presented the Irish question in these humanitarian terms, but also sought to build bridges between the Irish and the British working class on the basis that their enemies were the same. For the Irish, both at home and abroad, he was positing within Irish nationalism a counter-culture to the prevailing Parnellism in Parnell's time, and later to the narrower ideology of Irish-Ireland. While he never sought to challenge Parnell's leadership or the fundamental ideas of the Party *tout court* prior to the Parnell split, the ideas he expressed were considerably more radical, secular and focused socially as well as politically, more open to international trends and issues than the dominant nationalist orthodoxies. His articles for American and Australian papers aimed to keep the Irish abroad in touch with developments at home, to create that consciousness of a wider identity that Davitt sought to promote. Perhaps his concern with working-class issues spoke more directly to the Irish abroad, many of whom were living urban, working-class lives, than the inward-looking nationalism that had emerged by the time of his death.

Sources for the history of the Irish poor law in the post-Famine period[1]

VIRGINIA CROSSMAN, GEORGINA LARAGY, SEÁN LUCEY & OLWEN PURDUE

The popular view of the Irish poor law is dominated by the image of the workhouse. Built according to a standard plan, Irish workhouses were imposing structures that became a significant architectural feature of the Irish countryside. As one writer noted in 1859, 'the first intimation of approach to any town or district of considera- tion, is the appearance on rising ground of the Tudor gables and lattice windows of the Union Workhouse'.[2] Prior to the Great Famine (1845–52), relief was only avail- able within the workhouse. Under the threat of mass starvation, the system was extended in 1847 to allow poor law boards to grant outdoor relief to the sick and disabled, and to widows with two or more legitimate children. The able-bodied, however, were still required to enter the workhouse in order to receive relief unless the workhouse was full or a site of infection. In the immediate post-Famine period, most boards of guardians sought to minimize outdoor relief, accepting the official view that this form of relief was expensive and demoralizing. As the century continued, however, numbers on outdoor relief rose and from the 1880s, relief outside the workhouse became an accepted element of the relief system in many unions.

Despite considerable local interest in the workhouse system, particularly during the Famine, the operation of the poor law remains under-researched and poorly understood. With so much attention focusing on the Famine, there is little awareness of the extent to which the system changed over the period of its operation. This limited awareness reflects the relatively under-developed state of social history in Ireland, but not, it should be emphasized, a lack of source material. As this chapter seeks to demonstrate, examination of the relevant sources can shed light not only on the relief system and those who used and administered it, but on wider issues of social and political change. This paper is divided into three sections, each of which takes as its focus a different part of the country and a different kind of source material. The first surveys poverty and poor relief in the western seaboard through an examination of boards of guardians' minute books and local newspapers. The second explores patterns of relief in the north, as revealed by workhouse registers, and the third employs a comparative analysis of workhouse registers and census returns to investi- gate poor relief in two southern unions.

---

1 This chapter draws on research generated by the ESRC project 'Welfare regimes under the Irish poor law 1850–1921'. **2** 'Begin at the beginning', *Irish Quarterly Review*, 8 (Jan. 1859), 1081.

POOR LAW ADMINISTRATION IN THE WEST OF IRELAND

Ranging from the northern Inishowen union in Co. Donegal to the southern Skibbereen union in Co. Cork, twenty-nine poor law unions had a western seaboard. This region corresponded with the poorest areas in the country and was marked by a small farm economy and low-value agricultural land. Frequent economic downturns and extreme distress on the western seaboard often placed the poor law system to the forefront of the concerns and needs of local society and 'by the end of the nineteenth century, emergency relief had become an integral element of the economy and culture of the west'.[3] Furthermore, the highly politicized nature of the region, particularly during the anti-landlord and nationalist agitations of the late 1870s and 1880, ensured that the poor law became intermeshed with the wider political situation.[4] This combination of poverty and politics made the poor law in this area central to broader societal transformations that occurred throughout the years 1850–1921. The sources for the poor law, largely in the form of minute books of the boards of guardians meetings, together with near-verbatim newspaper reportage on their activities, provide a wealth of under-researched material. These sources not only document the working of the poor law, but also offer valuable insights into the alterations that occurred in social, economic and political relations during this period.

Although poor law boards generated much written material, the surviving sources for unions on the western seaboard are somewhat limited. For example, unlike many of the unions in Ulster or in large urban areas such as Cork and Dublin, there are very few indoor registers available for western unions. The most extensive official source for poor law boards in the region lies in the surviving minute books.[5] The nature of information within the minutes was shaped by the bureaucratic administration of the poor law system. As Felix Driver has highlighted in his examination of the English poor law, the extension of nineteenth-century local government created permanent central authorities and 'the poor law led to a new... state apparatus of information gathering and inspection'.[6] The Local Government Board (prior to 1872, the Poor Law Commissioners) examined the minutes of each board of guardians on a weekly basis to ensure that unions were run according to official rules and regulations and that standards were maintained and enforced. Local guardians were required to keep account in the minutes of all resolutions passed, communications received and statistical breakdowns of the categories of inmates in the workhouse. Reports from various officials such as medical doctors, relieving

3 Virginia Crossman, *Politics, pauperism and power in late nineteenth century Ireland* (Manchester, 2006), p. 106.   **4** William Feingold, *The revolt of the tenantry: the transformation of local government in Ireland 1872–1886* (Boston, MA, 1984); Crossman, *Politics, pauperism and power.* **5** For the majority of unions there are minute books available for extensive periods. Many are deposited in local archives. The online database of the Women's History Project provides a catalogue of all existing poor law material, see www.nationalarchives.ie/wh/sources.html. **6** Felix Driver, *Power and pauperism: the workhouse system 1834–84* (Cambridge, 1993), p. 28.

officers, Poor Law Inspectors and auditors also frequently appeared in the minutes. In light of the lack of surviving source material from the central authorities (few records of either the Poor Law Commissioners or the Local Government Board remain) the minute books of the guardians are extremely important for exploring the poor law system.

The range of information within the minutes is extensive. From a statistical analysis of the categories of inmates, it is possible to highlight trends in workhouse admissions. As Figure 14.1 illustrates, by 1911 a higher portion of the elderly, the sick and males resided in the Tralee workhouse than in 1861, illustrating the development of the institution as a hospital and a place for the old. Furthermore, the minutes often reveal much of the prevailing social and moral attitudes of the period. By 1862, women in the Westport workhouse were divided into those of unblemished character, illegitimate mothers, and prostitutes. Fearful of moral degradation, each class had separate day rooms, dormitories and exercise yards and, in the words of the guardians, were 'never allowed to meet or associate with each other at any time of the day or night'.[7] The minutes also disclose information regarding the internal conditions of workhouses. In Westport during 1856, the inspector of schools complained of the 'damp clay floor' and 'excessive cold' in the classrooms and that 'the children were more intent on preserving the animal heat than in preparing their lessons'.[8] The regular communication between the Local Government Board and poor law boards often highlights competing interpretations of the poor law between local and central authorities. This was demonstrated in 1901, when the Tralee guardians passed a resolution informing the Relieving Officer not to grant passes to able-bodied persons to enter the workhouse. The Local Government Board, implementing the principle of the workhouse test in which willingness to enter the house was proof of destitution, overturned the local guardians' decision.[9] These examples highlight the extent and scope of material in the poor law minute books. Information on social attitudes, institutional conditions and care, and the relationship between central and local authorities can all be found in this source.

While the minutes provide a formal account of union activity, they do not record actual discussion on boards of guardians. However, provincial newspapers, of which 132 existed countrywide by 1883, frequently carried verbatim reports of board meetings.[10] These reports offer crucial insights into the motivations and opinions of guardians, popular discourses on poverty and prevailing notions of entitlement for relief among the poor. The provincial press widely reported the activities of local government bodies to a rate-paying reading public in the nineteenth century. The need to keep a public eye on such bodies was recognized as early as 1856, when the unionist *Mayo Constitution* declared 'the administration of the poor law and the

7 Westport Board of Guardians, 29 Aug. 1862, National Library of Ireland (hereafter NLI), MS 12,627. 8 Westport Board of Guardians, 24 Jan. 1856, NLI, MS 12,619. 9 Tralee Board of Guardians, 9 Jan. 1901, Kerry County Archives, BG/154/A/50. 10 Marie-Louise Legg, *Newspaper and nationalist: the provincial press, 1850–92* (Dublin, 1999), p. 125.

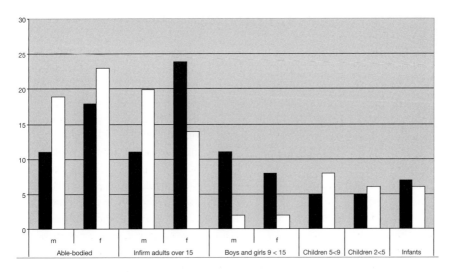

14.1 Percentage of inmates in various categories in the Tralee workhouse in 1861 (in black) and 1911 (in white) (source: Tralee Board of Guardians, 8 Jan. 1861, BG/154/AA/7, Kerry County Archives; Tralee Board of Guardians, 9 Jan. 1901, BG/154/A/50).

taxation it imposes are matters of deep interest to the general public and, consequently, it becomes our duty to give any information within our reach to our readers'.[11] In-depth reports on meetings, decisions reached or scandals in the workhouse made up much of the material published by the provincial press.

Within these reports, a wealth of material relating to local board activity is provided. Of particular interest is information that allows for the exploration of the criteria that guardians utilized to determine who deserved relief and how this changed over time. For much of the post-Famine period, Victorian values relating to thrift and self responsibility lay at the heart of the poor law and notions of entitlement.[12] This was demonstrated in Tralee in February 1880, when the guardians refused a Michael O'Sullivan relief on account of the fact that, although he was unemployed, he had up until Christmas earned a weekly wage of 12s. and yet owed £2.[13] The strategies of those seeking relief and the pressurizing of guardians can also be found in newspaper reports. During 1880, it was reported that distressed small farmers presented themselves before the Westport guardians, with one person stating that 'we want work, and if we don't get work or relief we cannot stand any longer. We are entitled to get it'.[14] During the same period in Kerry, a newspaper report described how over one hundred agricultural labourers demonstrated at a board meeting of the Tralee guardians and demanded relief. Two of the demonstrators

11 *Mayo Constitution*, 17 June 1856. **12** For a discussion of the ideological basis of the poor law system, see Crossman, *Politics, pauperism and power*, pp 6–7. **13** *Tralee Chronicle and Killarney Echo*, 20 Feb. 1880. **14** *Connaught Telegraph*, 10 Jan. 1880.

carried black flags with the inscriptions 'The Flag of Distress' on one side and 'Erin Lamenting' on the other.[15] Such insights into the attempts of the poor at seeking aid and the criteria utilized by guardians in granting relief are largely unavailable in the minutes, while the newspapers regularly published these occurrences.

Newspapers are vital to exploring the politicization of local poor law boards during the political and agrarian agitations of the 1880s.[16] Provincial newspapers such as James Daly's *Connaught Telegraph* and Timothy Harrington's *Kerry Sentinel* were pivotal to orchestrating nationalist successes over landlords on poor law boards. In the latter newspaper, Harrington went to the extreme measure of publishing the names of voters and how they voted in Tralee during the 1881 poor law election after the Land League marginally failed to gain control of the board.[17] Throughout this period, boards of guardians became intermeshed in landlord-tenant tensions and a focal point for localized nationalist agitation. Furthermore, in response to the extreme distress and destitution that prevailed on much of the western seaboard, the government introduced temporary emergency legislation, which allowed able-bodied persons to receive outdoor relief from boards of guardians in unions experiencing exceptional distress.[18] This measure, combined with the nationalist attainment of control on poor law boards, transformed the poor law system in the region. Between 1871 and 1881, the total number in the workhouses increased from 225,510 to 363,844, while the numbers receiving outdoor relief jumped from 282,492 to 590,067.[19] Increases in outdoor relief were most drastic in the poorer and politically volatile unions on the western seaboard. This was demonstrated in the strongly Land League organized Tralee region, where the number on outdoor relief increased from just one case in 1871 to 7,541 cases in 1881.[20] The dispersion of this relief became a central aspect of the Land War period and radically altered the position of the poor law in local society. The provincial press reporting of the activity of boards of guardians during the 1880s is a much neglected source for exploring this highly formative period. There were few people living on the western seaboard in the latter part of the nineteenth century whose lives were untouched by the poor law system, whether through rate-paying, receiving assistance, or political activism. The wealth of sources on poor law activity throughout the years 1850–1921, and particularly during the turbulent 1880s, makes

---

15 *Tralee Chronicle and Killarney Echo*, 23 Jan. 1880.   **16** The importance of this under-researched aspect of the period was originally highlighted in W.L. Feingold, *The revolt of the tenantry*. It has been further explored in Crossman, *Politics, pauperism and power*.   **17** See Feingold, 'Land League power: the Tralee poor law election of 1881' in Samuel Clark and J.S. Donnelly (eds), *Irish peasants, violence and political unrest, 1780–1915* (Manchester, 1983), pp 285–310. For a wider analysis of the Land League in Tralee and Co. Kerry, see Seán Lucey, 'Land and popular politics in County Kerry, 1872–86' (PhD, NUIM, 2007).   **18** *Circular, February 1880, by Local Government Board for Ireland to boards of guardians, relating to out-door relief to families of persons occupying land*, H.C., 1880 (9), lxii.377.   **19** *Commissioners for administering laws for relief of poor in Ireland, twenty-fifth annual report, appendix*, H.C., 1871 [c.577], xxix.1; *Local government board for Ireland, ninth report, appendix*, H.C., 1881, [c.2929] [c.2926–1], xlvii.269, 305.   **20** Ibid.

this material a rich resource for historians not just of the administration of the poor law but of wider social, economic and political transformations within the region.

THE POOR LAW IN THE NORTH

Those seeking to research poor relief in the north of Ireland are relatively fortunate when it comes to official sources. While little of the vast amount of paperwork generated by poor law administration remains for many unions in the south and west of Ireland, a substantial amount of the material relating to northern unions has been collected together and deposited in the Public Record Office of Northern Ireland. Among the most important sources available for the study of the administration and utilization of poor relief are the indoor registers of the union workhouses. These registers record every person admitted to or born in the workhouse and provide basic biographical information on each of them: name, age, gender, occupation, religious denomination and, occasionally, place of residence. They also record the date when they left the workhouse or died, allowing us to ascertain how long each person remained as an inmate. Careful examination of the registers can shed light on how the workhouse was being used and by whom, as well as the ways in which the role of the workhouse varied from one union to another and changed over time. Taking two Co. Antrim poor law unions as examples, the following section seeks to explain how workhouse registers can provide insight into patterns of relief, as well as revealing the diverse ways in which workhouses were being used.

Looking firstly at the indoor registers for Ballycastle union,[21] one valuable function that the registers serve is to explain the sudden and surprising upsurge in numbers seeking relief in this small union during the early 1880s. According to the published government statistics, 862 people, or about 41 per thousand of the population, were admitted to the workhouse in 1880 (fig. 14.2), demonstrating that it was not only the western seaboard that experienced a dramatic increase in the numbers seeking relief in this period.

When we turn to the indoor registers and examine the details of those being admitted, one of the reasons for the high number of admissions becomes evident. Most of the people admitted to the workhouse in 1880 and, indeed, in subsequent years, did not actually come from Ballycastle Union itself, but had travelled there from other parts of Ireland. One of the peculiarities of the Irish as opposed to the English poor law is that there was no law of settlement. While under English law, a pauper had to prove that he or she had been resident in the union for a minimum of five years in order to be eligible for relief, in Ireland, as long as the workhouse had capacity, it was obliged to admit any eligible pauper who sought shelter. This accounts for the large number of 'floating paupers', which seems to have become a

21 Indoor Registers, Ballycastle Poor Law Union, Public Record Office of Northern Ireland (hereafter PRONI), BG/3/G.

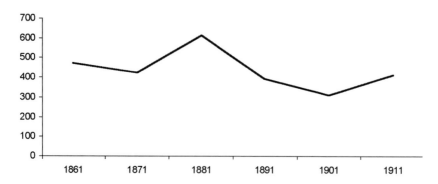

14.2 Number of admissions to Ballycastle workhouse, 1861–1911
(source: Annual Reports for the Poor Law Commission, 1851–71,
and for the Local Government Board for Ireland, 1872–1910).

particular problem throughout Ireland towards the end of the nineteenth century. While in 1861 the vast majority (90 per cent) of those admitted to Ballycastle workhouse were resident in the union, by 1879 those admitted to the workhouse from within the union were in the minority (figure 14.3).

Not only were large numbers coming to Ballycastle workhouse from outside the union, but they also came from a very wide geographical area. Large numbers of those admitted in 1879 – 12 per cent of the total admissions – had been resident in Belfast, while thirty-four people were admitted from Derry. Many others came from Dublin, Cork, Limerick, Waterford and Galway, while some were registered as having been resident in Scotland and England and even as far away as New York and the West Indies.[22] As Ballycastle was one of the main ports close to Scotland, and therefore offered ease of access between Ireland and Britain, it is most likely that large numbers were using the workhouse as a convenient stop-over on their way to or from Britain or elsewhere in search of work. Going back to indoor registers, this can be confirmed by analysing how long those from outside the union remained in the workhouse. In 1879, most of those admitted who were resident in Ballycastle Union remained in the workhouse for more than two days, generally weeks or months, and were there because they were ill, infirm or destitute. On the other hand, 85 per cent of those admitted, who were resident outside the union, remained for one or two nights only. Furthermore, although no marked seasonal trend in workhouse admissions is apparent when taking Ballycastle admissions as a whole, if those admitted from outside the union are examined in isolation, there is a marked increase in the numbers admitted each year between July and September, when travel in search of seasonal labour would have been at its height.

Thus, while simple statistics seem to indicate a large rise in the numbers from the Ballycastle area using the workhouse during the 1880s, a closer analysis reveals that

22 Ballycastle Indoor Register, 1879, PRONI, BG/3/G/3.

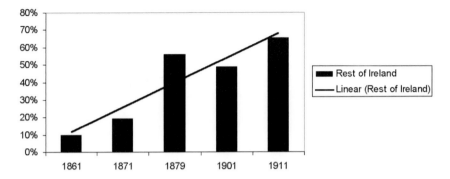

14.3 Those admitted to Ballycastle workhouse who had previously been resident
in other Irish unions, as a percentage of the total admissions, 1861–1911
(source: Ballycastle Indoor Registers, 1861–1911, PRONI, BG/3/G/2–6).

by this stage there were two entirely different groups of people using the workhouse,
for two completely different purposes. There were the paupers from within
Ballycastle Union who used the workhouse as they always had, as a longer term
shelter from sickness and destitution; the numbers of these admitted to the workhouse, while rising slightly, did not suddenly escalate. There was also, towards the end
of the century, a rapidly increasing number of people from outside the union, for
whom the workhouse represented a convenient place to spend a night and it is the
admission of these people that pushes the annual number of admissions so high.

Looking at Ballymoney Union, a similar story emerges. Again, the number of
those being admitted to the workhouse rose rapidly from the early 1870s onwards
and again the indoor registers reveal that there were two entirely different groups of
people, with contrasting profiles, who used the workhouse for different purposes, and
that this changed over time. In 1851–61, most of those who were admitted were in a
state of real destitution; the most vulnerable in society, the elderly and the young.
Large numbers of entire families or women with children were admitted, and most
of those who used the workhouse were female. From 1881 onwards, the indoor registers show that the number of annual admissions was being inflated by a very large
number of people who used the workhouse for one or two nights. These people
were generally adults aged between 16 and 59, single and male. They nearly all had
some kind of skill or trade and there is no evidence that they came from within
Ballymoney union.[23]

All this points to significant change; firstly, there was a change in the function of
the workhouse. From being a place where only the absolutely desperate sought relief,
it gradually became somewhere that offered people travelling through convenient
accommodation for the night. Secondly, there was a shift in popular perception of
the workhouse. By 1900, while there were still sections of the community for whom

23 Ballymoney Indoor Registers, 1861–1911, PRONI, BG/5/G/2–11.

the workhouse retained a terrible stigma and who would die rather than seek relief within its walls, there were also large numbers of people who had no compunction about using it as a temporary solution to the problem of where to spend the night.

This is simply one example of the ways in which detailed analysis of the indoor registers for a workhouse can help to build up a picture of experience and the administration of poor relief in a union. In this case, the indoor registers for the unions in question explain apparent anomalies in the official statistics, and suggest that the use of the workhouse was developing in a way that was at variance both with the original conception of how the poor law should work and with commonly held perceptions of how it turned out in reality.

WORKHOUSE ADMISSIONS IN NORTH DUBLIN AND THURLES, CO. TIPPERARY

The final section of this chapter compares data from workhouse registers and census returns for the North Dublin and Thurles Poor Law Unions for the year 1911.[24] Through an analysis of the records of these two unions, one located in the centre of the capital city, the other in a southern rural county, we can come to an evaluation not only of the experiences of poor people and the operation of the poor law in rural and urban Ireland, but of the nature of the sources themselves. Information on matters such as gender and age reveal significant differences relating to the composition of the workhouse population, differences that are functions of the source rather than anything to do with the experience of poverty itself. Each source contains some information lacking in the other. Thus the census provides information on literacy and Irish language skills of workhouse inmates not included in the registers. Only the registers, however, allow the historian to calculate the length of stay of individual paupers, as well as the admission of family groups.[25] The registers also contain, on occasion, very useful pieces of information regarding reasons for admittance, such as eviction.[26] Workhouse registers and census returns are thus complementary sources that together offer a rounded picture of Irish pauperism. Approached comparatively, they present an interesting perspective on the workhouse population and on institutional populations in general.

24 The Census of Ireland is only available for the years 1901 and 1911 at the moment. The Census return for Dublin for 1911 is currently available online at www.nationalarchives.ie. General reports on workhouse inmates are published in the reports of census between 1841 and 1891. See E. Margaret Crawford, *Counting the people: a survey of the Irish censuses, 1831–1911* (Dublin, 2003). Both census and indoor registers contain information on health but that is beyond the scope of this short piece.   **25** In 1911, the Thurles workhouse contained nine people who could speak Irish. The North Dublin Union workhouse housed seventeen Irish speakers.   **26** In 1910, the Conroy family entered the North Dublin Union workhouse following their eviction. The Rogers children were admitted following the eviction of their parents who were 'drinking about': National Archives of Ireland, Indoor Registers, North Dublin Union, BG/78/G/1–114.

The Thurles workhouse contained 209 inmates on census day, 2 April 1911. In Table 14.1, we see that of these inmates one hundred were men and 109 were women. Such figures suggest little gender difference in the experience of poverty in this part of rural Ireland. However, this conclusion is challenged by the picture presented in admission registers. The Board of Guardians admitted 1,202 people to the Thurles workhouse during the period 30 September 1910 to 29 September 1911; of these, 805 were male, whereas only 385 were female.[27] While the census presents a slight preponderance of women in the workhouse population, the pattern of admissions suggests a very different picture; approximately two thirds of all admissions to the Thurles workhouse were male. A similar though less dramatic picture emerges when we compare the census and indoor registers for North Dublin. There, of the 7,491 admissions recorded between September 1910 and 1911, 4,193 or 56 per cent were male, whereas 3,296 (44 per cent) were female. In the census, this picture is reversed, with 49 per cent being male and 51 per cent female. In the census returns for both unions, females comprised a greater proportion of inmates – as one would expect, given their greater vulnerability to poverty and distress. In the indoor registers, however, men constituted a greater proportion of admissions. The explanation for this apparent anomaly lies in the character of the source material. Inmates were captured on a single day by the census enumerators; admissions were those who used the workhouse over an extended time frame. In this way, the census acts as a photograph, a single moment in time; the register offers us a CCTV camera on the door of the workhouse, a moving image, a type of processional history.

Table 14.1 Male and Female Inmates (Census) and Admissions (Indoor Registers) in Thurles and North Dublin Poor Law Unions, 1911.

Union	Thurles		North Dublin	
Source	*Census*	*Indoor Registers*	*Census*	*Indoor Registers*
Male	100 (47.8%)	805 (67%)	1,141 (48.6%)	**4,193 (56%)**
Female	109 (52.2%)	397 (33%)	1,202 (51.2%)	**3,296 (44%)**
Total Number	*209*	*1,202*	*2,347*	*7,491*

When looking at admissions over a twelve-month period, it is clear that men used the workhouse in both rural and urban areas more frequently than women did. But what was the character of their usage; was it merely the same men repeatedly visiting the workhouse? The figures reveal that while repeat admissions in 1910–11 made up only 31 per cent of admissions in Dublin and 22 per cent in Thurles, the majority of those admissions (62 per cent for Dublin and 70 per cent for Thurles) were men. Therefore, men were more likely to revisit the workhouse than women, both in

27 These dates were chosen to correspond with the figures presented in the annual report of the Local Government Board for that year.

urban and rural Ireland. Among those who only entered the house once, there is a much greater difference between men and women in Thurles than in Dublin. This difference suggests a greater divergence in the experiences of men and women in rural Ireland than in the capital city.

Table 14.2 Duration of stay by admissions to workhouses of North Dublin and Thurles.

	North Dublin		Thurles	
	Men	*Women*	*Men*	*Women*
1 night–2 weeks	48.6%	38.7%	73.2%	67%
2 weeks–1 year	51.4%	61.3%	26.6%	33%

Figures also indicate that men used the workhouse for shorter periods than women in both Thurles and North Dublin (see Table 14.2), but the striking difference here is not between men and women but between rural and urban areas. In Thurles a significant majority of those admitted to the workhouse stayed less than two weeks, this was not the case in Dublin. Looking at the proportion of adults and children within the workhouse population again reveals differences between the registers and census returns. Table 14.3 shows a similar pattern occurring in both Thurles and Dublin with indoor registers recording a higher proportion of adult admissions than the census returns.

Table 14.3 Adults and children in the North Dublin and Thurles workhouses as recorded in the Indoor Registers and Census Returns, 1911.

	Indoor registers		Census returns	
	North Dublin	*Thurles*	*North Dublin*	*Thurles*
Adults	80.2%	81.3%	75.9%	73.2%
Children	19.8%	18.6%	23.4%	26.7%

The different pictures that emerge from indoor registers and census returns highlight an interesting distinction between these types of sources when studying institutional populations. The nature of the census, being a snapshot taken on one particular day, provides a useful, easily accessible and manageable cohort of inmates; one that can be used to construct a database with relative ease. However, there is no sense of the seasonality of workhouse use, which was clearly important in certain areas as has been shown for Ballymoney. Tentative conclusions can be drawn as to the types of people who suffered most from poverty during the census period, but statistics, so often presented as a true representation of the way things really were, are only as good as the source from which they emerge. Complementary sources deepen our understanding of the past, offering, in this case, a more enriched picture of Irish pauperism. The same is likely to be true for a wide variety of Irish institutions during the Victorian and Edwardian periods.

It is clear from this short survey that the workhouse was a more complex and less uniform institution than often is assumed. In many places, it provided both temporary accommodation for the travelling poor and a more permanent refuge for the most vulnerable groups in society, young people and the elderly and infirm. Moreover, while for the settled poor seeking admission to the workhouse was a last resort, for travellers it was a commonplace event. In the major cities where alternative temporary accommodation was available, there was less use of the workhouse as a hostel but a greater tendency to make repeat visits. This suggests that the workhouse was more closely integrated into the survival strategies of the poor in cities than was the case in rural areas where, once entered, the workhouse proved more difficult to leave. Workhouse records and related material provide a window on the changes and crises that occurred within the local community, the pressures outside the workhouse forcing people to seek shelter within its walls. Exploration of these forces enables the institution to be incorporated into a more community focused history, rather than being seen in an historical vacuum.

Two gentlemen of the *Freeman*: Thomas Sexton, W.H. Brayden and the *Freeman's Journal*, 1892–1916[1]

FELIX M. LARKIN

'There's a gentleman here, sir ... from the *Freeman*': with these words, the Director of the National Library of Ireland, T.W. Lyster, is summoned from his office to assist a visitor who has come to the Library on an errand connected with his work as an advertisement canvasser for the *Freeman's Journal*. The date is 16 June 1904, the visitor is Leopold Bloom and the incident is a scene in James Joyce's *Ulysses*.[2] It is one of many references to the *Freeman* in *Ulysses*: it occurs in the 'Scylla and Charybdis' episode of the novel. An earlier episode – the 'Aeolus' episode – is actually set in the *Freeman's* offices in North Prince's Street, beside the General Post Office, in Dublin.

The fact that the *Freeman* features so extensively in *Ulysses* reflects the central position it once occupied in Irish life. Published in Dublin from 1763 to 1924, it was the foremost nationalist daily newspaper in Ireland in the nineteenth and early twentieth centuries, and it was the semi-official organ of the Irish party at Westminster from the early 1880s until the 1918 general election. For a significant part of the latter period, it was under the control of the two men who are the subject of this essay: Thomas Sexton (fig. 15.1), chairman of the *Freeman's Journal* company, 1893–1912; and William Henry Brayden, editor of the newspaper, 1892–1916.[3] Historians who have written about the Irish party tend to depict the *Freeman* as almost *Pravda*-like in its relations with the party – normally passive, even supine.[4] The reality was quite

1 I acknowledge with gratitude the assistance of the late Desmond Brayden (1901–2006), a son of W.H. Brayden, whom I interviewed about his father in Apr. 1999 when he was aged 97. My thanks go also to the following, who assisted me in various ways: Dr Ian d'Alton, Philip Hamell, Dr James McConnel (University of Northumberland), Peter Lacy, Professor L. Perry Curtis Jr (formerly of Brown University, Providence, RI), Dr Mary Clark and Ellen Murphy (Dublin City Library and Archives) and Dr Patrick Maume.   2 *Ulysses*, 9: 585–6 (p. 164). The references to *Ulysses* here and in fn 16 below are to the chapter, line and page numbers in the latest printing of the text edited by Hans Walter Gabler (London, 2008 [1986; rev. ed., 1993], The Bodley Head).   3 I have written the entries on Thomas Sexton and W.H. Brayden in the Royal Irish Academy's *Dictionary of Irish biography* (Cambridge, 2009). On Thomas Sexton, see also the entries by Joseph Hone and Philip Bull in the *DNB 1931–40* (Oxford, 1949) and the *Oxford DNB* (Oxford, 2004) respectively.   4 *Pravda* (meaning 'Truth') was the official organ of the Russian communist party between 1912 and 1991. During the Cold War, it was well known in the West for its pronouncements as the authoritative voice of Soviet communism.

15.1 Thomas Sexton as Lord Mayor of Dublin (1888–9), portrait by Dermod O'Brien PRHA (*c.*1910), after H.J. Thaddeus, in the Dublin Civic Portrait Collection (courtesy of Dublin City Council).

different, and the complexity of the relationship between the party and the paper is a rich theme running through the intertwined careers of Sexton and Brayden.

Sexton was much the better known of the two: as a home rule MP from 1880 to 1896, his was a household name in Ireland.[5] He was born in Waterford city in 1847, the son of a constable in the Royal Irish Constabulary. Educated by the Christian Brothers at Mount Sion school in Waterford, he became a clerk with the Waterford and Limerick Railway when just 12 years old, and soon attained some local prominence as a member of the Mechanics' Institute and the Catholic Young Men's Society. In these forums, he began to develop the prowess in oratory for which he was renowned in later years – and which earned him the sobriquet 'silver-tongued Sexton', though he was sometimes caricatured as 'windbag Sexton'.[6] He also became an occasional correspondent for the *Nation* newspaper, and in 1867 moved to Dublin to join its staff. He was subsequently editor of its sister papers, the *Weekly News* and *Young Ireland*.

Encouraged by Parnell to stand for parliament, he was MP for Sligo County from 1880 to 1885 and then MP for South Sligo until 1886. One of Parnell's most trusted lieutenants, in early 1881 he played a notable part in the Irish party's obstruction of the bill to suppress Land League agitation by speaking for nearly four hours towards the end of a record 41½-hour continuous sitting of the House of Commons.[7] Moreover, he was imprisoned with Parnell in Kilmainham Jail in October 1881 (though released early because of ill health)[8] and he was one of the signatories of the 'no rent' manifesto of 18 October 1881. He enjoyed probably his greatest triumph with his speech on the second reading of the first home rule bill in the House of Commons on 1 June 1886[9] – a speech described by Gladstone as the most eloquent he had heard in a generation. Shortly afterwards, he was returned as MP for Belfast West in the general election of 1886 – his unexpected victory allegedly being due to the organizing genius of the young Joseph Devlin, himself later MP for the same constituency.[10] A member of Dublin corporation from 1886 to 1892, Sexton was lord

---

5 Sexton was, however, unknown when first elected: Conor Cruise O'Brien identifies him as one of a number of new MPs in 1880 'of whom little was known except that they were recommended by [Parnell]' (C.C. O'Brien, *Parnell and his party, 1880–90* (Oxford, 1957), p. 25). For Sexton's electoral contests from 1880 to 1895, see B.M. Walker (ed.), *Parliamentary election results in Ireland, 1801–1922* (Dublin, 1978), pp 312–13, 330, 353, 373, 433. 6 For 'silver-tongued Sexton', see J.S. Crone, *A concise dictionary of Irish biography* (2nd ed., Dublin, n.d. [1928]), p. 287. For 'windbag Sexton', see L.P. Curtis Jr, 'The battering ram and Irish evictions, 1887–90', *Éire-Ireland*, 42:3–4 (fall/winter 2007), 207–48 at 245. 7 *Hansard* (3rd ser.), cclvii, 2 Feb. 1881, cols 2008–28. J.B. Hall, a long-serving reporter with the *Freeman's Journal*, recalled Sexton's speech on this occasion as 'a marvel of completeness of diction, every word happily chosen and ... without one misplaced syllable' (J.B. Hall, *Random records of a reporter* (Dublin, 1928), p. 209). Hall was seconded from the *Freeman* staff to act as Sexton's private secretary when the latter was lord mayor of Dublin in 1888–9 (see *Irish Times*, 28 July 1931). 8 T.W. Moody and R. Hawkins (eds), *Florence Arnold-Foster's Irish journal* (Oxford, 1988), p. 300. 9 *Hansard* (3rd series), cccvi, 1 June 1886, cols 700–31. 10 See 'An Irishman's diary', *Irish Times*, 23 Oct. 2000.

mayor in 1888 and 1889, and during this double term in office he arranged a highly beneficial restructuring of the municipal debt. He was generally regarded as the Irish party's foremost financial expert, and served on the commission on financial relations between Britain and Ireland in the years 1894–6 and on the commission on Irish railways from 1906 to 1910. He was chairman of the *Freeman's Journal* company from 1893 to 1912.

William Henry Brayden was, by reference to his background, a most unlikely associate of Thomas Sexton. Born in Armagh city in 1865, Brayden was the son of a pawnbroker who later became manager of the local *Ulster Gazette* newspaper. His family was Church of Ireland and unionist. However, he converted to Catholicism in the early 1880s – perhaps to marry his first wife, Kate Devans (*c.*1863–92), of Newry, Co. Down[11] – and he also became an ardent home ruler. Educated at the Royal School in Armagh, he began his career as a journalist on the *Ulster Gazette* and then worked on the *Leinster Leader* in Naas, Co. Kildare, before joining the *Freeman's Journal* in 1883. In the same year, he enrolled in University College Dublin, where he studied ancient classics. He was among the first intake of students after UCD passed to the Jesuits, and later contributed a memoir of his teachers and fellow students – including the priest-poet and Professor of Greek, Gerard Manley Hopkins – to *A Page of Irish History*, the official history of UCD under the Jesuits, 1883–1909.[12] His studies were cut short when the *Freeman* sent him to London: he was a reporter in the House of Commons press gallery from 1885 to 1887. Next, he served as secretary to Edmund Dwyer Gray MP, the *Freeman's* proprietor – who was himself a convert to Catholicism – but he returned to the *Freeman's* Dublin staff after Gray's death in 1888.[13]

Following the Parnell 'split', Brayden was appointed editor of the *National Press*, established in March 1891 by the anti-Parnellites in opposition to the *Freeman's Journal*, which had initially supported Parnell. The *Freeman*, overwhelmed by this unaccustomed competition, quickly changed sides. The two newspapers were, therefore, merged – under the *Freeman's* more venerable title – in March 1892, with Brayden as editor.[14] He was then aged 26. Becoming editor of the *Freeman* so young was a remarkable achievement, albeit not without precedent: George Buckle had

---

11 They married in a Catholic church, in 1884. In 1895, Brayden married secondly Ethel Mary Shield (1872–1952), the daughter of a London publican. In all, he had eleven children – four by his first wife, seven by his second. The younger son of his first wife, Kevin (b. 1891), was killed in action with the London Irish Rifles in Palestine in Dec. 1917. The third son of his second wife, Basil Chrysostom (1904–95), became Dom Oliver Brayden OSB, a monk of Downside Abbey, near Bath, and later of Worth Abbey, Sussex.   **12** *A page of Irish history: story of University College, Dublin, 1883–1909*, compiled by Fathers of the Society of Jesus (Dublin, 1930), pp 123–6.   **13** For information on Edmund Dwyer Gray and his family, see F.M. Larkin, 'Mrs Jellyby's daughter: Caroline Agnes Gray (1848–1927) and the *Freeman's Journal*' in F.M. Larkin (ed.), *Librarians, poets and scholars: a Festschrift for Dónall Ó Luanaigh* (Dublin, 2007), pp 121–39.   **14** For details of the *Freeman's* tribulations in the immediate aftermath of the Parnell 'split', see Larkin 'Mrs Jellyby's daughter', pp 134–5.

become editor of the London *Times* in 1884 at the age of 29.[15] Brayden remained editor of the *Freeman* for twenty-four years until 1916, and was a director of the *Freeman* company from 1907 to 1916. He was called to the bar in 1894 and, despite his editorial responsibilities, practised occasionally on the North East Circuit. As editor of the *Freeman*, he makes a brief appearance in *Ulysses*. His arrival in the *Freeman's* building at about noon – presumably to begin his day's work – is observed by Leopold Bloom and others:

WILLIAM BRAYDEN, ESQUIRE, OF OAKLANDS, SANDYMOUNT

Red Murray touched Mr Bloom's arm with the shears and whispered: 'Brayden'.

Mr Bloom turned and saw the liveried porter raise his lettered cap as a stately figure entered between the newsboards of the *Weekly Freeman and National Press* and the *Freeman's Journal and National Press*. Dullthudding Guinness' barrels. It passed statelily up the staircase steered by an umbrella, a solemn, beardframed face. The broadcloth back ascended each step: back. All his brains are in the nape of his neck, Simon Dedalus says. Welts of flesh behind on him. Fat folds of neck, fat, neck, fat, neck.

'Don't you think his face is like Our Saviour?', Red Murray whispered.[16]

Joyce's friend, C.P. Curran, remembered Brayden 'as he sat in his dusty little editorial office in Prince's Street, a large, benevolent figure, with a perpetual air of weary omniscience'.[17]

Tim Pat Coogan, writing in 1966, claimed that 'more of the country's newspapers are coming to see their role as stimulators of the mind and not as retailers of received prejudices'.[18] When Brayden was editor of the *Freeman's Journal*, developments of that kind lay very far in the future. Brayden had not – and did not expect to have – the editorial freedom that many editors enjoy today. In his day, newspapers were highly partisan organs for particular points of view, usually those of their proprietors, and an editor was required to promote in reportage as well as in the leader columns the views of those who owned his paper. In fact, proprietors often acted as the editor themselves – or retained the editorship in name at least. Such was the practice on the *Freeman* until just a few years before Brayden became editor. The change occurred on the death of Edmund Dwyer Gray in 1888,[19] and was suggested by

15 See the entry on George Buckle by Stanley Weintraub in the *Oxford DNB*.   **16** *Ulysses*, 7: 38–49 (p. 97).   **17** C.P. Curran, *Under the receding wave* (Dublin, 1970), p. 99.   **18** T.P. Coogan, *Ireland since the Rising* (London, 1966), p. 174.   **19** Edward Byrne was then appointed editor (he had been *de facto* editor – without the formal title – since 1884), and held the post until 1891 when the *Freeman* switched sides in the Parnell 'split' and he resigned to become the first editor of the pro-Parnell *Irish Daily Independent*. His immediate successor as editor of the *Freeman* was William J. McDowell; after six months, Brayden displaced him when the *Freeman's Journal* and the *National Press* merged. For further information on Byrne and McDowell, see F.M. Larkin, 'The dog in the night-time: the

Parnell himself. Gray had died young and had no obvious successor, and the suggestion made by Parnell was 'to abolish the office of managing director [which had been
held by Gray] and, appointing an editor, simply manage the concern through the
board of directors'.[20] This was the structure within which Brayden worked.

Thomas Sexton was chairman of the *Freeman* company and unquestionably the
dominant figure on its board of directors for most of Brayden's period as editor. In
the 'split', Sexton had opposed Parnell on the grounds that his continued leadership
would mean the end of the Irish party's alliance with the Liberals on home rule.[21]
He was a director of the *National Press*, the anti-Parnell paper edited by Brayden; and
after it merged with the *Freeman* in 1892, he became a director and then chairman
of the *Freeman* company.[22] He lost his Belfast West seat in the 1892 general election;
but he had also contested North Kerry and sat for that constituency until 1896. The
early and mid-1890s was a time of relentless struggle in Irish politics – not only
between the pro- and anti-Parnellites, but also within the anti-Parnell ranks between
rival factions led by T.M. Healy and John Dillon, both MPs. The struggle in the anti-
Parnell camp was ultimately resolved in Dillon's favour, but not until 1896. Sexton,
though identified with Dillon more than with Healy, tried to remain above the row
– a difficult task, especially since it regularly spilled over into the *Freeman* boardroom.
Not surprisingly, both factions sought control of the *Freeman* – the organ of the anti-
Parnell party – so as to advance their interests.[23]

When Justin McCarthy MP quit as chairman of the anti-Parnell party in 1896,
Sexton was the unanimous choice of the party as his successor – a tribute to his
dexterity in remaining independent of the factions in the party. However, he
declined the position and instead supported Dillon for it. When Dillon was elected,
Sexton retired from parliament – giving as his reason 'the state of contention kept up
in the Irish party by a section of its members'.[24] Afterwards, he seemed to regret his
loss of influence, and he compensated for it by using the *Freeman* to try to impose
his will on his erstwhile colleagues. He was increasingly out of sympathy with them,
and this too was reflected in the *Freeman*. When Dillon complained about the paper's
attitude *c.*1899, Sexton's reply was that 'the people had lost interest in parliamentary

Freeman's Journal, the Irish parliamentary party and the empire' in S.J. Potter (ed.), *Newspapers
and empire in Ireland and Britain: reporting the British empire, c.1857–1921* (Dublin, 2004), pp
109–23 at pp 122–3. **20** Charles Stewart Parnell to Alderman Michael Kernan, 31 Mar.
1888, Cashel Diocesan Archives, Archbishop Croke papers, 1888/10. Kernan was a director
of the *Freeman's Journal* company and its largest shareholder after Edmund Dwyer Gray.
21 See F.S.L. Lyons, *Charles Stewart Parnell* (London, 1977), p. 518. In the tortured debate on
the question of Parnell's continued leadership in Committee Room Fifteen at Westminster
in early Dec. 1890, Sexton was the first speaker on the anti-Parnell side and – with all the
eloquence for which he was renowned – summed up the anti-Parnellite case with these
words: 'no service by any leader entitles him to ruin his cause' (quoted in O'Brien, *Parnell
and his party*, p. 316). **22** Regarding Sexton's election as chairman, see T.M. Healy, *Letters
and leaders of my day*, 2 vols (London, 1928), ii, p. 392. **23** F.S.L. Lyons, *The Irish
parliamentary party, 1890–1910* (London, 1951), pp 38–9, 44–5. **24** *Freeman's Journal*, 10
Febuary 1896 (quoted in Lyons, *Irish parliamentary party*, pp 60–1).

work'.[25] Subsequent events suggest that he was right about that and much more in touch than the parliamentarians were with public opinion.

The burden of managing the *Freeman's* day-to-day interaction with the party fell mainly on Brayden as editor and on his journalistic staff – most particularly J.M. Tuohy, the London correspondent, whose work brought him into close contact with the party's leaders when parliament was in session.[26] A letter from John Dillon to Brayden in 1898 provides some insight into the degree of control that the party sought to exercise over the newspaper and the extent of the party's dissatisfaction with it (fig. 15.2). The letter begins:

> It would have been well to have given a better show to the report of the West Mayo meetings – and to the Belfast Federation report. It is of the utmost importance that any activity on our side in the country should be well noticed in the *Freeman*. I understand that there are to be prosecutions in Westport today. Please give as good report as possible.[27]

Dillon goes on to refer to a recent speech by John Redmond, then leader of the pro-Parnellites, and outlines how the *Freeman* might criticize it. The letter is abrupt and testy, with Dillon making no attempt to hide his resentment that the newspaper was falling short in its support of the party.

Relations with the Irish party worsened after the reunification of the party under Redmond in 1900, and in 1903 Sexton and the *Freeman* were in open conflict with it over the land purchase scheme introduced by the chief secretary, George Wyndham. Wyndham's land act largely settled the Irish land question. It won broad approval from within the Irish party – and outside it. When it was going through parliament, however, Sexton denounced it in the *Freeman*.[28] He felt that the terms

25 'Extracts from a letter of Dillon to [Edward] Blake [MP], 8 Apr. 1904', National Library of Ireland, Dublin, John Redmond Papers, MS 15,182/6.   **26** James M. Tuohy was the *Freeman's* London correspondent from 1881 to 1912. For further information, see Larkin, 'The dog in the night-time', p. 121. I have written the entry on Tuohy in the *Dictionary of Irish biography*.   **27** John Dillon to W.H. Brayden, 3 Feb. 1898 (in the author's possession). I am grateful to the late Mollie Coghlan, who kindly gave me this letter along with several others from Dillon in a similar vein. The others, dated 1908–9, were addressed to Mrs Coghlan's father, Robert Donovan, a leader writer on the *Freeman's Journal* and first Professor of English in University College, Dublin (1909–34). Dillon's complaints to Brayden relate to reports of two meetings in Westport inaugurating the United Irish League (*Freeman's Journal*, 24 and 28 Jan. 1898) and of a meeting of party activists in Belfast chaired by Joseph Devlin (*Freeman's Journal*, 3 Feb. 1898); the prosecutions in Westport arose out of local land issues and were reported at length in the *Freeman* on 4 Feb. 1898.   **28** Philip Bull characterises the *Freeman's* opposition to Wyndham's land act as 'low-key' (Bull, *Land, politics and nationalism: a study of the Irish land question* (Dublin, 1996), p. 158), but Joseph V. O'Brien more accurately describes it as 'the thunder of that nationalist daily, managed by the hostile Sexton' (O'Brien, *William O'Brien and the course of Irish politics, 1881–1918* (Berkeley, 1976), p. 151) and F.S.L. Lyons refers to 'the raking fire the *Freeman's Journal* had been directing

15.2 First page of the letter from John Dillon to W.H. Brayden, 3 Feb. 1898.

offered to the landlords were too generous from a financial point of view. Once again, he was probably right: the financial terms were, in fact, modified by amending legislation in 1909.[29] Paradoxically, Sexton also feared that the proposed scheme would help the government achieve its avowed objective of 'killing home rule with kindness'. Unlike Dillon, who had similar misgivings, he was unwilling to moderate his opposition for the sake of party unity or even to acknowledge the undoubted benefits of the scheme. He had a personal grievance: William O'Brien, the Irish party MP who negotiated the scheme with a group of Irish landlords, had promised to consult Sexton about it but did not do so.[30]

After Wyndham's bill passed into law, Dillon joined Sexton in publicly rejecting the policy of seeking areas of co-operation between the party and the landlords – styled the policy of 'conciliation', but later characterized by William O'Brien as 'an olive branch in Ireland'.[31] Since 'conciliation' had brought about the land act, it was seen by O'Brien and others as offering the best hope of progress in Irish politics. Dillon and Sexton felt otherwise, their chief concern being that 'conciliation' would not deliver home rule. Redmond, while sympathetic to 'conciliation', refused to

against [Wyndham's] bill' (Lyons, *John Dillon: a biography* (London, 1968), p. 230).   **29** See Lyons, *Ireland since the Famine* (London, 1971), p. 215.   **30** Healy, *Letters and leaders*, ii, p. 462. See also S. Warwick-Haller, *William O'Brien and the Irish land war* (Dublin, 1990), p. 230.   **31** O'Brien's memoir of this period is entitled *An olive branch in Ireland, and its history* (London, 1910).

dissociate himself from those who opposed it.[32] As party leader, he was trying to avoid another split – but he did not succeed. O'Brien and Healy broke with the party because of Redmond's equivocation, and were never again in communion with it. So the policy of 'conciliation' failed, destroyed – at least in part – by the hostility of Sexton and the *Freeman*.[33] In fairness, it would probably have failed anyway – and it was the last formal attempt at co-operation between unionists and nationalists in Irish politics until the Sunningdale Agreement of December 1973, itself destroyed by the Ulster Workers' Council strike in the following May.

Sexton had to deal with an attempt by a London-based syndicate to acquire a substantial shareholding in the *Freeman* in order to change its stance on 'conciliation'.[34] The syndicate was led by Tipperary-born businessman, Edmond J. Frewen, a close associate of Wyndham and a relation of Brendan Bracken, Churchill's Minister for Information in the 1940s.[35] Sir Thomas Lipton – 'that boating grocer' (to quote Kaiser Wilhelm II),[36] whose family hailed from Co. Fermanagh – appears to have put up most of the money. Sexton frustrated the syndicate by blocking registration of the share transfers.[37] O'Brien and Healy both became involved with the syndicate, though to what extent is unclear. O'Brien's involvement with the syndicate was one of the issues in a libel action that he took against the *Freeman* in 1907; he won, but was awarded damages in the derisory sum of one farthing.[38]

The tension that defined the relations between the party and the paper during Sexton's chairmanship inevitably compromised the *Freeman*'s effectiveness as the organ of the anti-Parnell party in the 1890s and of the reunited Irish party thereafter. Of even greater concern to the party's leaders, however, was the fact that the *Freeman* was not in good shape financially. First, the *National Press* had inflicted grave damage

32 See P. Bew, *Conflict and conciliation in Ireland: Parnellites and radical agrarians, 1890–1910* (Oxford, 1987), p. 121.   **33** Wyndham himself wrote that 'Dillon, who is a pure agrarian sore-head; Davitt, who is a pure revolutionary socialist; [and] Sexton, editor of the *Freeman* [*sic*], who has been left out of parliamentary life, joined together to "spike" conciliation' (J.W. Mackail and G. Wyndham, *Life and letters of George Wyndham*, 2 vols (London, 1925), ii, p. 474).   **34** *Freeman's Journal*, 20 Nov. 1905. See also Bew, *Conflict and conciliation in Ireland*, p. 112; Bew there confuses Edmond Frewen with Moreton Frewen (MP for Cork North-East, 1910–11).   **35** C.E. Lysaght, *Brendan Bracken* (London, 1979), p. 25.   **36** See the entry on Sir Thomas Lipton by Ian d'Alton in the *Dictionary of Irish biography*. My thanks to Dr d'Alton for showing me a draft of this essay.   **37** See Sir Charles Russell to John L. Scallan (solicitor for the *Freeman's Journal* company), 23 June 1903 (copy), and Scallan's reply, 29 June 1903 (copy), Trinity College, Dublin, John Dillon papers, MSS 6805/230, 232. Sir Charles Russell, the second son of Lord Russell of Killowen, was the solicitor who acted for the syndicate.   **38** O'Brien, *An olive branch in Ireland*, pp 356, 361–73. Copies of the statement of claim in O'Brien's libel action against the *Freeman* and of the *Freeman*'s defence are in the T.C. Harrington papers in the National Library of Ireland (MS 8932). For proof of O'Brien's involvement with the syndicate, see Edmond J. Frewen to William O'Brien, 22 Feb. 1906, Boole Library, University College, Cork, William O'Brien papers, box AO; this letter is written on paper bearing the letterhead of Lipton Ltd, of Shadwell Basin, London Docks. For Thomas Lipton's involvement, see M. McDonnell Bodkin to William O'Brien, 15 Oct. 1902, Boole Library, University College, Cork, William O'Brien papers, box AM.

on it.[39] Then, after the merger with the *National Press*, it continued to face strong competition from the *Irish Daily Independent*, established in 1891 as a pro-Parnell organ when the *Freeman* changed sides in the 'split', but later – in 1900, following the reunification of the party – purchased by William Martin Murphy, an associate of Healy.[40] As a result, the *Freeman* lacked funds for investment; and Sexton, afraid of losing control, would not raise new capital. It was not, therefore, in a position to take advantage of the growing demand for newspapers in Ireland, as elsewhere, at that time.[41] Murphy seized the opportunity this presented to him, and in 1905 transformed his paper into the modern *Irish Independent* – at half the price of the *Freeman* and with a more popular, less partisan style. In effect, he copied what Lord Northcliffe had done in London in 1896 when he launched the *Daily Mail*, the first mass circulation newspaper in these islands.[42]

The *Freeman* was fatally undermined by the success of the new *Independent*. Its circulation – at between 30,000 and 35,000 copies per day – was still much the same as it had been under Edmund Dwyer Gray in the 1880s, and was quickly exceeded by the *Independent*.[43] With the consequent loss of advertising, the paper began to incur heavy trading losses and no dividends were paid to shareholders after 1908.[44] Sexton hung on as chairman for some time, but early in 1912 the Irish party leaders moved to save the paper and forced his resignation. What finally caused them to act was the knowledge that, if the *Freeman* failed, the party would be left without press support in Ireland for Asquith's imminent home rule bill. Moreover, if it did survive, the *Freeman*'s support for the bill was by no means certain with Sexton still in charge – given his record of deviating from the strict party line. He went quietly, thereby averting the public row that the party's leaders had feared.[45] Ironically, the only

39 The *Freeman*'s circulation fell by a quarter in 1891 and by a further 11 per cent in 1892 (Trinity College, Dublin, John Dillon papers, MS 6804/126–8). **40** P. Maume, 'Commerce, politics and the *Irish Independent*, 1891–1919', unpublished paper read before the 24th Irish Conference of Historians held at University College Cork, 20–22 May 1999; my thanks to Dr Maume for making a copy of this paper available to me. **41** Total sales of daily newspapers in Ireland grew from 75,000 copies per day in the 1880s to over half a million in the 1920s (L.M. Cullen, *Eason & son: a history* (Dublin, 1989), pp 77, 307); I have assumed that about one-third of total sales of newspapers in Ireland were through W.H. Smith, the antecedent of Eason's (see Cullen, *Eason*, p. 355). Raymond Williams likewise calculates a sevenfold increase in aggregate daily newspaper circulation in Britain between 1880 and 1920 (Williams, *The long revolution* (paperback ed., London, 1965), p. 198). **42** Maume, 'Commerce, politics and the *Irish Independent*, 1891–1919'. **43** The circulation figures given here for the *Freeman* refer to 1915 (National Library of Ireland, Dublin, John Redmond Papers, MS 15,262/7). By 1915, the *Irish Independent* claimed to have a circulation of 110,000 (*Newspaper Press Directory*, 1915). Regarding the *Freeman*'s circulation *c*.1885, see Larkin, 'Mrs Jellyby's daughter', p. 130. All estimates of newspaper circulation in Ireland in the nineteenth and early twentieth centuries should be regarded as extremely tentative: circulation figures were generally neither published nor independently verified. **44** *Freeman's Journal*, 29 Apr. 1912. **45** *The Times* (London), 19 and 20 Mar. 1912. The annual general meeting of the *Freeman* company at which Sexton resigned was held on 26 Mar. 1912, and afterwards Valentine Kilbride wrote to Dillon: 'Everything went well at the *Freeman* meeting

person to lament his fate was his old adversary, William O'Brien: O'Brien's paper, the *Cork Free Press*, commented that 'another intellect has been cast beneath the wheels of the modern juggernaut of so-called party discipline'.[46]

The *Freeman* was subsequently run by a small group of party stalwarts and was subsidized from party sources.[47] It was no longer commercially viable, and its parlous condition was exacerbated by the destruction of its premises during the 1916 Easter Rising. It was sold off after the party's defeat in the 1918 general election.[48] The *Freeman's* weakness in the years immediately before and after 1916, and its less-than-wholehearted support for the Irish party during Sexton's chairmanship, were important factors in the party's decline and fall. As early as 1907, John Dillon had written to Redmond that

> ... the chief weakness of the party lies in the management of the *Freeman*, and the *Freeman* is ruining itself as well as injuring the party by the manner in which it is being managed and edited ... I do not believe it is possible to maintain the Irish party without some newspaper in Dublin which can be counted on to give it loyal, active and intelligent support.[49]

Though reluctant to accept the new dispensation at the *Freeman* after Sexton's departure, Brayden continued as editor for four more years until 1916. He had hoped to succeed Sexton as chairman, but John Redmond vetoed that.[50] Sir Walter Nugent MP, who became chairman instead, found him 'awkward'[51] – while another new

today. Sexton did not face the music [i.e. he did not attend the meeting] ... At last, we have control of [the paper] and can dictate its policy. Are not the actions of public men strange? When you and I think of the work we went through in getting [Sexton] into the chair and now so glad to get rid of him.' (Valentine Kilbride to John Dillon, 26 Mar. 1912, Trinity College, Dublin, John Dillon papers, MS 6772/446). Kilbride was a Dublin-based solicitor and attended the meeting probably as Dillon's personal representative, Dillon being a substantial shareholder in the company.   **46** *Cork Free Press*, 19 Mar. 1912; quoted in *The Times* (London), 20 Mar. 1912.   **47** For details, see 'Note of moneys advanced to *Freeman's Journal*, 27 January 1919' in the John Dillon papers (Trinity College, Dublin, MS 6805/306). This shows that, in the period 1913–18, the Irish party arranged funding for the *Freeman* company from various sources amounting to over £28,000 (excluding interest accrued on the funds) – of which £6,500 related to the years 1913–14. The total moneys advanced to the *Freeman* are equivalent to well over £1 million sterling today.   **48** Lyons, *John Dillon*, pp 389–90, 419, 457–8. For information on the subsequent history of the *Freeman's Journal* (1919–24), see F.M. Larkin, 'A great daily organ: the *Freeman's Journal*, 1763–1924', *History Ireland*, 14:3 (May/June 2006), 44–9 at 48–9.   **49** John Dillon to John Redmond, 31 July 1907, National Library of Ireland, Dublin, John Redmond Papers, MS 15,182/15. Confirmation of the *Freeman's* role in the decline and fall of the Irish party is to be found in an anonymous memorandum, also in the Redmond papers, which concluded *c.*1916 that 'the press was the weakest side of the constitutional movement' (MS 15,262/1).   **50** John Redmond to John Dillon, 2 May 1912, Trinity College, Dublin, John Dillon papers, MS 6748/493.   **51** Sir Walter Nugent to John Dillon, 4 Oct. [1912?], Trinity College, Dublin, John Dillon papers, MS 6758/1351.

director, John Muldoon MP, complained that 'Brayden needs constant getting at, or important things slip'.[52] His exit was, however, precipitated by policy considerations rather than doubts about his competence. Immediately after the Rising in 1916, both Nugent and Brayden wanted the *Freeman* to take a harder line against the rebels than the Irish party leaders would countenance. Nugent resigned in protest,[53] and Brayden was replaced. Brayden became actively involved in military recruitment in Ireland in the remaining years of the First World War, and for this he was appointed OBE in 1920.[54] He undertook some anti-Sinn Féin propaganda work for Dublin Castle in 1918–19,[55] and was employed as a correspondent for the Associated Press of America, the Chicago *Daily News* and the English Catholic *Universe*. He was a trustee of the National Library of Ireland from 1923 until his death ten years later, on 17 December 1933.[56]

Sexton lived for twenty years after leaving the *Freeman*. He withdrew from politics, but retained business interests as chairman of Boland's Bakery and the Irish Catholic Church Property Insurance Company. He was a devout Catholic, perhaps influenced by the fact that he had reported on the apparition at Knock in 1879 as a journalist for the *Nation*.[57] He never married, though Florence Arnold-Foster noted in her journal in November 1881 that he was engaged to be married.[58] Shy and reclusive despite his gift for oratory, he was described by F.S.L. Lyons as 'a man who almost ceased to exist when he stepped down from the public platform'.[59] At the end of his life, he was a relatively wealthy man[60] – but he had known severe poverty, especially in his early years as an MP. Speaking in Dáil Éireann in 1940, James Dillon – John Dillon's son – recalled that Sexton had

> ... served in the British House of Commons and lived in a tenement room on the Vauxhall Bridge Road [in London] because he had not the wherewithal for a better lodging, and although he was the equal of any when he championed the cause of Ireland in the presence of the mighty, when he went

52 John Muldoon to John Dillon, 25 Aug. 1912, Trinity College, Dublin, John Dillon papers, MS 6734/159. **53** Sir Walter Nugent to John Dillon, 15 May 1916, Trinity College, Dublin, John Dillon papers, MS 6758/1363. This letter is referred to in Lyons, *Dillon*, p. 383. **54** *The Times* (London), 31 Mar. 1920. **55** For details, see PRO, London, CO 904/168/1222–35, 1239–44, 1265–70 (published on microfilm by Harvester Microform Publications in *The British in Ireland, part five: public control and administration, 1884–1921*, reel 91 [Brighton, 1985]); my thanks to Brian P. Murphy OSB for bringing these papers to my attention. **56** Obituaries were published in the *Irish Independent*, *Irish Press* and *Irish Times*, 18 Dec. 1933, and in *The Times* (London), 19 Dec. 1933. For details of Brayden's association with the National Library of Ireland, see D. Ó Luanaigh, 'A gentleman of the press: William J.H. Brayden OBE (1865–1933)', *Dublin Historical Record*, 47:1 (spring 1994), 103–4. Brayden's full name was William John Henry Brayden, but he rarely – if ever – used John. **57** P. Bew, *Ireland: the politics of enmity, 1798–2006* (Oxford, 2007), p. 315. **58** Moody and Hawkins (eds), *Florence Arnold-Foster's Irish journal*, p. 300. **59** Lyons, *Parnell*, p. 123. **60** The *Oxford DNB* records his wealth at death as £23,371 0s. 11d., equivalent to about £900,000 sterling today.

home at night he went home to poverty and sometimes even to hunger because he had no money to purchase the luxuries which fortified his rivals in that struggle.[61]

He died on 31 October 1932, the last survivor of the band of talented young men whom Parnell gathered around him in the early 1880s.[62] He supported Fianna Fáil in the 1932 general election because of its protectionist economic policies, and shortly before his death was quietly consulted by the new government about the land annuities question and the possibility of a claim against Britain in respect of excessive past taxation.[63]

In *Seven Winters*, her memoir of her early childhood, Elizabeth Bowen says of Edwardian Dublin that 'the twentieth century governed only in name; the nineteenth was still a powerful dowager'.[64] The *Freeman's Journal*, under the duumvirate of Sexton and Brayden, was part of that nineteenth-century Dublin that lingered well into the twentieth century. The *Freeman* had failed to modernize and, when Sexton quit in 1912, it was already too late to save it. Its rival, William Martin Murphy's *Irish Independent*, had by then an unassailable market advantage. In contrast to the *Freeman*, the *Independent* had embraced the new economics of newspaper production in the twentieth century. When the *Freeman* ultimately ceased publication in December 1924, its assets – including the title – were bought by the *Independent*, and for decades afterwards the *Independent* carried in its masthead the legend 'Incorporating the *Freeman's Journal*'. It was an ignominious end for one of Ireland's most notable newspapers.

---

61 *Dáil Debates*, 81, 11 Dec. 1940, col. 1079. See M. Manning, *James Dillon: a biography* (Dublin, 1999), p. 143.   **62** Obituaries were published in the *Irish Independent, Irish Press, Irish Times* and *The Times* (London), 2 Nov. 1932.   **63** *Irish Press*, 3 Nov. 1933. The report, by a special correspondent (possibly Eamon de Valera himself), stated that 'one of the last – probably the very last – times [Sexton] left his home was little more than a week ago when he met one of the members of the government who was engaged in preparing ... the claim of Ireland against Great Britain on account of over taxation' and Sexton is quoted as having remarked to the minister in question: 'Ireland has an unanswerable case against Great Britain on the grounds of over taxation and also on the land annuities question. If the government will only stand firm and if the people of Ireland stand firmly behind them, victory is certain.' **64** E. Bowen, *Seven winters: memories of a Dublin childhood* (London, 1943), p. 31.

The Melbourne Advocate, 1868–1900: bastion of Irish nationalism in colonial Victoria

PATRICK NAUGHTIN

When the *Advocate* was launched as a weekly newspaper in Melbourne on 1 February 1868 to represent 'the large section of this community who are Irish or Catholic', there could have been little expectation that it would endure for well over a century.[1] There had been three previous short-lived attempts to establish an Irish or Catholic newspaper in the new colony of Victoria and there was little reason to believe that the *Advocate* would be any less ephemeral than its predecessors. The *Advocate*, however, defied such expectations and survived by securing the support of the Catholic church, while at the same time maintaining independence for the first fifty years of its existence under the lay proprietorship and management of the Winter family.[2] During these first decades of its existence, the *Advocate* led the Irish nationalist movement in Victoria, at times being almost the sole bastion of Irish nationalism in this distant antipodean colony. As the main voice and vehicle of the movement, the *Advocate* was constantly assailed by powerful opponents, particularly in the Melbourne daily press where the so-called 'Irish question' was regularly brought to the forefront of colonial interest. As the *Advocate* was also a Catholic paper, promoting Catholic causes and depending on the support of the Catholic Church, opponents were provided with ready opportunities to equate Irish nationalism with Catholicism. The political ramifications of this extended well beyond the cause of Ireland's nationhood to local colonial affairs and to the political and social standing of Irish Catholics in the colony. Irish nationalism, while a rallying force for some colonial Irish, could be readily exploited by opponents as a divisive force and a potent factor to be used in restricting the extension of Irish Catholic political power in the colony.

From the outset, the *Advocate*'s political mission was made apparent to all. With a general election to be held in Victoria during the week following its launch, the *Advocate* urged unity in the Irish Catholic vote, particularly with regard to the contentious issue of funding of Catholic schools. Irish Catholics represented a

1 *Advocate*, 1 Febuary 1868. The *Advocate* finally ceased publication in 1990. 2 Samuel Vincent Winter (1843–1904) was managing proprietor of the *Advocate* from 1868 until 1872, when his brother Joseph (1844–1915) took over this role until his death. In 1919 the *Advocate* was purchased by the archdiocese of Melbourne.

substantial political presence in this new British colony. Victoria was not only the most populous of the Australian colonies, with its population increasing tenfold in the first twenty years of the colony's existence from 1851, but it was also the most Irish. Continued high immigration and high birth-rates during the 1860s had tended to proportionally increase the Irish component, so that by the 1871 census there would be just over 100,000 Irish-born, or about one in every seven people in the colony, with Catholics also increasing significantly to comprise almost a quarter (23.4 per cent) of the colony's population.[3] Oliver MacDonagh, in his insightful study of colonial Victoria, drew attention to the peculiar situation of the Irish in this new society, that was 'unusually fluid and unfixed', being comprised almost exclusively of direct immigrants or their immediate descendants 'in whom identification with country of origin or extraction was extremely powerful'.[4] Given their large numbers and the relative recentness of their arrival, the Irish, particularly the great bulk of whom who were Catholics, were an inescapably prominent element in this new society that represented, for many, a challenge to English and Protestant ascendancy.

The circumstances of the *Advocate*'s foundation and the background of its small group of founders determined the direction that the newspaper would follow, and to a large extent be locked into, for the remainder of the nineteenth century. The presence in the founding group of Charles Gavan Duffy (1816–1903), the member of the Victorian parliament with the most colourful and controversial past, ensured the notice of the Melbourne daily press, which had reminded its readers of Duffy's disloyalty as a Young Ireland leader in the rebellion of twenty years before. Duffy, whose political designs would soon see him leading a short-lived government in the colony in 1871, was mainly responsible for the *Advocate*'s political prospectus and the first editorial setting out Irish Catholic demands in the impending general election. This was not the first attempt by Duffy, one of the founders of the *Nation* in Ireland, to establish an Irish newspaper in Victoria. In 1862, he had launched the *Victorian*, a newspaper that struggled for two years before folding. A crucial factor in its collapse was the loss of episcopal patronage, with the bishop of Melbourne, the Cork-born James Goold (1812–86), declaring in 1863 that the newspaper had 'ceased to be the exponent of Catholic opinion in Victoria'.[5]

Patrick O'Farrell, the prominent historian of Irish Australia, has contended that the only Irish newspapers to enjoy continuity in Australia depended on clerical approval, content and involvement.[6] Certainly the backing of the Catholic Church was considered vital by the small group of men who founded the *Advocate* at a meeting in January 1868 at St Ignatius' Church in the Melbourne suburb of Richmond. Joining Duffy in this founding group was his close parliamentary colleague Michael O'Grady (1824–76), a prominent Catholic, originally from

3 Oliver MacDonagh, 'The Irish in Victoria, 1851–1891: a demographic essay' in T.D. Williams (ed.), *Historical Studies VIII* (Dublin, 1971), pp 82–92.   4 Ibid., pp 76–7.   5 W.T. Southerwood, *Planting a faith in Melbourne: colonial era, 1839–1899* (Sydney, 1973), p. 24; Cyril Pearl, *The three lives of Duffy* (Sydney, 1979), p. 199.   6 Patrick O'Farrell, *The Irish in Australia* (Sydney, 2000), p. 108.

Roscommon, who had been associated with Duffy in London before each left for Victoria in 1855.[7] Also present were two prominent Irish Jesuit priests, Joseph Dalton (1817–1905) from Waterford, and Isaac Moore (1829–99) from Limerick, members of the Jesuit mission established in Melbourne two years before. Dalton not only hosted this inaugural meeting in his parish church, but seems to have been responsible for initiating the idea of the *Advocate*, having been in Tasmania six months before, when the *Catholic Standard* was launched in Hobart, on which occasion he deplored the fact that Victoria's much larger Catholic population had no newspaper.[8] The Jesuit priests and O'Grady, particularly, were primarily driven in this newspaper enterprise by their commitment to the cause of separate Catholic education. O'Grady was the Catholic parliamentary member on the colony's Board of Education and a leading member of Bishop Goold's Education Committee, while Dalton and Moore were educationalists of considerable achievement, the former leaving his mark as a great builder of schools in Melbourne and later Sydney, while the latter returned to Ireland and, in a distinguished career, was at one time vice-rector of University College Dublin.[9] The active commitment on the part of these founders of the *Advocate* to the cause of Catholic education, the critical Catholic political issue at this time, ensured the all-important support of Bishop Goold, who agreed to the fledgling paper being distributed from parish churches on Sundays.

While these Irish founders of the *Advocate* may have been primarily driven by local Irish Catholic political purposes, they were also united in their endeavours by a common thread of Irish nationalism borne of their experiences in Ireland. Michael O'Grady had strong links to nationalists in Ireland, organizing the resettlement of evicted Irish tenants in Australia several years before, his work being praised by the celebrated Irish nationalist and journalist A.M. Sullivan.[10] Isaac Moore, since his youth in Limerick at the time of the Young Ireland rebellion, had been a strong supporter of Charles Gavan Duffy as, indeed, had been the *Advocate*'s foundation editor, William Henry Gunson (1828–1901), also a native of Limerick, who reportedly had associations with the 1848 movement.[11] There would seem to be more than a little basis for the *Advocate*'s assertion many years later that it 'might rightly claim a legitimate descent from '48 ancestry'.[12] William Gunson, editor of the *Advocate* until his death in 1901, had migrated to Australia in 1852 with his brother John, later an Irish nationalist leader in Adelaide.[13] 'Cultured and gifted', William Gunson's influence was of profound importance in maintaining not only the literary quality of the *Advocate*, but also its direction as an Irish paper, more so than a Catholic one, though

7 Janice Burns Woods, 'O'Grady, Michael (1824–1876)' in *Australian Dictionary of Biography*, 5 (Melbourne, 1974), p. 360.   **8** *One hundred years of the Advocate, 1868–1968 centenary souvenir*, *Advocate*, Febuary 1968.   **9** G.J. O'Kelly, 'Dalton, Joseph (1817–1905)', *Australian Dictionary of Biography*, 4 (Melbourne, 1972), pp 11–12; David Strong, *The Australian dictionary of Jesuit biography* (Sydney, 1999), p. 224.   **10** James F. Hogan, *The Irish in Australia* (London, 1887), p. 293.   **11** Morgan Jageurs, 'Joseph Winter: pioneer pressman, patriot and publisher', *Austral Light* (Jan. 1916), p. 44.   **12** *Advocate*, 23 Sept. 1899.   **13** Sally O'Neill, 'Gunson, John Michael (1825–1884)' in *Australian Dictionary of Biography*, 4 (Melbourne, 1972), p. 308.

he himself was staunchly Catholic, having converted from the Anglican faith of his English father.[14]

The final member of the *Advocate*'s founding group, Samuel Vincent Winter (1843–1904), had little in common with the Irish founders, apart from his strong Catholic background.[15] Born in Victoria, 24-year-old Samuel Winter was little more than half the age of his Irish co-founders and yet, as managing proprietor, he was to be the driving force in meeting the practical challenges of what was to be a turbulent infancy for the *Advocate*. Though his father was an English Protestant, Winter and his three younger brothers had been raised in the strict faith of their Irish Catholic mother in Richmond, then an Irish stronghold in Melbourne. Within a few years of his father's death when he was only 11, both Samuel and the next eldest brother, Joseph (1844–1915), were apprenticed in the printing trade. Remarkably, within a decade of this apprenticeship, the Winters' former employer, W.H. Williams, was printing the *Advocate*, of which Samuel Winter was the first registered proprietor and manager, as well as being a journalist.[16] Winter's key role was later attested to by Charles Gavan Duffy in a letter both defending the *Advocate*, which he acknowledged 'was established by a young Catholic printer', but also distancing himself from some of the *Advocate*'s expressed opinion, suggesting that 'perhaps it was rather overdone by persons new to journalism'.[17]

Despite having never set foot in Ireland, Samuel Winter was driven by an Irish nationalist ardour and activism that, influenced undoubtedly by his relative youth and inexperience, was demonstrative and provocative. Forthright and flamboyant, as secretary of the Melbourne St Patrick's Society, he reportedly led the St Patrick's Day parade mounted on a white horse.[18] Just a month before the *Advocate*'s founding, the *Argus* newspaper reported Winter's role in marshalling the funeral procession for a boy fatally shot by Orangemen during a sectarian disturbance outside the Protestant Hall in Melbourne. The funeral for the young victim, William Cross, who was neither Irish nor Catholic, became a political demonstration against sectarian violence, with the *Argus* report describing the procession of an estimated one thousand mourners as 'one of the most melancholy and imposing spectacles which Melbourne has witnessed since the funeral of Burke and Wills [the ill-fated explorers]'.[19] Samuel Winter, who had himself been near the Protestant Hall with his brother Joseph at the time of the shooting, was strongly influenced by this incident and led the *Advocate*'s indignant outcry when the accused Orangemen were later acquitted.

The timing of the *Advocate*'s launch provided an early opportunity for opponents

14 Jageurs, 'Joseph Winter', p. 44.   **15** Geoffrey Serle, 'Winter, Samuel Vincent (1843–1904)' in *Australian Dictionary of Biography*, vol. 6 (Melbourne, 1976), pp 425–7.   **16** Thomas A. Darragh, *Printer and newspaper registration in Victoria, 1838–1924* (Wellington, 1997), p. 142.   **17** *Advocate*, 18 Apr. 1868. This was a reprint of Duffy's letter dated 26 Mar. 1868 to William Dunne, Vicar-General of Tasmania, which was first published in the Hobart *Mercury*.   **18** Neryl Jensen, 'Unlawful assemblies and party concessions' (MA, University of Melbourne, 2000), p. 82.   **19** *Argus*, 16 Dec. 1867.

to link the new Irish Catholic newspaper with extremist Irish nationalism. Only a month after the *Advocate*'s launch, the Australian colonies were engulfed in the so-called 'Fenian scare', a period of heightened tension precipitated by the attempted assassination of Prince Alfred, the son of Queen Victoria, by an alleged Fenian in Sydney on 12 March. The would-be assassin, Henry O'Farrell, was from Victoria, heightening suspicions of a Fenian association in the colony. Attention immediately turned to the recently launched *Advocate*, with the question of its complicity in Fenian activity raised in the Victorian parliament when one member, George Paton Smith, alleged that there was 'a publication in this city which was the organ of Fenianism'.[20] While the *Advocate*'s denials that it supported Fenianism went largely unheard, the Fenian tensions of early 1868 ensured a prominence for the *Advocate* in its stormy infancy which was hardly in keeping with its small circulation.[21]

Allegations of the *Advocate*'s links with Fenianism were heard regularly from opponents of Irish nationalism over the coming years. Samuel Winter himself provided further fuel for such attacks when, in 1869, he established and operated through the *Advocate* a Released Irish State Prisoners Fund, raising the not inconsiderable sum of £5,000 to assist recently pardoned Fenian prisoners who had been transported to Western Australia two years before. When the remnant of Fenian prisoners in Western Australia was dramatically rescued several years later, in 1876, by an American whaleboat, the *Advocate* was again accused of being a Fenian journal after publishing a lengthy, and not disapproving, account of the rescue.[22]

The alleged Fenian threat, and attendant anti-Irish publicity, also gave the *Advocate* a foretaste of the powerful opposition it faced from the colonial press, notably the major Melbourne dailies, the *Age* and the *Argus*. The opposition of the *Argus* was the more straightforward and expected. As the conservative organ of the colony, it carried the reports of the London *Times* and generally equated Irish nationalism in its reports with a disloyalty that would lead to dismemberment of the British Empire. The hostility, however, of the *Age*, the widely circulated and influential penny newspaper, was more complex and virulent. As the professed champion of civil and religious liberty, it had long opposed any extension of Irish Catholic political power in the colony, leading a 'No Popery' campaign in the early 1860s.[23] Papal condemnation of liberalism had intensified the *Age*'s resolve to restrict the political influence of Catholics in the colony. For the *Age* and so-called liberal supporters, the principles of liberalism were embodied in the issue of secular education. The decision of the Catholic hierarchy meeting in Melbourne in April 1869 to promulgate new decrees on education that fully endorsed the papal condemnation of liberalism and specifically the principle that 'education should be subjected to the civil and political power', only served to intensify the forces of opposition to Irish Catholic causes led by the *Age* and its imperious proprietor, David Syme.[24] Syme's preoccupation with

---

20 *Age*, 14 Mar. 1868. **21** Early circulation figures are unavailable but by the end of its first year, the *Advocate* was advertising its readership as 20,000. *Advocate*, 16 Jan. 1869. **22** *Argus*, 12 June 1876; *Advocate*, 17 June 1876. **23** Margaret Pawsey, *The Popish Plot: culture clashes in Victoria, 1860–1863* (Sydney, 1983), pp 106–11. **24** A.G. Austin, *Australian education, 1788–*

curtailing the extension of Catholic political influence saw the *Age* show itself repeatedly throughout the nineteenth century ready to exploit any opportunities afforded by Irish nationalist politics to rouse anti-Irish Catholic sentiment in the colony. The *Advocate*'s unwavering support for separate Catholic education sacrificed any hope of enjoying the support of the powerful *Age* for Irish home rule, which the *Advocate* argued in frustration was also a liberal cause. The conflict only intensified in June 1871, when Charles Gavan Duffy became premier of Victoria, leading a short-lived government that was widely condemned in the Melbourne daily press for its alleged Irish Catholic patronage.

The *Advocate*, however, had prospered during these early years of sectarian conflict under Samuel Winter's management. It increased its size and circulation, being assisted by a share of government advertising when Duffy was in power, and also conducted the major Catholic bookshop in Melbourne from its offices. Samuel Winter, however, sought a new challenge for his entrepreneurial talents and found this in the form of the ailing evening newspaper, the *Herald*, where as editor he 'judiciously tempered his sympathies' in Irish Catholic matters.[25] In 1872, management of the *Advocate* was handed over to Winter's brother Joseph who, a year younger, was the antithesis of his outspoken and very public brother. Joseph was reserved and not renowned as a public speaker, shunning the limelight. However, despite this lack of a public profile, the names of Joseph Winter and the *Advocate* were to become almost synonymous during the period of over forty years that he was managing proprietor until his death at his desk in 1915. An incessant worker, Joseph Winter was recognized by the 1880s as the key figure of the Irish nationalist movement in Victoria, not only in providing the means to propagandize Irish causes through the *Advocate*, but also for his organizational work as treasurer or secretary for a multitude of these causes.[26] Irish nationalism was his particular focus and motivation and, in the words of Geoffrey Serle, the foremost historian of colonial Victoria, Joseph Winter was to be 'the heart and soul of the Home Rule movement in Victoria for thirty years'.[27]

In the early years of the *Advocate*, however, there were limited opportunities for the likes of Joseph Winter to express this Irish nationalist support in an active and meaningful way. Direct intrusions of Irish nationalist politics into colonial affairs were rare in the 1870s. It was difficult enough for Australian colonists to get information on Irish affairs, let alone to have any sense of participation in them. Colonial interest and involvement in Ireland's political issues were restricted by the most obvious factor of all – the very real, apparently insurmountable, obstacle of distance from the motherland. For virtually all Irish immigrants to the Australian colonies, unlike their counterparts who went to North America, the distance factor meant making a decision of permanent, irreversible exile from Ireland. The immense

1900: church, state and public education in colonial Australia (Melbourne, 1977), p. 203; Stuart Macintyre, *A colonial liberalism: the lost world of three Victorian visionaries* (Melbourne, 1991).
25 Serle, 'Winter, Samuel Vincent', p. 425. **26** O'Farrell, *Irish in Australia*, p. 223.
27 Serle, 'Winter, Samuel Vincent', pp 425–7.

distance and difficult, infrequent communications necessarily diminished home ties and, in so doing, diluted Irish issues. For the great bulk of immigrants, Ireland and its problems were increasingly only to exist in the memory of a distant past.

In the *Advocate*'s first years, the colonial press could only carry news from Europe that was at least two months old, that being the time it took for mail to reach the Australian colonies. However, developments in transport and communications during the 1870s were to revolutionize links between the colonies and England and Ireland. With more efficient steamships travelling via the newly opened Suez Canal, by the late 1870s the average passage of mails between London and Australia was half the time it had taken in the 1850s. Of more revolutionary import, though, were the developments in communications during the 1870s which saw the Australian colonies finally linked by telegraph to Britain. Information that had previously taken several weeks to be sent to and from Britain and Ireland could now be transmitted in hours. Almost overnight, in a very real, physical sense, the distant antipodean outreaches of the British empire had been linked with the old world. The consequences for the colonies were immense, as access to more current news fostered an awakening of interest in the politics of the old world. Control of this cabled news, however, contributed further to the domination of the major daily newspapers like the *Age* and the *Argus* and served British imperial interests well, with almost all Australian cable news being 'filtered' through London.[28] This British imperial press system reinforced 'an overarching sense of Britishness', leading the *Advocate* to caution its readers about the 'poisoned sources' responsible for the cabled news on Irish affairs.[29]

Generally, the 1870s were years when local issues dominated Irish Catholic politics in Victoria rather than Irish nationalist issues. The *Advocate* regularly carried items from Irish newspapers dealing with the growing Home Rule movement under Isaac Butt's leadership but the *Advocate*'s fervent support for home rule does not seem to have aroused great interest in the local Irish community or even stirred a reaction from the colonial press. This changed abruptly, however, at the end of the decade when the Irish famine crisis of the winter of 1879–80 focused Australian attention on Ireland's problems and ushered in the decade of the 1880s when the 'Irish question' was frequently at the forefront of colonial interest. The *Advocate*'s voice was the first in the Australian press heard calling for Irish famine relief.[30] The colonies raised the massive sum of £95,000 in just a few months, the success of this appeal being indisputably because of its non-political and non-sectarian character. The *Advocate* argued, however, that there was an inescapable political dimension to Ireland's impoverished condition and expressed its support for the agrarian agitation that the newly formed Land League was leading in Ireland.[31]

The prosecution of Parnell and other Land League leaders in November 1880

---

28 Simon J. Potter, *News and the British world: the emergence of an imperial press system, 1876–1922* (Oxford, 2003), p. 33.   **29** Ibid., p. 28; *Advocate*, 25 Dec. 1880.   **30** *Advocate*, 6 Dec. 1879.   **31** *Advocate*, 10 Jan. 1880.

provided the opportunity for local Irish nationalist supporters to participate directly in the Irish political agitation. Again, Joseph Winter and the *Advocate* led the way, opening a Land League Defence Fund on 27 November, the first such fund in the country. This was the forerunner of branches of the Parnell Defence Fund and Land League in the colony. However, it was not until the arrival in June 1881 of the Land League envoy, John Walshe, a cousin of Michael Davitt, that the Land League was firmly established throughout Victoria. Walshe and Winter worked closely together and a picture of a unified nationalist leadership was presented to colonial audiences, with little evidence in the *Advocate*'s reporting of the tensions appearing in Ireland between the agendas of Parnell and Davitt. With Winter's organizing ability and the promotion of the *Advocate*, the Land League movement spread rapidly throughout Victoria and into southern New South Wales. Just as much of the provincial press in Ireland had 'performed a central and essential role in the spread of Land League activity', so too now the *Advocate* had become the principal organ of the Land League at the antipodes.[32] As such, the *Advocate* was again accused of links to violent Fenianism, being attacked not only in the press but in the Victorian parliament. Brandishing a copy of the *Advocate*, James Brown Patterson, the chief Orange spokesman in the Legislative Assembly, declared that the Irish Catholic paper was engaged in 'disseminating the vilest treason' in the colony.[33]

A further upsurge in anti-Irish feeling was generated by the colonial press with the arrival in February 1883 of the Redmond brothers, John and William, on a mission to raise funds for the Irish Party and to reorganize the local Land League movement into branches of the newly formed Irish National League. Despite intense opposition from the colonial press and Orange movement, and despite being shunned by prominent Irishmen and the Catholic hierarchy generally, the mission was successful in achieving its objectives, enjoying solid support from working class Irish. Joseph Winter, now national treasurer of the reorganized Irish National League, and John Walshe were singled out by John Redmond as the individuals primarily responsible for the mission's success.[34] In making a special presentation to Winter on behalf of Parnell and the Irish National League, Redmond asserted that 'there was not a better or more intelligently conducted Irish national journal than the *Advocate*'.[35]

Without the input of Irish envoys or a major impetus from Ireland, however, the local Irish nationalist movement struggled to maintain support, despite the efforts of the *Advocate* in engaging John Redmond and Michael Davitt as regular correspondents to promote the successes of Parnell and the Irish Party. In 1886, Gladstone's endorsement of home rule greatly boosted support for the Irish nationalist cause in Victoria as elsewhere, winning respectability to the cause for many colonists. With the *Advocate*'s promotion and Winter as a key organizer, Melbourne witnessed the

---

32 Marie-Louise Legg, *Newspapers and nationalism: the Irish provincial press, 1850–1892* (Dublin, 1999), p. 119. **33** *Victorian Parliamentary Debates, Legislative Assembly*, 39, 9 May 1882, 205. **34** *Advocate*, 10 Nov. 1883. **35** *Advocate*, 17 Nov. 1883.

largest public rallies until then seen for Irish political causes. In June 1886, several thousand rallied in support of Gladstone's home rule measures. Twelve months later, an even larger anti-coercion public rally protested against the British government's policies in Ireland. By 1888, with Parnell and the Irish Parliamentary Party itself threatened by the Special Commission in London investigating the *Times* allegations against Parnellism, the *Advocate* was strongly promoting the Parnell Defence Fund. Winter by this time was facing his own legal challenge, with a lawsuit against the *Age* newspaper's allegations of his mishandling of Irish funds. Though vindicated, innuendo and dissidence associated with the lawsuit led him to resign all Irish nationalist positions for the next four years. Despite Winter's withdrawing from public activities, however, the *Advocate* was soon leading the promotion of the next Irish political mission, the 1889 Australian mission of Irish Party members led by John Dillon. The Dillon mission was a resounding success despite the hostility of the Melbourne daily press, with Dillon marvelling at the powerful influence of the *Age* and the cable press agencies[36] The substantial sum of £35,000, desperately needed to save the Plan of Campaign agrarian agitation in Ireland, was raised. The Dillon mission also provided a much-needed rallying focus for local Irish nationalists, resulting in a reorganization of the Irish National League in Victoria under the leadership of Dr Nicholas O'Donnell (1862–1920), Australian-born of Limerick parents, who would lead the local movement for more than a quarter of a century.[37]

The early 1890s, however, were years of disillusionment and decline for the Irish nationalist movement in Victoria, as elsewhere, following the split in the Irish party, though the neutralist attitude of the local league under O'Donnell and its support by the *Advocate* meant that Victoria largely avoided the divisions that beset the movement elsewhere, notably in Sydney. These were also years of severe economic depression in Victoria – far removed from the boom times of the 1880s – and this exacerbated fundraising difficulties for Irish causes. A brief revival of Irish nationalist sentiment occurred in 1895, with Michael Davitt's visit, strongly promoted by the *Advocate*. Davitt forged a close relationship with Winter and later acknowledged Winter as 'the most earnest and active worker for Ireland among all the staunch volunteers in Australia'.[38] However, disillusionment with the continued factionalism in the Irish party saw the Irish nationalist movement virtually disappear in the Australian colonies in the last years of the century. Only in Victoria did a remnant of the Irish National League survive, relying heavily on the energies of Nicholas O'Donnell and Joseph Winter. O'Donnell was now increasingly driven by the inspiration of the Gaelic Revival in Ireland and within a few years was regarded as Australia's leading Gaelic scholar, conducting a Gaelic column in the *Advocate* with type imported from Ireland, the only Australian newspaper to do so.

---

36 John Dillon Notebook, 14 Sept. 1889, Dillon Papers, TCD, MS 6562. **37** Chris McConville, 'O'Donnell, Nicholas Michael (1862–1920)' in *Australian Dictionary of Biography*, 11 (Melbourne, 1988), pp 60–1. **38** Michael Davitt, *The fall of Feudalism in Ireland or the story of the Land League Revolution* (London, 1904), p. 384.

The year 1900 marked the unification of the Irish Party under John Redmond and the establishment in Victoria of the United Irish League, which the *Advocate* supported as staunchly as it had done its predecessor, the Irish National League. However, January 1900 also saw the beginning of a new Catholic weekly newspaper in Melbourne, the *Tribune*, which marked a significant departure from the *Advocate*. The new penny newspaper emphasized its 'national' focus for the new Australian nation and, pointedly, there were no Irish news items in its first issues.[39] The *Tribune* represented the reality that, with now only five per cent of the population Irish-born, the great majority of Australians of Irish extraction were more concerned with the reality of an emerging Australian nationhood than with a floundering nationalist movement in Ireland.

The Irish nationalist movement generally in colonial Australia, let alone the specific role of the Irish Catholic press in this movement, has received little attention from historians. Few have commented on the role and influence of the *Advocate*. One historian of the Catholic church in colonial Victoria, Terry Southerwood, was plainly unimpressed with the *Advocate* as a Catholic paper during this period, when he dismissed it as being for most of the nineteenth century 'little better than an Irish nationalist magazine'.[40] This brief assessment, while a gross over-simplification, is an acknowledgment that the *Advocate* during this period was first and foremost an Irish paper, under lay management and editorship, with the majority of the paper devoted to Irish items, followed by a few pages of 'Catholic intelligence'. Yet, despite its emphasis on Irish political items, the *Advocate* was sufficiently balanced in its reporting to succeed in maintaining the confidence of the Catholic hierarchy in Victoria, from the aged and difficult Archbishop Goold to his successor, the erudite Archbishop Thomas Carr, former bishop of Galway, who admired the *Advocate*'s literary quality and supported its home rule political stance.[41] Geoffrey Serle, however, is dismissive of the *Advocate*'s influence, writing that it 'was read widely by the faithful but had little broad impact'.[42] Serle's brief evaluation must be questioned. A newspaper's influence is particularly difficult to assess for the nineteenth century, when newspapers were kept for long periods, passing through many hands, so that actual readership was typically several times the paper's circulation. In acknowledging the *Advocate*'s wide readership among Irish Catholics, as Serle seems to have done, its political influence must also be acknowledged, particularly during the Parnell decade of the 1880s, when it was the mouthpiece and main vehicle for promotion and defence of the Irish leagues, of which Joseph Winter was the key organizer. The Irish nationalist movement in Victoria was generally more active and enduring than elsewhere in Australia for this one key reason – the unwavering support of the *Advocate* and its resolute proprietor.

Consistently during the last decades of the nineteenth century, the *Advocate* was

---

39 *Tribune*, 13 Jan. 1900.   **40** Southerwood, *Planting a faith*, p. 24.   **41** T.P. Boland, *Thomas Carr: Archbishop of Melbourne* (Brisbane, 1997), p. 210.   **42** Geoffrey Serle, 'Winter, Joseph (1844–1915)', p. 427.

a more committed champion of the Irish nationalist cause than any other Irish Catholic newspaper in Australia. The Sydney-centric perspective of Patrick O'Farrell, the dominant historian of Irish Australia, has undoubtedly influenced others in obscuring the importance of the Irish nationalist movement in Victoria and particularly the role played by the *Advocate*. The only newspaper of comparable influence was the Sydney *Freeman's Journal*, but, as Susan Pruuhl has noted in her comparative study of the Irish in colonial Australia, it lacked 'the total commitment of the *Advocate*' for the Home Rule movement.[43] The recent contention of Dermot Meleady, in reference to the early 1880s, that the Sydney *Freeman's Journal* was 'the principal Australian newspaper that made a reasonable effort to keep up with events in Ireland' has little basis in fact.[44] In his defence, Meleady has the excuse, like other historians working in Ireland or Britain, that the *Advocate* is not accessible there, unlike the Sydney *Freeman's Journal*. But historians in Australia have no such excuses. It is now four decades since Gregory Tobin's pioneering unpublished study of the Home Rule movement in Victoria and New South Wales, which he based largely on accounts in the *Advocate* and Sydney *Freeman's Journal*, implicitly recognizing the importance of this Irish Catholic press for colonial Irish nationalism.[45] However, there still has been no comprehensive analysis of Irish nationalism in colonial Australia. More particularly, the *Advocate*'s rightful place as the leading Irish nationalist voice in late nineteenth-century Australia has yet to receive the acknowledgment it deserves in the published histories of both Australia and Ireland.

43 Susan Pruuhl, 'The Irish in New South Wales, Victoria and South Australia, 1788–1880' (MA, University of Adelaide, 1979), p. 383.   44 Dermot Meleady, *Redmond: the Parnellite* (Cork, 2008), p. 66.   45 Gregory Tobin, 'The sea-divided Gael: a study of the Irish Home Rule movement in Victoria and New South Wales, 1880–1916' (MA, Australian National University, 1969).

A new stage for the stage Irish: Sydney, 1844: Lanty O'Liffey and *The Currency Lass; or My Native Girl*

KIERA LINDSEY

In 1843, 'a genuine "Emeralder" of very jovial temperament and much devoted to his bottle and his lass' strutted the boards of the Royal Victoria Theatre in Pitt Street, Sydney.[1] His name was Lanty O'Liffey and he was the creation of Dublin convict Edward Geoghegan, who was serving a sentence in the British penal colony of New South Wales. Geoghegan's play *The Currency Lass; or My Native Girl* was the first in the colony to contain significant local content.[2] It was also the first time a stage Irish character had been written specifically for the Australian stage.

Following its three-night season at the Royal Victoria Theatre in 1844, Geoghegan's play slumbered in the Colonial Secretary's archives for over a hundred years.[3] Its discovery in 1964 inspired a smattering of responses, but since then, with the exception of Australian drama theorist Veronica Kelly, *The Currency Lass* has attracted little critical attention.[4] The local content of this frothy musical farce has inspired the majority of scholars to contextualize Geoghegan's play within an early canon of Australian literature. This paper seeks to situate *The Currency Lass* within a broader set of references that acknowledge Geoghegan's Irish origins.

In 1844, *The Currency Lass* was the first play to hold a mirror up to Sydney society. Now, the same play offers a window into a world that was undergoing rapid social transformation and was intent upon self-conscious reinvention. Such a perspective reveals that Geoghegan's construction of Lanty O'Liffey and the play's 'Currency Lass', Susan Hearty, replicated alliances between two similarly marginalized groups within the colony, that is the ex-convict Irish and first-generation European Australians, also known as the native-born, rising colonists, cornstalks and currency

---

1 Character notes on Lanty O'Liffey, Edward Geoghegan, *The Currency Lass, or, My Native Girl: a musical play in two acts*, ed. Roger Covell, The National Theatre (Sydney, 1976). **2** Eric Irvin, 'Australia's first dramatists', *Australian Literary Studies*, 4:1 (1969), 28. **3** Albert B. Weiner, '"The Hibernian Father": the mystery solved', *Meanjin Quarterly*, 4 (1966), 456–64; Helen L. Oppenheim, The author of the Hibberian Father: an early colonial playwright', *Australian Literary Studies*, 2:4 (1966), pp 278–88; Janette Pelosi, 'Colonial drama revealed, or plays submitted for approval', *Life and letters in early Australia* (July–Aug. 2003), 1–7. **4** Veronica Kelly, 'Hybridity and performance in colonial Australian theatre: the Currency Lass' in Helen. Gilbert (ed.), *Post-colonial stages: critical and creative views on drama, theatre and performance* (Hebden Bridge Dangaroo, Austraia, 1999), pp 45–50.

lads and lasses. This paper examines how Geoghegan fashioned Lanty and Susan in response to a highly stratified society in which the Irish and the native-born often shared common feelings of abjection. Such an examination reveals how the alliance between the Irish servant and the Currency Lass fostered the potentially conspiratorial link between these groups, while also mimicking behaviours that both demographics were described as exhibiting in real life.[5] Indeed, while Lanty assumes the fool's mask of the stage Irish servant, acting out what I am calling 'the mask of the oppressed', that is to act subservient, while maintaining autonomy, Susan employs disguise and theatrical versatility to deliver a form of audacious exhibitionism that disorients and seduces her colonial masters. Such performances offer insight into the nature of colonial society during this period, suggesting that while both groups experienced varying degrees of class exclusion and derision, they also enjoyed sufficient self-expression to articulate their frustrations and negotiate a degree of mobility for themselves. By making Lanty and Susan the central characters of *The Currency Lass*, Geoghegan not only places fleeting moments of resistance at the heart of the play's plot, drama and comic drive, he also presents a vision of his new home as a society where evasion, audacity and occasional subterfuge exist and are, to some extent, compatible with this particular manifestation of British Imperial order.

By examining Lanty within the broader tradition of stage Irish characters, we can also see how Geoghegan's *Currency Lass* stimulated social tensions within the colony regarding Irish and English identity. The stage Irish servant had been a familiar fixture on English and Irish stages since the seventeenth century, where these characters frequently featured in the work of British playwrights such as Thomas Dekker (1604), George Farquar (1702) and John Baldwin Buckstone (1828) as both loyal dupes and braggart servants. As these plays were often set on English soil, a lack of familiarity with English customs was accentuated to make these characters the brunt of English ridicule. Thus, they were also relegated to the sub-plot. Such Irish servant characters were, as David Krause notes, the theatrical descendant of the parasite slave from Roman theatre.[6] By the second half of the nineteenth century, however, stage Irish characters were being re-appropriated by Irish playwrights for more subversive purposes.[7] Dionysius Lardner Boucicault is largely recognized as the first to do this.[8] In his 1867 play, *The Shaugraun*, Boucicault restored the stage Irishman to home territory and to the central plot. The stage English or Anglo-Irish were recast as absurd and malign, while the stage Irishman was celebrated for his love of women, whiskey and songs, his natural wit and the ability to right all wrongs.

5 G.B. Earp, *The gold colonies of Australia: comprising their history, territorial divisions, produce, and capabilities: also, ample notices of the gold mines, and how to get to them: with every advice to emigrants* (London, 1852); Alexander Harris and W.S. Ramson, *The emigrant family, or, the story of an Australian settler* (Canberra, 1967); James Francis Hogan, *The Irish in Australia* (London, 1887); Godfrey Charles Mundy, D.W.A. Baker, *Our Antipodes* (Canberra, 2006). **6** David Krause (ed.), *The Dolmen Boucicault: the theatre of Dion Boucicault* (Dublin, 1964), p. 13. **7** Annelise Truninger, *Paddy and the Paycock: a study of the stage Irishman from Shakespeare to O'Casey* (Bern, 1976), pp 32–44. **8** George Chester Duggan, *The stage Irishman: a history of the Irish play and stage character from the earliest times* (Dublin and Cork, 1937).

Thirty-one years before *The Shaugraun*, Geoghegan's stage Irish servant represents an earlier, but transitory moment in the evolution of this character from loyal dupe to transgressive fool. Lanty has more freedom than previous stage Irish servants, and his linguistic and physical agility serve as a stark contrast to the rigidity of the stage English characters in the play. And yet, while *The Shaugraun* offers a critique of the English and Anglo-Irish, Lanty's interaction with these English characters in the play is always playful and light-hearted. He enjoys some autonomy but, ultimately, he is content to exist with them within the social order of the British colony.

These new developments in the stage Irish servant were possible, precisely because New South Wales represented foreign ground, but not quite neutral territory for both the stage Irish and the stage English. Although New South Wales was a British colony, it was still unfamiliar ground for Irish and English newcomers, both of whom lacked knowledge of local customs, social attitudes and linguistic nuances. In *The Currency Lass*, Geoghegan depicts two of three English characters – Miss Catherine Dormer and Samuel Simile – as 'fresh off the boat'. The romantic lead, Edward Stanford, possesses many of the traits of the typical British New Chum, and conducts himself in this new environment according to awkward 'old world' manners. In contrast, Lanty is in the 'know'. Although he is Stanford's servant, he rarely performs any of the tasks that Stanford sets him, but instead conspires with Susan to deliberately 'ruffle the equanimity' of Stanford's uncle, the aging British thespian Samuel Simile, who Kelly has correctly identified as the play's symbol of imperial authority.[9]

By forging Lanty's alliance with this Currency Lass and the wider native-born population, Geoghegan placed his stage Irish on familiar ground within the colony and simultaneously reconfigured the stage English as outsiders. In doing so, Geoghegan's play attempted to win favour and build alliances with the native-born. In the process, however, *The Currency Lass* alienated the growing number of British Isles free settler immigrants who were becoming increasingly influential in Sydney's public sphere.

SYDNEY IN THE 1840S

With its extreme isolation, as well as its shifting status from penal outpost to free settlement, New South Wales in the 1840s offered a unique, even exotic environment for Geoghegan's exportation of the stage Irish. At first glance, Sydney was like many other British colonies with a bustling urban centre not unlike Dublin and perhaps even slightly more modern. Gas lighting had been introduced to the streets in 1841, and visitors were often impressed by the evidence of civilized life. It was, as some noted, 'on the verge of becoming a grand centre of civilization'.[10] Indeed, many

9 Kelly, 'Hybridity and performance', p. 43. 10 G.B. Earp, *What we did in Australia: being the practical experience of three clerks, in the stock-yard and at the gold fields* (London, 1853), pp 39–40.

noted that it had grown at a rate 'without parallel in ancient or modern times'.[11] In contrast, Dublin in the early 1840s had been relegated to the level of a provincial British city due to the evacuation of significant numbers of political and aristocratic classes who had left after the Act of Union in the early 1800s. The city could still boast an extensive Georgian legacy of 'broad thoroughfares, impressive squares and outstanding civic architecture', but crime, poverty and uneven policing had lead to significant urban decline.[12]

Sydney provided Geoghegan with a fertile laboratory for his experimentation with the stage Irish. This was a deeply fissured society with numerous tensions simmering beneath the surface. It could also be volatile and unpredictable. The city craved civility and respectability but was reluctant to wean itself off cheap convict labour. Severe drought in the early 1840s had lead to economic depression, causing a record number of insolvencies and highly agitated public meetings. Men shame-lessly jostled for position, and snobbery was rife. Charles Darwin had visited the place in the 1830s and hated it, describing Sydney as a society that was 'rancorously divided ... on almost every subject'.[13]

The end of transportation to Australia's eastern coast settlements in 1840 had been a harbinger for major social change. As the convict population gradually decreased, the native-born assumed that they would naturally become the dominant social group in the colony.[14] Instead, the desire to restructure the penal outpost into a free settler society led colonial authorities to encourage the immigration of free British Isles settlers and, by the early 1840s, Sydney's immigrant population had more than trebled.[15] The rapid growth in the number of British Isles immigrants tipped the balance in favour of these newcomers, simultaneously dislodging the native-born from the social privileges and land grants that many felt was their natural birthright.

Consequently, this dramatic influx of free immigrants produced several uncom-fortable irritants. Not only did the colony continue to suffer a degree of imperial abjection associated with its convict past, newcomers were also prone to upset the locals by excluding those they assumed were tarnished with the convict taint, while also scrutinizing the native-born for their moral character.[16] Social cohesion within

11 William Pasco Crook, Letter to a friend in England, 31 Dec. 1804, Parramatta, Missionary Society Papers, Samuel Marsden Private letters, pp 537–8. Mitchell Library, NSW. **12** Pat Dargan, *Exploring Georgian Dublin* (Dublin, 2008), pp 25–6. **13** Charles Darwin, *Narrative of the surveying voyages of His Majesty's ships, Adventure and Beagle between the years 1826–1836, describing their examination of the southern shores of South America and the Beagle's circumnavigation of the globe* (London, 1836), 2, pp 443–4. **14** Beverley Kingston, *A history of New South Wales* (New York, Cambridge, 2006), p. 19; John Molony, *The native born: the first white Australians* (Melbourne, 2000), pp 46 and 149. **15** Manning Clark, *A history of Australia: the beginning of an Australian civilisation, 1824–51* (Melbourne, 1973), 3, p. 158. The number of immigrants arriving in New South Wales rose from 4,275 in 1837 to 13,358 in 1839. At the same time, with the end of transportation in 1840, the number of convicts also tapered off, from 3,425 in 1837 to 3,073 in 1838 and 2,293 in 1839. **16** Peter Cunningham, *Two years in New South Wales* (London, 1827), vol. 1. See also G.B. Earp and Joseph Fowles, *Sydney in 1848: a facsimile of the original text and copper-plate engravings of its principal streets, public buildings and churches,* the colony was predicated on the notion of rehabilitation, and many successful busi-nessmen had arrived in New South Wales as convicted felons.[17] Such backgrounds required a degree of discretion, and by the 1840s, even while convicts like Geoghegan were still serving their sentences, much of the vocabulary associated with the penal colony had been eradicated or replaced with euphemisms. Emancipated convicts were now referred to as 'Old Colonists'. Thus, debates associated with the possible resumption of transportation produced a further sensitivity that required delicate negotiation.[18] While newly arrived free settlers were outspoken in their support or rejection of transportation, convicts and their descendants were not. Like new arrivals, these long-term residents longed to rid their streets of the spectre of chain gangs but − to speak out against transportation was to condemn their own past. Ambivalent silence was their best and perhaps their only option.

Consequently, many long-term residents were uneasy with the volume and confidence of these new immigrants. Such tensions were particularly manifest in the territorial behaviours of a demographic known as the Cabbagers. Named after the cabbage-tree hats they wore, which became the well-recognized 'emblem of their order', this group, which consisted mainly of working-class native-born men, had a reputation for publicly pranking 'Jimmy Grants', a rhyming slang term they used to refer to immigrants.[19] They derived particular pleasure from hanging about Sydney theatre doors and knocking black beaver hats off the heads of these immigrants attempting to make their way to the stalls and boxes.[20]

While the Cabbagers were reputed to dress in long spurs, tight breeches, brightly coloured checked shirts and waistcoats, 'finished with a red kerchief and a Van Dyke beard', the formal dark-coloured suits and black beaver hats of these 'New Chums' antagonized the native-born.[21] The tribal behaviours exhibited by these Cabbagers was conducted, quite literally, in the threshold entrances of the Sydney playhouses, a visual manifestation of how the theatrical and public sphere frequently blurred during this period. The behaviour of these Cabbage-tree hat mobs, as they became known, also suggests that within the colony, relief from complex social frustrations were frequently sought in performance, both in the playhouse and in the streets.

Such behaviours reflect how numerous mechanisms, including clothes and

chapels, etc., from drawings by Joseph Fowles (Sydney, 1973).   **17** See John B. Hirst, 'An oddity from the start: convicts and national character', *The Monthly* (July 2008), 12–15; Brian H. Fletcher, *Colonial Australia before 1850* (Melbourne, 1976). The Australian Dictionary of Biography contains numerous examples of this, while my PhD is concerned with an emancipist called Martin Gill who arrived in the colony as a transported felon in 1820 from Dublin and was a successful businessman by 1836.   **18** A comprehensive survey of this debate is offered in Peter Cochrane, *Colonial ambition: foundations of Australian democracy* (Melbourne, 2006).   **19** These terms are recorded by contemporary observers, including Louisa Ann Meredith, C.G. Mundy and Townsend, cited below.   **20** William Baker, *Heads of the people: an illustrated journal of literature, whims, and oddities* (Sydney, 1847).   **21** Molony, *The native born: the first white Australians,* p. 56; Joseph Phipps Townsend, *Rambles and observations in New South Wales: with sketches of men and manners, ... Aborigines, ... scenery, and some hints to emigrants* (London, 1849).

language, were used to assert or undermine authority and social position. Indeed, while the physical boisterousness of the Cabbagers was a relatively new phenomenon, language had played a pivotal role in identity politics within Sydney since the early 1800s. The term 'Currency' was a local nickname coined in the first decade of the nineteenth century in reference to first-generation European Australians. It alluded to the inferior quality of the native-born, contrasting local currency unfavourably to the good 'sterling' pounds associated with British migrants. By the 1830s, the native-born had embraced the term, wearing it, as one newspaper editor observed, 'like a boastful appendage'.[22]

The topic of land grants was a particularly sensitive issue to many native-born, whose sense of birth-right made them increasingly resentful about having their applications for land regularly overlooked in favour of these new arrivals. In response to this, first-generation Australians appropriated the term 'native-born' from Aboriginal 'natives' who henceforth became known as 'blackfellows'.[23] In the process of becoming the colony's new 'natives', the native-born linguistically relegated the Aborigines to the margins of white colonial society, where they were reduced in the colonial imagination, to 'dingy divils' described by Samuel Similie in the play, as 'perambulating the streets wearing little more than 'skins and squalid blankets'. Of course, beyond the city boundaries, Aborigines were a much more threatening reality. The newspapers frequently recorded violent conflicts between Aborigines and settlers. These became known as 'the Black Wars' and were a real source of ambivalence about the implications of colonial settlement in New South Wales.[24]

As such examples indicate, however, public behaviour, language and re-appropriation were integral to early nineteenth-century New South Wales identity politics. It is therefore not surprising that such devices are also central to Geoghegan's play. Indeed, confusion about the terms Aboriginal and native provides the ambiguity upon which the plot depends. This functions as an in-joke, which serves to highlight the outsider status of new arrivals as well as the social otherness of the Aborigines. In doing so, Geoghegan affirms the 'proudest boast' made in the play by Susan's brother, Harry Hearty, that *only* the native-born are 'privileged to claim their birthright as "natives" of the soil and children of Australia!'

Geoghegan uses numerous techniques to pitch his play at the native-born, even more specifically, the Cabbagers crowding the pit designed to earn their admiration. Harry Hearty is prone to patriotic outbursts, while Susan's versatile performance is designed to earn our admiration. Three songs are dedicated to the native-born; Stanford sings 'My Native Girl' at the opening, while 'The Boy with the Cabbage-tree Hat' and 'The Currency Lass', which concludes the play, are both sung by Susan. Together, these songs assert the distinctive characteristics of the native-born,

22 Horatio Wills, *The Currency Lad newspaper*, 2 Aug. 1832. **23** K.S. Inglis, *Australian colonists: an exploration of social history 1788–1870* (Melbourne, 1993), p. 40; Louisa Ann Meredith, *Notes and sketches of New South Wales during a residence in that colony from 1839 to 1844* (London, 1844). **24** Numerous examples of this exist in M.F. Christie, *Aborigines in colonial Victoria, 1835–86* (Sydney, 1979).

simultaneously revealing, however, a need for 'applause' and 'plaudits' from the audience. In 'The Boy with the Cabbage-tree Hat', for instance, Susan declares:

> His heart ever true to his friend and his lass,
> To honour the fair his first duty,
> The Currency Lad never flinches his glass
> While he pours the libations to beauty.
> Let others then seek by each exquisite air
> To win your applause and all that, sir.
> They may make the attempt but they ne'er can compare
> With the boy in the cabbage-tree hat, sir!

For all the bravado of this rousing celebration of the Colony's Currency Lads, the play concludes with a much more tentative proffering of the female of the species:

> And now kind friends may we presume
> (On you our fate depending)
> To hope your smiles will banish gloom
> 'The Native Girl' befriending.
>
> No terrors vexing
> Cares perplexing
> Joy to each endeavour
> Your plaudits give
> If you receive
> The Currency Lass with favour.

In these two songs we might detect the 'push-me, pull-you' of a self-conscious nascent nationalism, which desires, on one hand, to defiantly assert its individuality, but on the other, still craves recognition and approval. As a result of these inherent tensions perhaps, the play's central character, Susan Hearty, requires back-up in the form of being part of a double-act. Thus, she depends upon Lanty to help her secure her man and ensure a happy ending. To do so, Lanty employs the pranks of the stage Irish servant. While Lanty is not the central plot's key protagonist, he is integral to it and is therefore the only other character who sings two songs, both of which express a love of whiskey, women and fighting. Lanty also remains on stage throughout the unfolding drama, using numerous tricks to maintain the dramatic momentum required between Susan's dazzling displays and costume changes.

The cross-pollinations between the theatrical and 'the real' within *The Currency Lass* and colonial society invites consideration of the intersections between the theatrical and public sphere in Sydney and how the relatively new phenomena of the playhouse may have influenced new modes of public expression. Throughout the Georgian era, playhouses in England and Ireland had been synonymous with insurrection, riots and social disorder.[25] Playhouses, indeed all things theatrical, had been strictly prohibited within the penal colony of New South Wales since its inception in 1788 until the mid-1830s.[26] Popular theatre was little more than ten years old when Geoghegan's play premiered in 1844 and the Colonial Secretary still insisted upon examining all scripts before production. Plays were to be sourced from London, eliminating the possibility of subversive local content and convicts were strictly prohibited from any form of participation.[27] With the support of Irishman Francis Nesbitt, one the colony's most popular tragedians, Geoghegan thwarted all these regulations. He submitted his play to the Colonial Secretary under a pseudonym and secured his play's production at the Royal Victoria Theatre, Sydney's largest and most respectable playhouse.[28]

Geoghegan had written the part of Susan Hearty for an accomplished 15-year-old currency lass called Matilda Jones, who had become a popular actress in the late 1830s and early 1840s, before retiring from the stage in late 1843 to marry. When the play premiered in May 1844, Madam Louise, a 'cockney import', stepped into the role of the currency lass, while the role of Lanty, which had been written for Nesbitt, was performed by Joseph Simmons, a British actor celebrated for his performances as Irishmen and sailors. Even patriotic Harry Hearty was played by another of the Royal Victoria's English actors. Thus, a series of homogenizing cultural practices, which demanded the use of British actors in the colony's playhouse, absorbed and diffused the potentially divisive distinctions between the different nationalities represented in the play.

Veronica Kelly has indicated that during this period in New South Wales, popular theatre provided a safety valve for social tensions as well as a laboratory for the rehearsal of new identity configurations.[29] While Kelly argues that Geoghegan's interest in national and local distinctions made a particularly strong contribution to identity configurations within the colony, my reading instead acknowledges the limited impact of this so-called 'intervention'. Although reviews of the play's premiere suggest that the native-born rumbustiously delighted in Geoghegan's depiction of colonial life and celebration of nascent Australian nationalism, a critic writing for the *Sydney Morning Herald* condemned *The Currency Lass* as being 'truly colony, indeed – rather too colonial for my liking'.[30] This attitude seems to have been

25 John Greene, 'The repertory of Dublin theatres, 1720–45', *Eighteenth Century Ireland*, 2 (1987), 133–48; Robert Jordan, *The convict theatres of early Australia, 1788–1840* (Sydney, 2002), see 'Ch. 3: The Sydney theatre, 1796–1804/7' and 'Ch. 6: Convict theatre, 1807– 1830', pp 24–45; 65–82. Marc Baer, *Theatre and disorder in Late Georgian London*, (Oxford 1992). **26** Eric Irvin, *Dictionary of the Australian Theatre, 1788–1914* (Sydney, 1985), p. 66; Harold Love and Australian Theatre Studies Centre, *The Australian stage: a documentary history* (Kensington, 1984), p. 89; Helen L. Oppenheim and Mitchell Library (NSW), 'Colonial theatre the rise of legitimate stage in Australia, 1824–1847', microform unpublished PhD thesis. **27** Pelosi, 'Colonial drama revealed, or plays submitted for approval', p. 2. **28** Roger Coghill, xvi. Currency Lass, introduction. **29** Kelly, 'Hybridity and performance', p. 42. **30** 'Review of the *Currency Lass; or My Native Girl*', *Sydney Morning Herald*, 16 May 1844.

shared by the increasingly respectable middle-class immigrant audiences of Sydney, for after a short season of only three nights, Geoghegan's play was replaced with standard fare from London and there are no records to suggest that it ever enjoyed a reprisal. The limited popularity of *The Currency Lass* signals the play's ability to strike a nerve within the colony, and makes it all the more interesting as a historical document. Indeed, read as a contested and contesting text, the play points to particular flashpoints and sensitivities within the colony that in turn reveal something about the distinctive way that Geoghegan fashioned his Irish servant for this new world audience.

THE PLAY IS THE THING

The play begins in 1843 in the Sydney drawing room of Edward Stanford, who has just decided to marry his 'faithful and unsophisticated native girl' as soon as he has the approval of his best friend, Susan's brother Harry Hearty. Having returned from a 'tour of Europe', this proud patriot bounds onto stage with 'redoubled zest' for his native city. 'Many Wonders have doubtless met my view and excited admiration', Harry eulogizes to Stanford,

> ... but my own country still possesses advantages surpassed by none. Let Italy boast her cloudless skies and beauteous dames – the skies of Australia are as pure, our native girls far more lovely. France may pride in her courtly airs and polished graces – but to me the blunt sincerity and cordial frankness of a currency lad are far more grateful ... oh ever may they, like myself, prefer my native Australia to any other clime or nation under the sun!'

Hearty endorses the union between his sister and Stanford, confiding that he too is ready to succumb to 'the delights of wedded love', having met 'a fair shipmate' on the boat called Miss Catherine Dormer. As Harry and Stanford dress for their prospective proposals, Lanty reflects that he also 'has a mighty laneing' for women and 'a gra of the cordial', before breaking into a song entitled 'Whiskey and Love' about the inflammable nature of an Irishman's heart.

Stanford's flowery proposal is arrested by Susan, who requests 'a truce on raptures'. She rejects 'the restraints of fashionable prudery', preferring frankness and candour to uncalled-for reserve. She nonetheless has no hesitation in entrusting her confiding heart to his care. The newly engaged pair sing a love duet, before Lanty arrives with a letter from Samuel Simile, who is due to arrive in the colony from England determined to prevent his nephew's union with the native girl. 'What! Give your name to a Wowski? ... have a set of woolly headed little imps of darkness cambering about my knees calling me Grand Uncle', exclaims the appalled (and appalling) Similie. Lacking local knowledge and assuming that 'native' refers to Aboriginal, Simile demands that his nephew instead form a union with a woman of 'superior theatrical ability'. He even has one in mind, a woman called Miss Dormer who has just arrived in the colony too. Susan's ire is provoked and she decides upon a plan to

> completely mystify the old gentlemen … introduce a number of fictitious personages … intrude upon his retirement, interrupt his most serious avocations, upset his tranquillity … tease and torment him into compliance with all our wishes, even the marriage of Stanford with a 'native girl'

In her desire to demonstrate her theatrical prowess, Susan embarks upon a 'duplicity' of dances and disguises, enlisting Lanty to distract Simile during her costume changes, with wild yarns and even wilder songs. Lanty approaches this task with relish. No longer the blundering stage Irish servant – this new world Irish servant undermines the stage English with a raft of devices, which illustrate his quick-wittedness. Irishness, in the hands of Lanty, becomes a powerful weapon. While Lanty's English masters ascribe him with stock stage Irish traits, both men appear rigid, naïve and dull, next to lithe linguistic tricks that allow Lanty to function, as Kelly notes, as a moving target that constantly evades and exceeds 'the fixed gaze of imperialism'.[31] Witness, for example, Lanty's arrival at the opening of the play, predicated by Stanford, bellowing for his servant. Lanty finally arrives, drunk. When Stanford asks him where he has been, Lanty responds:

> didn't you sind me to take places for you in the theaytre? And whin they directed me to the next door, d'ye think I cold lave the place with the curse ov the fair upon me, as we say in Donnybrook, and it with the Queen's name over it? No, in troth! So I left them Her Majesty's picture (bless her!) and got a dhrop ov the right stuff in exchange and staid listenin' to them devils of play actors gosterin' and jokin' at the bar.

In this playful patter, the audience learn about the true nature of Lanty's servant role. He *may* perform his tasks, but at his own pace and pleasure. In the process, he will offer only passing respect to Queen Victoria and the images of her that adorn the theatre. The bumbling stage Irish servant is thus combined with the reluctant convict servant (not unlike Geoghegan himself), who was well-documented in colonial Sydney as one who infuriated his master with his indifference or deliberate inaptitude to work.[32] Sydney's extreme labour shortage meant that masters were frequently at the mercy of servants who were more than capable of manipulating the terms of their employment. Indeed, at the end of this scene, as in many others, Lanty exits without performing any of the tasks requested. Despite this, or perhaps even because

31 Kelly, 'Hybridity and performance', p. 52.   **32** Inglis, *Australian colonists: an exploration of social history, 1788–1870*; Clark, *A history of Australia: the beginning of an Australian civilisation, 1824–51.*

of it, Lanty achieves the affection of both his master and the audience. Here, again, is Lanty reporting back to Stanford about the arrival of Similie:

> Och, Masther Edward, shure and it's the ould gintleman himself that's come. As soon as he arrived, he opened his writin' desk and sets to work quill dhrivin for the bare life. 'Does your honour want anyting?' sis I – manin' to be quite civil and polite. 'Don't taze me', sis he. 'I won't', sis I. 'Where's your Masther?', sis he. 'He's out', sis I. 'Go', sis he, and pints to the door. 'Where?', sis I. 'To the divil', sis he. 'Thank you for nothin', sis I and off I set to you, sir.

In these scenes, Geoghegan turns the tables on the expected roles of the stage Irish and English, reconfiguring the stage English characters as straight men who are duped by Lanty's playful license. Similie is out-of-touch and ill-informed when it comes to local matters. His ignorance renders him foolish and antiquated. Stanford is also slow on the uptake. His future union with Susan Hearty is therefore left in the hands of the Currency Lass and the Irish servant, who are thankfully equipped with an entertaining number of skills and schemes.

No sooner has Simile arrived in the colony, than he receives a visit from Susan disguised as Frank Foretop, a 'mad midshipman' who has come to warn Simile off Miss Dormer, 'a tight little craft' who he has 'cut from her moorings ... and now intends to take in tow'. He has heard of Simile's plans regarding Miss Dormer and Stanford, and challenges both uncle and nephew to a duel. As Susan leaves, Lanty regales Simile with stories about the 'beautiful sport' of duelling, before breaking into another 'Raal Ould Irish Rollicker' song, liberally punctuated with Irish phrases. As Lanty concludes, Susan appears again, this time disguised as a glamorous French actress who wants Simile to write her a part which will 'set all Sydney de blaze of happiness'. As Mademoiselle Bellejambe, Susan performs a song-and-dance routine that progresses from French dance, to British hornpipe, Highland Fling and Irish Lilt before concluding with a German Waltz. It is a dazzling display of theatrical ability that demonstrates the versatility of the Currency Lass. At the conclusion of this scene, a rapturous Simile observes that he would have forgiven his nephew's indifference to Miss Dormer if he had 'set his affections upon such a creature ... but a Native! Psha!'

Susan returns to Simile, this time as Cabbager Charlie Clackit, who has come to arrange the duel between Simile and Frank Foretop. Charlie describes the simple pleasures of life and how most nights will find him with his friends – 'stationed in the front rank of the pit'. To this crowd, as Clackit/Susan sings 'The Boy in the Cabbage-tree hat', while Miss Dormer arrives in 'showy' finery and determined to 'tie the knot' with uncle or nephew, depending on who has the most 'tin'. Horrified by this vulgarity and terrified by the prospect of a duel with Foretop, Simile calls upon Stanford to rescue him. In his desperation, he withdraws all objections to his nephew's union with the native girl.

The play thus concludes with the native girl reappearing, not as 'the Hottentot Venus' or a 'Princess of Timbuctoo', but as a native-born, whose 'complexion is

European' and theatrical skills have been more than demonstrated. A delighted Simile proclaims of Susan, 'Advance Australia! Blessed be the land that gave existence to so bright a gem!' He immediately consents to Stanford and Susan's wedding and bestows a £200 reward upon Lanty, who has declared his love with Susan's servant Jenny. The play ends, with the unions between Susan and Stanford, Harry and Miss Dormer and Lanty and Jenny all secured. Imperial authority has given its blessings to the genetic and cultural continuum of the colony. With the assistance of Lanty, the Currency Lass has secured her prize and the Rising Colonists have demonstrated that they are indeed the legitimate inheritors of the land.

CONCLUSION

By writing the first play with local content in the colony of New South Wales and making the character of Lanty central to its plot, Geoghegan created a new stage for the stage Irish. This was a stage where neither the Irish nor the English could assume 'home ground'. To occupy this territory, Lanty had to appear better equipped with local knowledge and more connected to the legitimate locals than his English counterparts. To do this, Geoghegan makes Lanty integral to the plot and antics of the Currency Lass – and simultaneously assigns his English characters with the roles of New Chums and Newcomers. To reinforce this, Lanty shares with Susan the task of undermining the British symbol of imperial authority, Samuel Simile.

Like Lanty's support of Susan, Geoghegan's connection with the Cabbagers is one that engages in transgressive play, but simultaneously seeks to exist within the social order. The play delights in the mercurial and the audacious, but never endorses the incendiary. Rather than offer tactics for rebellion, *The Currency Lass* presents techniques for survival and accommodation. Geoghegan's play proposes that, like Lanty, colonists assume the mask of the oppressed using sly civility to side-step authority and acquire a certain degree of mobility. 'Act subserviently, but be autonomous', Geoghegan seems to prompt in a stage whisper. Susan's behaviour also offers audiences both a deeply liberating response to the imperial gaze as well as another model of how legitimacy might be asserted through self-conscious exhibitionism.

The short season of *The Currency Lass* indicates, however, that Geoghegan's play did not find favour with the majority of his audience. By playing to the Cabbagers in the pit, Geoghegan failed to consider the sensibilities of other increasingly influential audience members seated in the stalls and boxes. Having braved their way across the threshold of the Royal Victoria Theatre, perhaps suffering public ridicule from Cabbagers in the process, such audiences were unlikely to share Geoghegan's appreciation of their tribal patriotism of the native-born Cabbagers. These immigrants came to the Royal Victoria Theatre with the expectation of seeing British actors performing plays from the London stage. It was a chance to bring close that which was at a distance, to temporarily dissolve the spatial and temporal reality of living in a remote British colony. While such audiences were no doubt familiar with stage Irish servants who suffered the brunt of British jokes, the character of Lanty did not conveniently conform to these reassuring and familiar stereotypes. Instead, he playfully outsmarted his British masters, simultaneously destabilizing their authority and even their sense of place within the colony. Instead of providing these audiences with a respite from reality, Geoghegan's play revealed some of its more unstable elements. The mirror he held up to colonial society accentuated its least favourable and most fractious features.

The remote and transitional nature of Sydney in the 1840s nonetheless provided a unique environment for the stage Irish servant. Previously based on British soil and made the brunt of British ridicule, Geoghegan's stage Irish servant acquired a new degree of licence on Australian shores. Lanty O'Liffey could use language to undermine and tease. He could develop alliances and local knowledge that equipped him with greater mobility and importance. Such features promoted him from sub-plot to central plot. There, he joyously sang, danced, fell in love and won the affection of his audience. In the evolution of the stage Irish servant from seventeenth-century buffoon to late nineteenth-century Shaugraun, Lanty O'Liffey therefore represents a fleeting but threshold moment. Regardless of its short season and limited popularity, this Dublin Convict can be celebrated for creating in this foreign land a new and significant style of performance for the stage Irish.

'The emigrants' friend'? Guides for Irish emigrants by clergymen, *c.*1830–82

SARAH RODDY

The effect that increasing levels of education and literacy had on emigration from nineteenth-century Ireland has been much considered. Explorations of the role of the proselytizing letters of previously departed family members in fostering chain migration are many, and the ubiquity of advertisements for emigrant shipping lines – even in newspapers that purported to oppose emigration – has also been noted.[1] What is more, as early as 1868, one Catholic bishop sharply observed with reference to the National School system that 'Educated youths who have had the maps of the world before their eyes for years are not likely to sit down for life on a patch of potato garden.'[2] Few of the three million people who left Ireland between the granting of Catholic Emancipation and the onset of the Land War can therefore have done so without the opportunity to garner information about the process of emigration and their ultimate destination.[3]

Yet there remains at least one under-appreciated feature of the swirl of data that surrounded would-be emigrants. Throughout the period, publishers eager to cash in on what appeared to be an endless potential readership produced a steady stream of emigrant guidebooks. The British Library catalogue alone contains upwards of seventy such publications, their authors varying from gung-ho adventurers and gold prospectors to sober colonial bureaucrats and jobbing journalists.[4] A number of anonymously written guides of questionable objectivity were also specially commis-

---

1 See William Forbes Adams, *Ireland and Irish emigration to the New World from 1815 to the Famine* (London, 1932), p. 218; Joel Mokyr, *Why Ireland starved: a quantitative and analytical history of the Irish economy, 1800–1850* (London, 1983), p. 247; Kerby A. Miller, *Emigrants and exiles: Ireland and the Irish exodus to North America* (Oxford, 1985); E.R.R. Green, 'Ulster emigrants' letters' in E.R.R. Green (ed.), *Essays in Scotch-Irish history* (London, 1969), pp 87–103; David Fitzpatrick, *Oceans of consolation: personal accounts of Irish migration to Australia* (London, 1994); David Fitzpatrick, *Irish emigration 1801–1921* (Dublin, 1984), p. 24; Arnold Schrier, *Ireland and the American emigration, 1850–1900* (Minneapolis, MN, 1958), p. 179. 2 David Moriarty, Bishop of Kerry, to Lord Dufferin, 23 Mar. 1868, PRONI, D107/H/B/H/M. 3 See Dympna McLoughlin, 'Information flows and Irish emigration: the image of America in Ireland, 1820–1870: a study of parliamentary papers, newspapers, pamphlets and emigrants' lore' (MA, NUIM, 1983). 4 John Capper, *The emigrant's guide to Australia, with a new map of the gold fields* (London, 1852); Colonial Land and Emigration Commission, *The emigrant's guide to New South Wales, Van Diemen's Land, Lower Canada, Upper Canada and New Brunswick* (London, 1832); Anon., *The Emigrant in Australia, or Gleanings from the Gold-Fields by an Australian journalist [with maps]* (London, 1852);

sioned by competing shipping companies and given away or sold by return of post via their press advertisements.[5] In the Irish case, however, arguably the most significant sub-genre comprised manuals written by clergymen, who offered what readers might have hoped would be trustworthy, impartial and, above all, useful advice.

A need for such advice certainly existed. While the letters of those who had previously departed were the main source of information for most intending emigrants, offering, as David Fitzpatrick has noted, 'a far wider range of questions and answers than the public discourse of the emigrant handbook',[6] they could still present problems. There was almost certainly an element of exaggeration of anticipated successes on the part of many correspondents, while some others surely obfuscated to cover inevitable failures. The personal could also be political; as Fitzpatrick notes, letters could be 'designed to influence and sometimes manipulate readers. Writers often selected facts and expressed sentiments purposefully rather than sentimentally, knowing the probable consequences of their advice for recipients'.[7]

Aware of such shortcomings, some clergymen, including Father John O'Hanlon, saw fit not only to caution people against believing inflated accounts in 'American letters', but also against writing similar letters home on their own arrival.[8] Revd John Brown was in agreement, warning in a popular sermon that 'Exaggerated views should never be given of success and prosperity, lest others should have cause to repent of following to their serious injury'.[9] By contrast, Brown's fellow Presbyterian minister John McCleery, was enraged by an opposing tendency, which he perceived in some emigrant correspondence, prompting him to attack those who sent 'whining letters across the Atlantic in which they pour forth pitiful complaints about the death-like loneliness of bush life, the indescribable toils and pains of chopping wood, the intolerable severity of the heat in Summer, and the cold in Winter ... I respectfully caution your readers not to be so indiscreet as to form their opinions of Canada from the dismal growls of such malcontents'.[10]

This intimate knowledge of the content of emigrant letters was a result of the practical involvement many Irish clergy had in the emigration process. Both letters and remittances routinely went through the local pastor, giving him a unique overview of the fate of local emigrants. He was often called upon to read aloud the emigrants' usually glowing accounts of their new homes, and perhaps even had the sense to gauge their accuracy by how much money was enclosed. One visitor to Ireland even noted that many Catholic emigrants sent their remittances not to their own parish priest, but to the local Protestant clergyman, which, while saying little for the perceived trustworthiness of the former, says much for the extent to which clergy were regarded as the natural facilitators of emigration.[11] Furthermore, several

5 [Griffiths, Newcombe & Co.], *Handbook for Australian emigrants* (London, 1854); [Willis, Gann & Co. Shipping], *New Zealand handbook* (London, 1861).   **6** Fitzpatrick, *Oceans of consolation*, p. 25.   **7** Ibid., p. 24.   **8** Revd John O'Hanlon, *The Irish emigrant's guide for the United States* (Dublin, 1851), pp 178, 255.   **9** John Brown, *Jacob: a sermon on emigration* (Londonderry, 1865), p. 22.   **10** John R. McCleery, *Emigration letters on Canada by a Presbyterian clergyman late returned from that country* (Belfast, 1874), p. 8.   **11** H.D. Inglis, *A*

clergymen, including James Warren Doyle, the Catholic bishop of Kildare and Leighlin, noted before parliament that nobody left their parish for America without first calling on them for a letter of reference.[12] This gave clergy an opportunity to impart informal advice, derived not only from reading the letters of others, but also, increasingly, from personal experience, from the 1850s, Irish clergymen of all denominations began visiting emigrant destinations, particularly in North America, in their droves. These visits could be for reasons varying from fundraising, to temporary parochial transfer, to simply a vacation, but they gave ministers an opportunity to see for themselves the places they had so often read about.

If some of them, like John O'Hanlon and John McCleery, saw a mismatch between the countries they visited and the perception of them being formed via emigrant correspondence, it is hardly surprising that they sought to provide what they believed to be a more accurate picture. The clergyman, to a greater degree than the colonial official or the journalist, had a claim to speak directly to the needs of intending Irish emigrants. There was a recognition that a pastor was, as one author put it, 'bound to aid his fellow countrymen by every means in his power and if he has information from personal experience which is necessary to the well-being of others, it is his duty to impart that information to as large a number of people as possible'.[13] Indeed, as early as 1825, Bishop Doyle had speculated that at some point the Catholic hierarchy would have to distribute pastoral letters 'explaining the advantages of emigration ... [and] pointing out the route'.[14]

This sense of priestly duty bore fruit in the form of the thirteen emigrant guides here examined; six by Catholic priests, five by Presbyterian ministers, and two by Anglican clergymen.[15] Most of the manuals are penned by Irish clergy, whether based in Ireland or abroad, but a few are by clergy from Great Britain and are included as their advice is aimed at least in part at Irish readers, who, with their high emigration levels, formed a disproportionate slice of any guide's potential market.[16] On that note, before delving into the content of these guides in more detail, an important question needs to be dealt with. That is, precisely how receptive was the audience of would-be emigrants in Ireland to these publications?

This question is, unfortunately, impossible to answer comprehensively, since few

---

journey throughout Ireland in the spring, summer and autumn of 1834 (London, 1835), p. 346. **12** *Second report from the select committee on the state of the poor in Ireland*, 1830, H.C. (654), vii, p. 396; *Poor Inquiry (Ireland): appendix (c): report on the city of Dublin, and supplement, containing answers to queries; with addenda to appendix (a) and communications*, 1836, H.C. [35], xxxiv, p. 219. **13** Revd D.M. Maclise, D.D., *The dominion of Canada as a field for emigrants from the United Kingdom* (Ottawa, 1882), p. 3. **14** J.K.L., *Letters on the state of Ireland; addressed by J.K.L. to a friend in England* (Dublin, 1825), p. 115. **15** The guides are listed throughout the footnotes and break down as follows: Catholic – O'Kelly, Peyton, O'Hanlon, Cahill, Dunne and Byrne; Presbyterian – Brown, McClure, McCleery, MacKenzie and Maclise; Anglican – Doyle and Warr. **16** George Warr was a Church of England rector based in Liverpool; David MacKenzie was a Church of Scotland minister sent to Australia under the Colonial Mission; while it is unclear whether D.M. Maclise, a clergyman based in Canada, was of Scottish or Ulster-Scots background.

of the works make reference to their print-runs or circulation. What can be said is that the first of the guides, Martin Doyle's *Hints on Emigration to Upper Canada*, first published in 1831, went to at least three editions, amounting to 15,000 copies, and was even plagiarized by a publisher in Castlebar who produced his own version.[17] John O'Hanlon's guide, meanwhile, had the distinct advantage of being cited as further reading in the preface to Vere Foster's *Penny emigrant's guide*, the most widely distributed emigrant's manual of the era.[18] A sixth edition of Foster's work claimed 280,000 copies had been printed – many of them given away rather than sold – so if even a fraction of those readers followed the advice to seek out O'Hanlon's guide, that too could have boasted a relatively high distribution.

Advertising and review columns can offer further hints as to circulation. Just under half of the guides were advertised in the popular national press or reviewed in periodicals and newspapers. Along with those by Doyle and O'Hanlon, guides by George Warr, Patrick Dunne, Alexander Peyton and David MacKenzie have left such traces, with, notably, only Warr's book on Canada appearing to have garnered positive reviews in both the Protestant and the Catholic press, chiefly because of its reasonable price.[19] Perhaps more significantly, the guides by Peyton, Daniel Cahill, John McCleery, D.M. Maclise and William McClure each started out as articles or letters in newspapers or periodicals – the *Cork Examiner*, the *Catholic Telegraph*, the *Northern Whig*, the *Witness* and the *Evangelical Witness* respectively – thereby suggesting a wider, although to some extent a more ephemeral readership than that won by stand-alone books.

Word of mouth also seems to have been in operation. This explains the gap between John Brown initially giving his emigration advice sermon in 1850, and its eventual publication as a pamphlet in 1865.[20] It also seems reasonable to speculate, along those lines, that manuals coming from the pens of prolific and otherwise popular authors would have naturally found an audience. Martin Doyle published many other manuals and works of fiction that went through several editions; John O'Hanlon produced a number of popular historical and religiously themed books; and Daniel Cahill was an inveterate letter-writer and lecturer, whose popularity was such that readers of the *Catholic Telegraph* were at one point given the opportunity to purchase a likeness of him.[21] It has not been possible to ascertain the distribution of the remaining guides, but we might reasonably assume that they too had their readerships. Certainly, it appears reasonable to say, based on the above, that emigrant manuals written by clergy were often among the most popular such publications.

Turning to the kind of advice offered in the guides, it may come as little surprise that clergymen had a knack for compiling lists of 'don'ts' rather than 'dos'. In so

17 Martin Doyle [Revd William Hickey], *Hints on emigration to Upper Canada especially addressed to the middle and lower classes in Great Britain and Ireland* (London, 1834), p. iii. **18** Vere Foster, *Work and wages; or, the penny emigrant's guide to the United States and Canada* (London, 1851). **19** *Freeman's Journal*, 8 May 1847; *Belfast News-Letter*, 1 June 1847. **20** James Norman Ian Dickson, 'More than discourse: the sermons of evangelical Protestants in nineteenth-century Ulster' (PhD, QUB, 2000). **21** *Catholic Telegraph*, 7 Apr. 1860.

doing, they were, consciously or not, following the lead of what Kerby Miller has identified as the very first Irish emigrant's guide, the Revd James MacSparran's *America dissected* (1753). MacSparran was a Presbyterian-turned-Anglican minister from Co. Londonderry who emigrated to Boston in 1718. According to Miller, he wrote his guidebook 'not to encourage or facilitate departures, but 'as a caution to unsteady people who may be tempted to leave their native country'.[22] This seemingly hypocritical formulation was employed repeatedly in later guides written by clergy. Yet, while there is certainly an obvious contradiction inherent in guides to emigration whose prefaces tell the reader *not* to emigrate, what most authors stressed – quite reasonably – was that only certain classes could thrive in whatever region they recommended. They reserved their strictest warnings for the 'unsteady' others who they felt would do better to stay at home. Fr Patrick Dunne, for example, cited a list of those who ought not to contemplate emigrating to Australia:

> the intemperate; wild young men; would-be gentlemen; those not used to hard labour; those with no trade or profession; clerks and people expecting government situations; governesses and single females who have not been in domestic service at home; married people with a large family of young children.[23]

In Dunne's estimation, therefore, both those aiming too high – would-be gentlemen and government officials – and those aiming too low – drunks and unskilled women – were deemed unsuitable for emigration.

The advice for those hoping to go to North America was little different. Soberness was invariably emphasized as a necessary virtue for those hoping to 'get on'. The Irish, as Stephen Byrne asserted, were possessed of 'a social and convivial spirit which, if not kept within due bounds, is apt to result in excesses of which no one ever dreamed'.[24] The 'grog shops' of the port cities, according to Peyton, represented an 'abominable system of entrapping into misery and destruction' newly arrived immigrants.[25] Meanwhile, female emigrants were told that experience of domestic work would be invaluable. Fr Cahill even mused upon a way to give young

22 Kerby A. Miller, 'Revd James MacSparran's America dissected (1753): eighteenth-century emigration and constructions of "Irishness"', *History Ireland*, 11:4 (2003), 17–22; Kerby A. Miller, Arnold Schrier, Bruce D. Bolling and David Doyle, *Irish immigrants in the Land of Canaan: letters and memoirs from colonial and revolutionary America, 1675–1815* (Oxford, 2003), pp 59, 19.   **23** Revd P. Dunne, *The emigrant's guide to Queensland and the other Australian colonies: being a compendium of useful information for intending emigrants before they leave home, during the voyage, and after their arrival in Australia* (Dublin and London, 1863), p. 8.   **24** Stephen Byrne, *Irish emigration to the United States: what it has been and what it is. Facts and reflections especially addressed to Irish people intending to emigrate from their native land; and to those living in the large cities of Great Britain and the United States* (New York, 1873), p. 52.   **25** Alexander J. Peyton, *The emigrants' friend or hints on emigration to the United States of America, addressed to the people of Ireland* (Cork, 1853), pp 32–3.

women the kinds of skills that would allow them to bypass the lower reaches of
domestic service, where the work was hard and the wages were low. Since, he
asserted, most poor Irish girls would not know how to clean silver, Irish nuns and
bishops should make arrangements to remedy the deficiency; this dubious kindness
presumably involved allowing intending female emigrants to spring clean the
convent or the episcopal palace before they departed.[26]

Those emigrants to America who aspired to be among the silver-owning, rather
than the silver-cleaning, classes were also cautioned. As Alexander Peyton wrote:

> There is one dangerous rock, on which many young men, with brilliant
> prospects, have been ship wrecked. When they get into a situation, and money
> becomes flush ... they assume independent, I should say aristocratic notions,
> they forget what they had been at home ... and ... from an anxiety to appear
> as gentlemen, as free and independent citizens ... they are hurried on by evil
> companions into the gaping jaws of destruction.[27]

Even those with more modest ambitions were warned against aiming above their
station. John O'Hanlon pointed out that anyone hoping for a situation as a shopman
or clerk would be disappointed; they would get nowhere without personal recommendations that could confirm their trustworthiness.[28]

The reader who did not fall into any of the above traps – he generally was among
Daniel Cahill's frequent addressees, the 'small tenant farmers, tradesmen and
labouring classes' – had still to contend with more warnings. The advice to be wary
of fraudsters, to avoid slipping into drunkenness and to work hard was clearly sensible,
and conducive to, if not necessarily a guarantee of, success. Other recommendations
seemed less so. Almost without exception,[29] clerical guide authors instructed their
readers to avoid settling in cities and towns, and especially in the large cities on the
eastern seaboard of North America to which so many sailed. As the Belfast pastor
James Strain noted in 1871, 'the Eastern States are getting very nearly as populous,
and the competition for the means of subsistence as great, as it is with ourselves'.[30]
Such places, moreover, were deemed too full of vice and temptation. New York may
have been a 'magnificent' city, in Fr Cahill's opinion, but it was also one whose seedy
underbelly, largely peopled by impoverished Irish immigrants, he had witnessed in
his tours of the wretched almshouses.[31]

---

26 D.W. Cahill, *Fourth letter from the Revd D.W. Cahill, D.D. to the small tenant farmers,
tradesmen and labouring classes of Ireland* (Dublin, 1860), p. 4.   **27** Peyton, *The emigrant's friend*,
p. 5.   **28** O'Hanlon, *Irish emigrant's guide*, pp 124–5.   **29** The single-minded Patrick
O'Kelly, who wrote his eccentric guide with the support of both Irish and American clergy,
seems to have felt that his primary duty was neither to emigrants nor the Irish church, but
to the growing American church, and recommended that immigrants settle near any of the
many magnificent cathedrals being built in places like Baltimore and New York. Patrick
O'Kelly, *Advice and guide to emigrants going to the United States of America* (Dublin, 1834), p. 25.
30 James K. Strain, *The story of a visit to America: a lecture* (Belfast, 1871), p. 42.   **31** D.W.

All but one of the authors of guides to America therefore implored their readers to proceed directly to the interior as soon as possible after landing and acquire farms. Those who wrote about Canada or Australia largely did so precisely because land was often more plentiful or easier to secure than in the USA. There are a number of problems with this advice, which became clearer over the course of the decades, but which did not prevent it being repeatedly given. The most obvious is that land requires considerable capital, if not always to acquire then certainly to develop, and the great majority of Irish emigrants in this period did not have any. Neither would many Irish emigrants have had the farming skills required. There was, as Oliver MacDonagh has pointed out, a world of difference between tending a potato garden in Ireland and farming an enormous and isolated holding on the American frontier, or indeed in the Australian bush.[32] How could most Irishmen, used to toiling on 'miserable little patches of land, which by stretch of charity and an abuse of language we call "farms"',[33] be expected to make the leap to clearing and farming hundreds of acres in the new world?

A few authors did recognize and grapple with this discrepancy as time went on. In 1860, Daniel Cahill, informed by anyone he consulted that it would be 'ruinous' to engage in farming in America without an independent capital of at least five or six hundred dollars, acknowledged that those Irish who had that kind of money available to them would be better to remain at home.[34] Fr Peyton had earlier noted that wealthy would-be emigrants might find land more easily in the Encumbered Estates Court.[35] A few years later, William McClure, the head of the Presbyterian Church's Colonial Mission, showed a keen awareness of the amount of hard work required to make a success of oneself in the colonies and pondered whether 'It might be well for [would-be emigrants] to [see] if the amount of labour they must expect to be called upon to expend in a foreign land would not be equally effective at home'.[36]

Yet the dream of one day becoming an upright and prosperous farmer – often presented as the only alternative to ending up an urban misfit – continued to be held out to readers of these guides. 'It should be the aim and ambition of all emigrant labourers', according to Alexander Peyton, to be placed in such 'an independent, respectable position'.[37] Both Peyton and Daniel Cahill made something of an

Cahill, *Second letter from the Revd D.W. Cahill, D.D. to the small tenant farmers, tradesmen, and labouring classes of Ireland* (Dublin, 1859), p. 4; D.W. Cahill, *Important letter from the Revd Dr Cahill on old England and young America* (Dublin, 1860), p. 9. **32** Oliver MacDonagh, 'Emigration during the famine' in R. Dudley Edwards and T. Desmond Williams (eds), *The Great Famine: studies in Irish history, 1845–52* (Dublin, 1956), pp 319–88 at p. 384. **33** McCleery, *Emigration letters*, p. 6. David Noel Doyle, 'The Irish as urban pioneers in the United States, 1850–1870', *Journal of American Ethnic History*, 10:1–2 (1990), 36–59. **34** D.W. Cahill, *Important letter from the Revd D.W. Cahill, D.D. to the small tenant farmers, tradesmen, and labourers of Ireland* (Dublin, 1860), p. 4. **35** Peyton, *The emigrant's friend*, p. 36. **36** William McClure, 'Suggestions to intending emigrants', *The Evangelical Witness and Presbyterian Review* (Apr. 1864), 104. **37** Peyton, *The emigrant's friend*, pp 16–17.

attempt to deal with the difficult reality of most emigrants' situations by suggesting that those who were prepared to keep their heads down, work hard on the railroad or as agricultural labourers, and save their money rather than spend it all on drink and tobacco, might still aspire to own their own small farm one day. If this was an especially literal case of 'Blessed are the meek, for they shall inherit the earth', it did not often come to pass. In the USA at least, a scant 6 per cent of Irish emigrants realized this ambition, with one historian memorably suggesting that 'The Irish rejected the land for the land had rejected them'.[38]

There is of course a great irony in clergymen, of all people, advising emigrants to settle on the land rather than in urban centres. As most of the authors readily acknowledged, those who did so were likely to be beyond the reach of religion. This is especially true of the earlier part of the period, when surviving letters show that emigrants could often be as much as a day's journey from a church of their own denomination, even along the relatively well-developed east coast of America.[39] In many parts of the interior, settlers might, if they were sufficiently committed and lucky, see an itinerant minister just a few times a year.[40] Yet, even as late as 1873, Fr Stephen Byrne, while confident that 'Churches and priests are now sufficiently numerous to give to all the opportunity of receiving the sacraments', reckoned that 'a journey of twenty-five or fifty miles once or twice a year' to a church might still be the best many could expect.[41] It is impossible to calculate how many such emigrants therefore resigned themselves, given the new world's much-vaunted religious freedom, to any port, or even no port, in a storm; a prospect that was greatly feared by many Irish clergy.[42]

This problem was magnified in the even vaster and more sparsely populated Australian bush. David MacKenzie, a Church of Scotland minister, related an extraordinary tale that illustrated the distances and difficulties some faced in getting to a church even for important occasions. A fellow Presbyterian minister unwittingly conducted a wedding where the groom was unavoidably detained; his brother and best man stepped in, being 'unwilling to return home from the parson, after having come so far, without doing some business by way of "securing the woman"'. Incredibly, the man was under the impression that he could simply transfer the bride to his brother on returning home that night. Sadly, it is not recorded who the unfortunate wife eventually settled with, but as MacKenzie noted, 'This is ... the greatest extension of 'a power of attorney' that I have ever known given in this colony'.[43]

38 McDonagh, 'Emigration during the famine', p. 383; William V. Shannon, *The American Irish* (London, 1963), p. 27. **39** Patrick Fitzgerald, Albion, Orleans Co., New York to Michael Cahill, Quebec, 1846. Ulster American Folk Park, Doc. no. 9601014. **40** See Right Revd John England, *A brief account of the introduction of the Catholic religion into the states of North Carolina and Georgia, USA* (Dublin, 1832). **41** Byrne, *Irish emigration to the United States*, p. 49. **42** Byrne repeated the contention, almost certainly erroneous, that millions of Irish Catholics had been lost to the faith in the US – his estimate was two thirds of the total. Byrne, *Irish emigration to the United States*, p. 50; cf Gerald Shaughnessy, *Has the immigrant kept the faith? A study of immigration and Catholic growth in the United States, 1790–1920* (New York, 1925), pp 224–31. **43** David MacKenzie, *The emigrants' guide or ten years'*

That was clearly an extreme example, but the problem was a very real one, and one which it might be thought clergy writing guides that explicitly directed emigrants to remote, largely unchurched areas would have felt a responsibility to address in some depth. There were certainly enough references in the anti-emigration press, both Protestant and Catholic, to Irish emigrants 'dying without the consolation of religion' for the issue to warrant attention. Few guide-writers offered practical solutions. Protestant clergy, however, in many ways had the easier task. Martin Doyle was able to suggest that 'the good Christian has always a *Friend above*, to whose willing ear he may address himself', while also encouraging young vicars to consider emigration to supply the spiritual wants of settlers.[44] David MacKenzie could note that 'In the wilderness you may live near to Him, enjoy His favour, hold daily communion with Him, and experience that peace of mind and joy in believing, which the world can neither give nor take away'.[45] For Protestant emigrants of all denominations, a personal relationship with God, perhaps enhanced by a proximity to nature in an as yet unspoilt landscape, may have been seen as an acceptable temporary substitute for having a church or a parson nearby.

Catholic priests clearly had much less scope to suggest the same, and although the issue loomed large, it tended to be addressed in a variety of problematic ways. For some authors, it was a question of waiting. Emigrants might be without spiritual guidance for a few years, but in time, as the population grew, chapels would be built and priests would be found. In the meantime, emigrants were expected to attend to their religious duties at least once a year, at Easter, and instruct their children in the Catholic faith.[46] Stephen Byrne suggested that rich New York Catholics should fund and create a million-strong Catholic colony in the southern states, a hopeful proposal that owed much to the only patchily realized (and even at that smaller-scale) dreams of certain American bishops.[47] Others felt that clever forward planning was needed. John O'Hanlon envisaged his readers consulting the US Catholic almanac to find where churches were located in the interior, while Daniel Cahill stated that 'care and correspondence' could elicit the same information.[48] Given the likelihood that the most forward planning an emigrant did was to read one of these guides, such suggestions seem optimistic, to say the least. Most Catholic guide authors therefore failed plausibly to reconcile their temporal and spiritual advice to emigrants.

To what extent, then, did these manuals fulfil their brief to be trustworthy, impartial and useful? On the whole, the basic information offered is accurate. One edition

practical experience in Australia (London, 1845), pp 62–3. **44** Doyle, *Hints on emigration*, pp 14, 70. **45** MacKenzie, *The emigrants' guide*, p. 274. **46** Dunne, *The emigrant's guide to Queensland*, p. 27; O'Hanlon, *Irish emigrant's guide*, pp 159–60; Peyton, *The emigrant's friend*, p. 29. **47** Byrne, *Irish emigration to the United States*, p. 56; See also James P. Shannon, *Catholic colonization on the western frontier* (New York, 1976); John Lancaster Spalding, *The religious mission of the Irish people and Catholic colonization* (New York, 1880); Mary Gilbert Kelly, *Catholic immigrant colonization projects in the United States, 1815–1860* (New York, 1939). **48** O'Hanlon, *Irish emigrant's guide*, pp 103–4; D.W. Cahill, *Important letter ... to the small farmers*, p. 6.

of O'Hanlon's guide suggested that it 'abounds' with 'sound advice and wise suggestions' and that 'the errors of fact which are noted are of no real consequence'.[49] The
modern critical reader might well be tempted to differentiate between those guides
written on a short visit and those penned by clergy who had lived and worked for
many years in the country of which they wrote, but most of the authors took their
self-assumed duty seriously, consulted widely and produced manuals that would have
safely guided from port to port any reader looking to emigrate.

As to their impartiality, there is less certainty. It is clear that for the most part,
Catholic authors aimed their advice at Catholic readers, Protestant authors at
Protestant readers. One senses therefore, that certain party lines had sometimes to be
followed. It is significant that, in those guides where a specific destination was recommended, Protestant clergy invariably urged that emigrants settle within the Empire,
while Catholic clergy, with only one understandable exception,[50] recommended that
readers emigrate to the USA. It speaks volumes, however, that Alexander Peyton,
who wrote his book with the approval of Archbishop Paul Cullen, and at whose
behest he had gone to North America collecting for the Catholic University in 1851,
clearly wanted to recommend Canada over the USA, but was able to do so only in
passing, with a reference to 'the apprehension that many Irishmen may feel about
settling in British territory' and in a book whose title and main body favour the USA
as an emigrant destination.[51]

Yet there can be no doubt that for all their faults, emigrant guides written by
members of the clergy were useful. The very uniformity of their content – especially
the emphasis on 'what not to do' – suggests that they were accumulations of hard-
won and often much-tested knowledge. That meant, however, that the less sage
advice was also routinely recycled. Furthermore, there is a sense in which many of
the authors sought primarily to present their own very personal visions of how
emigration *should* be. Hence, most of the emigrant manuals written by Irish clergymen are a mixture of practical advice and wishful thinking. They were useful up
to a point and for some, but ultimately, perhaps, they were not rooted in the reality
facing most Irish emigrants.

49 Edward J. Maguire, *Reverend John O'Hanlon's* The Irish emigrant's guide for the United
States: *a critical edition with introduction and commentary* (New York, 1976), p. 25.   **50** Dunne
wrote his guide as part of his involvement with the Catholic Bishop of Queensland's
colonization project. See Jennifer Harrison, 'From King's County to Quinnsland' in William
Nolan and Timothy P. O'Neill (eds), *Offaly: history & society, interdisciplinary essays on the
history of an Irish county* (Dublin, 1998), pp 831–54.   **51** Peyton, *The emigrant's friend*, pp 42–3.

'Mar is fánach mac a' teacht go cruinn mar ' athair': Dáibhí de Barra's surviving translations[1]

SEÁN Ó DUINNSHLÉIBHE

In his survey of literature in Irish from the Act of Union to the Gaelic League, Gearóid Denvir refers to the marginalization of contemporary Gaelic literature in most English-language studies of literature written in Ireland in the period. He attributes this disregard to a tendency among many commentators and scholars to read nineteenth-century Ireland solely 'in anglocentric terms'.[2] Regrettably, this bias is compounded by the fact that within Irish-language studies Gaelic literature of the pre-Famine period has been under-researched compared to the attention that writing originating in earlier phases of the tradition has received.[3] In recent times, a counterpoint to this trend has come in the form of insightful commentaries and studies carried out by a number of scholars (most notably Neil Buttimer) who have sought to highlight the importance of pre-Famine Gaelic writings as a source from below and from within, indispensable to scholars of social history and literature alike. The writings of Dáibhí de Barra are one such source and only in the last thirty years or so have his writings – his prose works in particular – come to receive fuller attention from critics.

Born in the late 1750s, de Barra enjoyed a long life spent entirely in the Carrigtwohill district of east Cork, where he died in 1851. As Breandán Ó Conchúir has pointed out in his seminal study of Cork scribes, *Scríobhaithe Chorcaí*, the south-

---

1 The Irish quotation is taken from the preface that de Barra included in his translation of *The Death of Abel* (Fermoy MS F PB 5: p. 1), the first line of which is quoted in the title of this paper. The opening couplet reads: 'Mar is fánach mac a' teacht go cruinn mar ' athair // is mar sin bhíonn an tslí in iompó leabhair', which may be translated as follows: 'Since a son seldom comes forth exactly as his father // so too is the case when translating a book'. The spelling of extracts from manuscript sources quoted in this essay has been normalized in an effort to render quotations more intelligible to contemporary readers, but only insofar as the linguistic integrity of the extracts is not compromised. I should like to thank Dr Mícheál Briody and Prof. Seán Ó Coileáin, who read an earlier draft of this paper and made several helpful suggestions. **2** Gearóid Denvir, 'Literature in Irish, 1800–1890: from the Act of Union to the Gaelic League' in Margaret Kelleher and Philip O'Leary (eds), *The Cambridge history of Irish literature*, vol. 1, to 1890 (Cambridge, 2006), pp 544–98 at p. 544. **3** This trend has been most recently commented upon by Dr Neil Buttimer in his essay 'Literature in Irish, 1690–1800: from the Williamite Wars to the Act of Union' in O'Leary and Kelleher (eds), *The Cambridge history of Irish literature*, pp 320–71 at p. 321.

east part of the county was an important centre for scribal and literary activities throughout the eighteenth century.[4] Constrained by the routine demands of his life as a small farmer, de Barra seems to have had limited contact with antiquarians or fellow scribes in Cork city or surrounding areas, although he tells us that in later years a handful of antiquarians were in the habit of calling on him from time to time.[5] The extent of the patronage he received was trifling and infrequent, amounting to little more than the occasional gift of a book or pen. What we know of his life and work has been garnered mostly from marginalia and colophons scattered throughout a dozen or so manuscripts of his that survive, and also, to a lesser extent, from his own creative writings, some of which reveal personal or political sentiments.[6]

In Denvir's survey, de Barra's literary work is singled out as exemplifying the range of native learning in the nineteenth century,[7] and Buttimer has ranked his writings second only, in terms of volume and detail, to those of de Barra's contemporary, the celebrated diarist, Humphrey O'Sullivan of Callan.[8] His creative *oeuvre* can be broadly divided into three categories: poetry; original prose works; and translations. The bulk of his poetry remains unpublished and therefore has yet to receive proper critical literary attention. It is in his prose writings, however, that de Barra comes into his own. *Párliment na bhFíodóirí* ('The Parliament of Weavers') and *Cath na Deachún ar Thráigh Rosa Móire* ('The Tithe Affray at Rossmore Strand') are his only substantial original prose works: the former is a colourful and biting satire on Cork weavers, while the latter work takes the form of an amusing and spirited account of a tithe disturbance in his locality. These two works display a similar imaginative engagement with events of the day: through skilful employment of a range of registers and effective use of a mock-heroic style, contemporary events are refracted through satire or parody to ridicule what he regards as the overweening ambition and sense of self-importance of his targets – weavers and tithe officials alike.

DE BARRA'S TRANSLATIONS

The third and final category of his *oeuvre*, his work of translation, forms the subject of this paper. My researches thus far have uncovered thirteen translations made by him. The matter of identification is complicated by de Barra's practice of not

---

4 Breandán Ó Conchúir, *Scríobhaithe Chorcaí* (Dublin, 1982), p. 194.   **5** See the letter, dated 1 July 1841, which he sent to Philip Baron. The only extant copy of this letter was made by one of Dáibhí's sons, and is now preserved in Fermoy MS F PB 3, pp 129–30.   **6** See Ó Conchúir *Scríobhaithe Chorcaí*, pp 8–13, for an account of de Barra's life. An account of his poetry is provided in M.R. Ó Táthain, 'Amhráin is dánta Dháibhí de Barra' (MA, UCD, 1931–2).   **7** Denvir, 'Literature in Irish, 1800–1890: from the Act of Union to the Gaelic League', p. 567.   **8** Cornelius G. Buttimer, 'Early nineteenth-century Cork poems in Irish', *Journal of the Cork Historical and Archaeological Society*, 90 (1985), pp 158–85 at p. 167. Another of O'Sullivan's works – his previously unpublished botany book – was described in Neil Buttimer's contribution to the SSNCI conference in 2008.

acknowledging some of these works as translations. It is important to emphasize that this study is very much a work in progress, as the sources of a number of these works have only recently been identified, and other translations may lie among his writings, similarly unacknowledged. All thirteen are listed below (Table 19.1), along with information on the original work and time of writing or, in cases where the exact time of writing is unknown, the date of the earliest known manuscript in which the translation occurs is given. It is also important to point out that this is not a complete list, because at least two translations of his are now lost.[9] At all events, this aspect of his work remains largely unresearched despite its particular significance for our understanding of de Barra's formation and development as a writer. As is clear from the table, the act of translation continued to appeal to him at various stages in his career. There are gaps in the chronology but it would seem that external factors account for the years of inactivity between c.1780 and 1825 (between the completion of translations 2 and 3) and 1835–c.1847 (between the completion of translations 12 and 13). We know from notes in a number of de Barra's manuscripts that these gaps coincide with periods in his life when he scarcely engaged in writing of any kind, a curious fact for which he offers no fully satisfactory explanation, apart from oblique references to the busyness of his daily life and to intermittent ill health. In total, we know of three periods during which de Barra did not engage in any sustained writing, viz. c.1791–1821, 1835–9 and c.1844–9. Ó Conchúir has cited other possible reasons for these periods of literary inactivity, among which were de Barra's relative seclusion from scribal centres and the declining status of the Irish language in the community in which he lived. Ironically, he was roused from this inactivity by the rise of proselytizing (or Bible) societies in his locality which sought to use the Irish language as a medium of instruction in their work.[10]

While still in his teens (in the mid- to late 1770s), he completed his first two translations: that of the familiar *Merchant's Tale* by Geoffrey Chaucer and of *Female Policy Detected* by Ned Ward, which is known less widely today. In the only extant autograph copy of *Corraghliocas na mBan Léirmhínithe* (*CBL* hereafter; his translation of *Female Policy Detected*), we have recorded for us, in a note added subsequently by one of de Barra's children, a reference to the work's time of writing: the note indicates that *CBL* represents de Barra's first serious essay at writing. The timing of the translation is not without significance. Speaking about English-language writers in the context of the British (and mainland European) literary tradition, translation scholar Susan Bassnett explains how in the early nineteenth century, 'translation was still regarded as a serious and useful method for helping a writer to explore and shape his own native style, much as it had been for centuries'.[11] Given the time of writing,

---

9 A letter, held in Maynooth Library (MC 100 (d) (1)), dated 13 Apr. 1817, which was sent by Seán Ó Cinnéide, living in Enniscorthy, to Pádraig Ó Loingsigh, resident in Dublin, mentions 'some English prayer books' which de Barra had translated into Irish (quoted in *Scríobhaithe Chorcaí*, p. 251, fn. 78). None of these prayer books is known to have survived. **10** See *Scríobhaithe Chorcaí*, p. 251, fn. 64. **11** Susan Bassnett, *Translation studies* (London, 1980 [2002]), p. 13.

Table 19.1 Translations by Dáibhí de Barra, with titles and authors of original works and years of translation.

	Translated work by Dáibhí de Barra (1757/8–1851)	Original work/source (and author)	Year(s) of writing/ earliest MS copy of translation
1	Corraghliocas na mBan Léirmhínithe	Female Policy Detected (Edward Ward)	c.1775–80
2	Scéal January agus May	The Merchant's Tale (Geoffrey Chaucer)	c.1775–80
3	In Aimsir Bhess do Bheith 'na Beanríoghain Álainn	England's Reformation from the time of K. Henry VIII to the end of the Oates's Plot (excerpt; Thomas Ward)	1825
4	Más Mithid é, Tráchtfad ar Bhás na Beanríoghan Eilís	ditto	1825
5	Sómpla Diadha	Historia Ecclesiastica (Book V, chapter xiii; Bede)	1827
6	Agallamh Dís Marbhán	Dialogues of the Dead: Dialogue VI (George Lyttelton)	1827
7	Scéal ar an Ridire Beartrad	Sir Bertrand: a Fragment (Anna Laetitia Barbauld)	1827
8	Cnoc na nEaladhan	The Hill of Science: a Vision (Anna Laetitia Barbauld)	1827
9	Nithe Cianainteartha agus Bás Abel	The Death of Abel (Mary Collyer) / Der Tod Abels (original work; Salomon Gessner)	1829
10	An Giaour	The Giaour (excerpt; Lord Byron)	c.1828–30
11	Scáthán na hAimsire (agus Rejoinder/Aguisín leis)	Speculum Seculi (and Postscript) from History of the Life of Thomas Ellwood (Thomas Ellwood)	1835
12	Feartlaoi nó Epitaph Tory	An Epitaph on Jeremy Ives from History of the Life of Thomas Ellwood (Thomas Ellwood)	1835
13	The C[h]aracter of a Miser	Some Account of Mr Vandille (author unknown)	c.1847–9

it seems highly likely that when testing his pen seriously for the first time, de Barra would choose the activity of translation with such a purpose in mind, favouring the comparative safety of translation over the more daunting prospect of going it alone, as it were.

His translations are invariably in one direction, from English to Irish. In the surviving correspondence between de Barra and amateur antiquarian William Hackett of Midleton, the writer alludes on two separate occasions to his halting command of English, which makes him, as he says, 'shy in writing anything but my mother tongue'.[12] This should not necessarily be interpreted as modest understatement (considering his attempts, at such a young age, to translate Chaucer's tale and Ward's 'pocketbook'), but rather as an explanation of his decision to translate only into his native tongue and, for the most part, to compose only in Irish. Although his earliest two translations were made in the eighteenth century, all of his other extant translations belong to the second quarter of the following century. The present confines do not allow me to make more than very general observations about the range and quality of this work and so the account that follows will begin by touching on the question of reception before focusing on de Barra's best known translation, *Corraghliocas na mBan Léirmhínithe*. The concluding section looks generally at the writer's motivations and, in so doing, attempts to draw these disparate translations together somewhat, in the context of the writer's career and times.

QUESTION OF RECEPTION

The reception that de Barra's writings would have enjoyed needs to be understood in the context of rapid and profound change taking place in the second half of the eighteenth century and, in particular, in the first half of the nineteenth. For instance, the influence of print culture was steadily increasing during de Barra's lifetime and, as is often remarked, this growing influence brought with it gradual changes to the make-up of Gaelic manuscripts in terms of materiality and presentation of content, as scribes became increasingly familiar with print norms.[13] Certainly de Barra's familiarity with such norms is clear from an examination of his surviving manuscripts: some of these contain standard print conventions such as title-pages, tables of contents (*cómhthímpsiúghadh*, to use his own term), end of page notes etc., and in the particular case of manuscript F PB 6, which comprises a large body of devotional poetry by de Barra, an earlier printed work, Timothy O'Sullivan's very popular *Pious Miscellany*, would appear to have acted as inspiration for the compilation of de Barra's handwritten collection.[14] By the end of the eighteenth century, other significant

12 RIA MS 12 C 1: p. 26. The other reference to his imperfect command of English occurs on p. 10 of the same manuscript. 13 See Neil Buttimer, 'Manuscript and book in pre-Famine Gaelic Ireland', *Newsletter of the School of Celtic Studies*, 5 (1992), 23; Meidhbhín Ní Úrdail, *The scribe in eighteenth- and nineteenth-century Ireland: motivations and milieu* (Münster, 2000), pp 199–225. 14 This manuscript (F PB 6) dates to the year 1835. For an account of

changes had begun to take effect: the traditional scribal milieu was in irreversible decline, as was the availability of individual patronage; despite such changes, scribal tradition in Cork persisted down to the middle of the nineteenth century.[15] Allied to these changes, levels of literacy in the Irish language had been in free fall from the middle of the eighteenth century.[16] Paradoxically, as Buttimer has implied, greater literacy in English may have led to both 'the promotion of English and curiously the survival and enrichment of Gaelic culture itself',[17] as literacy in English, in some cases, facilitated the ability of scribes to acquire a similar competence in Irish.

In view of such changes, it is interesting to note that many of de Barra's works circulated in manuscript and some, we know, enjoyed a good deal of popularity. Although the tradition retained a certain degree of vigour until the middle of the nineteenth century, local structures for the exchange of manuscript materials had effectively broken down by the 1830s, as Meidhbhín Ní Úrdail has pointed out.[18] Accordingly, it makes more sense in a short account of reception such as this to focus primarily on de Barra's earliest translations, as these would have had longer to circulate. Four copies of *CBL* have come down to us, the oldest of which was made by Cork-city-based scribe Tadhg Ó Conaill in the early years of the nineteenth century, and the last in 1840 by the Clare scribe, Mícheál Ó Mongáin.[19] In addition, we know that this translation circulated widely in de Barra's locality during his lifetime and was copied there frequently: a note to that effect occurs at the very beginning of NLI manuscript G 654.[20] His other early translation, that of *The Merchant's Tale*, survives in five copies – although not all are complete – one of which made its way into the library of Cork scholar and antiquary, John Windele (1801–65). Interestingly, this copy was made by well-known scribe Seosamh Ó Longáin at the behest of his patron Windele and occurs in RIA manuscript 24 C 2, where we also find two other translations by de Barra in Ó Longáin's hand. This compendium is made up of manuscript scraps originally written by several scribes but gathered together to form a miscellany of sorts. The contents consist, in the main, of an assortment of poetry and prose interspersed with lithographs of various subjects of antiquarian interest. A goodly number of the texts are translations, among which are renderings into Irish of works

O'Sullivan's *Pious miscellany*, see Niall Ó Ciosáin, *Print and popular culture in Ireland, 1750–1850* (London, 1997), pp 118–31.   **15** The definitive account of this tradition is Ó Conchúir's study, *Scríobhaithe Chorcaí*.   **16** See Louis Cullen, 'Patrons, teachers and literacy in Irish: 1700–1850' in Mary Daly and David Dickson (eds), *The origins of popular literacy in Ireland: language change and educational development, 1700–1920* (Dublin, 1990), pp 15–44 at pp 29–40, for an account of literacy in Irish. See also Ó Ciosáin, *Print and popular culture in Ireland, 1750–1850*, pp 25–51, for a further discussion of the topic.   **17** Cornelius G. Buttimer, 'Gaelic literature and contemporary life in Cork, 1700–1840' in Patrick O'Flanagan and Cornelius G. Buttimer (eds), *Cork history and society: interdisciplinary essays on the history of an Irish county* (Dublin, 1993), pp 585–654 at p. 640.   **18** Ní Úrdail, *The scribe in eighteenth- and nineteenth-century Ireland*, p. 221.   **19** The textual tradition of the work is described in greater detail by Breandán Ó Conchúir in his edition of *Corraghliocas na mBan léirmhínithe* (Dublin, 1991), pp xiv–xv.   **20** This note is quoted in full in Ó Conchúir, *Corraghliocas na mBan léirmhínithe*, p. xiv.

by Thomas Moore, J.J. Callanan and Walter Scott, for example. This is the only known manuscript in which several of de Barra's translations were chosen (and perhaps drawn together from different sources) by another scribe/patron for inclusion in a miscellany.

Although *The Merchant's Tale* needs no introduction, the other two translations by de Barra would not be generally as well known to readers today. The first of these, *Scéal ar an Ridire Beartrard*, has as its source the short gothic tale *Sir Bertrand: a Fragment* by the English poet and essayist Anna Laetitia Barbauld, while the second work, *Agallamh Dís Marbhán*[21] (an account of a verbal exchange between an English duellist and a North American savage), is a rendering of the sixth dialogue from George Lyttelton's work, *Dialogues of the Dead*. De Barra's source for the originals was the educationalist and writer, Vicesimus Knox's anthology, *Elegant Extracts: or, Useful and Entertaining Passages in Prose*, an extremely popular work, which reached its tenth edition in 1816. Ó Longáin's copy of the three works in RIA manuscript 24 C 2 was made in 1848, just a few years before de Barra died. The translated texts in the manuscript consist mostly of verse, with the majority of the Irish poems being accompanied by the English original. As Ní Úrdail has pointed out, manuscripts of this kind, not uncommon among Ó Longáin's scribal material, were put together for patrons or readers 'whose literacy in the Irish language was limited, if not negligible'.[22] The three works by de Barra are not accompanied by their originals in this instance, however.

We have more detailed information about one of his longer, and later, translations, *Nithe Cianaimseartha agus Bás Abel* (Table 19.1, no. 9), only because de Barra himself has left behind an account of its fortunes.[23] The work in question is a rendering into Irish of Mary Collyer's English-language translation of the German prose-poem *Der Tód Abels*.[24] The original, based on the Cain and Abel theme, was written by Swiss writer and painter Salomon Gessner. The most striking feature of the translation is de Barra's choice of medium: the translation is made up entirely of rhyming couplets, and so departs from the prosaic form of Collyer's translation and Gessner's original. Such marked formal transformation of the source text was a strategy that de Barra had already employed some years before, in the case of his translation of Lyttelton's sixth dialogue, *Agallamh Dís Marbhán*. Given his impecunious state and growing ill health, de Barra found himself in the difficult position of having to sell his translation of the *Death of Abel*. His first attempt brought him to the Society House in Midleton, an interesting but not unlikely choice, given the religious nature of the text

---

21 This work is given the title *Comhrá an Sabhage agus an Sacsanach* in the Ó Longáin copy. In the body of the autograph copy, NLI MS G 656, in which the original writing occurs, the work is untitled; however, de Barra gives *Agallamh Dís Marbhán* as its title in the *cómhthímpsiúghadh* (or table of contents) at the end of the manuscript.   **22** Ní Úrdail, *The scribe in eighteenth- and nineteenth-century Ireland*, p. 132.   **23** References to *Nithe Cianaimseartha agus Bás Abel* can be found in RIA MSS 12 C 1: pp 1–18 and 23 H 28, fo. 115.   **24** Collyer's English translation stands at almost 160 pages while the Irish version runs to *c.*4,400 lines of verse.

and the Society's interest in using Irish-language material. The degree to which de Barra's circumstances had been reduced is reflected in his decision to appeal in this way to members of the Society House given his avowed antipathy to their faith, but not meeting with the success he had hoped for, he ventured further afield to Cork city. He tells William Hackett in their correspondence of his lack of success on the second attempt, although indications are that some interest was shown in the work. He explains the difficulties he encountered as follows:

> . . . and as there is no Irish type in Cork they wouldn't buy it unless I'd write it over in English caracter and that would be too much for a man in my situation. But, Sir, I conjectured in my own mind that you could forward it for me, being acquainted with people in the North that might buy it. And if you wish to take my case in hand give your commands to John Hyde Habberdasher [sic] in the New Street, Cork Road, Middleton who will forward them here.[25]

This letter, written almost ten years after the translation was completed, illustrates the frustration that the lack of a Gaelic or Irish type in Cork occasioned for writers such as de Barra. Attempts were made earlier in the century to introduce an Irish type to Cork city, but these proved largely unsuccessful.[26] We do not know with certitude how Hackett responded to the aforementioned request, but it is of interest here that one of the two other extant copies, apart from the autograph text, was made by the same scribe, John Siefield Hyde (alias Seán Ó Seitheacháin), although this copy was made much later, in 1865. To judge from the surviving manuscripts, it would seem, however, that no copies circulated outside Cork during the period.

'CORRAGHLIOCAS NA mBAN LÉIRMHÍNITHE (CBL)'

CBL is the only substantial translation of de Barra's to have been published; it is also the only one to have received a reasonable amount of critical attention. The original work, *Female Policy Detected* (*FPD* hereafter), was completed by Ned Ward in 1695. Ward, a tavern-keeper and writer, is now more famous for his colourful and original Hudibrastic sketches of London life. However, *FPD* is a very different kind of work, having been written 'as an amusing contribution to the contemporary debate on women, the famous *Querelles des Femmes*'.[27] It proved immensely popular in England and North America.[28] As the title indicates, *FPD* seeks to lay bare the conniving ways

25 RIA MS 12 C 1: p. 11.   26 For a discussion of the individuals involved with this project, see Ní Úrdail, *The scribe in eighteenth- and nineteenth-century Ireland*, pp 206–8.   27 Mary O'Dowd, *A history of women in Ireland, 1500–1800* (London, 2005), p. 241.   28 For an account of its author and the popularity of the work in England, see Howard William Troyer, *Ned Ward of Grub Street: a study of sub-literary London in the eighteenth century* (Harvard, 1946), and for a short account of the reception of the work in North America, see Clare A. Lyons,

of women, and was styled by Ward as a pocket companion for young male readers, intended to serve 'as armour to defend them from the darts thrown by wanton and designing women'.[29] De Barra completed his translation some time between the years 1775 and 1780; the original translation (now lost) was later reworked and the only surviving autograph copy dates to 1834.[30]

The original work has a tripartite structure, while de Barra's translation is made up of only two books. The first book of *FPD* is translated quite faithfully, which may indicate that de Barra did, in fact, begin the translation as a *probatio pennae*. Only very occasionally does de Barra depart from the source text: one notable category of divergence consists in the translator's tendency to gloss references to mythological characters cited in *FPD*, whereas Ward refers only to the characters without offering any explanation of the original context. Two examples occur in *CBL* at ll. 355–64 and 523–56, where references to Sisyphus, and Echo and Narcissus respectively are glossed by de Barra. These minor divergences notwithstanding, faithfulness to the source text is the most salient feature of the first part of *CBL*. Soon into the second book, however, his writerly instincts emerge, as he sets about rewriting and reorganizing parts of the original text in place of the method of faithful translation that he had followed up until then. Part of this rewriting involved the substitution of native examples of unfaithful or treacherous women, such as Bláthnaid, wife of Con Raoi (who was instrumental in the death of her husband) or Aoife, cruel stepmother to the children of Lir, for some of the examples from Classical and Christian literature cited by Ward. The choice of native female figures such as these was obviously made with a local readership in mind.

An interesting example not drawn from Gaelic literature but incorporated by de Barra into the later version of his translation is that of Queen Elizabeth I. She is presented to us as obsessively lustful, and he recounts a tale of how her jealousy led her to put the Earl of Essex to death because he had sought the affections of another woman over her. The figure of Elizabeth features prominently in two other translations made by de Barra (Table 19.1, nos 3 and 4) in which she is portrayed in an equally unflattering light. As already mentioned, the account of Queen Elizabeth occurs only in the 1834 reworking of de Barra's original translation and, given the date of translations 3 and 4 (1825), it is plausible that his inclusion of the story in *CBL* reflects his reading on the subject in the interim. De Barra's decision to include in the later reworking of *CBL* his translation of the Hamlet story may also be accounted for in a similar fashion;[31] this particular rendering of the story emphasizes the role of

Sex among the rabble: an intimate history of power and gender in the age of revolution, Philadelphia, *1730–1830* (Chapel Hill, NC, 2006), p. 298.   **29** Edward Ward, *Female policy detected* (London, 1695), The Epistle Dedicatory to the Apprentices of London. For a discussion of the representation of women in the Irish-language translation, *CBL*, and of parallel descriptions in other Irish-language literary genres, see Máirín Nic Eoin, *B'ait leo bean: gnéithe den idé-eolaíocht inscne i dtraidisiún liteartha na Gaeilge* (Dublin, 1998), pp 126–40 in particular.   **30** Ó Conchúir, *Corraghliocas na mBan léirmhínithe*, pp xii–xiii.   **31** This account is in effect a translation of the first three quarters of 'Plan of the tragedy of Hamlet' from *The Tales of*

Gertrude, Hamlet's mother, in her husband's death, and she is portrayed throughout
as treacherous and unfaithful. Taken together, the inclusion of native and non-native
female literary or historical figures in this way suggests that de Barra empathized with
the misogynistic message of the original, as feminist historian Mary O'Dowd has
argued.[32] This conclusion is supported by the fact that the other work he set to translating in his teens was *The Merchant's Tale*. Central to Chaucer's story is the infidelity
of young May who goes to great lengths to convince her credulous old husband,
January, that he has imagined her unfaithfulness. The tale clearly echoes some of the
descriptions of perfidious and unfaithful women described in Ward's work.

In the poetic epilogue that accompanies the translation, de Barra gives us the
clearest indication – indirect as it may be – that *CBL* is not his own work. The admission comes in the fifth verse, the opening two lines of which go as follows:

> Dá mbeadh mo lámhsa a' scríobh, is go scaoilfí an glas dem béal // trian gníomhartha
> drochmhná ní chuirfinn síos lem shaol

> If my hand had written and the lock had been loosed from my mouth // a
> third of the deeds of evil women I should never recount[33]

In the remaining couplet of the quatrain, de Barra offers an explanation for his
focusing almost entirely on the conniving ways of women, by arguing that only those
rightly deserving of criticism, namely women of bad character, are singled out in
CBL.[34] The element of special pleading here could, perhaps, be attributed to a desire
to assuage his mixed feelings at having made available to a native audience a work
which many of the opposite sex would find displeasing. He may also have hoped to
soften the reaction of female readers (and listeners) to his work in the process. The
two lines quoted above clearly point to an ambivalence that he felt in this case
towards the act of translation. Tellingly, it is the only allusion in the entire work to
the fact of its being a translation. Nowhere else does he mention the question of
authorship as directly. This absence of acknowledgment shows through in other
translated works: well over half of the translations listed in Table 19.1 lack any reference to an original.[35] Even in those cases where the original is acknowledged, de
Barra was not usually in the habit of prefacing such translations with an account of
the original work or of how he set about translating it. The only exception is the
preface (in verse form) to *Nithe Cianaimseartha agus Bás Abel*, but this is in part a

William Vadé. These tales were published as part of *The Works of M. de Voltaire, translated from
the French, with notes, historical and critical,* which were compiled by T. Smollett, MD, T.
Francklin, MA and others. A Dublin edition of the work appeared in 1772–3 and Vadé's tales
occur in vol. 19. The relevant portion of the Hamlet story occurs on pp 1107–17. **32**
O'Dowd, *A history of women in Ireland, 1500–1800,* p. 242. **33** Ó Conchúir, *Corraghliocas na
mBan léirmhínithe,* p. 90. **34** This line of reasoning echoes a similar defence put forward by
Ward at the end of his preface to *Female policy detected.* **35** Nos 2, 6, 9 and 10 in the table
are the only works which carry an unambiguous acknowledgment.

reworking of the preface that accompanied the original, so the idea was not his own. De Barra alludes therein to the context and content of the translation and explains the didactic purpose he had in mind, stating his hope that readers will gain lessons from the work.[36] Glimpses of this kind are rare, however. The absence of any clear acknowledgment in the case of *CBL* could perhaps be explained by the extent to which de Barra had appropriated the original: in rearranging the format of *FPD* and abridging sections or on occasion enlarging them with examples of his own choosing, he may well have considered *CBL* to have been nativized, not only in terms of language but also in respect of content. Conversely, several faithful translations fashioned by him do not carry an acknowledgment either. In order for us to understand this practice of his, de Barra's entire corpus of translations needs to be surveyed in greater detail, case by case.

Ní Úrdail has remarked on the dual transference at work in the translations (mostly for Cork bishop, John Murphy) carried out by de Barra's contemporary, Mícheál Óg Ó Longáin, owing to the fact that he was translating not only from one language to another (from English to Irish) but also, in terms of medium, from printed exemplar to manuscript form.[37] This is also true of all of de Barra's translations, as none of them was published in his lifetime, being limited to circulation in manuscript form. With regard to the latter transference, that of medium, de Barra goes as far as to copy the original printed work, *FPD*, in several distinctive ways. In those sections which he translated faithfully, *CBL* contains many of the same print norms as the original, with de Barra's inclusion of headings, subheadings, paragraph indentations, chapter divisions etc.[38] The most striking influence, however, can be seen in the relatively small dimensions of the 1834 manuscript: the work, bound in linoleum, approximates a medium sextodecimo size. This format sorts well with the purpose of the original work, which was intended as a 'pocketbook' or companion, to be carried about by its young male owner and consulted as occasion demanded.[39] It seems that de Barra had such a practical consideration in mind when choosing a format for his own *compánach beag póca* ('little pocket companion').

INFLUENCES AND PURPOSE

In very simple terms, the works he translated give us an insight into the range of printed material in English to which he had access, at least a number of which he would have first encountered at school: *FPD* is most likely one such example. Apart

---

36 The introduction is to be found in Fermoy MS F PB 5: pp 1–4; the didactic purpose is mentioned on p. 2.   **37** Ní Úrdail, *The scribe in eighteenth- and nineteenth-century Ireland*, p. 218.   **38** These norms are found throughout the manuscript but are adhered to more closely in the first book.   **39** The manuscript's dimensions, as recorded by its cataloguer, are 15½cm × 9cm. Although slightly smaller than the chapbooks or 'burtons' of his time, the physical appearance of the manuscript is nevertheless reminiscent of their format and obviously designed for portability.

from de Barra's young age when translating the text, this is also suggested to us from the fact that Ward's work is known to have been used as reading material in some of the hedge schools of the early nineteenth century.[40] In addition, de Barra informs us in his correspondence with Hackett that he had in his possession copies of many other printed works (in English and Irish) unrelated to those listed in Table 19.1. And his own writings – prose and poetry – contain references to an assortment of religious and political works as diverse as Denis Taafe's *An Impartial History of Ireland*, 4 vols (1809–11) and Flavius Josephus' *Antiquities of the Jews*. His scribal activities involved the transcription of native works of a very different kind: among his surviving manuscripts are copies he made of saints' lives, and eighteenth- and nineteenth-century poetry, as well as numerous traditional prose romance tales. Distinct influences can be seen to come together at times in his translations, particularly in those cases where de Barra attempts to domesticate the English-language original. A clear example of this is his translation of Anne Barbauld's short gothic tale, *Sir Bertrand: a Fragment*, throughout which he uses the style and language of the aforementioned native romance tales. This was a style well known to de Barra from his scribal work, and he uses it to great effect to recreate the distinctive atmosphere of the original, giving *Sgéal ar an Ridire Beartrard* a flavour of the gothic, but rendering it more familiar to native readers in the process. A short representative extract is given below to illustrate the point:

> After a short parley with himself, he entered the porch, and seizing a massy iron knocker at the gate, lifted it up, and hesitating, at length struck a loud stroke – the noise resounded through the whole mansion with hollow echoes. All was still again – he repeated the strokes more boldly and louder – another interval of silence ensued – A third time he knocked, and a third time all was still. He then fell back to some distance, that he might discern whether any light could be seen in the whole front – It again appeared in the same place, and quickly glided away, as before – at the same instant a deep sullen toll sounded from the turret. Sir Bertrand's heart made a fearful stop – he was motionless; then terror impelled him to make some hasty steps towards his steed – but shame stopt his flight; and urged by honour, and a resistless desire of finishing the adventure . . .

> . . . *tar éis beagán machnaimh dhéanamh dho, do chuaidh isteach sa phóirse agus beireas 'na láimh ar bhuailteoir throm iarainn do bhí ar an ndoras agus tógas suas é go dtug bloscbhéim go ró-áibhseach de ar an gcomhlainn go dtug fuaim agus macalla tré shleasaibh na bruíne uile, agus níor fhreagair aon do ann, agus tug an dara béim agus an treas bhéim agus ní bhfuair freagra ar bith. Drideas an Ridire air sin beagán ar gcúlaibh, dá fhéachain an bhfaic[e]adh aon tsolas in aon bhall. Air sin ad-ch[o]nairc an solas san*

---

40 See *First Report of the Commissioners on Education in Ireland*, H.C. 1825 (400), xii, Appendix no. 221, p. 557.

*áit chéanna 'na bhfeacaidh é roimhe, agus go ha[i]thghearr do imthigh arís gan tuairisc,
go mba chomhchlos do an chreill ag bualadh le fuaim uaigneach agus le iomad iarg[h]nó
insa chaisleán, air sin glacas uamhan agus imeagla mhór é go ndeachaidh a chroí in
anbhainne, agus gluaiseas go haosga i ndáil a eich, gur smaoin 'na íntinn gur mhór an
náire agus an briseadh onóra dho gan dul air agha[i]dh san ngnó sin do ghaibh do
láimh ...*[41]

Most notable among the stylistic conventions that de Barra uses in order to lend his
translation the quality of a native romance tale (some of which can be found in the
extract above), are his inclusion of occasional archaisms; his tendency to put verbs
into the absolute third singular (later) preterite form in order to suggest quick action
or movement, and his use of repetitive and sometimes alliterative formulae, often
where no such repetition occurs in the original (e.g. *'uamhan agus imeagla mhór'* for
'terror' in the passages quoted above).[42] The excerpt also demonstrates de Barra's
willingness to depart from the source text where necessary in the interests of fash-
ioning a more communicative translation.

The question of de Barra's motivation or purpose in carrying out these translations remains. I have already touched on the importance of translation in helping de
Barra to explore and shape his own native style, as we saw in the case of *CBL*. Other
purposes are evident. His translations of several shorter tales (the aforementioned
gothic tale included) were apparently made for the entertainment of younger
readers.[43] A note by de Barra in the middle of the manuscript in which they occur
relates this intention, as does the general preface he includes at the beginning of the
book.[44] Not all of his translations, however, were fashioned to prove his pen or for
the amusement or edification of prospective (anonymous) readers; at least one translation was the product of a direct request, and it is likely that others, too, were made
to order.[45] We know, for instance, that he translated a short portion of Lord Byron's
popular Oriental Romance, *The Giaour*,[46] for a certain John Cummins,[47] then resident in de Barra's locality. The fact that he had been requested to translate it may
suggest that de Barra had acquired something of a reputation, locally at any rate, for
this kind of work. The inclusion of three of his translations by Seosamh Ó Longáin

41 The excerpt in Irish occurs in NLI MS G 656, pp 229–30.   **42** For an account of the
stylistic features of Gaelic romance tales, see Alan Bruford, *Gaelic folktales and native romances:
a study of the early modern Irish 'romance tales' and their oral derivatives* (Dublin, 1969), pp 33–44.
43 The shorter tales in question are translations nos 5–8 listed in Table 19.1.   **44** NLI MS
G 656, pp 126 and v–viii respectively.   **45** The prayer books mentioned in fn. 9 above may
well have been put together for local readers. Ní Úrdail has argued that the production of
such prayer books implied a growing interest in bilingual reading practices which
encouraged an acquisition of literacy in the two languages: see *The scribe in eighteenth- and
nineteenth-century Ireland*, p. 223 and fn. 112.   **46** Translation no. 10 in Table 19.1.   **47** One
John Cummins is recorded in Public Record Office, Dublin: *Tithe Applotment Books*, Cork,
par. Caherlag and Little Island (1833), tld Lackanvoe. Cummins may have been a relative of
Nicholas Marshall Cummins, resident at Dunkettle House, who gave de Barra the gift of a
book (now Fermoy MS F PB 1) in 1844 to use in his scribal work.

in the manuscript put together for Windele would seem to support this, and the aforementioned note at the beginning of the nineteenth-century manuscript copy of *CBL* states that this translation was often borrowed and copied in his locality.

Considered in the context of contemporary literary activity in Irish, de Barra was one of only a handful of scholars engaged in translation work of this kind in Cork in the 1820s and 1830s: others involved in similar work included Mícheál Óg Ó Longáin, Seán Ó Coileáin and Fr Mat Horgan.[48] Translations into Irish were being made by Gaelic scribes and writers in Cork from the end of the seventeenth century down to the 1830s or so, and consisted primarily of devotional material, a fact that reflects the close relations between scribes, scholars and clergy after the enactment of the penal laws. The majority of these translations circulated solely in manuscript form; Ní Úrdail, for instance, cites only two examples from the eighteenth century, and one from the first half of the nineteenth, of Irish translations fashioned contemporaneously in Cork which made it through the printing press.[49] As already mentioned, the prohibitive cost of printing, the relative unavailability of an Irish type and vastly reduced levels of literacy in Irish all played their part in this. The general tide was very much running in the opposite direction, as new (and very often non-native) audiences sought English-language translations of Gaelic material, and the many Gaelic translators who responded to this demand looked upon their work as an act of retrieval in the wake of a dying culture.[50] The category of translator to which de Barra belonged could not have hoped to make any deep or lasting impact.[51] At all events, whoever his intended readership (diminished as it was), whatever his motives, the extent of his translation work, and his abiding interest in this creative endeavour, mean that we cannot overlook this dimension of his writing when assessing de Barra's *oeuvre* or the progress of his career as a writer.

48 For biographical information on Ó Longáin, see Ó Conchúir, *Scríobhaithe Chorcaí*, pp 91–133 and Ní Úrdail, *The scribe in eighteenth- and nineteenth-century Ireland*, pp 43–99; for Ó Coileáin, see *Scríobhaithe Chorcaí*, pp 41–6, and Bláthnaid Uí Chatháin, *Éigse Chairbre: filíocht ó Chairbreacha i gco. Chorcaí agus ón gceantar máguaird, 1750–1850* (Dublin, 2006), pp 19–36, and for Horgan, see *Scríobhaithe Chorcaí*, pp 83–4. Translations by Ó Coileáin and Horgan also feature in the aforementioned miscellany, RIA MS 24 C 2. **49** Meidhbhín Ní Úrdail 'Aistriúcháin ó Chorcaigh i lámhscríbhinní déanacha na Gaeilge' in E. Poppe and L.C.H. Tristram (eds), *Übersetzung, adaptation und akkulturation im insularen mittelalter* (Münster, 1999), pp 319–36 at p. 331. **50** For a discussion of this, see Michael Cronin, *Translating Ireland* (Cork, 1996), pp 91–131. **51** To judge from surviving manuscripts, several of de Barra's translations scarcely circulated to any significant degree and three others, nos 5, 8, and 13, have come down to us in only one copy.

Index